ISLAM AND DISSENT IN POSTREVOLUTIONARY IRAN

RENEWALS 458-4574
DATE DUE

D1739344

WITHDRAWN
UTSA Libraries

WITHDRAWN
UTSA Libraries

ISLAM AND DISSENT IN POSTREVOLUTIONARY IRAN

Abdolkarim Soroush, Religious Politics and Democratic Reform

Behrooz Ghamari-Tabrizi

I.B. TAURIS

LONDON · NEW YORK

To Silenced Voices

Published in 2008 by I.B.Tauris & Co Ltd
6 Salem Road, London W2 4BU
175 Fifth Avenue, New York NY 10010
www.ibtauris.com

In the United States of America and Canada distributed by Palgrave Macmillan,
a division of St. Martin's Press, 175 Fifth Avenue, New York NY 10010

Copyright © Behrooz Ghamari-Tabrizi, 2008

The right of Behrooz Ghamari-Tabrizi to be identified as the author of this work
has been asserted by the author in accordance with the Copyright, Designs and
Patent Act 1988.

All rights reserved. Except for brief quotations in a review, this book, or any part
thereof, may not be reproduced, stored in or introduced into a retrieval system,
or transmitted, in any form or by any means, electronic, mechanical, photo-
copying, recording or otherwise, without the prior written permission of the
publisher.

International Library of Iranian Studies 16

ISBN: 978 1 84511 879 2 HB
         978 1 84511 880 8 PB

A full CIP record for this book is available from the British Library
A full CIP record is available from the Library of Congress

Library of Congress Catalog Card Number: available

Printed and bound in Great Britain by TJ International Ltd, Padstow, Cornwall
from camera-ready copy edited and supplied by the author.

**Library
University of Texas
at San Antonio**

Contents

Acknowledgments

I always knew but never truly understood how difficult it would be to write a few words of gratitude to acknowledge those who contributed to the birth of this work. Writing a book is a collective work. It is the outcome of the interaction between complex layers of networks, accommodations, intellectual exchanges, emotional connections, and yes, everybody's omnipresent concern, financial support. Acknowledging every person and institution that supported this work is impossible.

I must begin by recognizing my teachers, those from whose knowledge and wisdom I have benefited. The very first time that I had to find my way in the meandering world of ideas, Hossein Zahiri, known to all his friends for his immense knowledge of history and philosophy simply as *Doktor*, inspired me and taught me how to be an engaged intellectual. I was admitted to graduate school at the University of California in Santa Cruz merely because a number of faculty members in the department of sociology trusted that I was up to the task. Bill Domhoff and Andrew Szasz recognized my intellectual thirst and made sure that bureaucratic barriers did not hinder my academic ambitions. Paul Lubeck has always championed my work and offered insights at moments I most needed them. Edmund Burke III made sure that my conceptual world would stand the test of history and my history was framed by plausible concepts. I thank him for allowing me to be greedy with his time. R. W. Connell taught me the possibility of thinking from the margins and surviving in the mainstream. I was truly blessed to be a part of a vibrant intellectual community in Santa Cruz where I could learn from scholars such as James Clifford, Donna Haraway, James O'Connor, Dana Takagi, Johan Brown Childs, Craig Reinerman, Mark Traugott, and Walter Goldfrank.

Many others, in casual talks or formal meetings, have posed questions and offered me answers throughout the years of working on this project. Mentioning their names will not suffice to express my appreciation, Asef Bayat, Linda Herrera, Ali Rahnema, Minoo Moalem, Saba Mahmood, Sami Zubaida, Farzin Vahdat, Valentine Moghadam, Michael Burawoy, Ahmad Sadri, Charles Kurzman, Richard Martin, Armando Salvatore, Fatemeh Keshavarz, and Ahmet Karamustafa. I am also indebted to many who post comments on the list serve of Study of Islam Group of the American Academy of Religion. I thank Omid Safi and Jonathan Brockopp for being the force behind this endeavor.

I received an invaluable joint fellowship from the SSRC and *Wissenschaftkolleg zü Berlin* for two sessions of a summer institute. The institute conveners Thomas Philipp, Serif Mardin, Said Amir Arjomand, and Charles Butterworth were most gracious hosts who facilitated discussions with utmost integrity and vigor. I learned immensely from every member of the group in the formative stages of my project.

I have also received generous funding from other academic institutions, the University of California Regent's IGCC Fellowship, United States Institute of Peace, NEH Summer Fellowship, Georgia State University Research Initiation Grant, and a residential postdoctoral fellowship from the Center for the Humanities at Wesleyan University. Elizabeth Traube, the Director of the Center, created the best working environment one can wish for, from the elegance of the office space to the rigor of weekly lectures and discussions. While at Wesleyan, I enjoyed the company and friendship of Sepideh Bajracharya, Khachig Tölölyan, Jed Esty, and Andrea Goulet.

I would like to thank faculty members in the Sociology Department and the Middle East Studies Institute for their friendship and support, especially Chip Gallagher, Wendy Simonds, Ralph LaRossa, Toshi Kii, Donald Ried, Dona Stewart, and John Iskander. Selma Poage made departmental life much easier. Maggie McMillan and other staff members of the Interlibrary Loan office miraculously fulfilled my most obscure requests. Without the help of Nikki Siahpoush, Taka Ono, and Bill Holland, I could not manage filing and cataloguing endless pieces of documents and papers. In Atlanta, I also met Supriya Gandhi, Kaveh Kamooneh, and Roji Aldashi, and Diane Bennett whose friendships I cherish.

When I moved to Illinois, I did not realize that I had stepped into one of the most intellectually vibrant campuses in the country. I thank my colleagues in the History Department and in Sociology for making me feel at home so fast and so easily. I would especially like to thank Zohreh Sullivan and Jim Hurt for their generosity and love. I would also like to thank Faranak Miraftab, Rajmohan and Usha Gandhi, Hadi Esfahani, Niloofar Shambayati, Richard Powers, Peter Fritzsche, the Salonistas, David Prochoska, Bruce Levine, and Poshek Fu, David Roediger, Antoinette Burton, Tamara Chaplin, Ken Cuno, Marilyn Booth, Tim Liao, Jan Nederveen Pieterse, Markus Schultz, Michael Rothberg, Matti Bunzl, Barbara Sattler, and Hairong Yan. I especially thank Jane Kuntz for reading my rough manuscript patiently and offering invaluable editorial assistance. I would like to thank my editor Rasna Dhillon at I.B.Tauris for her enthusiastic hard work to make this book a reality.

Through my academic work I have also found friends whose presence in my life has made this effort more meaningful, among them are Jung Ha Kim, Zsuzsa Gille, Niloufar Haeri, Ian Fletcher, and Mazyar Lotfalian. My old friends have always offered tremendous support and encouragement, Tannaz Jafarian, Niloofar Dasti, Khosrow Khorrami, Fereshteh Ahmadi, Said Sharif, Afsaneh Khajavi, Shahin Sakhi, Asad Kabir, Shokoufeh Sakhi, Nancy Hormechea, Qumars Hakim, and Anoush Khoshbatn. I would like to thank my sister Behjat, and brothers Behdad and Bijan and my mother who all taught me the meaning of selfless love. For many years Sharon Ghamari has offered me her love, friendship, and intellectual wisdom. She has been a true friend and my most sincere critic. Nothing I have written in the last decade has been made public without her close reading and thoughtful comments.

1

Introduction:
Ideological Certainties,
Past and Present

My first serious encounter with Islamic literature was during my imprisonment from 1981 to 1985. I read the Qur'an for the first time in its entirety while I was in the *Towhid Committee,* an underground prison that the Islamic Republic's Revolutionary Guards inherited from the notorious SAVAK.[1] At *Towhid*, torture was common and, according to the government's estimates, more than 75 per cent of political prisoners detained in *Towhid* between 1981-82 were eventually executed.[2] Later, in the gruesomely infamous Evin prison, as part of the regime's indoctrination programs cum 'ideological education,' I read contemporary writings on Islamic philosophy, economy, and politics. Needless to say, I was not exposed to Islamic literature in an encouraging environment. By this unusual opening, I do not intend to add to the drama of the book. Rather, my purpose is, first, to locate myself vis-à-vis the subject of my study, and second, to emphasize my own awareness of the stakes in proposing a critique of 'universalizing' narratives of history.

As a student activist against Mohammad Reza Shah's US-backed dictatorship, like many of my fellow students, I considered myself a Marxist-Leninist. As a dominant ideological foundation of national liberation movements around the world, Marxism-Leninism envisioned a speedy bypass from the characteristic 'pre-capitalist' conditions in the Third World to socialism. Marx predicted that the transition to socialism would be realized through the advancement of the forces of production which would eventually supersede the fetters of capitalism. This formula considered the most advanced capitalist societies to be the forerunners to the establishment of socialism, a path which was to be followed by less-developed countries. Leninism (and Maoism) turned this prediction

upside down and regarded anti-imperialist liberation movements as the
engine of the world revolution. Lenin turned Marxism into an attractive
ideology within which, while remaining faithful to the grand historical
commitment of establishing socialism, my comrades and I could justify
our nationalist pride. By virtue of this ideology the Third World became
the torchbearer of progress towards socialism; the most advanced
industrial societies were to follow *us*.

While the 1978-79 revolutionary movement reinforced my ideological commitment, losing the post-revolution power struggle to the
militant clergy planted the seeds of doubt in my mind and generated
deep schisms in the Iranian Left. Two major leftist parties supported the
establishment of the new Islamic regime.[3] By 1980, only one year later,
the question of acceptance or rejection of the legitimacy of the Islamic
Republic became the wedge issue that divided the Left into two distinct
camps. Although the rift within the Left seemed deep, and the two
positions were growing increasingly antagonistic, both sides remained
faithful to their socialist ideals. On the one hand, the supporters of the
regime believed that the Islamic Republic, with its petit-bourgeois anti-
imperialist propaganda and its rhetoric of social justice, would take
Iranian society a step closer to socialism,[4] while the opponents argued
that the petit-bourgeoisie exhausted its revolutionary potential upon
assuming political power. Therefore, for the latter group, the Islamic
Republic hindered the establishment of socialism and had to be toppled.

I was associated with the second current; I organized student
groups, wrote propaganda pamphlets and theoretical position papers,
and orchestrated demonstrations against the Islamic regime. I was
arrested in 1981. Soon, the leftist supporters of the government endured
the same fate. They were persecuted, imprisoned, and executed by the
thousands. The government's indiscriminate suppression of the Left
solved at least one problem: the Islamic regime was not heading towards
socialism, or if it were, it did not regard the Bolshevik Left as its ally.

In prison, in addition to extreme violence, we were subjected to
constant indoctrination cum 'ideological training.' Watching three hours
of Islamic educational television every morning from 9 to 12 was
mandatory, reading books was optional. It was an open secret, however,
that torture had proven to be more effective than education in
'converting' Marxists to Islam. Tehran's Chief Revolutionary Prosecutor,
Asadollah Lajevardi, once confided to a group of us on death row that
converts did not enjoy the respect of the regime. 'They are like weeping

willows,' Lajevardi chastised them, 'which tremble with winds blowing from any direction.'

The great majority of people do not experience matters of faith and ideology in such extreme circumstances. But, both temporally and spatially, prison was a condensed and, at the same time, exaggerated version of everyday life. Ideological commitments in prison were literally a matter of life and death. It is not clear to me why, even in the face of death, some of us chose to remain faithful to our ideology. But ideology is a totalizing discourse through which one defines one's historical and social location. It is a dogma that provides certainty and comfort, especially in the times of crisis. I was sheltered against my captors' ideological training, for I was immunized by my certainty about the legitimacy of my Marxist convictions. I regarded anything outside my Marxist worldview, especially religion, as either false consciousness (in cases where I did not question the intentions of the actors) or mere deception. I considered myself to be a part of an irreversible force of history, a part in the unfolding of an historical necessity.

My second encounter with Islamic literature was during my graduate education. Stressful though it was to fulfill the requirements for the doctoral program in sociology, this time I did not feel coerced to study the material. Contrary to what the cliché of 'studying your captors' might suggest, from the beginning of my graduate training I was interested in reexamining my *own* convictions rather than those of my captors. Of course, soon the two became indistinguishable as totalizing ideologies. Another distinction in my second encounter was the collapse of communism and the spectacle of all those nations who had fought admirably to de-link from global capitalism and who were now struggling to rejoin the fold. It was time I came to terms with the idea that rather than a bridge between capitalism and communism, Bolshevik socialism was a transitional period from feudalism to capitalism.[5]

Totality, Utopia, and Foundationalism

The shattering of certainty is a traumatic experience. The pain of this trauma is radically alleviated if one totalizing system replaces another: Marxism giving way to liberalism, or to conversion to Islam. In recent years, thanks to religious revivals of different sorts, certainty has also been associated with fundamentalism: free-market fundamentalism;[6] Enlightenment fundamentalism;[7] Christian-Jewish-Islamic fundamentalisms; etc. Accordingly, I redefined my previous convictions as Marxist-Leninist fundamentalism. The pejorative association of certainty with

fundamentalism (or less pejoratively with foundationalism) was related
to the rise of, to be playful with the concept, a fundamentalist assertion
of indeterminacy in social life and history.

Indeterminacy raises the fear of chaos and legitimizes the quondam
counter-culture notion of *anything goes*.[8] Without foundational per-
suasions, rather than a 'natural' progressive movement with identifiable
laws, history becomes a contested realm of human subjectivity with the
possibility of infinite formations. This brings me to my second concern in
writing this book: *the stakes of a relativist approach.*

A few years ago, an old friend who knew that I was searching for a
theoretical framework for making sense of Islamist movements pleaded
with me: *we should not allow postmodernism to cross the border into Iran! If it
does, it would have disastrous consequences.* Although he was not specific
about how it was possible to close the borders against the spread of an
idea, he passionately elaborated on the disaster he anticipated. If it is
true that *anything goes*, then the Islamic regime in Iran may legitimize its
atrocities according to their own cultural codes. How would it be
possible to criticize the Islamic Republic's violations of the human rights
without recourse to a universally accepted normative point of reference?

My friend's concern, in spite of its simplicity, in many ways
resonated with foundationalist critiques of post-structuralism. Although
it is unlikely that Ayatollah Khomeini was ever aware of the post-
structuralist critique of humanism, his response to his western-minded
critics about violations of human rights was that he respected neither
western notions of humanity nor western conception of rights. The
regime candidly opposed the universal declaration of human rights and
western notions of democracy. While despotic regimes often try to
commit their atrocities behind closed doors, the Islamic Republic was
unashamedly blunt about its bloody crackdown on the opposition in
1981 and thereafter. Government-sponsored daily papers published the
names of the executed—a list that occasionally consisted of 100-150
people per day in the summer and fall of 1981.[9]

Although my friend's fear that the Islamic Republic might justify its
oppressive anti-democratic politics through appropriating (co-opting)
postmodernism suggested a scene from the theater of the absurd, it
points to an ongoing academic debate about the risks of losing the
universal referent. Of course, none of the theorists of postmodernism or
post-structuralism would ever endorse any regime's massacre of its
dissidents as a legitimate particularist position. Nevertheless, the anxiety

that a Derridian post-foundationalist position generates both for the progressive Left and for the liberal humanist needs to be appreciated.[10]

The question is how the non-western subject may translate the politics of difference or the negation of 'White mythologies'[11] into an emancipatory politics, without reference to the various foundational myths: History as the March of Man, Reason, Civilization, Progress, Modes-of-Production?[12] Is an emancipatory politics conceivable without a careful look at 'what are we emancipating ourselves into?'[13] From this rhetorical question, one may conclude that without a totalizing conception of a good society (Utopia), 'emancipation becomes a Nietzschean act of pure autonomous will [...] a struggle purely internal to the consciousness of those who resist and only represented by them.'[14]

Conversely, politics without foundational myths convey *emerging* processes of emancipation, through which the concept of the good society is constructed. This view inevitably negates the position that where there is a *totality*, there exists a mapping, cognitively drawn by a *totalizer*.[15] In this context, not only is an *a priori* knowledge of the totality, into which we are stepping, problematized, but also the relation between those who *resist* and those who *represent* the resistance is re-imagined and reconstituted. Both Gramsci and Foucault influenced this debate by distinguishing between 'traditional versus organic' and 'universal versus specific' intellectuals, respectively. In their view, intellectuals can emerge from any social class or group. Whereas for Foucault specific intellectuals operate in a more modest social sphere, Gramsci's organic intellectuals act more universally and historically. But for each the new type of intellectual is also an acknowledgment that the masses do not need to have understanding thrust on them from above.[16] Contrary to what O'Hanlon and Washbrook contend, this does not mean the end of representation altogether. For the fact remains that the assertion that oppressed subjects speak, act, and know *for themselves*, 'leads to an essentialist, utopian politics.'[17]

Totality and totalizing conceptions of history depict the *problematique* of postmodern politics. Of course, it is plausible to argue that postmodernist approaches are themselves built around a form of totalizing abstraction that 'distinguishes postmodern culture,' as Jameson once wrote, 'by its logic of difference and its sustained production of random and unrelated subsystems of all kinds.'[18] While the philosophical foundations of critique of totalizing conceptions of reality lie elsewhere, the political motivation of the 'war on totality,' as Jameson observed, rests on 'a fear of Utopia that turns out to be none other than our old friend

1984, such that a Utopian and revolutionary politics, correctly associated with totalization and a certain 'concept' of totality, is to be eschewed because it leads fatally to Terror . . .'[19]

There are numerous examples where revolutionary movements, once having attained political power, turned into totalitarian regimes of terror. Totalizing emancipatory visions, be they revolutionary movements of the oppressed, or the self-proclaimed 'liberating' forces of colonialism, have most often been realized violently against perceived reactionary social and historical elements. But does this imply, as Jameson rhetorically asked, that the 'revolutionary, Utopian, or totalizing impulse is somehow tainted from the outset and doomed to bloodshed by very structure of its thoughts?'[20]

Or, conversely, does the negation of ideological totality imply, as Habermas maintains, a reactionary, neo-conservative political function?[21] The *potentiality* for a reactionary politics of course is not uniquely a characteristic of postmodernism. Liberalism, humanism, Marxism, and other post-Enlightenment rationalities have already demonstrated their oppressive and violent potentials. Islamism, like other political ideologies, does not offer an alternative free of repressive tendencies. Does a 'good' politics only emerge through the spirit, or what Derrida called the 'metaphysics,' of the project of Enlightenment (either the instrumental or the humanist sides) in which absolute and unified explanations of political, economic, and cultural processes are produced? If we accept the proposition that there is an inescapable association between Utopia and Terror, between imagining an ideal society and totalitarianism, are we not suggesting the end of all that is political?

One can argue that the essence of distinctly *political* thought is the imagining of the good society as a whole. Mannheim once predicted that 'the utopias of today become the realities of tomorrow,' and 'the road of history leads from one *topia* [existing social conditions] over a utopia to the next *topia.*' Mannheim imagined a history in which existing orders give birth to utopians who continuously envision utopias 'which in turn break the bounds of the existing order, leaving it free to develop in the direction of the next order of existence.'[22] He rebuked those who rejected the conception of totality and warned that on that basis

Utopia disappears [and] history ceases to be a process leading to an ultimate end. The frame of reference according to which we evaluate facts vanishes and we are left with a series of events all equal as far as their inner significance is concerned [...] All those elements of thought which are rooted in utopias are now viewed from a skeptical relativist point of view.[23]

Ernst Bloch went even further to suggest that a society dispossessed of the narrative skill to envision alternative political, economic, and cultural relations is dead. However, Bloch's vision of utopia was distinct from Mannheim's, in that he linked the conception of utopia to the principle of hope. Whereas for Mannheim the blueprint of utopia was to be drawn up by the intelligentsia, Bloch located utopia in the 'Not-Yet-Become' of folklore, in the popular desire to hope and strive for a better life expressed in myth, fairytales and daydreams.[24]

From Fairytales to Nightmares

The absurdity of perceiving the Islamic Republic as a manifestation of a postmodern political logic is too obvious. However, the Rushdie Affair of 1989 once again highlighted the contradiction between 'plurality of terrains, multiple experiences and different constituencies'[25] and commitment to 'a fundamental human and intellectual obligation.'[26] I located both sides of this contradiction in the works of Edward Said to emphasize that the two positions are not divided into mutually exclusive camps. One might rightly argue, as Gyan Prakash does, that there is no contradiction in Said's position. There should be enough room for intellectual obligations of any sort in a plural terrain, room for both Salman Rushdie and his Muslim critics. The point however is whether a totality or a systemizing perspective (i.e. human rights, democracy) is necessary to accommodate plurality and difference. James Clifford once wrote that

> The privilege of standing above cultural particularism, of appealing to the universalist power that speaks for humanity, for universal experience of love, work, death, etc., is a privilege invented by totalizing Western liberalism.[27]

He further chastised Said for remaining 'ambivalently enmeshed in the totalizing habits of Western humanism.'[28] But this formula still leaves the point of reference in defending Salman Rushdie's rights opaque.

Although the Rushdie Affair became synonymous with Ayatollah Khomeini's *fatwa* calling for Mr. Rushdie's death, what is more intriguing in this case is the politics of British Muslims. Socio-political movements that thrive on the notion of cultural particularism, pose a conceptual as well as a political dilemma for those who distrust totalizing habits. In the case of the Rushdie Affair, the problem was that Salman Rushdie's 'cultural translation'[29] became the target of the wrath of a community whose culture was supposedly translated in his book, that of the émigré.[30]

In writing *The Satanic Verses*, Rushdie remarked, he ventured to converge his English and Indian parts, the part that 'loves London' and the part that 'longs for Bombay,' into a single self. 'But most of the time,' he commented, 'people will ask me—will ask anyone like me [the émigré, the exiled]—are you Indian? Pakistani? English? What is being expressed is a discomfort with a plural identity.'[31] Apparently, two opposing *totalizing* groups voiced this discomfort: the 'fundamentalist absolutists' and the 'liberal universalists.'[32] Neither the British government nor rioting Muslims in Bradford, according to Bhabha, 'represents the values of the multiracial society that we identify with, either as political ideal or as a social reality.'[33]

The liberals and conservatives alike moved promptly to defend tolerance versus the transgression of fundamentalism. They asked ethnic minorities not to insulate themselves in the host society, and invited them for 'proper integration' without 'abandoning their faith.' John Patten, the Home Secretary's deputy, in his open letter (July 18, 1989) entitled 'On being British,' attributed Britishness to 'those things which…we have in common. Our democracy and our laws, the English language, and the history that has shaped modern Britain.' To take advantage of being a British citizen, immigrant children, according to Patten, must command 'a clear understanding of British democratic processes, of its laws, the system of Government and the history that lies behind them.' No one had better captured the irony of Patton's assertion than Rushdie himself in the wonderful passage in *The Satanic Verses*: 'The trouble with the English is that their history happened overseas, so they don't know what it means.' The former subjects of the Empire lived a closer life to British history than their present white hosts. Gerald Kaufman was one of the first to expose the racism informing much of the national debate on the Rushdie affair. 'The liberals were prepared,' he wrote, 'to fight against racial discri-mination and stand up for Muslims so long as they conformed to liberal notions of acceptable conduct and did not get above themselves.'[34]

The second tendency was manifested in the British Muslims' demand for banning *The Satanic Verses*, which obviously did not elicit a sympathetic response from either the state, or the non-liberal supporters of Salman Rushdie. Khomeini's *fatwa* quashed British Muslims' demands and turned the local predicaments of the émigré communities into a global war over liberal principles of human rights and civil liberties. For example, on February 1, 1989, the British government rejected the demand to include Islam (in addition to Christianity and Judaism) under the existing blasphemy law. At the same time, the government refused to extend the same financial support that Christian and Jewish schools enjoyed to Islamic schools in Birmingham and Bradford.[35]

One of the major contributions of post-foundationalist cultural studies lies in its attempt to demolish the elitist notions of culture and the Marxian idea of false consciousness.[36] But the British Muslims' protest against Salman Rushdie posed a controversial question for these theorists---how to reconcile the émigré represented in *The Satanic Verses* with the protesters asserting themselves on the streets of Bradford. What did their assertion mean? Some observed the Affair through class-based Marxian eyes and attributed the Muslim riots to their 'rural origin with hardly any social awareness of city life even in Pakistan itself.'[37] Others, like Homi Bhabha, belittled the political, social, and cultural significance of Muslim protests by not even acknowledging their self described identity as British Muslims. He located himself, Rushdie, and others who identify with a 'values of the multicultural society' in 'black or Asian communities.'[38]

The Affair brought forth the inherent contradiction of postmodern politics. How can we defend the principle of free speech or a fundamental human obligation outside a unifying system and without reference to totalizing universalities? Although Rushdie so eloquently constructed an aesthetic plural self, in the aftermath of the Affair, in his *Realpolitik*, he located himself in one or another totalizing camps, and desperately sought their support.

In his editorial piece in the New York Times (February 15, 1997), 'Europe's shameful trade in silence,' Rushdie, wrote as 'a committed European,' to convince European governments that they should fight on behalf of freedom against 'the Zeus of Iran.' 'Like so many of my fellow Britons,' Rushdie remarked, 'I hope there will soon be a new Labor Government.' After conceding that European governments value trade, money, guns, and power more highly than the 'European idea,' he concluded by recommending that the Labor Party show its commitment to 'the true spirit of Europe—not just to [...] a monetary union, but to European civilization itself.' Rushdie, who has established his distinctive artistic vision as an outsider, a *diasporic* voice, has now emerged as a 'committed European,' brandishing the flag of its civil-izational heritage.

Earlier in his career, Rushdie established himself as a staunch critic of European colonialism. For example, in 1982, in *The New Empire Within*

Britain, he lambasted British culture for being tainted by 'Four hundred years of conquest and looting, four centuries of being told that you are superior to the Fuzzy-Wuzzies and the wogs, leave their stain. This stain has speeded into every part of the culture, the language and daily life; and nothing much has been done to wash it out.'[39]

He wrote that for the colonized Asians and blacks of Britain, a community of which Rushdie was a distinguished member, 'the police force represents that colonizing army,' and concluded his essay by reminding his readers of Mahatma Gandhi's response when he was asked during a trip to England what he thought of English civilization, 'I think it would be a good idea.' In 1990, chafing under the threat of Ayatollah Khomeini's *fatwa*, in a press release called *In Good Faith*, Rushdie put it bluntly and asserted that he was not a Muslim, thereby making the charges of blasphemy against him erroneous. As he said in *The Satanic Verses*, 'where there is no belief, there is no blasphemy.' However, in the same year, in 'Why I have embraced Islam,' he announced that he had converted to Islam. Although 'certainly not a good Muslim,' he admitted,

> I am able now to say that I am Muslim; in fact it is a source of happiness to say that I am now inside, and part of, the community whose values have always been closest to my heart. I have in the past described the furor over *The Satanic Verses* as a family quarrel. Well, I'm now inside the family. My real safety, I have long believed, lies in the attitude of the Muslim community at large.[40]

Then again in 1997, he stepped outside the family and turned the family quarrel into a civilizational war between Europeans—of which he was a committed votary—and the evil forces of the Iranian Zeus! Although I deeply sympathize with Rushdie's predicament, the Affair raises the question as to how it is possible to conceive of politics from a heterogeneous standpoint. How are plural selves manifested in social and political movements? The answer is definitely not in Rushdie's opportunistic vacillation between different totalities.

The Topic of this Book
During a casual lunchtime chat, one of my colleagues raised a fantastic question. 'If you could decide,' he asked, 'which historical period and place would you have chosen to live in?' 'Vienna of the turn of the century,' one said; 'Paris, no matter when,' said another; 'New York of the Harlem Renaissance,' sighed another colleague. 'What about you?'

they inquired, turning their heads toward me. I thought for a split second and replied, 'Well,' I bought some more time, 'I can't decide.' The fact was that I was very certain that I had no desire to have been born in another time or place. I was born at the right time and in the right place. This cliché could not be discussed over our lunch break. As a fearless, radical, utopian, and young student, I lived through one of the greatest revolutions of modern times. I actively helped to organize, participated in, and was later shaped by the revolution and the consequences of its tumultuous force.

In 1977, I was a student in one of the most respected engineering schools in Tehran. I studied textile engineering, a field so alien to me that even after many years of attending school I remained aloof to its scope and technical principles. At the time I began my university years, everything in the Iranian political panorama, albeit superficially, pointed to the relevance of Amir Parviz Pouyan's doctrine of the 'two absolutes': 'the *absolute* domination of the regime, which finds its reflection in the minds of the workers as their *absolute* inability to change the established order.'[41] In less than one year, from the early days of 1978, the fundamental absurdity of this doctrine became evident.

In a process that virtually defied all existing general theories of revolution, massive demonstrations swept major cities in the country.[42] Neither did the revolution substantiate theories of political violence, nor did it confirm any historical/structural theories of revolution. The general consensus among the theorists of revolutions was that all the elements of revolutionary movements, from the inability of the state to continue its rule to the mobilization of social networks necessary for its sustenance, converged in Iran to give rise to the revolutionary movement of 1978-79. A further consensus emerged that Islam had become the hegemonic ideology of the revolution in the absence of the systematically suppressed secular leftist ideologies.[43] Many pointed out that the clergy had seized the leadership thanks to their ability to mobilize the masses of recent rural-urban migrants to major cities through their extensive networks of mosques and the financial support of traditional merchant classes concentrated in the Iranian bazaars.[44]

Theoretical frames never correspond to immediate experiences or first-hand knowledge of events. There are too many exceptions, moments, conjunctures, and faces that do not fit the abstract models. But my objection to these theories of revolution also goes beyond my individual experience.

At the time that the Iranian revolution occurred in 1979, despite their theoretical and ideological differences, theories of revolution pre-supposed a linear progressive schema of modernity. Revolutions were considered to be a rupture that would ultimately serve as a vehicle to bring societies more in line with a teleologically conceived path of progress. The Iranian revolution, particularly after the institutional-ization of the Islamic Republic, posed a conceptual and historical riddle. It intensified the age-old debates on modernity and religion, democracy and its relation to secularism, and more broadly the issue of the social contract and the origins of rights. The Iranian revolution was one of the first world historical events which directly challenged the foundational binaries of modernity, often constructed on mutually exclusive concep-tions of the modern versus the traditional. The revolution rebuked in practice the commonplace view that conceived modernity as an inherent-ly western condition that was supposed to 'have swept us away from *all* traditional types of social order.'[45]

Revolutions were supposed to make societies more 'modern' and inescapably more western in the constitution of their social relations and institutions. For all theoretical and practical purposes, to a modernist eye, the establishment of a 'theocracy' in Iran near the end of the twentieth century appeared more as a *counter*-revolution than a *real* revolution. A chorus of sociologists and historians voiced their skept-icism about what they called an 'Islamic cultural reaction (rather than a Marxist political revolution) to the Shah's modernization in Iran.'[46]

Before the Iranian revolution, theorists of modernity, with their emphasis on the perpetual processes of social differentiation, argued that religion has played an integral role in traditional societies, and that in order to modernize, political leaders must displace 'the authority of religious leaders and in other ways devalue the importance of traditional religious institutions.'[47]As Alasdir MacIntyre observed, in this evolution-ist progressive view, reason will inevitably undermine the authority of tradition, and rationalism will appeal to universal principles undeniable by any rational person—thus the independence of rationality of all social and cultural particularities. Any attempt to provide a radically different alternative standpoint is considered to be inimical to the standpoint of the Enlightenment itself. 'Hence,' MacIntyre reiterated, 'it is inevitable that such an attempt should be unacceptable to and rejected by those whose allegiance is to the dominant intellectual and cultural modes of the present order.'[48]

Dominant voices among sociologists and historians were disconcerted by this bold *return* of religion to the political scene—as if it had gone away, never to return. This confusion was often colored with a hostile inheritance from Orientalist conceptions of Islam and the Muslim world. Western scholarship traced the 'Roots of Muslim rage' to Muslim societies' incapacity to cope with the socio-cultural consequences of modernity, most notably, as Bernard Lewis remarked, democracy and individualism. Lewis and other Orientalist ideologues psychologized the revolution and linked it to the 'humiliation' suffered by Muslims during the time of the Crusades.[49] For them, the Iranian revolution and its ensuing Islamist social movements amounted to a reactionary retreat from a rapid modernization that threatened the unchanging 'essence' of Islam. They located the ideological basis of contemporary Islamist movements in the despotic and anti-modern core of the Islamic dogma. They warned about the perils of Islamic fundamentalism, locally as well as globally, and its devastating interruption of the general progressive project of modernity.[50]

A more sympathetic view, however, regarded the revolution to be modern in its constitution and in its political doctrine.[51] Its proponents argued that the Iranian revolution was the result of an uneven modernization project that combined large-scale industrialization plans and urban development with an unchanging despotic monarchical rule. As it remained oblivious towards the demands of political participation of a growing, prosperous urban middle class, this 'royal modernization' left large segments of the population unaffected or disgruntled.[52] Thus, rather than a *reaction to,* they considered the Iranian revolution to be a *consequence of* the modern restructuring of society.

Whether as a *reaction to* or a *consequence of* modernity, the revolution in Iran was as mysterious to its critics as it was to its agents. Although it was retrospectively reconstructed as an Islamic revolution, even days before its decisive victory in February 1979, its leaders continued their commitment to a broad coalition of social and political groups whose alliance was based on the most general demands of liberty and the right to self-determination.[53] Rather than posing an obstacle, the ambiguities of revolutionary slogans advanced the unity of the opposition. Neither the clerical leadership nor other influential leaders of the revolution offered with any certainty an affirmative content for the future direction of the revolution. That, they all emphasized in their revolutionary communiqués, was to be decided after the collapse of monarchy.[54]

It is true that each participating political faction in the revolution had its own vision of the ideal postrevolutionary regime. The communists saw the revolution as a democratic step towards the establishment of a socialist dictatorship of the proletariat, Khomeini believed that the revolution would *ultimately* pave the way for the emergence of *velāyat-e faqih,* and liberals, the reluctant supporters of Republicanism, hoped that the restoration of moral-religious legitimacy to the state would herald the arrival of an independent democratic Iran. Immediately after the final armed uprising of February 9-11, 1979, within each competing bloc, differing interests began their struggle first to be dominant in their own sphere and then to impose their hegemony on other factions.

But before discussing these power struggles, in Chapter Two, I will situate the Islamic response to the Pahlavi Monarchy in the postcolonial context of the twentieth century. One of the consequences of the colonization of vast regions of the Muslim world was the creation of Islam as an ideology of liberation and political identity. Colonial encounters had a paradoxical significance of the colonized subjects. While using the newly acquired colonial language of nationhood and religious identity, the colonized rose to emancipate itself from the yoke of colonialism. Islam was thus transformed from diverse ritual and religious practices into a universalizing anti-colonial political discourse. In this chapter, I will discuss four constitutive historical moments in the development of Islamism before turning my attention to the postrevolutionary Iran.

In Chapter Three, I will discuss the contingencies of drafting the constitution of the Islamic Republic. I will demonstrate that far from a premeditated and deliberate plan by the young clerical militants to constitute a political system under the supreme authority of a *faqih* (a high ranking jurist and a source of emulation), the ratification of *velāyat-e faqih* (the Guardianship of the Islamic Jurist) was the outcome of a power struggle between different political factions. Through a close reading of the minutes of the Constitutional Assembly meetings in the summer of 1979, I shall illustrate that the new constitution was Islamic neither in its sources of legitimation, nor in its historical reference.

In Chapter Four, I introduce Abdolkarim Soroush as a new breed of Muslim intellectual *par excellence* who, on the one hand, became central in legitimizing the new regime intellectually, and on the other hand, planted the seeds of dissent from within the new polity. Soroush's controversial role in the Cultural Revolution and its aftermath captured the contradictions inherent in the project of the consolidation of power. Chapter Five draws a political map of competing dominant factions and how they effectively solidified their power. Together these varying factions eliminated the opposition groups by mass executions, exile, and cooptation. As I stress in Chapter Five, three important projects brought this otherwise unlikely polity together: (a) their unabashed interest in the suppression of liberal and secular Left contentious politics; (b) their entrenched commitment to defend the country against Saddam Hussein's aggression; (c) their unwavering allegiance to Khomeini. With the disappearance of the threat against the new Republic both from Iraqi invasion and the opposition groups, and with the passing of Khomeini in 1989, the solid foundation that cemented the dominant coalition melted into air. In this chapter, by close scrutiny of the debates on amending the constitution, I also discuss how the emerging reformists failed to advance a democratic rendition of *velāyat-e faqih*.

In Chapter Six, I revisit the liberation theology of Ali Shari`ati and write about how his counter-hegemonic project of revolutionary Islam was now transformed into a movement of cultural and intellectual politics reminiscent of the Gramscian concept of the 'war of position.' I also describe how the critique of *westoxication*, the kernel of the Islamist revolutionary discourse, was transformed in this period from a total rejection of the West to a critical engagement with modernity. One of the first intellectuals who advanced a systematic and philosophically sophisticated critique of Shari`ati's conception of Islam as a revolution-ary ideology was Abdolkarim Soroush. Chapter Seven is devoted to the critical writings of Soroush. It begins with the distinction he makes between religion and ideology and his critique of Shari`ati's 'ideologization' of Islam. I also explain Soroush's theory of the 'silence of the *shari`ah,*' and its political implications. Here I show how Soroush laid the theoretical foundation of the reform movement, which was manifested in the presidency of Mohammad Khatami in 1997. Chapter Eight engages with later writings of Soroush and his self-imposed exile. I argue that Soroush's theory of religious pluralism, on the one hand, advances a radical epistemological break with all movements of Islamic revival, and on the other hand, reflects his disillusionment with the Iranian reform movement.

The Iranian revolution, along with many revolutionary movements in Latin America inspired by Liberation Theology, redefined the public role of religion in modern societies. The revolution generated its own intellectuals whose main preoccupation is a critical engagement with modernity and its contingencies. Postrevolutionary developments in Iran generated new understandings about participatory democracy, democratic politics, and secularism.

This book examines the significance of public Islam and Muslim intellectuals in shaping contemporary Iranian society. However, I need to emphasize that the Iranian intellectual landscape is not limited to Islamic hermeneutics. The fact that I have not examined the works of public intellectuals who do not justify their ideas with references to Islam, should not obscure their significance.

2

The Islamic Roots of Modernity
and the Modern Roots of Islamism

The great 'myth of the European miracle,' to borrow from James Blaut, was built upon the idea that Europe has been inherently and uniquely progressive.[1] As Marshall Hodgson posited, the myth proclaimed that although its emergence was 'natural' only to Europe, modernity[2] became an all-encompassing global force which brought all 'isolated' parts of the world into the 'mainstream' of history.[3] Not only did the idea of the 'European miracle'[4] require the construction of Europe as existentially progressive, it also rested simultaneously upon a vision of an inherently *unhistorical* and static Other whose history was merely, as Hegel remarked, 'the repetition of the same majestic ruin.'[5]

Progress, with its presupposition of movement toward a goal, or a better life in the right direction, was seen as the essence of historical change in Europe. Progress became an ideological device (or a 'moral judgment' in Marshall Hodgson's words) through which the internal historical dynamics of the non-European world was portrayed as a mere digression. The genius of the European myth was in the transposition of a temporal-chronological scheme of modern versus pre-modern onto a spatial-ideological construct of the Occident versus the Orient. This ideological scheme turned the non-Western into the pre-modern, and established Westernization as the imperative of modernity. From South Asia to greater Anatolia, not only did the European colonizers advance and institutionalize this idea, but also local elites and their modernist apologists adopted this scheme as a progressive historical inevitability.

While the colonial conquest of the Muslim world reinforced the evolutionary European vision of historical change, it also created a counter-hegemonic discourse of modernity among the first generation of

Muslim intelligentsia. In this chapter I situate the Iranian revolution of 1979 in the context of four distinct moments in the construction of Muslim responses to European modernity: (1) the colonial encounter and Sayyid Jamal ad-Din al-Afghani's anti-imperialist *Salafiyyah*[6] movement of the late nineteenth century (1858-1921); (2) the collapse of the Ottoman Empire and the formation of *al Ikhwān al-Muslimun* (The Muslim Brethren) under Hassan al-Banna (1928-1947); (3) the establishment of Pakistan and Abul Ala Maududi's conception of the Islamic state, along with the establishment of the state of Israel and Sayyid Qutb's revolutionizing of *al Ikhwān*'s original platform, turning the bottom-up into a top-down project of social change (1947-1967); (4) and finally the Arab-Israeli war of 1967 and the Iranian Revolution of 1979.

In its initial construction, this counter-hegemonic ideology simply turned the European miracle inside-out and identified the spirit of progress as an essential feature of Islam. Proponents of this view, known as the *Salafiyyah*, argued that to achieve their scientific, techno-logical, and military superiority, Europeans emulated the great medieval literary and scientific renaissance of Islamic civilization. The time had come, they declared, that Muslims *return* to their own rational, scientific traditions and *reclaim* what Europeans have taken away.

The other counter-hegemonic move in the Islamic revival recons-tructed the European transposition of the binaries of modern/pre-modern onto western/non-western. Following Abul Ala Maududi, the advocates of this view rearticulated the historical period of *jāhiliyyah*, a reference to pre-Islamic Arabs, as a supra-historical state of being—a juxtaposition of a temporal concept with a spatial construct. They considered all secular and European states to be in the state of *jāhiliyyah* progressing toward the state of Islam.

Although diverse and multidimensional, there has been a common desire in Islamic responses to modernity to secure a connection between change and what they perceive as their Islamic identity. This was evident in the writings of one of the pioneers of the Islamic response to modernity, Sayyid Jamal ad-Din al-Afghani, whose vision of modernity left a lasting mark on his contemporaries as well as more recent advocates of Islamic modernism.

British Colonialism in India and the Islamic Modernism of Sayyid Jamal ad-Din al-Afghani (1838-1897)

Afghani was born in Iran in the village of Asad-Abad and died in Istanbul.[7] To enjoy universal appeal among Muslims of the entire region, he adopted the name al-Afghani to hide his Shi`ite Iranian roots. One of the most influential figures of the nineteenth-century Middle East, al-Afghani was introduced to English readers in 1968 by Nikki Keddie and Hamid Algar.[8] He represents the Islamic response to modernity for two reasons. First, he had a distinct understanding of the difference between modernity and westernization; and second, he led a cosmopolitan intellectual movement, which influenced political landscapes in a variety of urban centers from India to Egypt.[9] In India he was regarded as anti-colonial threat, 'a free-thinker of the French kind, a socialist, an advocate of 'liberty, fraternity, and equality,''[10] the Ottoman court initially regarded him a reformist at the service of the empire, and in Egypt and later in Paris he emerged as a vocal critic of Islamic traditionalism and an advocate of modernity. Curiously, he did not leave a notable intellectual mark in his native Iran. The rise of Islamic modernity and the spread of ideas of liberty and social democracy, which eventually provided an ideological foundation for the Constitutional Revolution of 1905-1906, occurred for the most part independently of al-Afghani's legacy.[11]

Though at times contradictory, these depictions describe accurately al-Afghani, for he is, in Keddie's words, 'in some sense the parent of various later trends that reject both pure traditionalism and pure westernism.'[12] Although sometimes exaggerated, his effect on the nationalist and pan-Islamist movements in the Middle East has been immense. As Keddie wrote,

> These range from the Islamic liberalism associated particularly with Afghani's most prominent disciple, Muhammad `Abdu, to the more conservative Islamic revivalism of the Syrian/Egyptian Rashid Rida and the Muslim Brethren, and include pan-Arabism and various other forms of Middle Eastern nationalism.[13]

W. C. Smith once described Islamic modernist movements as nostalgia for the departed earthly glory of pristine Islam.[14] If we subscribe to this description, then Afghani should be credited for giving birth to this movement at the heart of which was the romanticizing of the scientific and literary Renaissance of Muslim civilizations. While there are many Muslim modernists who trace back the roots of western scientific development to medieval Islamic science,[15] al-Afghani was indisputably 'the first to stress the "Islam-West" antinomy,' and to identify Islamic civilization as the origin of modern European rationality.[16]

By emphasizing the Islamic roots of modernity, on the one hand, al-Afghani developed a critique of those traditionalist *ulama* who regarded westernization as the inevitable consequence of modernity, and thereby condemned any attempt to rearticulate Islamic scriptures in the contemporary context.[17] On the other hand, al-Afghani chastised those who promoted modernity without emphasizing its Islamic distinctions. He particularly ridiculed Sir Ahmed Khan, whom Orientalists champion as the intellectual force behind the modernization of India.[18] Al-Afghani thus argued that modernity was a Western project neither in its origin, nor in its global implications. He believed that benefiting from Western science and technology must bring Muslims closer to, rather than alienate them from, their cultural identity. This assertion became a recurring theme in Islamic movements in the last century.

It is difficult to determine whether al-Afghani genuinely believed in the Islamic origin of modernity, or adopted an instrumental relation to Islam that originated in his fear of rejection by Muslim peoples. Whatever the case may be, he was convinced that advocating modernity as a Western project amounted to political suicide. The West, al-Afghani believed, was engaged in a two-fold relation with Muslims:

> On the one hand it was an aggressive conqueror and oppressor, which was renewing its territorial conquests in the Muslim world... [On the other hand] Westerners were bent on undermining the Muslim sense of identity by turning their conquered subjects away from their own proud tradition.[19]

Al-Afghani's insight into the nature of the colonial relation has been of particular relevance in recent years. His analysis enabled him to observe, in addition to the physical violence of the territorial conquest, as well as the colonialist project of acculturation through fundamental reconstitution of the colonized societies. By reinventing their colonial subjects, al-Afghani warned, anticipating Franz Fanon, the colonialists intended to transform them into strangers in their own lands, alienated from their own traditions and amenable to the demands of their oppressors.[20]

Al-Afghani had a rather distinct understanding of Muslim identity. For him, orthodox belief in Islam and dogmatic doctrinal convictions were not what determined Muslim identity. Rather, all ethnic-regional characteristics of peoples, among which he considered language to be primary, were part of their historical being. This belief was particularly apparent in his Indian writings, in which he advocated a linguistic or territorial nationalism, rather than a call for pan-Islamism. Rather than advocating the unification of Indian Muslims with the *ummah* (the global community of Muslims), he saw stronger foundations for the unity of Hindus and Muslims in India. Conscious of the irrevocable mark colonialism had left in mapping the new world, he asserted that 'there is no happiness except in nationality, and there is no nationality except in language.'[21] Conspicuously absent from his conception of happiness was religion. He argued for the primacy of language over religion as the unifying means of a nation, for he regarded language to be a more durable, stable, and persistent linkage between people than religion, whose forms and popular observance can change in different periods.

For some western observers, such as the French rationalist philosopher and Orientalist Ernest Renan, Afghani's embrace of modern science, technology, and the rational means of political administration, as well as his vehement rejection of colonialism, appeared to represent an inherent contradiction in his thought. Keddie for example, argued that 'the conflict between a desire to Westernize and a need to avoid identification with the West was one of the roots of the contradictions in Afghani's ideas.'[22] It would be hard to find a reference where al-Afghani expressed a desire to Westernize. He considered modernity to be an *Islamic* project. The fact that the West benefited from the philosophical and scientific achievements of medieval Islam did not make the modern technological and scientific advances a western accomplishment. For al-Afghani, whereas modernity in Europe was realized through a rupture with and the abolishment of the past, for Muslims it meant reclaiming a lost tradition via reconnecting with their past. For him, Westernization conveyed alienating cultural transformation and dependency.

In his 'Lecture on teaching and learning' (1882), he accused those who 'forbid science and knowledge in the belief that they are safeguarding the Islamic religion [to be] really the enemies of that religion.' He wondered how it was possible for Muslims to study with the greatest delight the sciences that are ascribed to Aristotle, 'as if Aristotle was one of the pillars of the Muslims,' when the study of Galileo, Newton, and Kepler was forbidden, since the *ulama* considered them to be infidels. 'There is no incompatibility between science and knowledge,' he reminded the traditionalist *ulama,*[23] 'with the foundation of the Islamic faith.' For Muslims, modernity is possible if it is connected to its Islamic origin. As Keddie noted,

> Like other nationalists, and like the Islamic modernists who followed him, his general argument for defending Islam, [and] modernism at the same time was to claim that modern virtues originated with Islam, and that the Muslims who rejected them were acting against the principles of their religion.[24]

At the same time, in terms almost as bold as his defense of modernity, al-Afghani criticized those, such as Sir Ahmad Khan in India, who were unable to see the distinction between modernization and westernization, and promoted cultural alienation of Muslim nations as a requirement of modernization. Ahmad Khan and his companions, al-Afghani remarked, invited people to reject their religion. '[He] disparaged to them the interest of their fatherland and made people consider foreign domination over them a slight thing, and strove to erase the traces of religious and patriotic zeal.'[25] They were an army for the British in India.

> They drew their swords to cut the throats of the Muslims, while weeping for them and crying: 'We kill you only out of compassion and pity for you, and seeking to improve you and make your life comfortable.[26]

Al-Afghani's modernist movement was based upon the desire to initiate a project of modernity without compromising Islamic traditions. For him and all other Muslim modernists, borrowing from Western science and technology was the first step towards the realization of that desire. In his articulation of the integral constituents of the Islamic modernist project and its relation to Western modern knowledge, Fazlur Rahman captures the core of al-Afghani's modernist project:

> [1] that the flowering of science and the scientific spirit from the ninth to the thirteenth century among Muslims resulted from the fulfillment of the insistent Qur'anic requirement that man study the universe—the handiwork of God, which has been created for his benefit; [2] that in the later medieval centuries the spirit of inquiry had severely declined in the Muslim world and hence Muslim society stagnated and deteriorated; [3] that the West had cultivated scientific studies that had borrowed largely from Muslims and hence had prospered, even colonizing the Muslim countries themselves; and [4] that therefore Muslims, in learning science afresh from the West, would be both recovering their past and fulfilling the neglected commandments of the Qur'an.[27]

Echoing the Orientalists' long-standing position, Rahman identified a decline of the spirit of inquiry as the main cause of Muslim societies' stagnation and deterioration. He was convinced that the scientific studies that brought prosperity to the West were largely borrowed from Muslims. He neglected, however, to recognize that the West's prosperity was directly related to the colonization of Muslim countries and other parts of the globe. Rahman and other Muslim modernists failed to view the Western scientific-technological progress and colonialism as an indivisible project.

In sum, al-Afghani's modernist discourse was constructed on the premise of the separation of modernity from Westernization—that is, the separation of modern science-technology from the socio-historical conditions within which it has arisen. Jamshid Behnam summarized this project with reference to al-Afghani's articles published in Paris in his 1884 journal *Al-Urwah al-Wuthqa*:

1. Returning to the pure tradition of primeval Islam and cleans-ing Islam from superstitions.
2. Condemning blind traditionalism and the conformist 'imitation' [of the *ulama*].
3. Advocating the unity of all Muslims against colonialism.
4. Resisting the absolute authority of the sovereign and accept-ing the principles of political philosophy of the West [rational political administration].
5. Appropriating modern science and technology as the only means of Islamic world's progress and strength.[28]

Al-Ikhwān al-Muslimun: The Birth of Political Islam

Both politics and Islam project social totalities. Indeed, political Islam is based on the assumption that there is an inherent link between 'Islam as a comprehensive scheme for ordering life' and 'politics as an indispens-able instrument to secure universal compliance with that scheme.'[29] Many western critics of political Islam have highlighted the authoritarian implications of this link. What is also of significance in this scheme is the absence of any specific political theory in Islamic thought. In pre-twentieth century Islam, politics was considered as only another part of the 'general outlook of Islamic values,' hence the Orientalist claims about Islamic political quietism. For much of their history since the dawn of Islam, Muslims had the religious obligation to obey their rulers. The collapse of the Ottoman Empire after the First World War and the subsequent end of the Caliphate rule resulted in the introduction of the idea of the Islamic state as an alternative to the Caliphate, which was now being declared, either implicitly or explicitly, not only by the Turkish secularists but also by Muslims of diverging outlooks, to be beyond resuscitation.[30]

In his revivalist movement, al-Afghani presupposed the hetero-geneity of Muslim (and non-Muslim) subjects of the Ottoman Empire. However, with its collapse, competing assertions of the homogeneity and authenticity of the nation informed the political discourses of secularists and Muslims alike. Turkish secularism, pan-Arabism, and emergent political Islam offered competing ideologies of nationhood.

They shared an affinity with German romantic nationalism in their search for pure ethnic Turkish identity, Arab linguistic communities, and the global community of Muslims, the *ummah*, respectively. What was *given* earlier as cultural diversity of Muslims now faced great skepticism from those who believed that colonial encounters had contaminated the purity of their faith and the cultural authenticity of its followers.

Rejecting the Kemalist secular alternative in Turkey and al-Saud's *Wahhabi* puritanism,[31] the movement of al-Afghani's disciple and companion Muhammad Abduh's *Salafiyyah* became the main impetus for a new configuration of political Islam. Established in 1928 by Hasan al-Banna (1906-1949), *al-Ikhwān al-Muslimun* (The Muslim Brethren) was the institutionalized and organized extension of al-Afghani's and Abduh's activism. Al-Banna was influenced by the kind of Islamic nationalism advocated in *Al-Urwah al-Wuthqa,* a journal published by al-Afghani and Abduh in 1884, and the ideas of his Syrian contemporary Rashid Rida, editor of the journal *al-Manar*. According to al-Banna, the mission of *al-Ikhwān* was, through a return to the wellsprings of Islam, to enable Muslims to restore their religion's power and stand firm against all 'intrusive tendencies,' such as secular liberalism and Marxism.[32]

The abolition of the Caliphate political system created a space outside the state for religio-political institutions. Soon after its inception, *al Ikhwān* occupied this space in Egypt and later in several other Arab countries. The existence of a religio-political organization outside the state apparatus raised new questions about the role of Islam in social change in the Muslim world. From the beginning, *al Ikhwān's* leaders faced the question of defining their role vis-à-vis the existing state. In a 1943 monograph al- Banna described *al Ikhwān's* objectives:

> My Brothers: [1] you are a benevolent society, not a political party, nor a local organization having limited purposes... [2] When asked what it is for which you call, reply that it is Islam, the message of Muhammad, the religion that contains within it government, and has as one of its obligations freedom. If you are told that you are political, answer that Islam admits no such distinction. [3] If you are accused of being revolutionaries, say 'We are voices for right and for peace in which we dearly believe, and of which we are proud. If you rise against us or stand in the path of our message, then we are permitted by God to defend ourselves against your injustice.' [...] If they insist on pursuing their oppression, say to them, 'Peace be upon you, we will ignore the ignorant.'[33]

As I enumerated, there are three significant points in this document, which incidentally served as a membership guideline. First, al-Banna argued against the description of *al Ikhwān* as a mere political party, from which, he believed, the objectives of his organization were broader and deeper. The project of *al Ikhwān* encompassed *all* aspects of social life, including politics. Thus, second, the realm of state politics was on the agenda of the Brothers, for in Islam there is no distinction between politics and religion. However, as al-Banna emphasized in his third point, the political action of the Brothers could not be realized through a revolutionary assumption of political power.

Although *al Ikhwān* occupied a unique space in the history of religious organizations in Islamic societies, al-Banna and other theoreticians of this movement did not abandon the fundamentals of orthodox teachings of the relation between religion and the state, at the center of which were the doctrines of *takfir* (the condemnation of the apostate or *kāfir*) and *jihad*.

One becomes a Muslim by professing the *shahādah* ('There is no god but Allah and Muhammad is His messenger'). Islam does not recognize any mediation between humankind and God. Thus, in the absence of priestly mediation, a self-proclaimed Muslim ought to be considered a Muslim. The unmediated relation with God and self-proclamation as the only foundation of Muslimhood, created the predicament of 'corrupt Muslim rulers.' Muslim theologians predominantly argued that the duty of Muslims was to obey their Muslim rulers. Regardless of how corrupt they might be, so long as they ascertain their Muslimhood, only through the *shahādah*, they should be recognized as the vicegerent of Allah. Inevitably, *takfir* of a ruler by the *ulama* has been a rare incident in the history of Islam. According to Islamic political orthodoxy, since *takfir* of a Muslim ruler cannot be justified religiously, there could be no just cause to defy a Muslim ruler.[34]

Al-Ikhwān al-Muslimun's position on the Islamization of society was not a direct challenge to this orthodox belief. The *Salafiyyah* movement and the founders of the Muslim Brotherhood, as John Esposito notes, were concerned with the 'effects of a Western secular form of modernization upon Islamic life and values and the failure of the government to address adequately the widespread socio-economic disparities in Egyptian society.'[35] A plan to seize political power was not included in this critique. In line with old orthodoxies, al-Banna believed that a good state will eventually emerge from a 'virtuous community.' As John O. Voll described al-Banna's political philosophy, 'although he believed that the power to reform was inextricably linked to the power to rule, al-Banna insisted that the Muslim Brotherhood was committed to broad-based social reform, not to the direct exercise of political power.'[36]

Evidently, in spite of its new social and historical location, the political Islam of the Muslim Brotherhood did not diverge from the belief that it was not the responsibility of a 'true Islamic state' to reconnect Muslims with their 'glorious past' and aid them in reestablishing their hegemonic position in the world. Rather, they believed, it is through the Islamization of Muslims' lives that the re-emergence of the 'true Islamic state' was to be realized. The difference, as al-Banna noted, is between a revolutionary assumption of political power and a thoroughgoing grassroots cultural transformation of the whole community.

Abul Ala Maududi (1903-1979): The Islamic State in Pakistan
The call for the establishment of an Islamic state came from Pakistan. Abul Ala Maududi's political teaching was the first systematic attempt to formulate the notion and necessity of an Islamic state. Although critical of such a notion before the partition of India and establishment of Pakistan in 1947, Maududi came to be recognized as the main theorist of the Islamic state.

Maududi emerged as a significant intellectual figure after the publication of his voluminous work *Al-Jihad fi al-Islam* (*Jihad in Islam*) in 1930. He became the editor of *Tarjuman al-Qur'an*, an influential monthly journal in the Indian subcontinent. In the 1940s and 1950s his scholarly works were translated into English and Arabic through which he became known among Arabs and other non-Indo-Pakistani Muslim intellectuals.

In contrast to al-Afghani's belief that Indians constituted a nation and should unite against the British colonizers as one, during the Indian anti-colonial movement Maududi maintained that any nationalist movement, either Indian or Muslim, amounted to a secular attempt to undermine Islamic values and ways of life. Thus, he argued, any attempt to establish an Islamic nation-state would violate fundamental principles of Islamic teachings on the global unity of the *ummah*.[37] However, the realization of the 1947 partition and the establishment of Pakistan had compelled him to revise his political philosophy. In March 1949, the new state adopted the Objectives Resolution and declared:

> Whereas sovereignty over the entire universe belongs to Allah Almighty alone, and the authority which He has delegated to the State of Pakistan through its people for being exercised within the limits prescribed by Him as a sacred trust...[38]

The resolution struck Maududi as an ideal point of departure for his new doctrine of the Islamic state. During decades of the Indian anti-colonial movement and in the early phases of the post-partition period, Maududi had argued that change in Muslims' lives should come from within, by soul-searching and the compliance of every individual Muslim with the teachings of the Qur'an. Maududi believed that politics began with the transformation of the self. Only a truly pious Muslim could act as the source of a just government. By distancing himself and barring his followers from participating in the Indian anti-colonial struggle, he often appeared as a British collaborator.[39] His initial thought on social activism resembles more closely the early *al-Ikhwān* agenda where he saw the main objective of Muslims in the formation of a virtuous (*Sālih*) community, whose expansion would give rise to the ideal *ummah*. It was within that frame that he called for the establishment of the *Jamā`at al-Islami* in 1941 in Lahore.

However, the dramatic revision of his position after the partition inspired *Jamā`at-i Islami* to reject political quietism and advocate a more activist interpretation in which the realization of the virtuous community proceeded entirely from top down. Not only was Maududi unperturbed by the authoritarian implications of his political philosophy, he believed that existing circumstances necessitated such a despotic rule. By 'circumstances,' he meant the state of *jāhiliyyah* (ignorance), originally a reference to the pre-Islamic conditions of the Arabian Peninsula. In Maududi's interpretation, *jāhiliyyah* did not refer to a particular historical period. Rather, it signified an omni-historical condition under the influence of which the *ummah* abandons its Islamic way of life and accepts the rule of apostates (*kuffar*). Thereby, Maududi considered all forms of nationalism, democracy, and secular states to be various sources of *jāhiliyyah*, thus subject to destruction.[40]

For the most part, Maududi enjoyed the support of the Pakistani *ulama* and had always been considered an insider. The organization he founded in 1941 as the alternative to the Islamic nationalist movement, *Jamā`at-i Islami*, played a major role in the formation of the independent Pakistani state. Hence, in the Pakistani context, Maududi's theory of the Islamic state was to legitimize an already existing political power. Although he espoused liberal ideas on the question of citizens' rights,[41] he remained an apologist for a totalitarian exercise of state power, skeptical of participatory democratic politics. As Hamid Enayat posits, 'despite the revolutionary methods recommended by him to fulfill the prerequisites of the Islamic state, his perception of the structure of the state itself is 'conservative.'"[42] Although Maududi's political doctrine is far from a revolutionary manifesto, his ideas outside Pakistan engendered a new mode of Islamic political expression at the center of which was the notion of *jāhiliyyah*. The most influential proponent of this new political discourse was Sayyid Qutb.

Sayyid Qutb (1906-1966): The Establishment of the State of Israel

The post-WWII era brought disillusion about the promises of modernity. The unprecedented atrocities committed by modern states stirred doubts and suspicion across the globe about the utility and benefits of modern technology and science. A definitive moment after the war in the Middle Eastern political landscape was the establishment of the state of Israel in 1948. Not only did the state of Israel become the ultimate manifestation of jāhiliyyah, but it also contradicted the long-standing modern/secular position on the separation of church and state.

Sayyid Qutb, one of the most influential Muslim political theorists, depicted the inherent contradiction in the notion of a Jewish state within the context of liberal political theory. In response to the critics who considered the idea of an Islamic state reactionary and pre-modern, Qutb offered the example of Israel as a nation 'founded on religion—and religion alone,' since, as he rightly pointed out, 'Judaism is not a nationality but a religion,' yet Israel was supported by the British, funded by the Americans, and accepted by the Russians.[43]

Qutb was born in the village of Mosha in the Assiyut district of Egypt to a farmer father and a devout Muslim mother. It was his mother who wished her children to memorize the Qur'an as Qutb recalled in the dedication of his book *Al Taswir al-Fanni fi al-Qur'an* (*The Artistic Imagery in the Qur'an*).[44] Although Qutb memorized the Qur'an as a child, and attended the local *madrasa*, his formal higher education was in Cairo's *Dar al-Ulum* (now the University of Cairo) from where in 1933 he earned his BA in Education. After graduation, he was hired as a lecturer at the same school, and later was employed by the Egyptian Ministry of Education as a School Inspector.

In 1949 the Ministry sent him to the United States to pursue his studies in education. The two years he spent in America profoundly transformed Qutb's consciousness. He saw first hand what he regarded as the 'insatiable greed for material things,' a racially divided (Qutb himself had a very dark complexion), and what he perceived as a 'sexually perverted' America. He was also appalled by the American media's support for the establishment of the state of Israel. He perceived the American support of Zionism to be inherently anti-Arab and anti-Islam. As M. Siddiqui observed, 'prior to his trip to the USA [...] he had not been committed to the Islamic movement in Egypt;' after his return he 'came to appreciate the deeper meaning of the Islamic teachings.'[45]

In 1951, at the same time as Qutb returned to Egypt, Maududi's writings were translated into Arabic and published in Egypt. Maududi's theory of *jāhiliyyah* found strong resonance in Qutb's state of mind. Disappointment in America, the establishment of the state of Israel, and the high fever of nationalism in Egypt had decisive effects on Qutb's politicization and his search for an Islamic alternative to what he, after Maududi, saw as the state of *jāhiliyyah*. As Qutb developed his theory, it became apparent that his analysis diverged from the original philosophy of the founders of the *Ikhwān* movement. He abandoned reformist efforts for cultural transformation, and instead, advocated the establish-ment of a vanguard party, *jamā`ah*, the prime goal of which was the revolutionary assumption of political power.[46]

Qutb challenged the *Ikhwānian* idea that the Islamic state emerges from the enlightened *ummah*. He argued that the *ummah* could not realize itself under the existing condition of *jāhiliyyah*. *Jahiliyyah*, he remarked, is an 'all-encompassing condition' which manifests itself in all spheres of social, cultural, and intellectual life.[47] 'We must free our-selves,' he asserted, 'from the cluthes [sic] of *jāhili* society, *jāhili* concepts, *jāhili* traditions and *jāhili* leadership.'[48] Qutb did not regard *jāhiliyyah* as a form of false consciousness. Rather, he treated it as an active movement that reproduced itself in action. He proposed that

> *Jāhiliyyah* controls the practical world, and for its support there is a living and active organization. In this situation, mere theoretical efforts to fight it cannot even be equal, much less superior, to it. When the purpose is to abolish the existing order and to replace it with a new system which in its character, principles and all its general and particular aspects, is different from the controlling *jāhili* system, then it stands to reason that this new system should also come into the battlefield as an organized movement and a viable group.[49]

Qutb called this viable group *jamā`ah*. Rather than through the gradual cultural transformation of the *ummah*, Qutb believed that 'the Islamiz-ation of the *ummah* can only proceed from the *jamā`ah* whose total existence is focused on the mission it has assumed.'[50] He thereby inverted the original mandate of the *Ikhwān* and contended that '[The

Muslim society] cannot come into existence simply as a creed in the hearts of individual Muslims.' Society changes top down.[51]

Sayyid Qutb's Schema of the Islamic Revolution

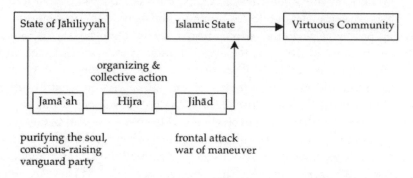

In his political philosophy, Qutb regarded reformist politics as a means of justification of the state of *jāhiliyyah*. The responsibility of the vanguard was to become 'independent and distinct from the active and organized *jāhili* society.'[52] Qutb called this period of struggle *hijra*, a reference to the Prophet Mohammad's migration from Mecca to Medina where he established the first Islamic state in 622 AC. A contemporary proponent of the Qutbian political thought, Abd al-Salam Faraj addresses the point in the following way:

> There are those who say one must establish an Islamic party modeled on the present political parties. Yet rather than destroying the godless state, such a party would bolster it further and enhance legitimacy through participation in its political life and sitting in parliaments that legislate without reference to Allah. Others still allege that Muslim [activists] should endeavor to occupy decision-making positions [...] so that by dint of having 'Islamic engineers,' 'Islamic doctors,' and the like in the upper echelons of government the regime will be transformed into an Islamic one . . . This is sheer fantasy.[53]

Qutb justified his call for *jihad* against the tyranny of the apostates, by calling the Arab nationalist states of Egypt and Syria the states of *jāhiliyyah*. He chastised the dominant interpretations of *jihad* as defeatist ideologies that exonerate the existing structures of *jāhiliyyah*. Qutb distinguished his articulation of *jihad* from earlier renditions in two ways.[54] First, rather than merely a theoretical/spiritual matter, he considered *jihad* to be a practical issue. *Jāhiliyyah* prevails over ideas and beliefs, it enjoys ideological hegemony while at the same time asserts itself in a 'practical system of life' maintained by political and material authority. *Jihad* thus needs to confront both ideological and practical features of *jāhiliyyah*, both reforming ideas and beliefs by persuasion, and, at the same time, utilizing physical power to abolish *jāhiliyyah.*

Second, *jihad* should be understood progressively, as a movement whose objectives and methods are not abstract and unchanging. In a hermeneutical approach, he chastised orthodox views of *jihad* and argued that

> Those who talk about *jihad* in Islam and quote Qur'anic verses do not take into account [...] the relationship of the verses revealed at various occasions with each stage [...] this is because they regard every verse of the Qur'an as if it were the final principle of this religion.[55]

Qutb castigated orthodox *ulama* for their rendition of *jihad* as either an individual soul-searching and purification or a 'defensive war.' By denying Islam its right to abolish 'all injustice from the earth,' he argued, the established religious institutions have reconciled with and have become integrated into *jāhiliyyah.*

Reviving a hitherto obscure opinion advanced by the esteemed medieval theologian, Ibn Taymiyyah (1268-1328), Qutb revisited the question of whether a self-proclaimed Muslim could be condemned as an apostate (*takfir*). Did the mere *shahādah* (professing the Islamic credo) suffice to make one a Muslim? Was Muslimhood only a matter of self-identification or should it be exercised in practice?[56]

Ibn Taymiyyah argued that a ruler would abandon his Muslimhood if he failed to enforce the *shari`ah* (the Islamic code of law and governing) and breaks major injunctions concerning 'life and limb, property, *jihad* and the status of non-Muslims, the sexual code of behavior, alcoholic prohibition, gambling.' Accordingly, Ibn Taymiyyah transformed the condition of Muslimhood from self-proclamation to a practice, most importantly of the just exercise of power, judged by other members of the community.[57] Unlike Qutb's revolutionary rearticulation, during the first two decades of the fourteenth century, Ibn Taymiyyah was more concerned with the inclusion of the *ulama* and the urban elite in Baghdad and Damascus under the Turkic Mamluk rulers. As Albert Hourani aptly observed, calling upon these newly converted rulers to enforce the *shari`ah* had a further implication: 'the local, Arabic-speaking population should be consulted and given their share in the process of government.'[58]

Although Qutb sought to legitimize his call with the unimpeachable authority of Ibn Taymiyyah, one should not misinterpret that as an indication of an unchanging continuity in Islamic political thought. Commentators such as Emanuel Sivan often disregard the historical context of Ibn Taymiyyah's doctrine and the socio-political contingencies of the postcolonial Islamism of Sayyid Qutb, to depict Islamic political philosophy as inherently totalitarian.[59] The notion of continuity in this context is pejoratively utilized to illustrate the anti-modern core of Islam and its political philosophy. Sivan puts it bluntly that, 'the core of Sayyid Qutb's ideas [...] consists in total rejection of modernity.'[60]

In contrast to Qutb's radical re-articulation through which he revolutionized Ibn Taymiyyah's theology, throughout the history of Islamic societies, Ibn Taymiyyah's teachings were understood within the framework of mainstream orthodoxy, the most famous example of which was the *Wahhabi* movement, which eventually led to the creation of Saudi Arabia. More than the sudden awakening to the revolutionary teachings of Islam, together the question of postcolonial statehood, national liberation movements, the Cuban Revolution, the revolutionary ideas of Che Guevara, can better explain the radical Islamism of Qutb and other Islamist religio-political theorists. Whereas western social theorists and historians have comprehended the Bolshevik doctrine of vanguard party or urban guerrilla warfare, the Islamic version of the same political tactics have appeared utterly unjustifiable within the modern context and its roots had to be linked to the radical core of Islamic dogma. As Olivier Roy observes, 'we have lost the common frame of reference, the Third World Marxist vulgate allowed some to 'understand' the Baader-Meinhof or the Red Brigades, even the Palestinian hijackers, but not the Hizbollah hostage-takers.'[61]

Not only was Qutb's condemnation of the contemporary *jāhiliyyah* conditioned by post-colonial politics, but also his political doctrine, as Roxanne Euben suggests, 'was a "dialectical response" to rationalism and Westernization, as a dynamic critique rather than a scripturalist reflex.' Qutb was a critic of post-Enlightenment rationalism, which he blamed for depleting modern life of any ethical norms and spiritual values. Like his political radicalism, Qutb's assertion of the failure of modernity resonated with Western political theorists from diverse political and moral perspectives, from Alasdair MacIntyre and Robert Bellah to Hannah Arendt and Daniel Bell. 'Such resonances suggest that Qutb's perspective is neither unfamiliar nor pathological but is rather one interlocutor among a chorus of voices attempting to capture the causes and character of what I have called the leaching of meaning from modern life.'[62]

Qutb viewed Islam as a 'pragmatic activist system of life.' In contradistinction to the Orientalist doctrine of genesis and decline, Qutb's Islam was engaged in the continuous reproduction of itself, and had limitless resources to provide solutions for contemporary social, economic, and political predicaments. He intended to transform Islam from 'a religion seeking an irrelevant, static, purely transcendent ideal to an operative force actively at work on modern problems.'[63]

Qutb diverged from the early modernist Islamic movements in two fundamental ways. First, he rejected hybridity as a violation of the comprehensiveness (*shumul*) of Islam. In his vision, a true Islamic society was not based on an amalgamation of western science and technology with Islamic values. Contrary to the modernists' belief, Qutb did not believe that by learning from the West, Muslims could reclaim their past socio-political and intellectual glory. He condemned neither learning western sciences nor appropriating its technology, but he did not speculate that by doing so Muslims would reclaim their past.

> If a proper atmosphere is not provided under which [...] sciences and arts develop in a Muslim society, the whole society will be considered sinful; but as long as these conditions are not attained, it is permitted for a Muslim to learn them from a Muslim or a non-Muslim and to gain experience under his direction, without any distinction of religion.[64]

Second, he advocated the assumption of political power as a precondition of social change. He contradicted al-Banna's thesis that a good state will eventually arise from a virtuous community. He proposed a 'Bolshevik' vanguard revolutionary politics in which a coalition of committed individuals (*jamā`ah*) would dedicate themselves to the materialization of the true Islamic society.

The Arab-Israeli War of 1967 and the Iranian Revolution of 1979

Sayyid Qutb was executed in 1966 by Gamal Abdel Nasser's regime. This act did not result in mass protest and his ideas remained eclipsed by Arab nationalist movements until the mid-1970s. The humiliating defeat of Egypt in 1967 the Arab-Israeli war for the first time raised questions about the effectiveness of secular nation-building projects in the Arab world, at the center of which was the defense of Arab lands against Zionist intrusions.

Qutb's influence spread beyond Egyptian boundaries. Some of his writings were widely translated into non-Arab Muslim and European languages. The translation of Qutb's early writings into Farsi (*Al-'Adala* and *Mashāhid* as well as parts of *Fi Zilal al-Qur'an*, his six-volume Qur'anic commentary) had a ubiquitous influence on the emergent Muslim intelligentsia in Iran. In his public talks, Ali Shari`ati (1933-1977), regarded by many as *the* ideologue of the Iranian revolution, employed a Qutbian political rhetoric and made Sayyid Qutb known to Iranian youth. Although Shari`ati's ideas and his audience differed from Sayyid Qutb's, he nonetheless adopted a Qutbian pragmatist and activist apprehension of Islam. Shari`ati invented a revolutionary Islamic lexicon that moved with ease from Fanonian concepts to Qur'anic verses and from Trotsky to the Prophet in addressing the predicaments of *Westoxication*. He galvanized an otherwise Marxist generation of young Islamists who played a major role in the overthrow of the monarchy in Iran.

By assuming political power, the Iranian revolution introduced a new direction for social change in the Islamic countries. Not only did it put an end to the monarchy, it also limited the influence of both secular Arab nationalisms and the old Islamic political quietism. The Iranian revolution was a compelling example of the feasibility of the Islamic alternative. It transformed the idea of top down change through the assumption of political power from a Qutbian fantastic idealism to a realized doctrine.

The revolution, however, had a paradoxical effect inside and outside Iran. Inside, it was institutionalized simultaneously via a Jacobin Reign of Terror, and through a period of constitutional and legal projects of legitimation. Outside, it became *the* signifier of revolutionary change in the Muslim world. Inside, from the heavenly discourse of justice and emancipation from the yoke of imperialism, the predicament of revolutionary Islam became the earthly criminal legal codes and family laws and other bureaucratic nuts and bolts of governance. Outside, a new generation of young activists around the Muslim world found new hope in their struggle against tyranny and injustice. In a pamphlet, published in 1979, entitled 'Lessons from Iran,' the Islamic Student Association of Cairo University saw the revolution as 'a vindication of the true nature of Islam as the sole, comprehensive guide for life and the basis of a just society.' The students declared:

> The first lesson is the influence of the creed on Muslims. A spirit
> has moved the being of this people, who appeared servile and
> submissive to injustice and tyranny. This revolution confirmed

for us that rulers who sold their countries were transformed into puppets in the hands of rulers of East and West.[65]

Perhaps the most important feature of the Iranian revolution was that it nationalized an Islamist movement that had been characterized by an anti-nationalist ideology. What made the Iranian revolution distinct was the dialectic between its transnational rhetoric (Muslim *ummah*) and its nationalist manifestation. Both rhetorically and practically the Islamic Republic defined itself within the boundaries of the modern nation state. Immediately after the triumph of the revolution, the Islamic Republic became more concerned with political and economic independence at home, as Henry Precht observed, than 'dominion abroad.'[66]

The assumption of political power in Iran brought forth an inherent contradiction of Islamism. The paradigmatic shift in Islamic revivalism from modernizing Islam to Islamizing modernity was based on the critique of modernity as the universal experience of westernization. The shift, therefore, was based on a call for pluralization of a politically, socially, and culturally contingent modernity. In its defining motto of 'neither Western, nor Eastern,' the Iranian revolution and the post-revolutionary regime set to constitute an alternative path of social change legitimized by Islam and manifested nationally.

If the concept of Islamized modernity presupposed the *plurality of modernity*, the experience of the Islamic Republic of Iran proved that it could not be sustained without accepting the *plurality of Islam*. The struggle to Islamize a society inevitably leads to the questions of *who the Islamizers are* and *to which interpretation of Islam they subscribe*. In other words, Islamization, or public Islam, ushers in either totalitarianism, the dominance of a singular understanding of Islam as the state ideology, or pluralism, the recognition of competing interpretations of Islam and the diversity of religious experiences.

In the following chapter, I will show how the early attempts to legitimize Islam against Marxism and liberalism as a competing ideology of social change shaped the debates in drafting the constitution. But more importantly, making Islam public generated a new space for the emergence of a new generation of intellectuals whose hermeneutical project became the foundations of a democratic movement. This movement engenders a transnational network of activist intellectuals who have established a sustained movement of social change and transformations in the institutions of civil society.

3

Legitimizing the Postrevolutionary Regime: The Genesis of the New Constitution

In the fall of 1980, more than one year after the triumph of the revolution, the state-sponsored Iranian television broadcasted a series of debates divided into three categories of ideology and belief, politics, and economy. The Supervisory Council of the Islamic Republic's Voice and Vision invited a diverse group of intellectuals and political activists, from Babak Zahra'i, the representative of a small Trotskyite socialist party to Mohammad Taqi Mesbah Yazdi, a conservative Shi`ite jurist, to participate in these primetime television conversations.

Although the postrevolutionary regime by then had established its constitutional authority, the contentious politics of competing factions, from within and without the polity, continued to disrupt the Islamic Republic's irrevocable consolidation of power. While soon after the triumph of the revolution the *ruhaniyyat*, the clerical hierocracy, took charge of the state's coercive means of oppression, they remained uncertain about their own intellectual vigor and ability to justify their rule for the greater population of urban and educated classes. In the opening session of the seven-part debates on religion and materialism, the moderator explained that the series was designed to emphasize that, 'one of the honorable attributes of the Islamic regime is to allow the proponents of other doctrines and ideologies to debate and challenge Islamic ideology.'[1] Mesbah Yazdi also began his introductory remarks by reiterating,

> With the Divine blessing and the beatitude of the Islamic revolution, today we have succeeded in discussing the important issue of ideology in a free and respectful environment. I hope that we will try to distance ourselves from personal prejudices and devote our efforts to the illumination of truth, so our esteemed audiences and the Iranian nation, who have borne the

weight of this revolution, may comprehend the truth better and more deeply.[2]

Questioning the motive behind the primetime show, several influential political parties and intellectuals refused to partake in these debates.[3] To bear out the openness of the new regime on national television by inviting dissenting intellectuals and political activists to engage with the representatives of the governing power seemed at odds with the state's policy of shutting down newspapers, harassing members of the opposition parties, organizing thugs to attack their headquarters and ransack their offices.

Those who appeared on television for the seven-part series on religion and materialism[4] were Ehsan Tabari, central committee member of the Tudeh Party, Farrokh Negahdar, the leader of the *Fada'iyān-e Khalq* Organization (the majority faction, a militant communist urban guerrilla group); Mohammad Taqi Mesbah Yazdi, from Qom Seminary, and finally a young philosopher and lay theologian Abdolkarim Soroush.[5] Although Soroush already had a presence in the postrevolutionary political landscape as a member of the Cultural Revolution Council, his eloquent oratory and mastery of sophisticated philosophical concepts introduced him for the first time to a wider audience. Notwithstanding his *intentions* for participating in these debates, with his ongoing responsibilities in the Cultural Revolution Council (CRC), Soroush exemplified the new regime's attempt to construct a hegemonic legitimacy for the Islamic Republic outside its traditional social base. He personified the postrevolutionary Muslim intellectual—learned in both western and Islamic philosophical traditions; scholastic, rather than revolutionary, in his disposition; dialogical, rather than provoca-tive, in his discourse.

Through these debates, the new regime hoped to strengthen its legitimacy by showing its commitment to 'free exercise of public reason,' as John Rawls would say, and an 'undistorted rational communication,' as Jürgen Habermas would imagine. Moreover, by allowing a non-seminarian philosopher such as Soroush to present an Islamic critique of philosophical materialism, the organizers also believed that the debates could limit the appeal of Marxism among young Iranian intellectuals.

The two Marxists who participated in the panel, Ehsan Tabari and Farrokh Negahdar, represented two influential organizations, both of which supported the radical anti-imperialism of the 'petit-bourgeois clergy' against the conciliatory liberalism of the 'bourgeoisie.' By their participation, they had also hoped that they could both contribute to the isolation and eventual elimination of the liberal faction in power and present a version of Marxist politics more congruent with the policies of the Islamic Republic. Indeed, during the debates they advocated the interests of the Islamic Republic more than their Muslim counterparts.

These debates were organized while Iraqi forces were invading large territories in the southwestern regions of the country. Whereas Muslims dismissed the significance of the war, Marxists qualified their presence in these debates by reiterating that they would rather be defending the revolution against the Iraqi aggressors than debating philosophy on national television. In contrast, Mesbah Yazdi, representing the Qom Seminary, argued

> It might appear that during this time of war, our audiences would not have the patience to follow philosophical discussions. One might argue that people's attention is directed towards the borders and their minds are preoccupied by the devastations of war, and therefore these types of discussions are unnecessary and fruitless [...] But all conflicts and wars are rooted in ideological differences [...] As Imam Ali said, even during wartime, we need to engage in ideological discussions.[6]

In his introductory remark, Ehsan Tabari responded,

> Under current circumstances, discussions about ideology are unnecessary. We believe that we can solve many urgent problems by discussing important political and economic issues. We agree that these are important issues, but this is neither the right medium nor the right time to discuss them.[7]

Farrokh Negahdar expressed the same sentiment about the wisdom or the necessity of these debates and further stressed the importance of 'unity among all anti-imperialist forces, despite ideological differences.' He began his remarks, with 'greetings to the country's toilers and with the hope of victory for fighters in the war imposed by the criminal regime of Saddam.' He also criticized those who refused to participate in the debates, and called for a unified front 'against imperialism and its allies.'[8]

Why would a regime which had successfully seized the repressive apparatus of the state and had already eliminated major contenders of power through two massive popular events, the 1979 invasion of the American Embassy in Tehran and the Cultural Revolution of April 1980, organize exhaustive, complicated, and obscure philosophical debates on primetime national television? Whom were they intended to persuade that their ideological discourse had a depth and breadth akin to its

Marxian counterparts? The primetime debates functioned as another state-building effort that combined an oppressive exclusionary politics with the construction of a persuasive hegemonic ideology of Islamic governance. This effort, to wed Islam and state power, and link governance and Islam *in practice,* was a new endeavor for the fledgling regime and its critics.

Not only was the collapse of the old regime with its military might unexpected to its ubiquitously western supporters, but more importantly, it came like a bolt from the blue for the clerical leadership of the revolution. The clergy was neither ready to assume power, nor was it clear about the actual organizational meaning of an Islamic Republic. Not only did the clergy lack confidence in their own administrative power to manage the colossal state bureaucracy, with few exceptions, such as Morteza Motahhari, they were also incapable of putting forward an effective intellectual discourse to legitimize the Islamic regime. This was evident when Khomeini decided to appoint Mehdi Bazargan, a longtime liberal Muslim political activist, to form the Provisional Government, or when he asked Hasan Habibi, a liberal civil jurist, to draw up the first draft of the new constitution. An amplified sense of the revolutionary *geist* led to an exaggerated sense of people's determination in pursuing their demands. That sense shaped the intentions of the post-revolutionary state during its initial power struggle. Major competing factions in postrevolutionary politics operated from an uncompromising position with the objective of eliminating their opposition.

Although the meaning of an Islamic state was outlined in Ayatollah Khomeini's 1971 manifesto,[9] its appropriation as a revolutionary demand was tentative and for the most part symbolic. I use the term symbolic not to suggest that Islam operated only as an ideology in the Marxian sense of false consciousness. Rather, it was appropriated by the leadership and internalized by the revolutionary actors as a symbolic and philosophical frame of social justice. When millions of Iranians chanted in the streets of the capital and other towns and cities, *Esteqlāl, Āzādi, Hokumat-e Islami* (Independence, Liberty, Islamic State) and *Barābari, Barādari, Hokumat-e `Adl-e Ali* (*égalité, fraternité,* Imam Ali's rule of Justice), they were plainly demonstrating their appreciation for an Islamic allegory of justice and liberty. Islam was understood but not spoken in practical and organizational terms. It was up to the new regime to render its tangible, mundane, and immediate voice.

The revolution created a 'new Man [sic],' in a Fanonian fashion, through a violent process by which people freed themselves from the yoke of a tyrannical regime.[10]   But the victory of the revolution also unequivocally ended the period of symbolic appropriation of Islam by a diverse spectrum of political parties and social groups. As Michael Fischer observed, 'political victory requires a spelling out in political and institutional terms of what previously could be left in vague philosophical and moral language.'[11] Which group was to become the voice of this symbolic frame was uncertain, even for the undisputed leader of the revolution, Ayatollah Khomeini. More than twenty-seven years after its establishment, the riddle of finding the institutional means of an Islamic social order remains the main paradigm of legitimacy in the Islamic Republic.

Many scholars of the Iranian revolution, most notably Said Amir Arjomand, have argued that the establishment of an autocratic theocracy in the form of an absolute authority of the *faqih*, was indeed the strategic goal of Ayatollah Khomeini. Arjomand ridicules Shahpour Bakhtiar, the last prime minister under the Shah, and Mehdi Bazargan, the head of the provisional government, for arguing that 'Khomeini did not know where he was leading the nation.'[12] Citing a 1979 interview with Oriana Fallaci, he illustrates Bazargan's blunder about Khomeini's true intentions:

> Something unforeseen and unforeseeable happened after the revolution. What happened was that the clergy supplanted us and succeeded in taking over the country [...] Yes, it was the lack of initiative by the laity that permitted the takeover by the clergy [...] In fact, it cannot even be said that they had it in mind to monopolize the country. They simply seized the opportunity offered by history to fill the vacuum left by us.[13]

It is indisputable that Ayatollah Khomeini believed in the establishment of an Islamic state from the first time he laid out its legal (*fiqhi*) justification in his five volume treatise *al-Bay'* in early 1960s. However, as indicated by the minutes from the meetings of the Assembly for the Final Examination of the Constitution of the Islamic Republic (the Assembly of Experts), which was convened in the summer of 1979, the role of the *faqih* in the postrevolutionary regime was neither institutionally nor ideologically predetermined. The discussions of the Assembly of Experts most visibly show that the clergy recognized that it was ill prepared to seize political power and invent a new Islamically-sanctioned political apparatus.[14] The minutes indubitably show that even the inner circles of power contested the meaning of an Islamic state as an undisputed idea of governance. Even the closest allies of Khomeini, most notably his influential disciple Morteza Motahhari, expressed doubts about the ability and legitimacy of the clergy to govern.[15]

While the leadership of Khomeini was incontrovertible, institution-alizing this leadership in the new constitution was met with great skepticism and confusion. Not only was the idea of bestowing direct political power upon the clergy controversial from a theoretical stand-point, but it also seemed implausible from the practical consideration of the legitimacy of the new regime. Although the *ruhāniyat* (clerical establishment) played a significant role in mobilizing the revolutionary movement, it lacked the intellectual depth and significant cultural capital to lead the urban middle and working classes. Scholars of the Iranian revolution often argue that the *ruhāniyat* in general and Ayatollah Khomeini in particular knowingly manipulated secular and other non-clerical intellectuals and deceived the public to advance their political agenda of instituting the *velāyat-e faqih*. This view, however, neglects the postrevolutionary contingencies of state-building and the social context within which *velāyat-e faqih* was constitutionally recognized as the foundational pillar of the new regime.

Undoubtedly, for Khomeini, *velāyat-e faqih* was the ideal form of governance. However, he and other advocates of the doctrine did not believe in its feasibility. In 1978 Khomeini became an advocate of Islamic republicanism not as a calculated effort at public deception, but rather as an attempt to establish an Islamic regime that could appeal to larger numbers of intellectuals and urban classes. He did believe that the new regime would eventually lead the society towards the realization of a virtuous *ummah* and the establishment of the *velāyat-e faqih*. But in his view, this was a long historical process whereby Islam was to become hegemonic in society. Khomeini believed that neither was Iranian society ready to accept the rule of the clergy, nor was the clergy prepared to take on the task of governance. Therefore, rather than a mere deception, his political strategy was a pragmatic attempt to assure the victory of the revolution with the widest possible popular support and intellectual justification. It was not ideological conviction, but rather the insecurities and uncertainties of the new regime that motivated the push to establish the *velāyat-e faqih* and its ratification by the Assembly of Experts, the Constitutional Assembly's *coup de théâtre*.

The Genesis of the Constitution and Its Ratification

In 1978, before his return to Iran, Ayatollah Khomeini commissioned Hasan Habibi, a noted political activist and liberal jurist, to draft the first version of the constitution in Paris. The first draft was based on Khomeini's recent assertion that the new regime would be an Islamic Republic highlighting its republicanism. On numerous occasions in his press interviews, Khomeini was asked to draw a distinction between an Islamic republic and other forms of republics. His response to a reporter for *Le Monde* was typical of his replies to the question of the reconciliation between Islam and the notion of a republic.

> *Le Monde*: Your Excellency wishes to establish an Islamic Republic in Iran. For the French people this is ambiguous, because a republic cannot have a religious foundation. Is your republic based on socialism? Constitutionalism? Would you hold elections? Is it democratic?
>
> Ayatollah Khomeini: Our republic has the same meaning as anywhere else. We call it 'Islamic Republic' because the conditions of its emergence are embedded in Islam, but the choice belongs to the people. The meaning of the republic is the same as any other republics in the world.[16]

Khomeini's positions prior to the victory of the revolution were merely informed by his shrewd political instinct. Not only was the notion of an Islamic Republic ambiguous to Khomeini's critics, it was also a political experiment for Khomeini himself. As noted by Mehdi Bazargan a few years after he resigned from his position as the head of the provisional government in 1979, neither Khomeini nor any other members of the Revolutionary Council had specified the institutional forms of the Islamic Republic or how to go about establishing them in practice.[17]

Ayatollah Khomeini took practical steps beyond his rhetorical endorsement of republicanism by bestowing the responsibility of drafting the new constitution to Habibi, who later formed a commission comprised by all civil experts in jurisprudence.[18] Hasan Habibi was profoundly influenced by French republicanism, particularly the Gaullist tradition of the Fifth Republic. Approved in a referendum in 1958, the constitution of the Fifth Republic gave unprecedented powers to the president and afforded the Constitutional Council the power of judicial review and the right to examine laws passed by the parliament. From a *parliamentary* republic of the Fourth Republic, the Fifth Republic converted France to *presidential* republicanism.[19] Habibi's affinity with Gaullist republicanism manifested itself in the document he drafted, in which he assigned absolute executive powers to the president and called for a Guardian Council to review the constitutionality of laws passed by the parliament in order to examine their compatibility with Islam.

The Revolutionary Council and the Provisional Council of Ministers under the supervision of Yadollah Sahabi, another prominent liberal politician and an advisor to the provisional government of Mehdi Bazargan, further revised the document and published the official preliminary draft on June 14, 1979.[20] This version revised the first draft by moving it towards a social-democratic constitution. They added provisions on women's rights, specifically the right to hold public office, on other social justice issues, participatory democracy, and further restricted the private ownership of industry. The published version limited the power of the president and increased that of the prime minister. More importantly, it recognized municipal and provincial councils as a major source of decision-making and executive power. Ayatollah Beheshti notably advocated the issue of women's right to run for all the elected offices of the government (including the office of the president) and Ayatollah Mahmoud Taleqani championed the elevation of municipal councils as the practical foundation of governance.[21]

Not only did Khomeini trust civic jurists to draft the new constitution, on several occasions he lent his support publicly to the published preliminary draft in which no mention of *velāyat-e faqih* was made.[22] For example, in a meeting with members of the Tehran Preachers' Society on June 17, 1979, he insisted on supporting the published draft and hoped that it would be approved and instituted shortly. Indeed, until *velāyat-e faqih* was passed by the Assembly of Experts on September 12, 1979, Khomeini remained faithful to his 1978 Paris declaration of Islamic republicanism, in which *ruhāniyat* was to assume an advisory role in the guidance and proctorship of the state.[23] According to Hasan Habibi, the Revolutionary Council approved the published version of the constitution with direct blessing of Ayatollah Khomeini, who had only expressed minor concerns about the consistency of the document with Islamic jurisprudence in matters of women's rights and the relationship between the Shi`ites and the minority Sunnis. In an interview with the *Kayhan* daily, Habibi argued that Khomeini believed that 'the realities of our society do not allow a full appreciation of *velāyat-e faqih*, our society is not ready to accept this.'[24]

Six days after the publication of the draft of the constitution, Khomeini invited all 'groups, *ruhāniyun*, intellectuals, and theologians' to participate in a public discussion of the draft. 'You have one month,' he declared, 'to examine this new [constitution] and write your opinions in existing newspapers about all the things you might deem useful for Islam and consistent with the Islamic Republic.'[25] In the months prior to the election of the Assembly for the Final Examination of the Constitution, diverse groups of jurists, public intellectuals, political activists, and theologians flooded daily papers and magazines with their commentaries in support or rejection of the draft.

As Shaul Bakhash illustrated,[26] the reaction to the published draft was wide, uncompromising, and divisive. While a small minority of political parties and activists, such as the secular liberal National Front, reluctantly supported the existing draft, most political parties of the Left castigated it as a betrayal of the goals of the revolution. This document, which had enjoyed the overwhelming support of the Revolutionary Council, the Council of the Provisional Ministers, and Ayatollah Khomeini, lacked the endorsement of the intelligentsia. It intended to satisfy simultaneously the disparate concerns of many factions from socialists to Islamists and liberals. But at the end, it failed to muster enough support from any single contender of postrevolutionary political power.

The most systematic critique came from a group of jurists and lawyers of the Iranian Lawyers Guild who organized the Seminar on the People's Expectations from the Constitution only three weeks after the draft's publication. They went as far as demanding to 'make the Universal Declaration of Human Rights part of the Iranian constitution, and to give international human rights organizations and lawyers the legal authority to defend Iranian nationals before Iranian courts [!]' They further called for limiting the powers of the President in favor of a participatory parliamentary democracy. They asked for a stronger emphasis on the rights of minorities, particularly the right of self-determination, through the empowerment of local and municipal councils. Additionally, they called for large-scale nationalization of land, large industry, and foreign trade.[27] Although the draft delegated limited powers to the clergy, nevertheless, it generated significant negative reaction among secular intellectuals, political activists, and the leaders of religious and ethnic minorities in Baluchistan, Khuzistan, and most importantly, Kurdistan.

During the first few months of the postrevolutionary regime, the *ruhāniyat* failed to assert itself as a formidable intellectual force. With the exception of Ayatollah Khomeini, the clerical leadership of the revolution did not possess a broad theoretical basis from which they could respond to the numerous critiques raised against the draft. The most influential clerics, such as Mohammad Beheshti, Mohammad Bahonar, Ali Khamene'i, Ali Akbar Hashemi Rafsanjani, while effective politically, initially did not counter arguments to secular critiques of the constitution. They feared that by advocating more institutionalized clerical power, they would strengthen the position of the traditionalist senior clerics. Younger clerics such as Rafsanjani, who believed that the draft of the constitution met the expectations of the revolution, advocated speedy ratification by referendum. Khomeini also supported the idea of quick and direct ratification of the constitution,[28] but his reason differed from these younger activists. Rafsanjani captured the attitude of the younger generation of clerics when he warned the liberal advocates of the constituents' assembly that such an assembly would be dominated by 'a fistful of ignorant and fanatical fundamentalists who will do such damage that you will regret ever having convened them.'[29]

Khomeini, satisfied with the basic premises of the document, was more troubled by the political gains made by the liberal-Left by their critique of the proposed constitution. He feared that a prolonged process of ratification would eventually lead to the marginalization of the clergy. Khomeini asked the *ruhāniyat* not to be intimidated by the intellectual vigor of the opposition and to engage in the debate on the evaluation of the draft. In his remarks to a delegation of preachers from Mashad at the end of June 1979, he declared:

> This right belongs to you. Those knowledgeable of Islam may express an opinion on the law of Islam. The constitution of the Islamic Republic means the constitution of Islam. Do not sit back while 'foreignized' intellectuals, who have no faith in Islam, give their views and write the things they write. Pick up your pens and in the mosques, from the altars, in the streets and bazaars, speak of the things that in your view should be included in the constitution.[30]

The *ruhāniyat* and other advocates of *velāyat-e faqih* responded to Ayatollah Khomeini's call and convened the Congress of Muslim Critics of the Constitution. In a resolution that was widely believed to have been authored by two conservative ideologues Hasan Ayat and Fu'ad Karimi, the Congress proposed that 'the duties of the president ought to be carried out by the ruling *faqih*. Otherwise, the constitution needs to specify the rights and responsibilities of the *faqih* in separate articles.'[31]

Under the leadership of Ayatollah Hossein Ali Montazeri, the clergy launched a campaign to promote the inclusion of *velāyat-e faqih* in the constitution. Grand Ayatollahs Golpaygani and Mar`ashi Najafi, who seldom spoke of political topics, declared that without *velāyat-e faqih* the new constitution was meaningless. The most well-articulated and precise position on this topic was put forward by Ayatollah Montazeri who questioned the basic premises of the published draft, such as the separation of powers and peoples' rights of self-determination. He argued that, both theoretically and practically, the idea of *velāyat-e faqih* was incongruent with the main principles of the proposed constitution. He further reiterated that the *faqih* ought to have the right 'to dissolve the parliament, [...] to declare war or peace, [...] to be commander in chief of the armed forces, [...] to nominate candidates for presidency and approve the president after a general election [...].'[32] On September 14, 1979, for the first time in a Friday prayer sermon, Montazeri raised the foundational significance of the *velāyat-e faqih*, and the worshipers responded by crying out '*velāyat-e faqih* is the protector of our revolution.'[33]

Although Khomeini invited the *ruhāniyat* to engage in the debate, he resisted their calls to endorse the idea of *velāyat-e faqih*. On several occasions, he deferred his decision to the final deliberation of the Assembly of Experts. For example, on July 8, 1979, in response to the complaint of an unspecified group of clerics about the absence of *velāyat-e faqih* in the draft constitution, Khomeini responded, 'these are matters in which I shall not intervene.'[34] Later, on the eve of the election-day for the Assembly Experts, he reiterated that 'I have my opinion about the constitution, but God willing I will convey it in the future.'[35] In all his declarations prior to the approval of *velāyat-e faqih* in the Assembly of Experts, Khomeini adopted a pragmatist approach to the role of the *ruhāniyat* in the Islamic Republic. He was neither certain that Iranian society was ready and willing to accept the rule of jurisprudence, nor was he convinced that he could gather enough enthusiasm and support among clerics, particularly the more junior among them. Although he was oblivious as to how this would be viewed on the global political scene, his intention was to avoid alienating the civil jurists and other secular intellectuals. His August 19, 1979, message to the opening session of the Assembly was indicative of his pragmatist strategy of speaking to both sides of the issue of *velāyat-e faqih*.

By the time the Assembly convened, the propaganda machine of the new regime had turned *velāyat-e faqih* into a foundational principle of the revolution and the Islamic Republic. However, in none of the six points he raised in his message did Ayatollah Khomeini mention *velāyat-e faqih* as the litmus test of the new constitution's compliance with Islam. In the first two points, Khomeini declared:

> 1. It is not hidden to any person who is knowledgeable about the Islamic Revolution in Iran that the main motivation for this revolution and the secret to its victory was Islam. By crying out 'Allah-o Akbar,' our people from even the remotest parts of the country demanded the establishment of an Islamic Republic, which was approved by their almost unanimous vote. Islamic as well as non-Islamic countries recognize us as the 'Islamic Republic of Iran.'
> 2. The constitution ought to be based on Islam. If even one article contradicts Islamic ordinances, it is a deviation from the Republic and the vote of the great majority of people [...].[36]

Although Khomeini insisted on the Islamic basis of the constitution, he considered peoples' votes to be the final measure of the legitimacy of these laws. He further bound himself by the final decision of the Assembly. In the third point of his message, on the one hand he entrusted 'the determination of what is consistent with and what contradicts Islamic rules in the constitution to the high-ranking *foqaha*,' and on the other hand, he deemed it necessary to consult the expertise of the civil jurists in matters of constitutional law. It is not difficult to read between the lines of the message that, although intrigued by the possibility of the establishment of the *velāyat-e faqih*, Khomeini did not intend to fulfill this agenda at the risk of alienating and eventually antagonizing its opponents.

> 3. The determination of what is consistent with and what contradicts Islamic rules belongs solely to the high-ranking *foqaha*, many of whom are present in this Assembly. Because this matter requires expertise, it is necessary to welcome the input of the expert representatives. There are learned and capable individuals among the respected representatives who are expert in legal, administrative, and political matters. Their expertise ought to be reflected in this constitution.[37]

Points four and five cautioned the assembly not to be intimidated by the propaganda of the Left and the Right and their international supporters. 'They see themselves defeated,' he asserted, 'and will not refrain from these clamors and controversies.' In his last point, Khomeini laid out the basic principles by which the constitution needed to abide.

6. The respected representatives of the Assembly of Experts must strive to their outmost to ensure that the constitution embraces the following characteristics:

    a.   Support and protection of rights and interests of all people without discrimination.

    b.   Providing for the needs of future generations in accordance to the divine laws.

    c.   Clarity and candor when it comes to the meaning of laws, such that they would not lend themselves to false interpretations and inferences to justify the despotic temptations of the self-idolizers of history.

    d.   Guiding and inspiring other Islamic movements by setting an exemplary model of an Islamic society.

At the end, I ask the omnipotent God for your success and I hope that with your dedication you will approve a truly Islamic and progressive (*moteraqqi*) constitution. [38]

One of the hallmarks of Khomeini's pragmatism was that he never wholeheartedly supported any political agenda before gaining the confidence that he had the means of carrying out the policy or position he preached. Khomeini's lukewarm support for including *velāyat-e faqih* in the constitution indicated that he was first of all uncertain as to whether the clergy-dominated Assembly could carry the vote to pass such a constitution. Second, he worried about losing popular support and did not want to be identified exclusively with one faction of the regime at the expense of eliminating the other. With the inclusion of the term *moteraqqi* (progressive), from the political lexicon of the left and liberals, in the last line of his message, he markedly demonstrated that he was not ready to abandon *in toto* the republicanism of the draft. Khomeini was aware of the basic contradiction of the rule of jurisprudence with the spirit of republicanism and the right of self-determination. Appointing a *faqih* with the qualification of being the *source of emulation* as the leader could institutionalize Khomeini's leadership, but as it was seen by many (I shall discuss this later), not only did such an addition to the constitution fundamentally undermine its main principles, but also, after Khomeini's death, the constitution could lose its relevance—Khomeini was irreplaceable.

In his letter to the Council for the Reappraisal of the Constitution on April 29, 1988, Khomeini revisited this issue, admitting that he did not think the *velāyat-e faqih*, with its required condition of *marja`iyat* (source of emulation) was politically feasible.

    I believed and insisted from the beginning that the condition of *marja`iyat* is not necessary. A righteous *mojtahid* who is endorsed by the respected experts [*khobregan*] ought to be qualified, if the people have given the *khobregan* the authority to choose their leader […] This was my position in the original constitution, but my companions insisted on the condition of *marja`iyat* and I consented.[39]

Thereby, Khomeini took the political debate over the administrative structure of the Islamic Republic back to its original post-revolutionary context.

The Politics of the Assembly of Experts:
The Final Draft of the Constitution

The first time that the clergy as an institution realized the extent of its social power was when, in a nation-wide referendum on April 1, 1979, more than 98 per cent of the electorate voted 'yes' to the establishment of the Islamic Republic. Different factions in the revolutionary leadership saw the referendum as the first opportunity to influence the construction of the postrevolutionary regime. While the religious factions did not question the Islamic character of the new regime, they sharply diverged on the institutional role of Islam and the *ruhāniyat* in managing the affairs of the country. Ayatollah Shari`atmadari, a grand ayatollah with wide support among Azeri Iranians, proposed an open-ended question for the referendum, rather than a simple 'yes' or 'no' plebiscite. A large coalition of clerics and liberal parties advocated a 'Democratic Islamic Republic,' which was an attempt to institutionalize public participation as the only source of legitimacy of the new regime.

Khomeini oscillated between two positions in his rejection of the addition 'Democratic' to the Islamic Republic. From one position he argued that the addition of democratic to the title of the state was redundant, that democracy was embedded in Islam and such an addition presupposed Islam was undemocratic. In this regard, he followed the logic put forward by his liberal disciple Morteza Motahhari. A few days before the referendum, in an interview with Iranian Television, in response to a question about deleting the term 'Democratic' from the Islamic Republic, Motahhari asserted that:

The word 'democratic' in the 'Democratic Islamic Republic' is tautological. Moreover, soon people will gain certain freedoms and democratic rights under the Islamic Republic, and some might believe that they have attained these rights because of the democratic principle of the regime, not for its Islamic essence

[...] When we speak of the Islamic Republic, naturally we recognize individual rights, freedom, and democracy.[40]

Several months later, in his interview with Oriana Fallaci, when Khomeini was asked about the reason for dropping 'Democratic' from the Islamic Republic, Khomeini followed the same logic. 'It is saddening to me,' he lamented, 'when Islam is emptied of its essence, and then some believe that we need to add a prefix, such as 'democratic,' to define it. Islam encompasses everything.'[41]

But most often in his speeches to revolutionary masses, Khomeini used his blunt anti-colonial discourse to reject the adjective 'Democratic' from the referendum's ballot. On March 1, 1979, upon return to Qom, he warned the welcoming crowd that democracy was a 'Western idea,' and that the next regime in Iran was not going to be 'the republic of Iran,' nor is it going to be the 'Democratic Republic of Iran,' or 'the Democratic Islamic Republic of Iran,' but just 'Islamic Republic of Iran, not a word more, not a word less.'[42] Khomeini's declaration was marred by contradiction. On the one hand, he adopted the modern idea of republicanism, and on the other hand, he castigated 'westoxicated intellectuals' and their supporters for borrowing the notion of democracy from the West.

Nothing in Khomeini's sermons or his allies' political positions indicated that they had anticipated overwhelming victory in the April 1 referendum. Even in his final message on the eve of the vote, Khomeini struck a conciliatory tone, hinting at the possibility of a third alternative. He stated that 'Tomorrow, step out of your homes and vote for the Islamic Republic [...] You are free to cast your vote for any form of government you wish. The fact that there are only 'Yes' or 'No' on the ballots should not limit your choice. You may write in any type of government on your "No" ballot.'[43] The fact that the advocates of the Democratic Islamic Republic or an open-ended referendum yielded to Khomeini's agenda explains the almost unanimous approval of the Islamic Republic. The opponents did not have organizational means to mobilize against the referendum, however, one can only suspect that the results could not have been fundamentally different had they widely publicized their opposition. Perhaps what contributed to this over-whelming victory for the 'Islamic Republic' was the ambiguity of the concept, which Khomeini deliberately maintained. An ambiguous concept spoke to the revolutionary spirit of the masses who continued to articulate themselves in terms of negation rather than an affirmative construction of a political system.

The referendum eased the uncertainties of the clergy and encouraged them to become more assertive in their demands for an institutional role in the postrevolutionary state. Moreover, the chaotic emergence of multiples sources of power—grassroots organizations in the factories, ethnic self-determination movements, revolutionary foundations (*nahādhā-ye enqelābi*), and state institutions—impelled Khomeini and his allies to accelerate their plans for the consolidation of power. The contradictions in Khomeini's positions regarding the institutional role of the *ruhāniyat* in the state are indeed explicable when contextualized in the postrevolutionary power struggle. Khomeini decided to put the Islamic Republic to a referendum and not the *velāyat-e faqih* because he still questioned the extent of his power to legitimize and the readiness of society to accept it. But despite these uncertainties, faced with mounting opposition, and the inability and unwillingness of the Provisional Government to exercise its Jacobin power in order to solidify its political leverage, Khomeini and his allies were forced to rethink their strategy.

The most important event that shaped the power struggle in the days immediately after the revolution was the rebellion in Kurdistan and the Kurdish provinces in Western Azerbaijan. The first signs of unrest appeared in the city of Mahabad, on March 17, when the armed guerillas of the Kurdish Democratic Party clashed with government militia over the control of community organizations in charge of security and the distribution of goods and municipal services. In only one day, the conflict escalated. Twelve people were killed and hundreds wounded. The central government, conscious of the history of Kurdish movements for the right of self-determination, acted hastily and without careful examination of the demands of the Kurdish parties. A one-day truce was broken on March 19, and violence spread throughout all Kurdish regions in western Iran. In the city of Sanandaj, the rebels took over government buildings and demanded specific recognition of Kurdish rights in the constitution. Intoxicated with the newly acquired powers of the air force and heavy artillery, the new government responded violently to the rebels' actions, it bombed their positions in the city. On March 19, 1979, the daily *Ettelāʿāt* reported that one hundred and thirty were killed and more than three hundred wounded. Many were arrested to be executed later in public.[44]

After the massacre in Sanandaj, on the Iranian New Year's Eve of 1358 (March 20, 1979), Khomeini and the Provisional Government sent a joint mission to the region for negotiation with the different factions of the Kurdish insurgency, the Kurdish Democratic Party, Kumeleh, and a widely popular and respected local imam, Sheikh Ezzeddin Hosseini. Recognizing the colossal significance of the bloodshed, the government dispatched its highest ranking and most prestigious representatives to the region to find a settlement with the Kurdish leaders.[45] Although the high-level composition of its delegates showed that the central government took the matter of Kurdish rights seriously, the negotiations failed to resolve the issue. Although the Kurds emphasized that they did not harbor a secessionist agenda, it did not deter the new regime from treating the resurgence as such. The new regime's excessive use of force radicalized the insurrection and allowed militant leftist groups to exploit this in order to stymie the regime's consolidation of power.

Earlier in March, Arabs of Khuzistan had also put forward the same demands for self-determination. On March 9, 1979, the Organization of Arab People of Iran convened in the town of Khorramshahr. In their final resolution, which was published in the daily *Ettelā`āt* (March 11, 1979), they called for:

1. The recognition of Arabic as the first language for the Arab speakers.
2. Freedom of expression and publication in Arabic.
3. The recognition of Arab courts as the only legitimate judiciary in the region.
4. Production and dissemination of Arabic radio and television programs.
5. Presence of Arab representatives in the *majlis*.
6. The appointment of Arab government ministers.[46]

Hojjat al-Islam Khamene'i represented the central government in the negotiations with the organization's spokesperson Sheikh Mohammad Taher Khaqani. Since the Arab community predominantly lives in the oil-rich region of Khuzistan, the government was resolute that it would not tolerate disturbances in the region. Arab riots followed, which were put down swiftly and brutally by the military.

In the northeastern region of Turkman Sahra, disputes over the distribution of land and access to sources of water for small farmers spiraled into full-scale urban warfare in the town of Gonbad Kavus. On March 28, the Pars News Agency reported than in only three days fifteen people had lost their lives and more than 400 were wounded in street battles between the leftist *Fadā'iyan-e Khalq* guerillas and military and paramilitary government forces. The Minister of Domestic Affairs sent a three-member commission to negotiate with the rebels, while at the same time, according to a *Fadā'iyan* organization flyer, they militarized the region by deploying soldiers into Gonbad Kavus.[47]

In major industrial cities, the Left organized, supporting workers' councils and advocating radical profit-sharing and management reforms. They helped to establish unemployed workers in major industrial cities. On several occasions, unions of unemployed workers clashed with government paramilitary forces and at least in one case in the city of Isfahan, an organizer was killed during a peaceful demonstration. Fearing the expansion of the Left's influence, the Islamic regime showed particular sensitivity to labor issues and the control of workers' organizations. The Provisional Government found itself paralyzed when faced with capital flight, while Islamists and leftists competed on the factory floor for the control of the production and distribution of goods. Ezzatollah Sahabi, who represented the Ministry of Industry in the newly formed Council for the Protection of Industry,[48] recalled that 'the Council worked like a war command center. There were several phones on each member's desk that were constantly ringing with the news of labor riots all around the country. Managers or owners of factories were taken hostage by the workers who demanded back pay and benefits.'[49]

Islamists considered Marxists their prime ideological competitor, both in their intellectual discourse and in their ability to lead labor movements. Thus, while they fought fiercely over the control of labor organizations, in order to build grassroots support for the new regime, the Provisional Government offered unprecedented benefits to workers in major industries. For example, under the powerful Minister of Oil Industry, Hasan Nazih, oil workers in the South gained a 40per cent increase in their average income in the first six months of the new administration.[50] At one point Ayatollah Beheshti (the future Vice Chair of the Assembly of Experts), influenced by the communists' egalitarian mantra, set the goal of the distribution of wealth in society to a one-to-three ratio between the lowest and highest income!

Although the transition of power in 1979 was relatively peaceful, during the first few months of the postrevolutionary period, the country fell into seemingly uncontrollable disorder. These events proved that the Provisional Government was unable to contain the Islamist and communist agendas of radicalization, and that the outcome of the postrevolutionary power struggle was far from certain. After the total consolidation of power, in 1981 Ayatollah Khomeini reflected on the predicament of the clergy two years before how his earlier position on the role of the *ruhāniyat* in the postrevolutionary state had been transformed. The following long citation captures Khomeini's shift:

> From the beginning of the revolution, my position, as I conveyed it in many interviews and declarations, in Najaf, Paris and upon returning to Tehran was that the *ruhāniyat* has a higher responsibility than do executive appointments. In case the revolution should triumph, I had suggested, they would return to their cherished responsibilities. But when we entered the political arena [after the revolution], we realized if we asked them to return to their mosques, the Americans and the Soviets would swallow up the country. We experienced and learned that those non-clerics who assumed power, albeit many of them were devout Muslims, failed to realize our basic desire for independence and being content with our bread and butter [...] Therefore, since we did not find a person who could be faithful to the cause for which this nation has sacrificed its youth, we felt obliged to accept clerics in the office of the presidency, or other government positions. I reiterate that we do not intend to run the country, and on the day we realize that non-clerics are able to manage the country according to God's desires, our respected [President] Khamene'i shall return to his spiritual duties. We [...] asked the *ruhāniyat* to attend to their spiritual and guiding roles after the revolution. *But we made a mistake,* and we should have the courage to admit our mistakes. We seek the realization of Islam, not the advancement of our own words. During the revolution, we thought that these educated, devout, and intellectual groups would advance the country according to the Divine Will, but we were mistaken. Many duped us; others had good intentions, but contradicted our ideas. We deviated from our earlier assertions and asked the *ruhāniyat* to run the country [...] If we suspect that the integrity of Islam is in jeopardy, under any circumstances, it is our responsibility to intervene. Let them accuse us of anything, let them broadcast that this is the country of mullahs run by an *akhundist* regime. This is propaganda to force us to leave. No! We shall not leave the scene.[51]

The idea of a seventy-five-member (reduced to seventy-two after the election) Assembly of Experts for the final ratification of the constitution emerged in the context of this growing uncertainty. It resulted from a compromise between two proposals, one that advocated a direct referendum (supported by Ayatollah Khomeini and the majority of younger revolutionary clerics), and the other that called for a 450-member Constituent Assembly (supported by Ayatollah Taleqani and the Provisional Council of Ministers led by Prime Minister Mehdi Bazargan). The compromise was to assure a speedy ratification which would end the chaotic period of transition and justify the legitimacy of the new regime against Marxist as well as Muslim traditionalist contenders for power.

The reduction of the number of members of the Assembly from its original four hundred fifty to seventy-two offered the new regime the means to control its composition and the boundaries of its negotiations. Through an ingenious redistricting measures, which mixed rural and urban regions, the organizers of the election ensured the victory of the clerics who ran against a diverse group of politicians and activists, many of whom did not accept the legitimacy of such an assembly to ratify the final draft of the constitution. The election was riddled with irregularities, particularly in rural areas with high rates of illiteracy. Mob groups repeatedly ransacked campaign offices of the opposition in the days preceding the election.[52]

On election-day, August 3, 1979, five months after the revolution, revolutionary fervor and massive enthusiasm that had marked the first referendum of the Islamic Republic was conspicuously absent. As Table 1 illustrates, the majority of the representatives were elected with more than 50 per cent of the popular vote. However, in relation to the first referendum, the percentages show an increasing division among the electorate. More importantly, 18 per cent of the candidates were elected with less than 35 per cent and two with only 17 per cent of the vote.

Table 1. Distribution of the Representatives of the Assembly of Experts Based on Percentage of the Vote

Percentage of the Vote	No. of Representatives
100-91	8
90-81	9
80-71	9
70-61	14
60-51	15
50-41	8
40-36	1
<35	8
Total	72

Source: *Mozākerāt*, Vol. 4, p. 411.

The assembly members from rural areas with little or no formal modern education formed a solid majority bloc (see Table 2). But they did not enjoy a strong mandate sine they were elected in their district with a small margin of victory over their opponents. In contrast, the candidates with postgraduate education as well as well-known revolutionary clerics, although in the minority, received a high percentage of votes in their districts.

Table 2. Distribution of the Representatives of the Assembly of Experts Based on Modern Education

Education Level	No. of Representatives
Lower than High School Diploma	44
High School Diploma	3
Associate Degree	1
Bachelor's Degree	7
Masters Degree	6
PhDs	10

Source: *Mozākerāt*, Vol. 4, p. 408

Khomeini positioned himself to retain his leadership in any outcome. Although forty-one members of the Assembly were seminarians who specialized in *ijtihad*, Khomeini remained skeptical of their ability to apply their expertise fully in devising a political system that could meet the needs of contemporary Iranian society. This skepticism later manifested itself in Khomeini's lingering conflicts with the Guardian's Council on the issue of *maslahat-e nezām-e islami* or the expediency of the Islamic system.

Velāyat-e Faqih and the Right of Self-Determination

> *A friend once told me that whenever he recites the Qur'an in private he makes no mistakes, but whenever he does so in front of others he makes twenty mistakes in every line. This is how I feel today in front of my distinguished colleagues. When I am in a mosque I have no problem expressing what is in my mind, but at this podium my tongue totters. Well, I am inexperienced in these matters. We have worked in mosques but are unseasoned in legislating or running a government.*
>
> Ayatollah Mohammad Saduqi

Ayatollah Saduqi's expression of his own position in the Assembly perfectly illustrates how ill-suited many of the traditionalist clerics felt in what was then the highest postrevolutionary institution of power. Critique of the ruhāniyat's new role in shaping the emerging regime came not only from secular outsiders, but the clerics themselves who conveyed a deep skepticism about their own legitimacy and ability to administer the country. This uncertainty was evident in the text of the Assembly pledge, which made a Persianized reference to God (parvardegār-e yektā) and to a revolutionary commitment to the 'heroic people of Iran' (khalq-e qahramān-e Iran) and to be faithful to the goals of the revolution. Both promises of the pledge were derived from the political lexicon of liberal nationalists and communist Left, respectively. It demonstrated that the new regime continued to rely for its legitimacy on the broader coalition that brought the revolution to its triumphant conclusion.

The young regime used its recently acquired executive powers to create a homogenous Assembly for the final ratification of the published draft of the constitution. Ayatollah Khomeini expressed his satisfaction with the composition of the Assembly and his optimism about the general agreement among its members on the draft's basic foundations, when he announced that there would be a one-month deadline for the constitution's final ratification. The fact that the Assembly extended the deadline twice, taking them more than four-and-a-half months to rewrite rather than revise the new constitution indicated that deep social and political divisions existed even among the most loyal factions in the new regime.

During the summer of 1979, the idea of *velāyat-e faqih* emerged as the defining principle of the new regime. From editorial pages to Friday prayers, *velāyat-e faqih* became *the* political dogma that distinguished the insiders from outsiders of the new regime. However, since Khomeini declined to invest all his political capital directly in advancing the cause of *velāyat-e faqih,* opponents of the idea from inside and outside of the clerical establishment voiced their dissent on the floor of the Assembly and in its subcommittees. At least one Assembly member highlighted the foundational significance of *velāyat-e faqih* when he called for the need to 'put it to a separate general referendum.' Moqadam Maraghe'i argued, 'If we change the fundamental basis of the legitimacy of the regime from popular vote to the rule of the *faqih,* then we need to revise all other articles [of the constitution] accordingly.'[53] Ayatollah Beheshti rebuffed Moqadam Maraghe'i's objection by arguing that there need not be a contradiction between the rule of the *faqih* and the sovereignty of people.[54] Article 5[55] generated long debates and, for the most part, left unresolved issues on four major topics: (a) the sources of the regime's legitimacy; (b) national interests versus the interests of the global Muslim *ummah;* (c) legislation and *ijtihad;* and (d) the limits and boundaries of freedom and democracy.

Although Assembly members of different factions shifted their positions on various topics, three main groups shaped the Assembly's political landscape. The proponents of *puyā* (dynamic) *ijtihad* formed the most influential faction. Along with Ayatollah Montazeri, the leading advocate of *velāyat-e faqih,* Beheshti represented this group in the Assembly. Its main agenda was the consolidation of power primarily through the elimination of the liberal opposition. Ayatollahs Meshkini and Saduqi represented a second group, which promoted a theocratic regime without regard to democratic processes. The third faction was composed mostley of those politicians and theologians whose main commitment was to the institutionalization of the right of self-determination within a general Islamic framework.

Sources of Legitimacy: The Faqih Meets Rousseau and Mao

During the summer of 1979, the proponents of *velāyat-e faqih* launched a political attack on the draft constitution as a western-inspired legal document that did not correspond to the main revolution's objectives. In response to this criticism, in his message to the opening session of the Assembly, Mehdi Bazargan, the head of the Provisional Government, argued that the draft's main premises did not in the least contradict the teachings of Islam. He remarked,

> All references to the principles of freedom, the right to criticism, self-determination rights, and majority rule in the proposed draft of the constitution are neither borrowed from the west nor imposed upon us by Westerners [...] Rather, these principles derive from the Islamic doctrine of free will, the notion of promoting good and forbidding evil, and the necessity of *shurā* [consultation]. These principles have Qur'anic roots and are consistent with Divine Providence.[56]

There was nothing novel about Bazargan's attempt to legitimize democratic principles of governance through references to the Qur'an. Since the early modern period, Muslim reformers in Iran and other parts of the Muslim world had devised the same discursive strategy to construct a modernist Islam through which the Divine text would enhance, rather than hinder, the social formations of modernity.[57] However, the introduction of *velāyat-e faqih* made this reformist position untenable. Whereas earlier reformers needed to justify the teachings of Islam as being consistent with the institutional principles of modern society, the rule of the *faqih* in the new constitution forced them to find legitimacy for a novel Islamic idea in the philosophical foundations of modernity.

The opponents of the *velāyat-e faqih* pointed to its inherent contradiction with the sovereignty of the people. For example, during the fourth session, even before the discussion on Article 5 began, Ezzatollah Sahabi warned that not only did the rule of the *faqih* violate the democratic spirit of the constitution, by bestowing 'divinity upon the ruler' it would also 'lead the society towards *shirk* [worshipping of idols].'[58] Opposition to *velāyat-e faqih* came from at least three different positions. The democratic position, such as Sahabi's, perceived the article to be foundationally unjustifiable. Alongside Sahabi, Moqadam Maraghe'i and Abolhasan Bani Sadr were among the most vociferous advocates of this view in the Assembly. They argued that *velāyat-e faqih* was neither desirable nor feasible in the contemporary world, and that it would alienate of the ruling class from intellectuals both at home and abroad, and from the community of nations. They argued that the exceptional charisma and leadership of Ayatollah Khomeini should not be institutionalized in the constitution. At the twentieth meeting of the Assembly, Bani Sadr reintroduced the problem of *faqih*'s rule and argued that any political institution whose function depends on the decisions of one person inevitably generated despotism.[59]

As the sole voice of opposition after Article Five was introduced at the fifteenth meeting of the Assembly, Moqaddam Maraghe'i warned that '[*velāyat-e faqih*] directly contradicts article III of the draft of the constitution which assigns the ultimate legitimacy of the government to the electorate.' He further reminded the members that their decisions should not be influenced or guided by the disturbances that had engulfed the country in the first few months of the new regime. 'The situation has changed,' he told his colleagues, 'from that of a few months ago.'

> There exists an exceptional situation in the country. The media are going through a period of transition. Political parties that took part in the struggle are now involved in troubles by now known to us all, and require no further discussion here. *But these special circumstances should not compel us to undermine the sovereignty of the people as it was envisioned and widely supported in the draft of the constitution.*[60]

The first group of opponents did not subscribe to the doctrine of *velāyat-e faqih,* and found it essentially unjustifiable. Others who were skeptical believed that although desirable, the implementation of *velāyat-e faqih* was socially and politically unfeasible. They believed that before its realization, *velāyat-e faqih* had to become the hegemonic idea of governance in society. Its adoption without mass consent would inevitably become coercive, and thus illegitimate. The distinction between the desirability of *velāyat-e faqih* and its applicability to Iranian society remained an unresolved topic in the Assembly. Weeks after its final approval at the Assembly's twentieth meeting, during the morning session of the forty-first meeting, in a lengthy address, Hojjati Kermani, the representative of Kerman remarked,

> The validity of *velāyat-e faqih* is not in question. The issue is what is in the interest of our society? I am not a *faqih* but this is a sociological problem that calls for diligent sociological examination. All we talk about here are abstract notions without real applicability in society. We need to understand what our society needs and how the notion of *velāyat-e faqih* may be implemented in ways that are acceptable and can be digested by our society.
>
> We are partly responsible for the rumors that these sectarian groups are spreading against the *ruhāniyat*. A few skilled anti-religion groups are fueling the fire by claiming that we are establishing a 'dictatorship of *akhunds*.'[61] We must demonstrate that we have no intention of instituting clerical despotism.
> Neither Ayatollah Montazeri nor Mr. Beheshti have despotic ambitions, but we need to think sociologically about these issues, not merely on the basis of our intentions. We have not been successful in fighting poverty, unemployment, homelessness, and soon these crowds of the dissatisfied will join the educated dissidents and form a large mass of discontents. We are alienating our educated and intellectuals by the way we are drafting our constitution [...] We should not forget that the Tudeh [Communist] Party, for example, took advantage of peoples' grievances and recruited them into their party. We need to have an expedient look at the notion of *velāyat-e faqih* and look at it from a sociological and psychological view. An architect who wants to design and build a building cannot be oblivious to the composition of the soil and other pertinent factors. We cannot establish *velāyat-e faqih* without considering the founda-tional conditions of its realization.[62]

Several other members of the Assembly shared Kermani's concern with the alienation of the masses and the new regime's intellectual and political vulnerability to criticism from both the domestic intelligentsia and foreign nations. In the first session of the Assembly, Sayyed Mohammad Khamene'i,[63] the representative from the state of Khorasan, reiterated that the constitution must reflect 'the international principle of the separation of the three branches of government.'[64] Although he supported *velāyat-e faqih*, he emphasized, 'We need a kind of republic that serves our Islamic mandate and saves our reputation in the world.' And further, 'We cannot be oblivious about what the world thinks of us.'[65] Ahmad Nurbakhsh, the representative from Chaharmahal Bakhtiyari, similarly chastised the proponents of the implementation of *velāyat-e faqih* for neglecting the image the constitution was generating in the world community. 'Unfortunately, we do not pay enough attention to the international situation and how we are going to relate our constitution to international laws.' He suggested that the revolution would eventually fail if 'we remain insensitive towards the conditions within which it is supposed to be implemented.' 'I have brought some foreign papers to show you how foreign governments are taking advantage of our oblivion and making a mockery of our constitution.'[66] Abbas Shaybani also pleaded to 'let the people of the world know that we do not intend to institute a dictatorship of *akhunds*.'[67]

The most passionate and fervent critique of the adoption of Article 5 came from Naser Makarem Shirazi, a long-time ally and disciple of Ayatollah Khomeini. A leading scholar of *ijtihad* and the founder of the Imam Amir al-Mu'minin school at Qom Seminary in 1975, Makarem raised similar objections to the institutionalization of Khomeini's leadership. He argued that the present revolutionary atmosphere had influenced the advocates of *velāyat-e faqih*. Their vision of the future political system in Iran was conditioned by the extraordinary charisma of Ayatollah Khomeini. '[Khomeini's] leadership,' he asserted, 'is an exception in history. We should not author a constitution that institutionalizes an exception, we must write it for all times and all places.' He continued,

> I have voted for *velāyat-e faqih* and will not change my mind about the validity of its principles. Nobody can accuse me of not understanding it—I have been in the *howza* for more than thirty years, twelve years of which I have dedicated to the study and discussion of the notion of *velāyat*. Therefore, I am well versed in this subject, and it is based on that credential that I speak here [...] [*Velāyat-e faqih*] in its current form is unrealistic and unattainable in the contemporary world. The most important reason for the unacceptability of a law is its impracticality. Our enemies inside and outside of the country are going to accuse us

of despotism [...] Do not allow our enemies to say that a bunch of mullahs sat there and wrote a constitution to justify their own rule. For God's sake do not do this. People might remain silent today, but as God is my witness, this would neither fulfill the interests of Islam, nor those of the revolution. We have recognized the right of self-determination in the previous draft. By consigning all the power to the *faqih*, do not turn the sovereignty of the people into a lion without the head, tail, and the body. For God's sake, do not do this![68]

In reply, Ayatollah Montazeri, the most outspoken proponent of *velāyat-e faqih*, sharply criticized those who doubted the political legitimacy of the rule of the *faqih*. Montazeri vehemently rejected the idea that linked the legitimacy of the constitution to the endorsement of 'intellectuals' or the support of 'the world community.' He reproached Makarem Shirazi in particular for his rhetoric of despotism and for his concern for the representation of the constitution in the western media.

I ask these gentlemen not to extol how things are done in the West, to concern themselves with what goes on in the world, and to worry that, if we behave in a particular way, they would ridicule us. We are rational human beings and our nation is conscious of its own decisions. Our nation has chosen the Islamic Republic. It is irrelevant whether [foreigners] like it or not. [...] If we cared for what the world thought, Mohammad Reza Pahlavi would still be ruling over us. They respected him, so why did we have a revolution?[69]

To show his unyielding position on Article 5 and Article 110 on the rights and responsibilities of the *faqih*, Montazeri tried and failed three times to further limit the powers of the President. He argued that the critics of *velāyat-e faqih* lacked confidence in the legitimacy of their beliefs and were more concerned with pleasing domestic intellectuals and western pundits. In an uncompromising attack, openly targeting Hojjati Kermani's oposition, he asserted,

Gharbzadegi (westoxication) is not limited to the way we dress or how we decorate our home, its most important manifestation is the loss of confidence and self-respect. One of the signs of our *gharbzadegi* is that we listen to the noises they make in Europe and America and look for their approval for actions we take in our own land. We are Muslims and ought to believe in ourselves and be mindful of our religious responsibilities. [The western media] want us to believe that our young people view [the *ruhāniyat*] as reactionaries. Unfortunately, the media show few infantile intellectuals who brand us as reactionaries and do not cover the millions who defend the Islamic regime.[70]

In response, Hojjati Kermani contended that the ambiguities of *velāyat-e faqih* as well as the conflicts it would generate among different social groups and political parties could not be explained away and suppressed by mere propaganda and political intimidation. He rebuked Montazeri for his infuriating remarks and retorted,

> I have spoken to respected members of this assembly, who are neither infantile, nor *gharbzadeh*, who disagree with this form of implementation of *velāyat-e faqih*. I am talking about grand ayatollahs and sources of emulation who disagree with this notion. This is not a sign of being influenced by Europe. Mr. Montazeri, you need to prove your case with substance, not accusations.[71]

Article 5 was approved more than one month earlier than these exchanges, but for the next three months that the Assembly remained in session, the foundations, meaning, and practicality of *velāyat-e faqih* continued to be a contested point. Although these reservations and unease were not reflected in the representatives' votes, in fifteen pre-session addresses, different members raised questions about its ambiguities and contradictions with the democratic spirit of the revolution. Moreover, Musavi Tabrizi put forward the more important critique of the *velāyat-e faqih* from the standpoint of the *ruhāniyat*. He objected to Section 4 of Article 3 of the constitution, which holds the government of the Islamic Republic responsible for 'strengthening the spirit of inquiry, investigation, and innovation in all areas of science, technology, and culture, as well as Islamic studies, by establishing research centers and encouraging researchers.' He argued that the establishment of research centers for the study of Islam by the government undermines the independence of the Shi`ite clergy and would eventually lead to a formal state-sanctioned religion. 'Do not infringe upon the Shi`ite clergy's freedom,' he asserted, 'and do not violate its independence [...] Do not consider the present time, this might be misused by the future governments.'[72] The point Musavi Tabrizi raised, the peril state-sanctioned religion and the loss of clerical independence from state oversight, became one of the pillars of the reform movement in the 1990s.

Although Ayatollah Montazeri later became the staunchest critic of the concentration of power in the hands of the clergy, during the first few months after the revolution he proved to be the most important theorist of the institutionalization of *velāyat-e faqih*. While he genuinely believed in the people's right of self-determination, he also adamantly adhered to the idea that such a right may be exercised only under the revolutionary leadership of Khomeini. He intended to institutionalize Khomeini's revolutionary leadership to save the revolution from stagnation. In a more literal reading of Khomeini's doctrine, Montazeri contended that the qualified *faqih* is the sole bearer of people's will and the exigencies of Islam. Moreover, in a direct conflict with the principle of the separation of powers, he believed that the *faqih* ought to act as an independent source of power above and beyond the responsibilities of the three legislative, judiciary, and executive powers. He lambasted the separation principle and accused its defenders of promoting a 'western-style of governance.' He went as far as to suggest that,

> It is even better if [the *faqih*] accepts the post of presidency; otherwise, the president should deliver his duties under the *faqih*'s guidance. The first draft of the constitution neglected the role of the sources of emulation and the just *foqaha*, who are the pivot of the Islamic regime—it marginalized them.[73]

While Montazeri's position was inspired by revolutionary street politics, others who defended the constitutional *velāyat-e faqih* did not follow his example. There were primarily two distinct groups who defended *velāyat-e faqih*. The first group, the traditionalist faction, supported the doctrine from a strict theocratic position. Two prominent figures, Ayatollahs Saduqi and Meshkini, justified the rule of the *faqih* from a *Shi`i* jurisprudential standpoint. They considered the consent to the rule of the *faqih* to be a religious duty rather than a right bestowed upon the *faqih* by his subjects. Although Montazeri and his faction did not promote the divinity of the *faqih* and linked his sovereignty to the people's right of self-determination, they welcomed the traditionalists' advocacy of theocracy. For example, Montazeri read a letter signed by forty clerics from Tehran and Qom to the twenty-sixth meeting of the Assembly, who had met at the residence of Ayatollah Ashtiani, an apolitical conservative jurist, without criticizing its patriarchal theocratic assertions. The signatories of the letter, which was addressed to Ayatollah Khomeini, demanded that the constitution state without any ambiguity that 'the just religion of Twelve Imamate Shi`ism ought to be the source of all laws and regulations of the country.' They further emphasized that 'the president must be Shi`ite, male, and a *faqih*.'[74] Ayatollah Saduqi derided those in the Assembly who emphasized the right of self-determination as the main foundation of the legitimacy of the regime. He asserted,

> A number of our colleagues show sensitivity towards the notion of *marja`iyat*. We know that people in this country have always followed a source of emulation. We cannot exempt the President of the Islamic Republic from the rule that he should also follow a source of emulation. So what is the source of this anxiety that these representatives show in regard to the relation between the President and the *faqih*? Do they think that *marja`iyat* contradicts the demands of God, or are they concerned about how foreigners would react to this principle?[75]

For the majority of Assembly members, the doctrine of *velāyat-e faqih* did not contradict the right of self-determination. Ayatollah Beheshti played an instrumental role in bridging the gap between the proponents of the *velāyat-e faqih* and its opponents. 'We should not create a division between the *ruhāniyat* and the educated, between the *akhund* and the intellectual,' he said, after the first time that Ayatollah Montazeri introduced his doctrine to the Assembly.[76] 'We have a referendum ahead of us,' Beheshti continued, 'and we need to realize that only a wholehearted acceptance by the majority of people would give validity to our constitution.'[77] Whereas Montazeri believed that he represented the masses in his insistence on *velāyat-e faqih*, Beheshti argued that the Assembly had the responsibility to explain this political doctrine to people 'through roundtable discussions and mass media.'[78]

The scholarship on the Iranian revolution emphasizes the ideological component of the establishment of *velāyat-e faqih* and the fact that the Iranian constitution was the implementation of Khomeini's 1971 treatise on the subject. However, in the entire sixty-seven meetings of the Assembly of Experts, only one member referred to Khomeini's book in one instance. During the fortieth meeting, Hamid Mir Moradzehi, a Sistan and Baluchistan representative, argued that 'according to a book called *Islamic Governance* by Kashef al-Ghata', the right of ruling belonged solely to the Patron Saints. After their passing, no ruler could enjoy divine sanction.'[79] Ayatollah Beheshti reminded representative Moradzehi that Khomeini authored that treatise under a pseudonym to escape the previous regime's censorship. More importantly, however, Hasan Ayat, one of the main ideologues of *velāyat-e faqih*, responded to Moradzehi by arguing that, first, he misinterpreted *Islamic Governance*, as Khomeini clearly stated that in the absence of the *imam* the responsibility of governance falls on the shoulders of the *faqih*. Second, that in order to defend *velāyat-e faqih*, we do not need to 'consult an expert of Islamic jurisprudence.' Ayat continued,

> If my colleagues have read Jean Jacques Rousseau's book, which I am sure they have, he based the foundation of democracy on a social contract. Rousseau argues that in the state of nature, human beings live individually and at some point they make a pledge to each other to relinquish some of their freedoms in exchange for the betterment of their lives. The whole foundation of democracy is based on this principle [sic].[80]

In another context, in response to questions raised by Khamene'i and Hojjati Kermani about the international dimension of the role of the *faqih*, Ayat also compared the office of the *faqih* to that of the leadership of Gandhi and Mao Tse-Tung. He remarked 'if there were no international problems for Chairman Mao, our *faqih* would not have any problem communicating with the rest of the world.'[81]

Other Assembly members justified *velāyat-e faqih* on the basis of a Hobbesian natural law philosophy. They viewed the rule of the *faqih* as the *Leviathan*, whose sovereignty, although absolute, was legitimate because people willingly relinquish their right of self-determination in exchange for a secure and prosperous life. For example, Mohammad Yazdi argued that 'the right of self-determination is a divine right. God has created human beings free and no power in this world can legitimately limit this freedom, except based on rational agreements between different groups of people [...] What we say in our constitution about the right of self-determination is the same concept that is accepted everywhere in the world.'[82] Yazdi's colleague, Abdolrahman Heidari, went even further to clarify this point with specific reference to the French Revolution.

> I wanted to share with the gentlemen, who perhaps are more knowledgeable than me, that the foundation of the right of self-determination comes from the third article of the declaration of human rights that was ratified more than two centuries ago in France. From what I remember, more or less, the article stated that 'the right of governance belongs to the people, no individual and no particular group or class of people has the right to govern except on behalf of their own subjects.'[83]

Heidari then explained that there is no contradiction between the asser-tions of the French constitution and the Islamic principle of *Khilāfah*, the vice regency of God. Therefore, in contrast to the traditionalists' theocratic position in which people's right of self-determination is mediated by the divine sovereignty of the *faqih,* this position recognizes the *faqih's* right of governance only in so far as it is exercised with the consent of the masses. In that case, the proponents of *velāyat-e faqih* saw no inherent contradiction between what they proposed and political self-determination. '*Velāyat-e faqih,*' Ali Morad Tehrani, the representative from Khorasan, observed, 'is founded on the basis of the right of self-determination, it is through the exercise of this right that the *faqih* establishes his legitimacy.'[84]

Several members of the Assembly argued that since 'the leadership of society requires expert knowledge of many complex fields of social affairs,' therefore, 'a social scientist would be more qualified to act as the *faqih* in society.' In response, another supporter, Mahmoud Rouhani,[85] justified *velāyat-e faqih* with reference to the humanist psychologist, Abraham Maslow. After reviewing Maslow's five categories of human needs, Rouhani asserted,

> As Maslow demonstrated, at the bottom lie physiological needs––such as eating and drinking—and the need for *self-actualization* defines the highest need of human beings [...] Now we ask, in order to guide a society, is there a more valuable expertise than the one which has roots in divine revelations and human spirituality? Certainly not! Accordingly, we believe that experts in teachings of Islam are more qualified to lead a society than any other experts.[86]

Even the most fervent supporters of *velāyat-e faqih* realized that in order to justify its implementation, they needed to legitimize it with references to non-Islamic sources. Although their radical political rhetoric and ideological commitments may have suggested otherwise, they were conscious of how the world community and different Iranian social classes, particularly the urban middle class who had played the most significant role in the revolution, would view the new regime. The advocates of *velāyat-e faqih*, led by Ayatollah Beheshti, emphasized the consistency of the foundations of the regime they promoted with modern conceptions of the nation-state. Beheshti articulated this position as the only representative who spoke in defense of Article 5 in the fifteenth meeting of the Assembly. 'Why are our people and our educated class anxious?' he asked. 'Our educated classes need to know that we have been faithful to our promises and to our allegiance with them. We are committed to the interests of our educated people.'[87] He criticized the opposition for misleading the public on the 'true' meaning of *velāyat-e faqih* and argued that once the constitution is complete, all these uncertainties will vanish. He further remarked,

> Does Article 5 negate the significance of the public ballot? Does Article 5 undermine basic liberties? Does Article 5 relegate all power to a particular group or social class? Does it suggest that the president and the prime minister from now on ought to be turban-wearing clerics? Never. I want you to pay closer attention to this article and show me where does it suggest any of these? (Makarem: *Tell us what velāyat-e faqih is, and that would clear all these ambiguities.*)[88]

Beheshti responded to Naser Makarem's query with a long discussion about the general distinctions between two types of social order, one liberal-democratic and the other socialist, that shape the political system of nation-states.[89] Under a liberal-democratic order, he opined, the electorates provide the source of legitimacy of the state. Presumably, the state carries out policies and legislates laws that reflect the desires of the voting public without consideration extra social or transcendental values or commitments to higher causes. Beheshti argued that all the liberal-democratic governments in Western Europe and the United States 'claim that they have created free societies in which people demonstrate their will through elections and that the state acts solely on behalf of the people.' However, this is a formal freedom. 'The critics of liberal-democracy have argued,' he ridiculed Moqadam Maraghe'i, the vocal liberal critic of *velāyat-e faqih*,

> In reality, people think they are free, but they are ruled by the capitalist class which controls all the bureaucratic instruments of the state and all the mass media. The ruling classes formally respect the electorate, but through the monopoly of mass media, they direct voting patterns of the public and shape public opinion. They respect the public only so long as it does not contradict the basic interests of the ruling class.[90]

After Ali Shari`ati's idiosyncratic invention of an Islamic ideology (see chapter six), Muslim intellectuals such as Beheshti had appropriated Marxist/Weberian political sociology in their critique of liberal-democracy. They found it plausible to Islamize the Marxist critique of liberalism both in its Bolshevik revolutionary form and its Gramscian style of cultural politics. Beheshti argued, 'all forms of political orders are ideological: some like liberal-democracy are ideological in disguise, some others openly commit to an ideology, like socialist countries.'

Velāyat-e faqih, according to Beheshti, resembled the latter case, a society and a political order with conspicuous ideological commitment to Islamic values. These values determine the limits and context of the rights of all citizens, just as Marxism and its philosophy of history had determined the limits of freedom in socialist countries. He asked rhetorically: 'Do not the constitutions of the Soviet Union and China recognize every right conditionally in accordance with Marxism, Leninism, or Maoism?' He suggested that instead of copies of Ayatollah Khomeini's treatise, *Islamic Governance*, the members of the Assembly should read the Farsi translations of the Bulgarian, Soviet, and Chinese constitutions. 'We asked you to read these constitutions, so you realize that what we are doing in Iran is not unprecedented.'

> It is clearly stated in the constitution of the Soviet Union, that power shall remain in the hands of the Marxist workers party, that is to say that they would not allow freedom without conditions, because their system is based on an ideology [...] Therefore, my dear critics should acknowledge that what we say about Islam in our constitution is exactly the same thing to which other 'doctrinal societies' subscribe. This is the story of all societies in which there is a specific commitment to an ideology, where public ballot is not the sole arbiter of the form of government. The point is not which dress the leader should wear, *ruhāni* or otherwise, what is at stake is our creed. Our people are sensitive about the protection of our religion, not about the garment of its guardians.[91]

Beheshti spoke at length against Moqdam Maraghe'i, who was the sole voice of the opposition allowed on the floor after the introduction of Article 5. He did not allow others to address the Assembly. A number of the members objected to his method of administrating the meeting, and accused him of using his position as the Vice Chair to advance his own agenda. In response, he did not allow opposing views to be heard on the floor and decided to end the discussion and put *velāyat-e faqih* to a vote. 'The Iranian people,' Beheshti derided his opponents, 'and our respected leaders reject your opinion. The day before yesterday, our leader urged us to speed up the process, we cannot continue these discussions.'[92] Article 5 was ratified, fifty-three votes to eight, with four abstaining.

The faction that legitimized *velāyat-e faqih* with references to other experiences of modern nation-states and their corresponding political philosophy remained ambivalent about the patriarchal theocratic assertions of the traditionalists. However, on the issues of national interest, civil and human rights (including women's rights), the fragility of the alliance between the two clerical factions became evident.

National Interests and the Interests of the Ummah

The inherent contradiction of writing a constitution for a nation which considered itself to be a part of the global *ummah* was immediately apparent in the Assembly's early debates. Jalal al-Din Farsi, an advocate of pan-Islamism and a zealous critic of nationalism, lambasted Article 2 of the constitution for its ambivalence towards the global mission of the Iranian revolution. Article 2 described the general responsibilities of the Islamic Republic and its duties in 'directing all its resources' to sixteen stated goals. Farsi specifically objected to section 11 which stated that the Islamic Republic of Iran has the responsibility of directing all its resources to 'all round strengthening of the foundations of national defense to the utmost degree by means of universal military training for the sake of safeguarding independence, territorial integrity, and the Islamic order of the country.' Farsi argued that 'this is too limited and incomplete, we need to make it clear that we will defend Palestine and other Muslim lands.'[93]

Although section 16 of the same article emphasized that the foreign policy of the country ought to be shaped on the basis of 'Islamic criteria, fraternal commitment to all Muslims, and unsparing support to all *mustaz`afin* [the disinherited] of the world,' Farsi believed that this political rhetoric needed to be backed by a military obligation to defend Muslims around the world. Beheshti was quick to dismiss Farsi's absurd assertion. He retorted, 'in today's world no country can mention such claims in its constitution. Have you ever seen in the constitution of any other country that its military is responsible for defending nations other than its own?'[94]

Ayatollah Meshkini raised similar objections when the Assembly discussed Article 4, which stated: 'All civil, penal financial, economic, administrative, cultural, military, political, and other laws and must be based on Islamic criteria...' Meshkini insisted that the Assembly needed to clarify whether the compliance of civil and criminal codes with *shari`ah* laws was applicable 'everywhere in the world, or just in our own country?'[95] Younger clerics and those who were elected for their political activism rather than their religious authority were conscious of the damage such an ignorance in authoring a constitution might inflict on the credibility of the Assembly. As the Vice Chair of the Assembly, in all instances of these traditionalist interventions, Ayatollah Beheshti did not permit such discussion to continue on the floor of the Assembly. Trying to maintain his calm, in response to Ayatollah Meshkini, one of the highest-ranking clerics from Qom, he replied, 'I think every reader knows that we are constituting laws for our *own* country and it is not necessary to reiterate that in each article of this document.'[96]

Legislating and Ijtihad, the Constitution versus the Shari`ah

> *It is undeniable that legislating is the basic right of the* majlis.
> Mehdi Karrubi

These words of the Speaker of the Parliament appeared on the front page on the daily *Aftab-e Yazd* on September 3, 2003, almost twenty-five years after the first constitutional discussions in the Assembly of Experts. Karrubi's comment points to the issue of Islamic constitutionalism, which has remained an unresolved predicament since the rise of the modern nation-state. With the exception of the Tunisian experience of 1861—whose short-lived Islamic constitutionalism collapsed in 1864—for the first time during the Iranian Constitutional Revolution of 1905-1911, the high ranking *ulama* of the Shi`ite seminaries debated the relation between the *shari`ah* and the constitutional nation-state. Similar to the postrevolutionary discussions in the Assembly, the debates suring Constitutional Revolution centered on the question of citizens' *rights* versus Muslims' *obligations*. High-ranking ayatollahs represented both sides of that debate.[97] While several influential clerics such as Sayyid Mohammad Tabataba'i, Mirza Mohammad Hossein Na'ini, Abdolrahman Kawakebi, and Mullah Abdolrasul Kashani advocated the establishment of a constitutional monarchy, other clerics, such as Mirza Ali Sistani and most notably Sheikh Fazlollah Nuri, lambasted the constitutionalists and called the revolution a betrayal of Islam.

Those who endorsed the Constitutional Revolution were divided in the way they justified their support. Whereas one faction of the clerical defenders supported the Constitutional Revolution without hesitating to acknowledge the European origin of the ideas of 'liberty and equality,' the other defending faction justified its support through references to Islamic sources. Sayyid Mohammad Tabataba'i, one of the most famous advocates of the first position, 'who had joined the movement out of his liberal convictions,'[98] asserted,

> We have never witnessed a constitutional system. However, based upon what we have learned from those who had experienced living under such systems, I have concluded that

constitutionality leads the country toward more security and prosperity.[99]

The second group, represented by Na'ini and Kashani, was more conscious of legitimizing the egalitarian ideology of the Revolution by linking it to Islamic ideals.[100] While Na'ini was familiar with European political thought, he was vexed by the brutality of colonialism. Therefore, in his description of politics, he equated the 'maintenance of the seed of Islam' with the 'protection of the homeland from the invasion of foreigners.' He argued that there is no contradiction between religious and secular/national politics, between the *ummah* and the homeland, and emphasized the importance of national independence.[101] Drawing from the notions of *shura* (consultation) and `*adl* (justice), Na'ini argued that the fundamental principles of the Constitutional Revolution, that is 'liberty and equality,' are essential tenets of Islam. In the absence of the infallible (*ma`sum*) Imam, Muslims faced two alternatives for governance: despotic or constitutional rule.[102] Mullah Abdolrasul Kashani went even further and located the idea of the separation of the judiciary, the executive, and the legislative powers *within* the Islamic tradition. He recognized the legislative power of the *majlis* (the parliament) and saw no conflict between the *shari`ah* and the laws forged by the representatives of the nation. In his *Resāle-ye Ensāfiyeh* (*The Credo of Fairness*, originally published in 1910) Kashani insisted that not only is there no contradiction between the creeds of the *Shari`ah* and the principles of 'equality before law,' 'freedom of expression and assembly,' and even the freedom to choose one's own dress, these principles enhance and strengthen the sustainability of these creeds.[103] He further assured the *ulama* that

> The National Assembly is not responsible for the matters of *halal* (religiously permitted), *haram* (religiously prohibited), or issues of worship and prayer. These matters are legislated by God Himself. The Assembly is concerned with the affairs of the country; therefore, the fear of some Muslims that the constitution threatens the integrity of Islam is unwarranted.[104]

But, as Janet Afary has pointed out, the support of the *ulama* for the Constitutional Revolution was initially based on their assumption that the division between secular and religious laws would be maintained under the new order. They expected the *majlis* to institutionalize laws regulating the commercial and political aspects of society, and would refrain from addressing personal and religious laws, which were to remain the legal domain of religious authorities. 'But,' as Afary remarked,

> The requirements of a modern society, new civil rights that curtailed the authority of the shah, the ministers, and the *ulama*, the demands for land reform, for women's education, and for equal legal rights of non-Muslim (male) citizens made the traditional distinction between the *shari`ah* and *`urf* [secular] laws impossible to maintain.[105]

One of the most influential clergymen to capture the contradiction in the constitutionalist *ruhāniyat* was Sheikh Fazlollah Nuri (1844-1909). Nuri insisted on the irreconcilability of the *shari`ah* with constitutional laws. He proposed a fundamental *shari`atization* of the constitution.[106] An early supporter of the Constitutional Revolution, Nuri became more suspicious of its premises and eventually declared it 'fundamentally antagonistic to the spirit of Islam.'[107] He berated the Constitutionalists for writing a 'document of perdition' based on two principles of 'liberty' and 'equality,'[108] both of which 'emanated from the West' and are 'alien' to Muslims.[109] The following excerpts from Sheikh Fazlollah Nuri's letters and essays, provide a summary of his opinion about four fundamental bases where the constitutional revolution contradicted the *shari`ah*:

> 1. <u>Forging new laws</u>: Legislating new laws is exclusively a prophetic mission [...] Even if the laws legislated in the parliament are consistent with our religion, we refute their legitimacy for two reasons: first, they are conceived purely on a rational basis; second, they are written by the shopkeepers and peasants who do not have any authority in these matters (p. 57). [...] We, the community of *imamiyyeh* [followers of the Shi'ite imams] possess the most impeccable divine law [...] Islam itself is the law of Muslims (p. 104).

> 2. <u>Equality and Egalitarianism</u>: One of the articles of that document of perdition [the Constitution] states that all the citizens of Iran are guaranteed equal rights according to the law. Men and women, Muslims and non-Muslims cannot enjoy equal rights under Islam (pp. 58-59). [...] Beware that constitutionality means that peasants elect their representatives to congregate in the capital to legislate laws based upon the desires of the majority, and to act upon the necessities of the present time without respect for the holy *shari`ah* (p. 64).

3. <u>Liberty</u>: This deceptive notion [of liberty] destroys all the divine laws, because the Qur'an is founded on the basis of restraining the pen and the word (p. 65). [...] By the acceptance of the idea of liberty we will allow all apostate parties to spread their heresies in speeches and legislation . . . and infuse the pure hearts of our innocent masses with doubts (p.60). [...] It is surprising to me that they [the constitutionalists] go through so much to prove that Islamists are despotic. We have to be despotic; not only Islam but all religions are based on despotism (p. 348).

4. <u>Un-Islamic Origins</u>: Constitutionality is a European idea that contradicts Islam and has to be stopped [...] The Iranian people must not become like Europeans: faithless, lustful for prostitution, and untouched by divinity and spirituality (p. 264).

In 1909, the hostility between the clerics who supported the Revolution and those who opposed it, reached a critical point. In July 1909, a military tribunal (consisting of five prominent leaders of the revolution, including the clerical faction) sentenced Sheikh Fazlollah Nuri, the highest-ranking cleric in Tehran, to death on the charges of treason, plotting and assisting the assassination of constitutionalists. The public and the leading mullahs supported the tribunal's decision and Nuri was hanged in public on July 31, 1909.

Although Khomeini envisioned the Islamic Republic as a constitutional state—with the recognition of universal suffrage for its citizens (men and women, Muslim and non-Muslim), electoral politics, and the legislative power of the *majlis*—upon assuming political power, he declared Sheikh Fazlollah Nuri to be the 'ideological father of the Islamic Republic.'[110] Rather than an ideological association, the rehabilitation of Nuri, by naming important highways, hospitals, and government buildings after him, was a political move to demarcate the end of constitutional monarchy in Iran. While in practice and in its political doctrine, the Islamic Republic was more congruent with the views of the constitutionalist clerics, Khomeini's depiction of Nuri as the grand ideologue of the Islamic Republic once again signified the contradictions with which the Assembly of Experts had to grapple.

From early meetings of the Assembly, those whom Hashemi Rafsanjani once called 'ignorant and fanatical fundamentalists' raised the issue of whether the Assembly had the right to legislate or whether it was only a body with the right to make existing *shari`ah* law and other Islamic ordinances applicable to contemporary circumstances. In the fourth meeting of the Assembly, with the support of Ayatollah Saduqi,

Jalal al-Din Farsi posed a rhetorical question: 'Does the Assembly recognize any body with legislative powers under the Islamic Republic?' Farsi, himself not a *faqih* with formal jurisprudent credentials, believed that 'the act of legislation belongs solely to God and we do not recognize the legitimacy of any other legislative powers. Therefore, rather than a legislative power, the *majlis* is an institution that interprets divine laws,' and for that reason 'every member of the *majlis* ought to be a *faqih*.'[111]

To contain the possibility of significant changes to the draft of the constitution emerging from a democratic position, other ideologues of *velāyat-e faqih*, such as Hasan Ayat, insisted on limiting the legislative authority of the Assembly, of which they were members, as well as the future legislative branch of the government. In his objection to Article 4, Ayat cautioned his colleagues

> We drafted this article with this idea in mind that not only should laws not contradict Islam, but they should also draw upon Islamic sources. The sources of any law should be only the Book and the *Sunna*. This article fails to convey that point unambiguously.[112]

While one group of clerics, such as Ayatollah Saduqi, fundamentally opposed the act of legislation, Hasan Ayat wanted to bar public participation democratic process, either in the executive or legislative branches of the government. As Makarem Shirazi argued in response to Ayat, 'This is an obsessive behavior that in each article we emphasize that our laws be based on the Book and the *Sunna* [...] As much as we give weight to the Islamic essence of this constitution, we also need to emphasize the significance of its public legitimacy, because in Islam there is no distinction between the two.'[113] Ayatollah Beheshti added, 'we cannot say that all laws ought to be derived from the Qur'an and the *Sunna*.'[114]

The discussion on the relation of *ijtihad* and the constitution arose after the introduction of Article 2 during the ninth meeting of the Assembly. Article 2 contained all the foundational elements that defined the points of contention between different factions of the Assembly. The preliminary draft of Article 2 suggested:

> Islamic Republic is a *towhidi* social order based on the authentic, *puyā* (dynamic), and revolutionary culture of Islam, with reliance on the value and integrity of the responsible human being; the foundational role of piety in his/her advancement; the negation of all forms of discrimination or cultural, political, and economic domination; and the necessity to utilize positive achievements of

the sciences and cultures of humanity with complete commitment to all divine teachings of Islam.[115]

When the Vice Chair introduced the article to the assembly, it generated objections from those who feared that, on the one hand, the opening line of the article, which identified the Islamic Republic, a la Ali Shari`ati, as a *towhidi* social order, alluded to socialism and a classless society. Others, such as Bani Sadr and Montazeri, objected that borrowing the adjectives such as '*puyā*' and 'revolutionary' from the political lexicon of the Iranian Marxists to describe the culture of Islam would add to the confusion of the ideological orientation of the new regime. Bani Sadr spoke at length about why the concept of *puyā* or revolutionary to describe Islam misleads the future readers of the constitution. '*Puyā* is the translation of dynamic,' he said, 'I have used the term before, but I have reached this conclusion that the term does not capture the reality of *towhid*. The term *puyā* may only be understood in a dialectical context, as something in the process of change which perpetually negates its own internal opposites.'[116] With that philosophical discourse, Bani Sadr tried to show the Marxist roots of the draft's language, and its authors tried to please the Left while writing an Islamic constitution.

Ayatollah Montazeri objected to the qualifier 'revolutionary' to describe Islam. He argued that although he considered himself a revolutionary and wholeheartedly participated in the revolution, he did not believe that the adjective was appropriate. He insisted that if they changed the wording, particularly the notion of '*towhidi* system,' nobody would mistake them for advocates of 'a communist classless society.'[117]

Ayatollah Beheshti once again intervened to contain the traditionalists. Although Bani Sadr and Montazeri were both critical of the theocratic tendencies of the orthodox Qom establishment, Beheshti feared that their attack on the adjectives of *puyā* and revolutionary to distinguish a politically appropriate *ijtihad* from a religiously dogmatic exercise would embolden the 'fanatics.' With his imposing stature and deep voice, Beheshti blocked the theocratic opposition to constitutional republicanism by emphasizing the need for what the final version of the article called 'perpetual *ijtihad*.' He explained matter-of-factly that in order to draft the constitution as a living document, they had to make *ijtihad* an unmistakable foundational principle of the republic. He reminded his colleagues that the new republic needed to be at the forefront of 'advances in science, technology, and other human experiences,' and a 'perpetual *ijtihad*' ensures the appropriation of these advances with neither 'dependency upon the East or the West,' nor 'the lose of our cultural heritage.'[118]

The Limits and Boundaries of Freedom and Democracy

Far from a scholastic debate, the struggle to define the scope and meaning of *ijtihad* reflected the factional divisions within the clergy over access to power. Whereas the adoption of a reified notion of *ijtihad* would have given the highest-ranking ayatollahs boundless political authority, 'perpetual *ijtihad*' meant that political authority could not spring from expertise in religious sources. The same factional division manifested itself in the discussion over citizens' rights versus Muslims' duties. Whereas a constitution based on religious obligations and duties could bestow sweeping powers upon the top echelons of the clergy, a rights-based document would constitute formal equality before law without regard to the religious privileges of the clergy.

The traditionalists believed that the responsibility of the legislator was primarily to interpret the existing laws and ordinances of the *shari`ah*. In effect, they planned to absorb the authority of the legislative body into the judiciary. As Jalal al-Din Farsi opined, rather than a forum for *qānun-gozārān* (lawmakers), the *majlis* was to be understood as the place of *qānun-shenāsān* (jurisprudents). Farsi correctly deducted from his own assertion that a *majlis* of jurisprudents would not be concerned with the question of rights, but the conditions for the observance of what Islam demands. He reiterated that 'people do not have rights, they have duties and obligations.'[119]

Although the contradiction between the principle of rights with the mandate of duties shaped the spirit of the new constitution, the specific debate on this issue began on September 18, 1979, during the 24th meeting when the Assembly started its deliberation on section 3 of the constitution, 'The Rights of the People.' As Ayatollah Beheshti had laid out earlier, under the Islamic Republic, the constitution could guarantee equality before law, civil liberties, and freedom of expression only so long as such guarantees did not undermine the ideological foundations of the new regime. Therefore, article 22 of the published draft which stated that 'All citizens, men and women, are equal before the law,' met with stern criticism of the majority members, particularly the defenders of patriarchal theocracy.

The Assembly was divided into three major factions on the question of rights. The first group, represented by Farsi, Ayat, and the other theocratic ideologues of *velāyat-e faqih*, did not believe that the constitution should recognize the rights of citizens, only their duties and responsibilities towards their leader. The second group, consisting mainly of liberal members, but not limited to them, defended article 22 and warned that too many qualifiers would render the recognition of rights meaningless. The third group, the majority, recognized the principle of rights, but restricted them within the boundaries of Islam, the definition of which remained opaque.

Bani Sadr spoke passionately on the need to allow freedom of expression as a test of the legitimacy of the Republic. The first president of the republic, he was educated in economics and sociology at the Sorbonne and had participated in debates within the Iranian exilic communities during the intense anti-monarchy political campaigns of the 1960s and 1970s in Europe. He did not share the wariness and uncertainties of the clerics who felt unprepared to mount an intellectual as well as political campaign against Marxist contestants for power. Bani Sadr believed that the new regime could justify its ideology and defend its legitimacy without resorting to constitutional trickery to restrict civil rights and political liberties. He told the Assembly that they should rid themselves of their 'Ancient Greek way of thinking' and allow other voices to be heard. He also informed his colleagues that Ayatollah Khomeini had supported his efforts to engage other parties with 'different ideological orientations,' and to invite them for public debates. 'We cannot prohibit other ideas,' Bani Sadr warned the Assembly. 'To defend Islam, we need to engage them. If we don't accept freedom of expression, it would taint the image of the Islamic Republic.'[120]

Mir Abolfazl Musavi Tabrizi, the representative from the state of Eastern Azerbaijan (not to be mistaken with Musavi Tabrizi, the so-called 'hanging-judge of Tabriz' in early 1980s), endorsed Bani Sadr's sentiment. He argued,

> Even a communist party should be free—that is the exact meaning of our assertion that God has endowed us with the gift of freedom. If political parties do not have opposing ideological orientations, then the plurality of parties becomes meaning-less.[121]

The representative of Isfahan, Taheri Isfahani, argued that his colleagues failed to see the distinction between rallies in the streets and debates on television and radio. Marching in the streets and shouting 'death to Islam,' he remarked, 'is not freedom of expression.'[122] Another representative echoed Isfahani's assertion and cautioned the Assembly that 'perhaps some women would gather tomorrow and say that they want to protest against the *hijab*. We cannot allow that.'[123]

Although the clerical leadership of the revolution doctrinally objected to liberalism, the postrevolution power struggle, civil unrest, and ethnic conflicts intensified their anti-liberal-democratic convictions. The civil war in Kurdistan was particularly significant during this period, as Monireh Gorji, the only woman member of the Assembly, warned her fellow members of the 'slippery slope' of recognizing the right of 'public gatherings and marches' (Article 27) without taking into consideration the intentions of the organizers. She chastised the Assembly members who defended the unconditional rights of free assembly and demonstration.

> I wonder about the recent demonstrations in Kurdistan, which have led to the murder of hundreds of our Kurdish brothers— was it not the case that it all began with a simple rally, where the protesters then armed themselves and caused this massacre? Had the government prohibited the first demonstration, none of this would have happened. We need to think of a solution that would prevent episodes like this one from recurring.[124]

Ayatollah Musavi Ardebili, the future chief of the Supreme Court, chastised Gorji and others who exploited postrevolutionary instabilities in order to restrict basic rights of expression. He declared, 'Freedom of assembly and expression cannot be contingent upon its consistency with Islam or any other law.' He reminded his colleagues, 'We wanted to include [these rights] in the constitution as a progressive (*moteraqqi*) principle.' But unfortunately, he continued, raising his voice above the members' rumpus,

> A number of gentlemen argued that to allow strikes, rallies, and gatherings for different political and religious groups would be contrary to the foundations of our religion. They should realize that adding different qualifiers would not solve their problem; they should agree to lift these conditions.[125]

The commotion continued on the floor after Musavi Ardebili ended his comments. Bani Sadr added to the chaos by speaking out of order, angrily charging the opponents of Article 22 with dishonesty about their true agenda.

> I think we should bluntly say that 'we enjoy the freedom [of expression] and others should not.' Why beat around the bush? Just say that we have the right of free assembly and others do

not. (Vice Chair Beheshti: You can cast your vote in opposition).
If your intention is that only Muslims have the right of
expression, you need to state that clearly. However, beware that
you might not always remain in power, tomorrow a military
bearded man may come to power and use these laws against
you. You are being shortsighted.[126]

Before the final vote, Monirodin Hosseini, a junior cleric representing the
province of Fars, opined that the problem of restrictions and
contingencies of civil liberties covers a wider range of issues than state
politics. In a remarkably candid admission, he lamented the inability of
the new regime to defend its ideological and cultural legitimacy against
the opposition's propaganda. He considered the restrictions on civil
liberties necessary to protect the high percentage of illiterates in the
country from the seduction of 'materialist life' promoted by
'intellectuals.' He unashamedly defended the state's right to suppress
civil liberties.

> We believe that our religion is right and just, we are certain of
> that, and even with a mathematical logic [!] we can easily prove
> that. It is not because of our logical weakness that we institute
> censorship, it is because of the objective realities in society and
> people's ideological dispositions that we deem ourselves
> vulnerable, for they [?] are very influential in the sphere of arts
> and culture. Do not take artistic issues lightly. They spend
> millions of dollars producing a film, and these films are very
> effective, especially those made by people who have materialist
> ideological convictions. We cannot compete against a powerful
> propaganda machine. The fact remains that half of our country
> is illiterate. One person with a suitcase filled with film reels may
> go to the countryside and attract them to his own ideology.
> Equipped with the weapon of the arts, they dupe uneducated
> masses. They are also skilled in accessible, simple writing and
> although we have begun to write in a more accessible way in the
> howzeh, we cannot compete with them. We are very weak in this
> field, our logic is rich and strong, but we are ineffective in the
> realm of arts and culture.[127]

The final version of the article was passed as the Article 20 during the
twenty-seventh meeting of the Assembly. It disregarded the assertions of
those who believed that the constitution should recognize only duties
and obligations. It thereby set the precedent in limiting citizens' rights,
making those rights contingent upon their congruity with the ambiguous
notion of 'Islamic criteria.'[128] As stated in other articles, citizens' rights
were recognized so long as they were 'not detrimental to the

fundamental principles of Islam' (Article 27). It was evident that even the expert members of the Assembly did not agree about what made a criterion Islamic or how to define the *fundamental principles of Islam*.

Nevertheless, the Assembly found these qualifiers the best means for concealing and reconciling their differences, and defering the practical meaning of these articles to the future *majlis* and judiciary. This approach proved successful in the first period of postrevolutionary state-building, but it also laid the foundation for future contentions over the legitimacy of the regime from within.

The Constitutional Referendum

After three months of negotiation and sixty-seven meetings, the Assembly completed its work on the new constitution on November 15, 1979. Its mission, which was supposed to have been a cosmetic effort to 'Islamize' the first published republicanist draft, set a different course for the new republic. This chapter demonstrated that the new constitution did *not* reflect Ayatollah Khomeini's calculated plan to implement his long-held ideological commitments to the principle of *velāyat-e faqih.* Rather, the constitution's theocratic spirit resulted from post-revolutionary circumstances. By all accounts, Ayatollah Khomeini did not divest himself of the published draft of the constitution and joined the chorus of the advocates of *velāyat-e faqih* after its ratification in the Assembly of Experts. The clerical establishment was threatened by its inability to govern, by its early realization that it did not have the discursive power to legitimize its rule, by civil war in Kurdistan, by unrealizable demands by other ethnic minorities and the working class, and finally by unprecedented civic freedoms which could undermine its social and political authority.

The first few months of postrevolutionary politics taught the clergy that in order to rule, they needed to accelerate the process of consoledation of power, and they had to legitimize their agenda to satisfy a wide-range of constituents who did not espouse their theocratic aspirations. Although *velāyat-e faqih* was to serve as the institutional means of consolidation of power, its supporters neither shared the same understanding of its meaning, nor did they agree on how to implement it. While the patriarchal theocrats paid little or no attention to the need for political legitimacy, the republican advocates of *velāyat-e faqih* sought to reconcile the public sources of legitimacy with the theocratic structure of the new regime. Both sides, however, failed to expand the social bases of the new regime.

The referendum on the constitution, held on December 2 -3, 1979, proved that the new regime's agenda to advance a new Islamic discourse of political authority based on an amalgam of theocracy, parliamentarianism, and direct participatory democracy did not resonate with a growing number of voters. According to official figures, out of 21-million electorates, 15,758,956 voted in favor and a negligible 78,516 cast their votes against the constitution. But the most importantly, 5,241,044 did not participate. In comparison to the first referendum on the Islamic Republic in March, the new regime managed to lose more than 27 per cent of the electorate in only nine months. Voter participation was down from 97.3 per cent to 75 per cent.

The more social impediments the Islamic Republic faced in its bid to solidify its political authority, the stronger its impetus became to utilize the repressive powers of the state. For another eighteen months, until June 1981, the Republic followed a state-building policy that combined *Jacobinist* coercive measures through formal and informal violence with haphazard *Girondist* efforts to generate a formidable ideological legitimacy against the liberal and Left contenders for power.

Not only did the militant Islamist factions purge the published draft of the constitution of its liberal-republican spirit through the institutionalization of *velāyat-e faqih*, they also intensified their struggle for the consolidation of power against the Provisional Government of Mehdi Bazargan. Bazargan's cabinet was the political manifestation of what the published draft envisioned as the Islamic Republic. But as a self-proclaimed 'knife without a blade,' Bazargan lacked the political authority and popular base to advance a liberal approach to the construction of the postrevolutionary regime. He became the target of a vociferous campaign of Marxist and Islamist populist groups, all of which considered his government inept and unwilling to realize the social justice and anti-imperialist aspirations of the revolution.

At the time that the Assembly of Experts began its final deliberations, a group of Muslim students organized one of the boldest steps towards monopolization of the state. On November 4, 1979, a crowd of 500 stormed the American Embassy in Tehran in order to demonstrate their discontent with the dawdling pace of the Provisional Government's implementation of revolutionary measures in domestic as well as international policies. The students and their influential supporters in the newly formed Islamic Republic Party (IRP) held Bazargan responsible for the failure to establish a transitional government that could overhaul the state bureaucracy, carry out redistributive social justice projects, and most importantly, eliminate the contenders for power on the Left. They believed that the conciliatory policies of the Provisional Government towards the United States betrayed one of the main objectives of the revolution, and justifying the leftist critique of the Islamic government as being 'soft on imperialism.' The seizure of the embassy forced Bazargan to resign, thus ending the first period of transition in the postrevolutionary regime.

From Sacralizing the State to Secularizing the Fiqh

> *At the bedside of a forlorn* faqih
> *I saw a clay jug overflowing with questions*
> Sohrab Sepehri

As Sami Zubaida once wrote, the Islamic Republic was 'the only example of an Islamic state installed through a popular revolution.'[129] This fact manifested itself in the inherent contradictions of the new constitution that corresponded to the charismatic leadership of Ayatollah Khomeini, while accommodating the Republic's need for popular legitimacy. The new constitution redefined the Islamic Republic based on the doctrine of *velāyat-e faqih,* declaring the new regime a constitutional republic whose legitimacy was to be maintained through electoral politics as well as the transcendental laws of the *shari`ah.* Since its formation, this contradiction has been the main source of conflict within the state, especially after Ayatollah Khomeini's death in June of 1989.

Not only did the new constitution create multiple sources of legitimation, it also engendered unintended socio-political and ideological consequences through its ambiguous references to 'Islamic criteria.' It intended to legitimate the 'Islamization' of society, its laws and institutions, but the *shari`ah* remained more as a point of *contestation* rather than a point of *reference.* By locating Islam in the public sphere, not only did the new constitution alter the political apparatus, legal system, education, and gender relations in Iran, it also transformed Islam from an *a priori* source of legitimacy into a contested body of discourses. In effect, in order to Islamize the postrevolutionary society, the *Islamizers* had to struggle continuously over the meaning of Islam and its bearing on specific contemporary social, economic, and cultural issues.

Prior to the establishment of the Islamic republic and the institutionalization of *velāyat-e faqih,* the Shi`ite clergy operated independently from the state, both financially and in its internal organization. Shi`ite clerical establishments lacked a Papal hierarchy through which a dominant discourse of *ijtihad* could canonize a dominant interpretation of the *shari`ah*. By extending the scope of traditional juristic authority to include previously unexamined matters of governance, Ayatollah Khomeini threatened the existing structures clerical independence. As Said Arjomand argues, Khomeini's theocratic theory of the state scandalized a great many influential Shi`ite *ulama,* because they believed their authority 'during the Occultation of the twelfth Imam cannot be extended from the religio-legal to the political sphere.' Moreover, they feared that his doctrine would eventually undermine the traditionally *pluralist* core of Shi`ite jurisprudence.[130]

Khomeini openly acknowledged the longstanding spectrum of legal interpretations, believing diversity of views would be enhanced and more accessible to the general public under the Islamic Republic. When a group of high-ranking clerics conveyed their displeasure on the 'popularization' of issues of jurisprudence and argued that the mass media were distorting the processes of *ijtihad,* Khomeini replied:

> The treatises of great *foqaha* of Islam are filled with differences of opinion, predilections, and interpretations on military, cultural, political, economic, and spiritual issues. In the past, these dis-agreements stayed behind the confines of the seminary, written in Arabic in specialist books. Inevitably, people were unaware of these debates, and showed no interest in engaging with them.
> Today, the Islamic revolution has brought the words of *foqaha* and other experts to the radio, television, and the newspapers, for there is an urgent need for such discussion, for example, on the limits and boundaries of individual and social liberties [...] and most importantly on defining and illustrating the principles of governance under *velāyat-e faqih.* These are only a small number of topics on which our *foqaha* have debated and dis-agreed with one another. If they encounter issues that do not have precedent, they need to address them through free thinking and *ijtihad.* Under the Islamic Republic the door of *ijtihad* ought to remain open. The nature of the revolution requires the free exchange of diverse opinions in *ijtihad* on different issues, even if they contradict one other; no one has the right to obstruct it.[131]

There is no doubt that for Khomeini free exchange of opinions did not include lay discussions on the relevance and contingencies of the *shari`ah*. However, with the establishment of the constitution as the legal framework for civil and criminal laws, it inescapably undermined the intentions of its authors. As Said Hajjarian observes,

The doctrine of *velāyat-e faqih* transformed Shi`ism into a state ideology. In contrast to its ostensible appearance in merging religion and the state, and thereby *sacralizing* the political sphere, *velāyat-e faqih* played the propelling role of a catalyst for the *secularization* of the Shi`ite juridical establish-ment.[132]

This apparent contradiction between the establishment of a theocracy and inner processes of secularization of Shi`ite jurisprudence became more evident in the late 1980s and early 1990s when a social movement for democratic access to the meaning of religion shaped Iranian politics and led to the emergence of what became known as the Khordad Second Movement and the Presidency of Mohammad Khatami in 1997. It was then that members of the parliament, community activists, lawyers, and a wider community of religious intellectuals questioned the exclusive authority of ayatollahs and other sources of emulation to interpret Islam.

The new constitution and the unprecedented position of Khomeini as a *vali-ye faqih* posed fundamental theological and jurisprudent questions among the high-ranking clerics who were apprehensive about the proposed relation between Islam and the State. They had two inter-related concerns: first, maintaining the independence of the *howzeh*, and second, highlighting the distinction between the decrees of Islam and the interests of the State (*maslahat-e nezām*). The first predicament, conveyed forcefully by Musavi Tabrizi during the twelfth session of the Assembly,[133] was, and remains, a significant point of tension between the Shi`ite seminaries and the office of the Supreme Leader. The appoint-ment of Ayatollah Khamene'i, a junior cleric, in 1989 to succeed Khomeini deepened the friction between the State and the *howzeh*, between the leadership of the republic and the institution of the clergy.

Even before assuming political power, Khomeini had long advocated that there could be no distinction between the interests of the state and Islamic credence, so long as the actions of the state resulted in the fortification of religion. But his new responsibility as the *vali-ye faqih* (the ruling jurist) compelled him to develop a new jurisprudence whereby he could navigate between the conventions and creeds of the *shari`ah* and the social and political needs of the nation-state. As Mohsen Kadivar and Jamileh Kadivar illustrated in their brilliant historical studies of Shi`ite political discourses, central to Khomeini's postrevolutionary reinvention of *velāyat-e faqih* was the rearticualtion of the notion of *maslahat* (utility, expediency, or concern for public welfare).[134]

Soon after the revolution, Khomeini realized the limits of jurisprudence in addressing questions of social justice, politics, and the

economy. In a letter to Khomeini dated September 27, 1981, Hashemi
Rafsanjani, the influential former speaker of the *majlis* and a founding
member of the Islamic Republic Party, addressed the new regime's
inability to make the 'contingencies of social policies' conform to abstract
juridical conceptions of the *fiqh*. The frustrated Rafsanjani wrote to the
Leader that 'under these circumstances, based on the teachings of the
shari`ah, many policies of the government would be unjustifiable.' He
closed by posing the question, 'Would it be possible to govern this
country with the existing interpretations of the *shari`ah?*'[135]

Khomeini responded that there was no contradiction between
discerning the contemporary practical necessities (*zarurat*) and the
'primary creeds' of the *shari`ah*. Indeed, under the Islamic government,
the former takes precedence over the latter. Khomeini also laid the
foundation for a forthright separation of the traditional Shi`ite hierocracy
and the elected *majlis* in the determination of these necessities. In a
speech addressed to the *majlis,* he delegated the responsibility of the
'discernment of *zarurat,*' to a two-thirds majority in the *majlis*.[136] Other
sources of emulation and grand ayatollahs perceived Khomeini's
controversial decision with great skepticism and warned him of the dire
consequences of integrating an *elected* political institution into the
process of *ijtihad*.

In a letter dated March 10, 1981, directly challenging Khomeini's
decree, one of the most influential sources of emulation, the grand
Ayatollah Golpayegani, warned the members of the *majlis* that 'their
responsibility is to reinvigorate Islam. They should not adopt policies
and pass legislation which unconsciously promote the interests of the
West or the East.' In his unusually lengthy correspondence, Ayatollah
Golpayegani rejected the idea that the affairs of the country needed to be
managed on the basis of *zarurat*. He wrote:

> My religious duty obligates me to inform you of my
> apprehension about the current situation in the *majlis* [...] From
> the beginning of the revolution, on the one hand, some
> *westoxicated* pundits pestered us that the decrees of Islam are not
> applicable to the contemporary world, or that the conditions for
> its implementation are not yet prepared, but with the help of
> God, their voices were silenced. On the other hand, with their
> propaganda machine, the leftists tried to transform the
> revolution and taint its authentic Islamic essence [...] Respected
> Gentlemen, to support the oppressed and the disinherited, to
> value the peasants and workers, and to improve the conditions
> of life in the country (even more than the city), all this is central
> in the teachings of Islam. It is not the case that primary creeds of

the *shari`ah* do not offer solutions to our current problems, so that we need evoke the idea of *zarurat* to remedy them, temporarily [...] As God is my witness that it would be regretful, in this atmosphere created by misguided groups, that we forsake the primary creeds under the banner of *zarurat*. I fear the day that they find a *zaruart* to violate commandments of God, a day that they turn God's *halāl* [permitted] into *harām* [prohibited] and His *harām* into *halāl* [...] I have informed Ayatollah Khomeini of my reservation about relegating the determination of *zarurat* to *majlis*, and I look forward to his reconsideration of the matter. [...] I believe that bestowing the authority of discernment of *zarurat* to the majority of *majlis*, or any other experts in that matter, is erroneous [...] In the determination of *zarurat* and the interplay of the *shari`ah* and the state policies, the *faqih* should not relinquish his power in favor of any other institution.[137]

By no means was Golpayegani alone in his concern for the integrity and independence of the clergy. The more the postrevolutionary state consolidated its power, greater numbers of ayatollahs voiced their displeasure with the expansion of state power into their offices. Many of these newly dissident ayatollahs had distanced themselves from the state in the earliest days of the revolution. Grand Ayatollahs such as Kho'i, Shari`atmadari, and Qomi, declared their opposition to the doctrine of *velāyat-e faqih* and its apparent contradiction with the sovereignty of people. But Ayatollah Golpayegani's objection invited a wider group of ayatollahs (Baha' al-Din Mahallati, Sadeq Ruhani, Ahmad Zanjani, Ali Tehrani, Morteza Ha'eri Yazdi) to express their unease with the growing primacy of politics over religion under the Islamic Republic.[138]

The increasing power of the *vali-ye faqih* undermined the authority of the sources of emulation (*marāji`-e taqlid*) in Qom and Mashad. This became more evident when in 1985 Ayatollah Khomeini chose Ayatollah Montazeri to be his successor and in effect shifted the center of the debate on *marja`iyyat* (qualification for assuming the position of a source of emulation) from the *howzeh* to Jamaran, his residence in Northern Tehran. Upon hearing the news of the succession, Ayatollah Sadeq Ruhani lamented that 'My duty is to say that I see Islam in danger, that *marja`iyyat* is in danger.'[139]

The danger Ayatollah Ruhani plainly spoke of was the paradox of the sacralization of politics in the establishment of an Islamic state. Danger was in subordinating the commandments of the *shari`ah* to the political needs of the state. Ayatollah Meshkini, the future head of the Assembly of Experts, unequivocally asserted, 'Political activity is an incumbent (*shar`i*) duty. Today, one of the most important acts of devotion (`ebādat`) is political activity [,] because without politics our religiosity (*diyānat*) will not last.'[140] However, Said Arjomand and other influential scholars of the Iranian revolution have often ignored the fact that by politicizing religion, Meshkini and other proponents of a patriarchal theocracy, unintentionally transformed Islamic dogma into a contested knowledge. That is why the pluralism of the religious sources of authority within the postrevolutionary political context, ultimately checked the emergence of the kind of totalitarian theocracy that many advocates of *velāyat-e faqih* envisioned.

I shall demonstrate in chapter five how Khomeini finally resolved his predicament, doctrinally, by advancing a new conception of *maslahat*, and institutionally, by establishing the Expediency Council to mediate between the Guardian's Council and the *majlis*. I will show how the postrevolutionary state politics inadvertently set into motion an idiosyncratic form of secularism which has shaped the processes of state-building in postrevolutionary Iran in the last quarter-of-a-century.

The young Islamic Republic initially launched the struggle to negotiate the boundaries of religion and state, *fiqh* and politics, by the brutal suppression of liberal and left contenders for power. However, it also put in place a genuinely irreversible process of secularization from within, which might prove to be more sustainable than similar experiences in other Islamic countries. As Hajjarian observes, the Iranian experience of secularization does not imply the separation of the church and the state; rather it emerged from an inevitable transformation of religion when its dogma and its institutions became contested in the public sphere.[141]

But before continuing this discussion, in the next chapter I shall introduce Abdolkarim Soroush and his early involvement with the postrevolutionary regime. Despite notable divergences with the ruling clergy in his philosophical ideas and political convictions, Soroush became a leading intellectual figure for a regime that increasingly relied on powers of coercion rather than persuasion. Soroush's mere presence damped the anxieties of the ruling clerics who feared that their lack of intellectual vigor would eventually jeopardize their legitimacy.

4

Abdolkarim Soroush:
The Intellectual Voice of the Islamic Republic

After Ayatollah Khomeini's death in 1989, Abdolkarim Soroush emerged as one of the most controversial intellectual figures on the Iranian political scene. At the core of this controversy was Soroush's rejection of the ideological claim of the Islamic regime as the sole bearer of 'true' Islam. Soroush's critique, developed in a three part essay entitled *The Theoretical Contraction and Expansion of the Shari`ah,* was particularly contentious for it was launched by the most respected spokesperson of the Cultural Revolution Council, and one of the most promising intellectuals *par excellence* of the postrevolutionary regime.

In this chapter, after a short biographical note, I will trace, through a discussion of a Soroush's early works, his emergence as a favored intellectual of the new regime. Despite the successful monopolization of state power, the Islamic Republic lacked the necessary vigor to justify intellectually its vision of an Islamic regime. Khomeini enjoyed an unparalleled social influence before and after the revolution, and could easily cause the political pendulum of events to swing towards his own agenda. However, the clergy believed that in order to legitimize its new Prince, it needed to cultivate an intelligentsia who could theoretically defend and substantiate the neither-East (against Soviet Marxism) and nor-West (against secular liberalism) premise of the new republic. By the time Abdolkarim Soroush returned to his homeland in the spring of 1979, the book of monarchy had been closed and power had already been transferred to the Provisional Government of Mehdi Bazargan. But with this return, he flew from relative obscurity of London to intellectual prominence of Tehran.

Although known to inner circles of Muslim students in England and to some leading clerics, most notably to Morteza Motahhari, Soroush was a marginal figure during the years preceding the revolution. He gained public recognition after Khomeini appointed him to the Cultural Revolution Council in 1980. In the fall of the same year he appeared in a series of debates on Marxism and Islam that were broadcasted on primetime Iranian television. In these debates, in which leaders of Leftist parties as well as representatives of the ruling clerics participated, Soroush chastised the Marxists for their pseudo-scientific claims about history, society, and culture. He scoffed at Marxian economic determinism and argued that political totalitarianism was inherent in the Marxian materialist conception of history.

Soroush was born in Tehran in 1945 into a lower middle class Muslim family. He was named Hossein,[1] for his birth fell on `Āshura, the day commemorating the martyrdom of Hossein, the third Shi`ite Imam. He attended Alavi High School in the early years of its establishment. Alavi was an alternative Islamic school founded by a group of bazaari merchants. At Alavi, many prominent Muslim intellectuals taught extra-curricular courses and offered seminars on Islamic law and exegesis. Alavi was not a traditional *madrasa* and followed the official Ministry of Education's curriculum, but the school hired teachers and invited students who were committed to their Islamic faith. The significance of Alavi becomes evident if one looks at the strong presence of Alavi graduates in postrevolutionary governments and other influential positions. The Speaker of the Seventh *Majlis*, Haddad `Adel; Ali Akbar Velāyati, the former Minister of Foreign Affairs and the Political Advisor of the Leader Khamene'i; Kamal Kharrazi, President Khatami's Minister of Foreign Affairs, and many other ministers in different administrations were graduates of Alavi high school.

While the founders of Alavi were motivated by anti-Pahlavi *political* sentiments, the religious mode of the school was primarily expressed in its at times violent anti-Baha'ism. Members of the Hojjatiyyah Society, known for its vicious campaign against Baha'is, were influential among Alavi students and faculty. Even their anti-establishment tendencies were inspired by the alleged freedom Baha'is enjoyed under the Shah's regime. According to his own account, Soroush attended only one Hojjatiyyah-organized 'training session,' after which he distanced himself from their often-violent campaigns.[2]

In high school, he majored in mathematics and went on to study pharmacology at Tehran University. After serving a two-year mandatory military deployment, which included fifteen-month of compulsory service in Bushehr, a deprived region of the country in the South, in 1972 he traveled to London to continue his education. Twenty years later, Soroush reminisced that in preparation for his journey abroad, he packed four books: Mulla Sadra's philosophical magnum opus *Al-Asfar al-`Arba`a*; the eight-volume set of Feiz Kashani's mystical *Mahajatol Beizā'*; the *Divan* of Hafiz; and Rumi's *Mathnavi*.[3] Of those books, Soroush recalled, 'the first fed his rational mind and the other three fulfilled the desires of his heart.'[4] Mulla Sadra (1571-1640) left a lasting mark on Soroush's quest for the articulation of a mystical rationality, in which reason was preeminent in an unfathomable universe.

He received his Master's degree in chemistry from the University of London. When he arrived in England, Soroush confided in me in an interview, he had never heard of the academic discipline called the Philosophy of Science.[5] He had always been interested in the question of where scientific problems come from: how does a scientist develop an experiment and reach certain conclusions? He has always considered these to be cognitive problems and topics of research in the discipline of psychology. He intended to study psychology when an advisor at the University of London suggested that he would find answers to his questions not in psychology but in the philosophy and history of science. Later, Soroush became interested in the subject of the indeterminacy of science and enrolled in a Ph. D. program in the History and Philosophy of Science at Chelsea College, where he studied for more than four years. He worked on a dissertation on the history of monomolecular reactions, but never finished his thesis.

While in London, Soroush became involved with the Muslim Youth Association (MYA) in the United Kingdom. With the growing protest movement in Iran in 1976, Iranian Muslim students established a religio-political center called Imam-Barah in west London. MYA invited prominent Muslim thinkers and activists to the new center where they delivered talks to large crowds of students from all over Europe. Ayatollah Beheshti and Morteza Motahhari were among those who addressed enthusiastic crowds at the center. Soroush often reminisces of his meeting and dialogue with Motahhari which occurred at that time. After the 1979 revolution, the Iranian government purchased the London center and renamed it *Kānun-e Towhid* (The *Towhid* Center).

During his association with the Muslim student movement in the UK, Soroush emerged as a popular speaker and later as a prolific writer. Like other Muslim intellectuals of his period, such as Morteza Motahhari and Ali Shari`ati, Soroush advanced philosophical argument primarily against Marxism. He considered Marxism to be the main intellectual threat that had estranged Iranian intellectuals from their own religion and culture. Unlike Shari`ati, who articulated an Islamic liberation theology, an Islam of *telos*, Soroush engaged Marxism outside its emancipatory politics. He focused on the logical inconsistencies of its philosophy and what he perceived as the totalitarian implications of the materialist conception of history. Shari`ati's indisputable success in containing the influence of communist groups on the younger generation of Iranian intellectuals afforded Soroush an eager audience who nevertheless remained oblivious to the fundamental distinctions between competing hermeneutics of Islam.

The result of Soroush's early preoccupation with the critique of Marxism was a series of books in each of which he chastised the 'illusive ideology of liberation' from a neo-positivist standpoint sheathed in Mulla Sadra's Islamic realism and the philosophy of Allameh Tabataba'i, who championed Mulla Sadra at Qom Seminary.[6] In the introduction of his treatise on Mulla Sadra's thesis of '(Trans)Substantial Motion' (*harkat-e jowhari*), he remarked,

> There are two reasons for my direct reference to Mulla Sadra and for utilizing his ideas. First, because of the richness of his philosophy, and second, to demonstrate the novelty of his philosophy and encourage others not to remain mere consumers of this or that school of philosophy, to generate a sense of self-sufficiency and independence in contemporary Islamic thought.[7]

He further lamented that contemporary generations of Muslims were gradually losing the courage to think independently, to be innovative and original. Soroush insisted, they had grown 'inept' and 'hopeless;' they had become 'timid and reluctant to consider positions on which foreigners have not inscribed their stamp of approval. Intellectual independence, the courage to think creatively, and *ijtihad* are the most urgent responsibilities that face Muslims today.'[8] The time had come, he declared in the same introduction, 'to emit the fragrance of our culture and offer it to those seekers who trust the aroma of a scent and are not bewitched by the promotional squawking of the scent seller.'[9]

The publication of *The Restless Nature* marked a defining moment in Soroush's intellectual and political life. First, by introducing Mulla Sadra to a new generation, he dismissed the Orientalist fallacy of the continuous decline of post-Peripatetic Islamic philosophy. He showed that more than three hundred years after the Golden Age of the Islamic Renaissance, in the early seventeenth century, Mulla Sadra brought together the rationalist philosophy of Ibn Sina (*Mashā`*), the Illuminationism (*Ishrāq*) of Shahab al-Din Suhrawardi, and the Gnostic teachings of Ibn `Arabi to create a meta-philosophy (*al-hikma al-muta`āliya*) through which he offered new resolutions to the centuries-old predicament of existence, reality, essence, and their relation to God.

Moreover, Soroush addressed these questions within the frame of Shi`ite theology, with significant stress laid on its principle of imamate and the imperative of *ijtihad*. Although Mulla Sadra subscribed to the basic Peripatetic motto, 'to be ignorant of motion is to be ignorant of nature,' he had developed his theory of (trans)substantial motion as a critique of Aristotle's famous dictum that 'All things that move are moved by something else.' By considering motion as an *inherent* feature of all things, Mulla Sadra put forward a solution to the complex problem of the prime mover in all Peripatetic Muslim philosophical traditions. As Soroush concluded his short but meticulously argued treatise,

> For the first time, the doctrine of substantial motion introduced two fundamental elements to Islamic thought: first, the historicity of existence; second the concomitant internal tumult and restlessness and external calm and tranquility of the phenomenon [...] Rather than being a thing, the world is an unremitting process of becoming [...] The inner transformation recreates the phenomenon anew in every given moment [...] God manifests his presence in the perpetual demise and birth of the universe.[10]

The young Soroush emerged as a brilliant exponent of this meta-philosophy, one who could creatively interlace his professional knowledge of the history of physics and chemistry into the philosophical contentions of Mulla Sadra.

Second, by regarding Mulla Sadra as the philosopher *par excellence* of Shi`ite theology, Soroush established himself as part of a philosophical tradition the main contemporary proponent of which was Ayatollah Khomeini. Many have argued that in his political philosophy, Khomeini drew substantially on Mulla Sadra.[11] As Michael Fischer commented,

> Both are inspired by a vision of simultaneous progress in social justice and spiritual consciousness. Both see the role of philosophical mysticism to integrate social norms...with higher

philosophical values, and thereby to give society a direction toward developing greater justice, equity, and fulfillment. Both maintain a creative tension between transcendent and ordinary perceptions. Both spoke out at critical historical junctures when there seemed to be a possibility of guiding public interpretations and symbols of man's destiny. Both deride literalist clerics, and defend the language of mysticism.[12]

However, Khomeini differed radically from Mulla Sadra on the role of *mujtahid* and his relation to the 'heedless masses.' In his metaphysics of being, Mulla Sadra believed in the unity of intelligence and the intelligible, of the knower and the known. But he recoiled from the idea that the *mujtahid's* transcendental knowledge makes incumbent upon him the task of guiding and transforming the masses. In contrast, Ayatollah Khomeini turned this metaphysics of being into a political doctrine, *velāyat-e faqih*, in which the *mujtahid* bears the responsibility of leading the masses towards the realization of the true Islam.

Whether or not Soroush shared Khomeini's political interpretation of Mulla Sadra, the publication of *The Restless Universe* brought the philosophical virtuosity of the young Soroush to the attention of the revolution's father. It has been said that with the encouragement of Morteza Motahhari, whose commentary on Mulla Sadra had influenced Soroush, Ayatollah Khomeini read the book and marveled at the erudition of its young author.[13]

During the two years that followed the publication of his first major treatise, from 1978 to 1980, Soroush published numerous essays and books, most of which were based on his lectures in the United Kingdom. In these publications, he demonstrated more clearly the extent to which Anglo-Saxon analytical philosophy and the post-positivism of Karl Popper had permeated his Islamic philosophical worldview.[14] He found himself at home with the non-revolutionary, elitist core of the British political tradition, as well as its liberal anti-Marxian propensities. Even at the height of the revolutionary movement in Iran, Soroush remained committed to his philosophical endeavors and academic rumination. If Ali Shari`ati's political discourse combined with his passionate oratory could inspire thousands of otherwise Marxist young Iranians to join the revolution, in a world apart, with his soft-spoken words and mono-tonous delivery, Soroush saw himself, and was accepted by the post-revolutionary regime, as the messenger of persuasion.

Soroush's rise to prominence in 1979-1980 soon after the triumph of the revolution, took place in a postrevolutionary context in which the new regime had realized that it could not expand and stabilize its authority through the coercive powers of the state. This became more evident with the significant drop in the popularity of the regime between two referenda. With its anti-imperialist agenda and focus on social justice, the new regime situated itself as an alternative to Marxist-inspired national liberation movements. To justify this position, the Islamic Republic launched a two-pronged assault on Marxism: first by hampering the activities of communist groups through a campaign of intimidation and suppression, and second, by positioning itself as a more authentic and legitimate anti-imperialist force. For the first part of their mission they organized *hezbollahi* mob groups, club-wielding thugs mobilized by the revolutionary guards. For the second front they relied on the emerging Muslim intellectuals such as Abdolkarim Soroush.

Soroush's philosophical investigations of Mulla Sadra, combined with his knowledge of history and philosophy of science, situated him as an authoritative intellectual. However, the revolutionary events of 1978 and the establishment of the Islamic Republic deterred him from his scholarly path, forcing him to leave the quiet of his mystic's love of philosophy for the boorish world of strident ideology. Like many contemporary Muslim intellectuals, he believed that the construction of a vigorous and engaging Islamic philosophy and an alternative discourse of social change would eventually weaken the ideological attraction of Marxism in Iran. Whereas earlier Muslim critics of Marxism advanced their discourse within the context of a struggle against a common enemy, the Monarchy and imperialism, Soroush's critique coincided with the strategy of the new regime to consolidate its power by eliminating its Marxist-Leninist and liberal opposition.

Soroush, Marxists, and the 'Eclectics'

Soroush based his critique of Marxism on the distinction between metaphysics cum ideology and science. In the introduction to the second edition of his main treatise on Marxism, he chastised 'those who transform science into metaphysics and demote metaphysics to the level of science.'[15] This distinction is of central significance to Soroush throughout his career. It is the collapse of this boundary between metaphysical claims and scientific facts that, he believes, renders Marxism a totalitarian ideology. He argued,

> Metaphysics and science convey two forms of knowledge with distinct foundations. Science observes *elements* of being, while life in its *totality* is the subject of metaphysics [...] experience is

the foundation of scientific knowledge, but irrelevant to metaphysics.[16]

Soroush places special emphasis on this distinction, for in his critique, he concentrates exclusively on vulgar varieties of Marxism with pseudo-scientific claims on the 'Laws of History' and the inevitability of communism. In his early treatises, Soroush attacked its scientism and warned about the dangers of the conflation of science and philosophy and its undesirable child, the so-called scientific philosophy. Following von Hayek's description of scientism as 'the slavish imitation of the method and language of science,'[17] he argued that Marxists invented the idea of scientific philosophy or scientific socialism in order to give legitimacy to their teleological view of history. 'In their minds,' he scolded, 'there is no distinction between scientific truth claims and what is right or legitimate.'[18]

> Now we can fathom why and how an outlandish creature called 'scientific philosophy' has come into being. The followers of general principles of dialectics intend to speak philosophically about all beings, while at the same time, by predicting the future, they draw practical conclusions from their philosophical assertions. Predictions need to be justified scientifically, thus the wedding of philosophy and science. [Marxists] boorishly blend science and philosophy, thereby giving birth to a bastard child named 'scientific philosophy' from the unwelcome marriage of philosophy and science.[19]

In contrast to his nuanced treatment of Mulla Sadra, his engagement with Marxism was polemical and narrow in scope. Whereas, in the former, he pursued genuine philosophical investigations, in the case of Marxism, his argument was primarily shaped by political considerations and the state of the Iranian communist movement. Rather than a serious engagement with Marxist philosophy, his critique was an attack on the political legitimacy of the Iranian communists.

Soroush divided his critique into three main categories: the logical inconsistencies of the dialectical method; anthropomorphism, scientism and historicism; and, elitist totalitarianism.

The Logical Inconsistencies of the Dialectical Method

Soroush devoted much of his critique of Marxist philosophy to the logical inconsistencies of the dialectical method. In his critique, he divided this contradiction into two logical and philosophical forms, both of which, he asserted, show the fallacies of the dialectical method. He subdivided logical contradiction into the categories of *taqābol-e tazād; taqābol-e tanāqoz; and taqābol-e tazāyef. Taqābol-e tazād* refers to contradictory attributes which cannot coexist in a single phenomenon, but a phenomenon may exist without either quality.[20] For example, a thing may not be black *and* white at any given moment, but could be neither white nor black. An individual may not be both an exploiter *and* exploited in relation to another individual, but may be neither exploiting nor exploited by another. In *taqābol-e salb va eijāb* (abjuration and exigency) two contradictory attributes may neither coexist nor could they be both absent in a single phenomenon, for example being and nothingness, silence and sound, or literate and illiterate.[21] And finally in *taqābol-e tazāyef* two contradicting attributes may not coexist in a phenomenon, but these attributions may be conceptually interdependent. For example, an individual may not be the father and the son of another individual, but fatherhood presupposes and depends on the existence of of children.

Philosophical contradiction, according to Soroush, points to the foundation of all motion in natural phenomena. He interpreted Mulla Sadra's often-cited assertion that 'Nothing would ever change and the exuberance of the benevolent God would not be sustained if there were no contradictions in existential reality,'[22] as interaction between *substantively distinct phenomena*. In this painstaking reading of Mulla Sadra, he intended to ridicule the leaders of the radical *Mojahedin-e Khalq*, a Muslim urban guerilla organization influenced by Marxist philosophy of history, for their 'misapprehension' of Mulla Sadra as a Hegelian dialectician who viewed contradiction as the *essential* feature of all phenomena.

A glance at the glossary of his book illustrates how Soroush advanced his critique against the straw man of crude mostly Soviet renditions of the dialectical method. He created a genealogy of the concept of dialectics from Engels' positivist elaborations in his *Anti-Dühring* and *The Dialectics of Nature*, Lenin's sketchy *Philosophical Notes*, Mao Tse-tung's *Four Philosophical Essays*, and Stalinist mass produced philosophical treatises such as Viktor Afanasiev's *Marxist Philosophy: A Popular Outline* and the rudimentary *An Introduction to Philosophy*, a French Communist Party primer for its adult schools.

Anthropomorphism, Scientism and Historicism
Soroush neglected the distinctions between different schools of Marxism in their interpretation of dialectics in favor of Engels's crude description

of dialectics as 'the science of the general laws of motion and development of nature, human society and thought.'[23] Engels collapsed the three most common emphases of the concept of dialectics, that of dialectics as method (epistemological); dialectics as a set of laws governing all forms of motion (ontological); and dialectics as the principle of historical change (relational), into the single determinist notion of dialectical materialism.[24] There is no doubt that the first generation of Marxists, beginning with Engels and leading to Plekhanov, Lenin, and later Stalin and, to a lesser extent Mao, advanced positivist, scientific dialectics. This perspective, which became dominant in the Second International, was influenced by the strong nineteenth century Darwinian tendency to extend the theory of natural selection to social theory and ideas of historical progress.[25] But it is a gross blunder to reduce, as Soroush did in his early critiques, social Darwinism, historicism, anthropomorphism, and Hegelian dialectics into a single worldview dubbed Marxism.

Even Engels, who was primarily responsible for the emergence of positivist Marxism, cautioned against using class struggle as the social manifestation of natural selection. While working on his *Dialectics of Nature,* in a letter to P. L. Lavrov in 1875, Engels disparaged his contemporaries who transposed the theory of 'the *struggle* for existence' in the state of nature to social competition as the essence of human society.

> The whole Darwinian teaching of the struggle for existence is simply a transference from society to living nature of Hobbes' doctrine of *bellum ominum contra omnes,* and of the bourgeois theory of competition together with the Malthusian theory of population. When this conjurer's trick has been performed [...] the same theories are transferred back again from organic nature into history and it is now claimed their validity as eternal laws of human society has been proved. The puerility of this procedure is so obvious that not a word need be said about it.[26]

Indeed, it was the British philosopher Herbert Spencer who in 1864 coined the phrase 'the survival of the fittest.' Social Darwinism had no connection whatsoever with the development of the Marxian theory of historical change. Rather, it was championed by the defenders of the system who found a justification for the brutality of nineteenth century capitalism in the extinction of species in natural selection, a marriage of Malthusian and Darwinian doctrines. Engels tried in his *Anti-Dühring* to save Darwinism from its bourgeois defenders, not because he believed that Marxism had to be understood as a Darwinian science of society, but because he intended *to deny* a scientific foundation for a natural philosophy of social inequality and injustice.

As much as Engels intended to repudiate scientific justifications for bourgeois ideas, he took it upon himself to legitimize a materialist conception of history on scientific grounds. For the first generation of Marxists, whose ideas were shaped by the later scientific writings of Marx in *Das Kapital,* science had emerged as the sole arbiter of truth, even in the realm of the humanities. In an allegorically appropriate moment, in his eulogy at Marx's graveside, Engels mourned the death of his intellectual companion by remembering him as the Darwin of social life. 'Just as Darwin discovered the law of development of organic nature,' Engels solemnly grieved, 'so Marx discovered the law of development of human history [...].'[27] The comment, however, does not suggest that he believed that in his materialist conception of history, Marx simply extended Darwin's doctrine of natural selection to social change. This idea found its most unambiguous expression for the first time in the work of the father of Russian Marxism. In his influential treatise, *The Development of the Monist View of History* (1895), Plekhanov unequivocally regarded Marxism as a Darwinist social science.

It was this monistic view of history, put forward by Plekhanov and his German counterparts Karl Kautsky and Eduard Bernstein, that congealed the ideological core of social democratic and later communist parties. The split in the Second International between Evolutionary Socialists and Bolshevik Revolutionaries showed that although this economic reductionist and determinist view dominated the International, the political meaning and the strategic consequences of this monism were anything but monolithic. The economic reductionism that shaped the philosophical core of the monist view of history, on the one hand, gave rise to Bernstein's conception of an *evolutionary* socialism,[28] and on the other hand, it afforded political legitimacy to the Leninist revolutionary communist movement and the establishment of a proletarian dictatorship.

The determinism in Marxist thought that Soroush rebuked in his early critiques has been the subject of a century-old debate among Marxists themselves. The Marxist philosophy of history, both in the writings of Marx as well as his disciples, bore an inherent contradiction in granting agency to human actors, on the one hand, and ceding it, on the other, to the historical inevitability of the collapse of capitalism and the emergence of socialism. Not only did this contradiction cause the first significant split in the first generation of Marxists, it also gave birth to humanist versions of Marxism often associated with Marx's earlier works on alienation. The latter group identified with the works of the Austro-Marxists,[29] later played an influential role in shaping the ideas of what came to be known as Western Marxism. The most prominent spokespersons of this group, Georg Lukács and Antonio Gramsci, led a movement in Marxian tradition that highlighted the non-determinist, subjective part of Marxism.

Long before Soroush discovered deterministic renditions of material-ist conception of history, Western Marxists had already advanced a critique of the vulgar determinism embedded in Marx's historiography. They regarded *Das Kapital* as a futile attempt to justify the materialist conception of history *scientifically*. An economically reductionist approach captured in Marx's prophesy in the first volume of the *Capital* that 'the country that is more developed industrially only shows, to the less developed, the image of its own future.' It was against this economic determinism that, after the Russian revolution of 1917, Gramsci famously called for a 'revolution against *Capital*.'[30] Both Gramsci and Lukács put forward a subjective theory of social change, rejecting determinist conceptions of consciousness and identity as the unmediated reflections of the conditions of production.

It is indisputable that divergent Marxian philosophies shared a teleological view of history. Their metaphysical core rests on the premise of the purposefulness of social life. Coming from an Islamic standpoint, Soroush did not question this messianic view, which has its roots in Abrahamic religious doctrines, until later in his career (see Chapter 8). The question for him was the predictability and inevitability of this desired future. Change, according to Soroush, is inevitable, but its direction and outcomes remain accessible only to God. Even if contradic-tion were regarded as the engine of change in society, he remained skeptical about whether such an assertion would analytically have any relation with the directionality of the historical processes. 'How do we determine the direction of change,' Soroush asked, 'there are so many types of contradictions in society, but which contradiction conveys *the* central [i.e. relations of production] one and which constitute the peripheral ones remain unfathomable.'[31] By conferring a scientific aura upon their philosophy of history, the Marxists are 'wedding Hegelian dialectics and Darwinian evolutionary theory,' in order to construct a scientifically sanctioned historicist position.[32]

Elitist Totalitarianism

Soroush's argument appeared more forceful and passionate when he discussed, in a Popperian way, the totalitarian consequences of an historicist position upon which Marxists ascertain what is right and what is wrong, what is progressive and what is regressive and reactionary with reference to their perceived March of History. Soroush often reads Hegel or Darwin through his own reading of Marx and projects vulgar Marxism back onto Hegel or Darwin. For example, in a short monograph written in early 1980, without any direct reference, he condemned Hegel for his lack of commitment to any ethics. 'What is good persists, and would be nourished by history,' Soroush paraphrased what he believed to be Hegel's ethical principle, 'and what is bad would be thrown into the dustbin of history.'[33]

Although Soroush adopted a Popperian view of history, he did not directly cite him. Popper defines historicism as 'an approach to the social sciences which assumes that *historical prediction* is their principle aim, and discovering the "rhythms" or the "patterns," the "laws" or the "trends" that underlie the evolution of history.'[34] In this general sense, there is nothing new about historicism, as the question *is there a plot to history, and if so, what it is?* has been asked, implicitly or explicitly, from the Bible and Homer down to our own day.[35] Modern historicism substitutes history for God or Nature, and the claims that history generates its own moral principles of right and wrong. Popper concludes that such a shift gave us the laws of historical determinism which transform 'sinners against God' into 'criminals who vainly resist the march of History.'[36] Following Popper, Soroush condemned Marxists for turning 'transcendental ethical principles' into the relative subject of historical progress. In their historicist lexicon, he contended, Iranian Marxists replaced '*mu'men* (faithful) with *pishrow* (progressive); *kāfir* (apostate) with *mortaje`* (reactionary); *haqq* (just) with *pirouz* (victorious); and *bātel* (unjust) with *shekast-khordeh* (defeated).'[37]

Marxism has an uneasy relation with historicism when defined as the unfolding of historical necessities based on a predetermined law of progress. The fatalism inherent in such assertion contradicts the very core of the Marxist philosophy of change most aptly evoked by Marx in his Thesis Eleven on Feuerbach: 'The philosophers have only *interpreted* the world in various ways: the point, however, is to *change it*.' Marx conceived his revolutionary standpoint against historicist ideas that gave history an internal logic independent from human action. Marx's ambiguities concerning the relation between human action and historical necessity gave rise to Marxian tendencies in which free agency was unnecessary in the march to inevitable communism.[38]

Following a Popperian liberal position, in his early writings, Soroush identified the philosophy of Marx with Stalinist totalitarianism. In his view, philosophers rule the world by producing ideas that would eventually shape human conscious or unconscious action. As Heinrich Heine warned after the end of the Jacobin Reign of Terror in France,

> Mark this, ye proud men of action: Ye are nothing but unconscious instruments of the men of thought who, often in humblest seclusion, have appointed you to your favorite task. Maximilien Robespierre was merely the hand of Jean-Jacques Rousseau...[39]

Expanding the idea of the philosophers' rule, Popper derisively rebuked Marx for 'his seizure of power, thirty-four years after his death, in the person of Lenin [...] an almost repetition of the seizure of power by Rousseau, sixteen years after his death, in the person of Robespierre.'[40]

Marxism seemed to be an uninterrupted continuum from Marx's ideas, communist utopia to Stalinist totalitarianism, operated as a *Satanic Ideology*.[41] Soroush called it a 'masked dogmatism'[42] that wrapped itself in the colorful sentiments of emancipation and freedom. Although he admitted that dogmatism 'conveys a method and not a belief,' it is difficult to see in his depiction the possibility of a non-dogmatic comprehension of Marxism. 'One cannot say,' he cautioned his readers, 'that some beliefs are dogmatic and others not, but rather that there are two ways of approaching ideas, one dogmatic, the other non-dogmatic.'[43]

He divided dogmatism into two forms: masked and unmasked. Whereas unmasked dogmatism manifests itself in *ta`ssob* (fanaticism) and violence, masked dogmatism hides behind emancipatory ideas. Those who believe that 'religious beliefs generate [unmasked] dogmatism,' derive their position from a dogmatic approach to religion. They conceive religion as a set of doctrines with fixed and unyielding applications.[44] Masked dogmatism (satanic ideology) divides societies into two groups: conscious, deliberate actors and unwitting masses. Satanic ideology 'considers people to be entrapped in the claws of mysterious elements of history and condemns their rationality to the manipulation of their subconscious or class-based motivations.'[45] At the same time, the bearers of dogmatic ideology bestow upon themselves mysterious powers, afforded to them by history, which enable them to lead the masses to their 'true destiny.' *Satanic ideology* (Marxism) draws its seductive powers from 'opening the arms at the expense of closing the mind, unleashing passion by imprisoning Reason.' *Satanic ideology* substitutes the 'clash of bodies,' for 'the encounters of minds.' Masked dogmatism 'would usher in the worship of power,' it would 'cast its opponents out of the scene and would legitimize itself based only on the power it holds.'[46]

Patterning himself after Popper's critique of the sociology of knowledge,[47] Soroush argued that rather than engaging with ideas, masked dogmatism (Marxism) is concerned with motivations behind ideas. To the advocates of this masked dogmatism, Soroush objected, what is said is incidental to who has said it. Masked dogmatism promotes an ideology in which 'the earthly devils rule over the soul and blood of all humankind.'

> Individuals believe that they think, reason, and go to war [...] but unconsciously, they respond to the demands of masters who rule over them, masters who instill in them war and peace, law and literature, politics and religion, thinking and reason. Irrationality governs their reason.[48]

These elements were irrational, especially the class interest that conditions one's ideas. The satanic ideology, or what Popper called 'reinforced dogmatism,' renders 'meaningless' the 'tenets of their opponents.'[49] As examples of the irrationality that haunts human the subject, Soroush mocked Marx's theory of consciousness and Freud's emphasis on unconscious in shaping human action. 'Freud invented a *jin* called the "complex" and Marx introduced another called "class,"' a *jin* that possessed human beings and drove their lives and guided their minds.[50] 'How,' he wondered, 'could one imagine people in a permanent state of unconsciousness and imprudence where they neither mean what they say nor realize what they desire.' According to this 'modern superstition of the possessed mind,' the words people utter or the actions they carry out only 'correspond to the falsity of their consciousness.' In order to become mesmerized by the promises of this *satanic ideology*, one needs to consent that one's faculties distort the realities in which one lives. To see *the* reality, one needs to transcend and believe that 'there exists another kind of science in the hands of a few who are gifted in deciphering the mysteries of life, those who can fathom the true needs and desires of humanity.'[51]

In his writings, Soroush often gives agency to ideas rather than to those who convey them, and when he doing so, he refers to them in the ambiguous third-person plural pronoun.[52] In 1979 and 1980, before and immediately after the revolution, when he was delivering these lectures against Marxism and its Iranian adherents, two ideologies of liberation competed for the allegiance of the masses and intellectuals, one Marxist and the other Islamist. Both ideologies were represented by varieties of political parties, some radical and others reformist. Reading Soroush almost twenty-five years later, the Orwellian tinge of his discourse is all but evident. At the same historical period that Soroush was alerting his audience to the 'worship of power' as the defining logic of Marxism as a *masked dogmatism*, organized mob groups of *hezbollahis*, known as the 'club-wielders,' were impinging upon the freedoms generated by the aftermath of the revolution. They attacked book vendors, torched bookstores, violated women's rights in public places, violently assaulted peaceful demonstrators, and launched a coordinated campaign of terror.

How did a philosopher who was inspired by the principles of the *open society* and respect for individual freedoms, who had grown weary of the totalitarian consequences of historicism and economic deter-minism, become oblivious to the emerging reign of terror in the first two years of postrevolutionary society? There is no doubt that communist groups in Iran and the *Mojahedin-e Khalq* Organization (MKO) based their operations on a totalitarian ideology. As much as the Islamic regime, they subscribed to Jacobin abolitionism. The communists believed that they were the bearers of history and their vanguard parties bore the responsibility of leading the masses to their inevitable destiny. In fact, the deceased leader of the Iranian Workers Communist Party matter-of-factly stated so in a recent interview. 'What people want in any given period, or what they say, does not have the slightest effect on what *we* say or what *we* want [...] we represent the majority of people!'[53] And with the increasing monopolization of power by the clergy, the MKO began their own reign of terror by a massive campaign of brutal assassinations of the key figures of the new regime. Any history of postrevolutionary Iran needs to highlight the atrocities committed by the MKO and the violence promoted by many communist groups. But how could we explain Soroush's ambivalence towards the bloody repression by means of which the new regime solidified its power and, to borrow from him, 'cast its opponents out of the scene'?

Although he rightly observed that dogmatism breeds totalitarianism, in two short essays *The World We Live in*,[54] and *Satanic Ideology and the Qur'an*, he himself advanced a theory of consciousness which in its general principles, mimicked masked dogmatism. Referring to Sura *al-Qasas* 28:50, 'If they do not accept your words, then you know that they obey their caprices,' he concluded that a pious person would never succumb to satanic temptations. 'Satan cannot delude a *mokhles* (pious, sincere) person.'[55] The sociological implication of these assertions is that societies are divided into two groups: the masses, who are vulnerable to temptations and susceptible to satanic ideologies (masked dogmatism), and the elite of *mokhles,* whose purity and devotion to God renders them impervious to those temptations.

Colonialism, Soroush observed, effectively restricted the universe of the colonized and 'created a condition of noncorrespondence between their worldview and their realities.'[56] Alluding to a Hegelian notion of alienation, he explained,

> Often individuals mistake his limited physical experience of the world for the totality of his universe [...] This is the moment that a human being acquires a false 'I' in place of the real 'I.' As our contemporaries [Hegel, Marx?] observed, he becomes 'alienated,' 'estranged,' and according to its more precise Qur'anic interpretation, he forgets his true self.[57]

Whereas in Marxian dogma in order to transcend the condition of estrangement one needs to realize historical necessities, in Soroush's schemata one cannot attain true consciousness 'without connecting to God.' Rather than history, the source of ethical values, the good and the just, is God.[58] But who would give earthly voice to the Divine's ethical principles remained unfathomed in Soroush's early writings. By all accounts, during the Reign of Terror, Soroush believed that the dominant clerical establishment offered a closer approximation of the Divine Will than those who became the target of its oppression.

Soroush and the Cultural Revolution

> *We fear neither economic boycott nor military intervention. What we fear is cultural dependence and imperialist universities that propel our young people into the service of communism.*
>
> Ayatollah Khomeini

> *The Cultural Revolution is not something that should take several years; it is only a one-hour speech.*   Mahdavi-Kani

> *Those who want to copy China's Cultural Revolution in Iran and think that they will remove or weaken [the President] are openly betraying the country.*   President Bani Sadr

Four months after the revolution, 105 newspapers and magazines were published in Tehran, the majority of which were non-Islamic.[59] Hundreds of book-vendors sold Marxist literature, communist pamphlets and journals on the sidewalks across from the Tehran University campus. While the newly established Committees of the Islamic Revolution (IRC), an armed militia organization, in cooperation with the organized mob of *hezbollah,* took control of law and order in others parts of the city, the vicinity around the university remained a liberated zone. It operated as a distribution post for opposition media. Large anti-government demonstrations were held on university campuses around the country, and prominent leaders of the opposition voiced their dissent in the university lecture halls. Despite arson attacks on bookstores and the brutalization of the street vendors by the 'club-wielders' of the *hezbollah*, the universities permitted a continuous flow of information and freedom of expression. In response, the state-owned media castigated them as breeding ground for communism. Leftist students appeared to be a major obstacle to the establishment of law and order in society.

Although the takeover of the American Embassy ended the short tenure of Mehdi Bazargan's Provisional Government and afforded the postrevolutionary regime a major step towards the consolidation of power, the election of President Abolhasan Bani Sadr in January 1980, a critic of the *velāyat-e faqih,* undermined the plans of the ruling party, the Islamic Republic Party (IRP), to monopolize all three branches of government. Similar to earlier attempts to eliminate their rivals in the executive offices, factions inside the IRP engaged in a series of destabilization plans to undermine the authority of the first president of the republic. In order to assure Bani Sadr's failure to govern, they rendered his office impotent by exploiting parallel sources of authority—revolutionary courts, Islamic associations at workplaces, revolutionary guards and committees, and the organized gangs of *hezbollah* thugs.

A Muslim intellectual, educated at the Sorbonne in sociology and economics, Bani Sadr had already proven his disdain for the principle of the *velāyat-e faqih* during the Assembly of Experts' constitutional debate. Influenced by the French New Left's skepticism of all forms of bureaucratic organizations, Bani Sadr developed an idiosyncratic view of Islamic governance, the basic characteristics of which contradicted the principle of *velāyat-e faqih.*[60] In his view, under the Islamic state, political authority should emerge from decentralized municipal politics, exercised through a network of mosques. Islamic governance, he believed, was antithetical to hierarchical organizations. Its main objective was to realize *ta`mim-e imāmat* or a 'generalized imamate,' where every individual Muslim could practice *ijtihad*. Any form of separation, whether ideological or organizational, between the leadership of the society and its constituents would inevitably lead to totalitarianism.

With his election as the first president of the republic, Bani Sadr entered a paradoxical position. The intellectual who advocated de-centralized power and nonhierarchical governance was transformed into a president whose survival depended on the massive centralization of power through undermining local and regional revolutionary centers of power. He embarked on a stupendous scheme to restore law and order by dissolving all parallel revolutionary organs into a regular military, a formal judiciary, standardized industrial management, and planned land reform. While his main objective was to contain and eventually disband the revolutionary committees, revolutionary guards, and revolutionary courts, he also targeted the communist opposition groups who instigated labor unrest and were active in ethnic self-determination movements around the country.

Communist groups heavily relied on their student organizations, and used university facilities (offices, printing, lecture halls, etc.) for organizing their political actions. They used these resources to radicalize the revolution through emphasizing its anti-imperialist core and issues of social justice and equality. Although many groups pursued different strategies, they generally shared the perception that the liberal advocates of law and order were the main obstacle to the expansion of the revolutionary reconstitution of society.[61] They asked their student organizations to sustain the insurgent environment of the universities, and expand their activism beyond campus walls. In a typical communiqué of communist groups to university students, in September 1979, *Razmandegān-e Āzādi-ye Tabaqe-ye Kargar* (Warriors for the Liberation of the Working Class) called upon 'revolutionary students' to engage in four areas of struggle. They identified each of these as obstacles to the realization of the main objectives of the revolution.

> [1] The Kurdish people are under brutal attack from the reactionary regime…; [2] progressive papers are closed down…; [3] inflation and unemployment are ravaging the lives of our workers …; [4] with a new mask, reactionary agents of imperialism are deceiving our masses and suppressing their resistance.[62]

Similarly, another communist opposition group, *Sāzmān-e Paykār dar Rāh-e Azādi-ye Tabaqe-ye Kārgar* (The Organization of Struggle for the Emancipation of the Working Class) issued a manifesto calling on Marxist-Leninist students to organize on behalf of the communist groups with which they sympathized. They divided the responsibilities of Marxist-Leninist students into two parts:

> The first responsibility is towards the radicalization of the democratic, anti-imperialist movement, and the other is to fight against liberal and petit-bourgeois tendencies among the Marxist-Leninist students.[63]

Bani Sadr had long urged the political parties to vacate the universities and allow the campuses to resume their educational mission. Although the President and the Islamic Republic Party agreed on the basic principle of the return to normalcy as a way of suppressing the Leftist opposition, under the leadership of Hasan Ayat, the IRP wished to turn the predicament of the universities into a means to destabilize Bani Sadr's government.

More than a year after the revolution, students and professors affiliated with the IRP were still in the minority on most university campuses. It became evident to the new regime that the problem of the universities could not be resolved from within the campus. In a conversation with the leaders of the Islamic Students' Association, Hasan Ayat, an ideologue of the IRP, revealed a decisive plan to reinvent higher education and put an end to the political dominance of the Left on university campuses. In editorial pages of daily papers, many other leaders of the IRP openly discussed the necessity of overhauling the higher education system. *Jomhuri-ye Islami*, the official paper of the IRP, published a series of editorials on the need for a cultural revolution. The first one appeared on February 12, 1980, written by Hasan Ayat. He wrote, 'In my opinion the greatest responsibility of the *majlis* is a cultural revolution [...] The *majlis* has to lay the foundations of such revolution.' Three days later on February 15, he reiterated that 'the mass media, such as radio and television, ought to be employed for the purpose of the cultural revolution.' On April 16, 1980, Mohammad Bahonar, another founding member of the IRP, identified the universities as the first targets of the Cultural Revolution. 'It is necessary,' he declared, 'to make fundamental changes in our universities, even if it meant shutting them down temporarily.'[64] What distinguished Ayat's position was that he linked the Cultural Revolution to an attack on Bani Sadr's presidency.

The *Mojahedin-e Khalq* Organization (MKO) leaked a tape recording of Ayat's private strategy meeting to the press. 'The universities in their present state,' Ayat was heard on the tape, 'should be closed down.'

> I assure you that the plan is ready for turning the situation around [...] Surely, after June 4 [1980, the last day of classes at the university] no exams will be administered, not a single university will remain open [...] We have organized a massive assault, so massive that it would completely paralyze Bani Sadr [...] This decision is made and is irrevocable, the universities shall be closed on June 4 and those greater than Bani Sadr can't stop it [...] We should not even whisper about this, we need to catch him off guard [...] but the Imam [Khomeini] has to be informed before we put our plan into action.[65]

Members of the *Mojahedin* delivered the tape of Ayat's plot to the President. In two editorials in his daily paper *Enqeláb-e Islami* (*The Islamic Revolution*) on April 20 and 21, Bani Sadr warned about the coming *coup d'état*. He took his case to the Revolutionary Council and was assured by its members that the planned Cultural Revolution had nothing to do with the legitimacy of his government. In his editorials, Bani Sadr reported that the Council justified the plan with three reasons:

> 1. The university has become the center for the activities of political groups, they have offices on campuses and use paper and copy machines at will. Universities do not resemble centers of academic learning, they have become a political marketplace in which different groups compete. The armed resistance [to the authority of the Islamic Republic] is conducted and coordinated from the universities.

> 2. There are three different types of faculty: the devoted Muslims (*maktabi*) about 10 per cent; second group, counterrevolution-aries, leftists and others, another 10 per cent; and finally 80 per cent who are ambivalent. Cleanse the universities of the second group and they would operate in an Islamic spirit with 90 per cent of their capacity.

> 3. We need to reform the curriculum; in its current state, it produces neither thinkers nor specialists. It produces burdens not experts.[66]

Bani Sadr's effort to block the plan to shut down the universities failed. Particularly since Ayatollah Khomeini had already lent his support for a Cultural Revolution in his New Year's message on March 21, 1980. Khomeini's thirteen-point message had a contradictory consequence. In his address he showed his willingness to recognize Bani Sadr's demands to restore order in the military, and contain the revolutionary courts' arbitrary verdicts in confiscation of property and execution of the associates of the *ancien régime*. However, apparently unaware of the IRP's plot to undermine Bani Sadr, he called for a cultural revolution to Islamize the universities and purge the 'Left and Right professors,' from them. He declared,

> A fundamental revolution must take place in all the universities across the country, so that professors with links to the East or to the West may be purged, and the university may provide a healthy atmosphere for cultivation of the Islamic sciences [...] I support all that has been said by the Revolutionary Council and the President of the Republic concerning the necessity for a purge of the universities and a change in the prevailing atmosphere in order to make them fully independent. I request that all of our young people not resist or try to sabotage the reform of the universities; if any of them do so, I will instruct the nation as to how to respond.[67]

Khomeini also distanced himself from the traditionalists' position against the main principles of higher education. He reproached 'certain gentlemen sitting on the sidelines' who accused the Revolutionary Council of not being aware of what they had embarked upon.

> They pretend that the Islamization of the universities rests on the assumption that the sciences are divisible into Islamic and non-Islamic varieties, so that we have Islamic mathematics and non-Islamic mathematics. Do they not know that some members of the Revolutionary Council hold doctorates and some are *mujtahids*? The place for the strictly Islamic sciences is the traditional *madrasa*; the other sciences are to be taught at the university. However, the universities must become Islamic in the sense that the subjects studied in them are to be pursued in accordance with the needs of the nation and for the sake of strengthening it [...] To Islamize the universities means to make them autonomous, independent of the West and independent of the East, so that we have an independent country with an independent university system and an independent culture.[68]

Despite the subtle but clear distinction between Khomeini's position and that of Hasan Ayat and his followers in the IRP, the New Year's message legitimized the launch of the campaign to close down the universities. At its April 18, 1980, meeting, the Revolutionary Council pledged that the universities would remain open and issued an ultimatum to the student groups to evacuate their political offices in a one-week period.

Despite these public declarations, after the Friday prayer on the same day, hundreds of *hezbollahis* attacked university campuses in Tehran and other major cities.

While representatives of the President negotiated with student organizations on the terms of evacuation, Bani Sadr could not contain the zeal of the IRP planners of the Cultural Revolution. He also failed to avert the attacks on university campuses. The leaders of the two major student groups, *Pishgām*[69] and the student organization of *Mojahedin*, had warned Bani Sadr of the pending coup against his government and had promised him to evacuate their offices in due time.[70] But on April 21 and 22, attacks on the universities reached a climax. This time thousands of *hezbollahi* club-wielders and ordinary people who were following their religious leaders' edict surrounded university campuses in Tehran and other parts of the country.

Although all campuses in Tehran—Polytechnique University, National University, Industrial University of Sharif, The College of Science and Technology, The Teachers' Training College, Mottahedin Women's College—were scenes of resistance, the focal point was Tehran University. Students inside the campus made an appeal to the people to help them save the last sanctuary of democracy. The armed Islamic militia prevented their supporters from approaching the vicinity. On the second day of the seizure of the campus, the militias of the Revolutionary Committees opened fire on students who refused to vacate their offices. Wounded students were smuggled out to hospitals; many of them, along with the doctors who treated them, were arrested. Positioned on the rooftop of several colleges, members of a radical faction of the *Fadā'iyan* fired back at the Islamic militia. A blood bath was in the making. Students decided to leave the campus before the number of killed and wounded increased.

Similar attacks occurred in the cities of Rasht, Mashad, Tabriz, Ahvaz, Isfahan, and Shiraz. The bloodiest clashes were in Rasht and Ahvaz. The government announced that twenty-four 'counter-revolutionaries' had been killed during the clashes. The opposition claimed the number of students killed during the Cultural Revolution was much higher. The government claimed that armed students opened fire on the revolutionary militia. However, a photograph showing armed *hezbollahis* firing at the students in Rasht, published in a *Pishgām* pamphlet, undermined the government's claim.[71]

Through a Bonapartist political maneuver, after failing to stop the spread of the Cultural Revolution, Bani Sadr led a large crowd of more than fifty thousand onto the campus of the 'liberated' Tehran University. While campus workers washed the blood off the buildings' walls, in the football field Bani Sadr inaugurated a Cultural Revolution, one of whose main purposes was to be his own ouster. In answer to a CBS reporter's question, 'Do you think the recent turbulences in the university is a threat to your government?' he tersely responded, 'Last night a friend described the situation in this manner: A train had left the station and was beginning to gather speed when you [the President] jumped into it and halted it.'[72]

Hasan Ayat and other ideologues of the IRP conceived the Cultural Revolution to be means of stifling the student movement and creating a crisis of legitimacy for the President. They failed on both accounts. Bani Sadr rode the wave of the masses and claimed the revolution as his own. After a few days of disruption, the students reopened the universities and resumed their political activities in their ransacked offices.

Abdolkarim Soroush and the Cultural Revolution Council (CRC)

> Officially and openly I seek absolution for my role in the Cultural Revolution.
>
> Professor Sadeq Ziba-Kalam
> Former Muslim Student Activist

On June 12, 1980, after the bloody attacks of the earlier month, Ayatollah Khomeini issued a decree announcing the formation of the Cultural Revolution Council. He appointed a seven-member committee, made up of Shams Al-e Ahmad; Abdolkarim Soroush; Ali Shari`atmadari; Mohammad Javad Bahonar; Hasan Habibi; Mehdi Rabbani Amlashi; and Jalal ad-Din Farsi, to carry out a systematic project to Islamize the universities. Admitting the failure of its initial phase, Khomeini reiterated that 'no effective measures have been taken for the realization of the cultural revolution.' He asked his appointees to devise a new plan for the 'restructuring of higher education based on Islamic culture.'[73]

If the Cultural Revolution shut the doors of the universities, it opened a door through which Abdolkarim Soroush entered the post-revolutionary political landscape. Although he served in the Cultural Revolution Council (CRC) for less than three years, his short tenure continues to be controversial, especially among Iranian expatriate intellectuals. At the time of his appointment to the CRC by Ayatollah Khomeini, Soroush was an unknown thirty-five-year old Muslim philosopher and lay theologian who had returned to the country a year earlier from England.

He was an anomaly in the CRC, having neither a significant history of political activism, nor an affiliation with any of the factions in power. The only apparent reason for his inclusion in the CRC was the affinity Khomeini felt with his account of Mulla Sadra's theosophy in the treatise he had authored a year before the revolution. Soroush believed that Khomeini had read the manuscript and had found it judiciously argued and insightful. [74] By appointing a diverse group of individuals, three of whom held postgraduate degrees, Khomeini intended to demonstrate that the Islamization of education did not pose a threat to the modern sciences. But in order to gain legitimacy, he needed a Council with intellectual vigor and commitment to the basic principles of the revolution. Despite his obscurity at the time, Soroush lent significant weight and legitimacy to the CRC and thereby emerged as an influential intellectual of the new republic.

Immediately after the formation of the CRC, Soroush distanced himself from the political context that had originally motivated the Cultural Revolution. For example, in an interview on June 28, 1980, he discussed the university (re)admission policy without a single reference to the CRC's mandate to purge 'unfit' faculty and students.[75] In recent years, Soroush has continued to depoliticize his responsibilities at the CRC and has rebuffed his critics' argument that through his role in the Cultural Revolution Council he contributed to the postrevolutionary regime's consolidation of power.[76] Not only does Soroush remain un-apologetic about his role, he considers his participation as a 'great honor to serve the people.'[77] In order to justify his membership in the CRC, Soroush points to four 'myths' about the Cultural Revolution and its relation to the formation of the CRC.

(1) He argues that his critics often confuse the events that transpired during the Cultural Revolution in April 1980 with the mandates of the Cultural Revolution Council, which was formed in June of the same year. In April 1980, at the time the raids on universities campuses occurred, the CRC did not exist. Therefore, the CRC could not be held responsible for the death and destruction caused by the attacks. However, while the Cultural Revolution preceded the appointment of the Council this does not mean that he condemns the violence perpet-rated against the students. He argues,

> The reason universities were shut down was that they were not
> actual universities. Armed opposition groups, which fancied the

overthrow of the state, were conducting wars and rebellions around the country from their positions on university campuses. When somebody speaks with the logic of force, the other side responds accordingly. Therefore, some clashes happened and those armed groups were forced out. That was the reason for the closure of the universities.[78]

In effect, Soroush holds the opposition groups and their student organizations unilaterally responsible for the bloodshed that marked the Cultural Revolution, without acknowledging the formal and informal violence that allowed factions in the IRP to consolidate their power. Although several student organizations did endorse the violent Kurdish insurgency, *none* supported the militarization of the university campuses. Elsewhere Soroush has acknowledged that 'the Cultural Revolution had political roots,'[79] but he limits his recognition of political objectives to the elimination of the armed radical campus groups, thereby ignoring the plot to undermine Bani Sadr's presidency.

(2) Soroush has also argued that the CRC was not responsible for shutting down the universities; rather, it was formed to investigate how to reopen them. 'At times,' he recalled, 'we even spoke of *behtar goshā'ei* (opening with improved conditions) rather than *bāz-goshā'ei* (reopening).'[80] He further defends his role by pointing out that

> At that time, there were people who seriously intended and actually attempted to keep the universities closed for an indefinite period. However, the Council, of which I was a member, did not want this to happen, and made every effort to compile and rewrite syllabi of various courses rapidly, and reopen the universities within a short period. The council succeeded in reopening the universities in less than two years.[81]

In contrast to Soroush's recollection of the mission of the CRC, Mohammad Javad Bahonar, a founding member of the IRP,[82] reported that in his meeting with the newly appointed CRC on August 9, 1980, for the first time, Khomeini insisted that the universities had to remain closed indefinitely, until they were reconstituted with Islamic principles. Contradicting recent recollections of Soroush, in response to a reporter's question in August 30, 1980, Bahonar, then the secretary general of the CRC, responded:

> In our last meeting with the imam [Khomeini], we discussed the issues related to the Cultural Revolution. The Imam emphasized that we do not have any obligation to keep the universities open. We insist that the universities should become consistent with the

goals of the Islamic Revolution [...] What is clear is that the universities will not open this fall.[83]

From the beginning Soroush justified his membership in the CRC by emphasizing the distinction between the Cultural Revolution and the responsibilities of the Council. For example, he remarked, 'we do not decide whether the universities will remain open or closed, rather, the Cultural Revolution, as an external force, will dictate either possibility.'

(3) In an interview with the daily *Jomhuri-ye Islami*, on July 21, 1980, he speculated that the universities might not reopen in the fall. And finally, on July 29, citing Soroush, the daily *Enqelab-e Islami* reported that the Council had decided to close the universities.[84] Soroush also contends that the CRC was involved with neither the Islamization of the curriculum nor the purges and cleansing of the faculty and students. Not only does he refuse to accept the formation of the CRC as an integrated part of the Cultural Revolution, he does not accept any responsibility regarding the purges and the exclusionary policies that followed the closing of the universities. Rather, he maintains,

> The dismissal of professors and the purging of the faculty had nothing to do with the Council. Rather, it was a movement that had started in all government offices, including the universities. We did not even know the members of the Cleansing Committees. Occasionally, we heard about it, and sometimes we acted against it and sometimes we did not. The revolutionary students were demanding the closure of the universities and dealing with them was an extraordinarily difficult task.[85]

On the question of the Islamization of the curriculum, he insists,

> The Islamization of the universities was not on the agenda, particularly at the beginning. We never discussed it. Later, when the council was expanded [and the High Council of the Cultural Revolution was formed] the issue [of Islamization] became one of the items on the agenda. But, as predicted, that also bore no fruit.[86]

Soroush's recent assertions conspicuously contradict Khomeini's June 12, 1980 directive for the establishment of the Cultural Revolution Council. In his message, Khomeini did not make any distinction between the Cultural Revolution and the responsibilities of the CRC. Rather, he saw the latter as an instrument for the execution of the former. He also laid out for the seven-member Council the guiding principles of future purges and the Islamization of the universities. Khomeini began his decree by emphasizing that the necessity for the formation of the CRC was dictated by 'our Muslim nation' during the Cultural Revolution. He stressed his expectation to see a university 'in the service of Islam and the country,' with no room for 'conspirators and other agents of colonial powers.'[87]

Like other postrevolutionary political institutions, the Council, in its earlier days as well as in its later configurations, reflected competing and contradictory tendencies. For example, in the summer of 1981, four major seminars were held in Mashad, Ahvaz, Kerman, and Shiraz to discuss 'the unity of the seminary and the university.'[88] None of the eighteen members or advisers to the CRC who delivered keynote speeches believed that the universities should open before they were completely Islamized. With the exception of Hasan Habibi, who spoke in Kerman, all the others firmly believed that higher education should be divided into the positive sciences and the humanities. The former would be taught at the universities and the howzeh would be responsible for the teaching of the latter.

Although Soroush never advocated such a division between the university and the howzeh, in the beginning of his tenure at the CRC, he did promote the Islamization of the social sciences. In the fall of 1981, he emphasized the urgent need to reconstitute the social sciences. Unlike experimental sciences, and proposed, 'social sciences are subjective, and as such they have roots in the land of their origin and the mind of their creators.' He regarded experimental sciences as 'rootless, they are sciences without land.' 'Mathematics [...] is the same in Germany, London, Moscow, and Washington,' but, 'just like a plant, [the social sciences] will be fed on the soil and the water of the land in which it has been planted.' He concluded, 'the question is how can we insert the taste and the smell of Islam into these sciences?' Soroush went on to say that 'if we cannot Islamize a discipline, it will remain closed.'[89] Although he belonged to the faction of the CRC that did not believe in the elimination of human sciences from the university, he certainly participated in the Islamization project, which reconstituted the curriculum and cleansed the campuses.

In the second edition of his short monograph *Bani Sadr, the Mojahediin Organization, and Hegelism,* published in 1983, three years after the Cultural Revolution, Soroush cautioned that revolutionary fervor could not sustain the revolution. In a reference to the President's exploitation of the invasion of university campuses as a vehicle to further his presidential authority, he purported that 'those who exploit people's raging passion and ride the waves of their zeal need to know that these passions will dissipate unless they embrace a strong theory.'[90] In sharp contrast with his later assertions, he defended the main objectives of the Cultural Revolution as the legitimate means of guiding peoples' passion by linking it to a systematic project of Islamization.

> During the Cultural Revolution, when we discussed the issue of the Islamization of the university, we underlined that an Islamic university is not merely a place of high academic achievement, though that would be desirable and we will strive for that. But we do not desire the kind of science practiced by detached, indifferent learned researchers. We intend to create legendary, passionate, and raging souls, who will hold the light of reason with one hand, and with the other spread the fire of their passion in the world.[91]

According to Sadeq Ziba-Kalam, a professor of political science at Tehran University, who was actively involved in the Cultural Revolution, and directly aware of the purges, Soroush chose not to interfere with the work of the Cleansing Committees. Ziba-Kalam recalls that in the early days of the Cultural Revolution there was a deep animosity towards those who were educated in Europe and the US. A degree from western universities became a liability for those who intended to restructure fundamentally the institution of higher education based on Islamic principles. Criticizing his own role, Ziba-Kalam reports that he and other Muslim students launched a vicious campaign of intimidation against any faculty who failed to demonstrate his or her loyalty to the Islamic Republic.[92]   He also asserts, after he began to question the wisdom of the policy of indiscriminate attacks on the faculty and students, he decided to take his case to Abdolkarim Soroush, the most sympathetic member of the CRC.

> [Soroush] did not endorse these actions, but unfortunately, he refused to take any action against the policy or even simply condemn the purges. In so many words he told me that there were more important matters […] He did not shed any tears over this issue, appeared unflustered, and left the matter behind nonchalantly. For example, I told him that a professor of mathematics, a graduate of Stanford University, is a treasure in this country, but he did not react, as if these events were happening in Afghanistan and they were not the children of this country walking away from their homeland.[93]

The distinction Soroush draws between his specific tasks as a member of the CRC and the general goals of the Cultural Revolution should not obscure the role he played in the consolidation of power by the clergy. As a young, western-educated, committed Muslim, he represented the kind of intellectual that the new regime desired in order to legitimize its actions for an urban middle class population.

Soroush, the Purged President, and the Obliterated Left

> This Nay sings with the wind of fire not of air,
> This fire will consume you, if its heat you cannot bear.
>
> Rumi[94]

Not only is Soroush unapologetic about the means and consequences of the Cultural Revolution, he believes that the postrevolutionary regime needed its fire to transform the educational system in Iran. In his recollections, he emphasizes the significance of his role in saving the humanities and social sciences from the onslaught of the orthodox factions within the Cultural Revolution Council. Historical memory is selective. It generates narratives that often highlight the significance of the narrator while concealing the scope and depth of other actors' experiences. In their selectivity, these memories generate continuity in the historical life of the narrator, portraying him as a conscious decision-maker who rises above circumstances in authoring his destiny. In addition to his selective memory of the Cultural Revolution, Soroush has consistently demonstrated his inability to perceive these events from the point of view of those who suffered its catastrophic consequences.

Soroush's early intellectual project focused on demystifying Marxism. He criticized Marxism as a determinist, totalitarian ideology, and more importantly, advanced a vehement critique of the Muslims such as members of the MKO, who had succumbed to the temptations of its emancipatory discourse. But during the late 1970s and early 1980s, Soroush remained oblivious to the fact that such a critique politically situated him on the side of the ruling factions whose measured encroachment into the state power would soon threaten the conditions of his own intellectual livelihood.

Although the Cultural Revolution achieved its main objectives of purging 'unfit' faculty members and students from universities around the country, it succeeded neither in generating social stability through the suppression of oppositional groups, nor in consolidating its power by marginalizing Bani Sadr. The instigators of the Cultural Revolution overestimated the significance of the campus offices of the opposition. Universities across the country were shut down in June 1980, but that did not dissipate the unrest. The civil war in Kurdistan intensified and continued to spread to larger areas of the Kurdish provinces, the MKO and other opposition parties continued to destabilize the new regime by simultaneous small and large demonstrations in the cities, and Bani Sadr's Bonapartist ride on the wave of the masses who occupied the campuses across the country turned the movement which was partly designed to undermine his authority into a vehicle for strengthening his political power.

In 1980, there were no disagreements about the need for stability in the country between the two main factions in power—the President and the liberal supporters of Bazargan's Provisional Government, and the Islamic Republic Party (IRP). They differed, however, over whose leadership would generate this stability. Bani Sadr came to power with the promise to consolidate all parallel institutions of power into a centralized system of governance. His centralization plan was a euphemism for stripping away the power of the revolutionary state institutions such as the Revolutionary Courts, the Revolutionary Guards, the Revolutionary Committees, etc.[95]

An early advocate of populist politics and a skeptic of large hierarchical organizations of power, Bani Sadr nevertheless realized that the survival of his presidency depended on the elimination of multiple sources of power. Earlier in his political career, he developed a pseudo anarchist theory of the state in which he had envisioned that the coming Islamic revolution would create the 'Government of God.'[96] As he had shown during the debates in the Constitutional Assembly, his notion of the Government of God was radically distinct from the doctrine of *velāyat-e faqih*. For Bani Sadr, the Government of God was to be maintained and municipally organized by a network of mosques, rather than through a hierarchical relation between infallible imams and their uniformed followers. He believed that in an Islamic society, leadership ought to become an unalienable right and imamate a sanctioned duty of every citizen. In this diffused conception of leadership and generalized notion of imamate, 'all become *mujtaheds* [jurists] and no one will need to ask his duty from another [...] Otherwise, religious tyranny will result.'[97]

The sobering experience of becoming the first president of the republic transformed Bani Sadr's anti-establishment political discourse into a comprehensive plan to eliminate multiple sources of authority, consolidate decision-making processes in the central government, and

most importantly resurrect the old military. The harder Bani Sadr tried
to consolidate power, the more the IRP and its allies intensified their call
for the revamping and purification of the old state bureaucracy. As Shaul
Bakhash noted, on 4 July, 1980, tens of thousands of supporters of the
IRP, the Mojahedin of the Islamic Revolution, the Revolutionary Guards,
the Crusade for Reconstruction, the 'Students of the Imam's Line,' the
Society of Qom Seminary Teachers, the Society of Militant Clergy of
Tehran, all rallied against Bani Sadr's centralization plans and called for
a 'new bureaucratic order.' They demanded the purging of all 'agents of
East and West' from the government, and the persecution of all 'godless
and eclectic groups' (referring to the Fadā'iyan and the MKO).[98]

Just weeks later, in September of 1980, after the Iraqi military
launched an all-out incursion into Iranian territory, Bani Sadr's agenda
became an urgent necessity. Saddam Hussein's military exploited the
chaotic political situation and overwhelmed Iranian defenses. The Iraqi
army advanced towards the Iranian oil fields with relative ease, despite
the vigorous resistance of the local militia and the disintegrated border
patrols. Although the war did not dampen factional political fighting, it
pushed it to the margins. Three weeks after the Iraqi assault, on October
12, 1980, Ayatollah Khomeini appointed Bani Sadr to the presidency of
the Supreme Defense Council and granted him unlimited powers to lead
the war effort. However, alarmed by the growing powers of the
President, the IRB and its allies in the Supreme Defense Council, Prime
Minister Raja'i, and the influential Minister of Justice, Ayatollah
Beheshti, contained Bani Sadr's authority by undermining his war plans.

Bani Sadr called back hundreds of purged high-ranking military
officers to duty, believing that the Iranian forces needed to unite under a
single command structure. Feeling the pressure of the opposition in the
capital, he moved to the front and led the war effort closely from his new
command post in the southern province of Khuzestan. Although this
proved to be successful in halting Iraqi advances and soon thereafter
recapturing parts of lost territories, the President's absence from the
capital left the political scene vacant for his opposition. With the consent
of Prime Minister Raja'i, the opposition quietly assumed control of all of
the executive powers of the office of the presidency. From the time he
moved his office to the war front to the final moment of his demise in
June 1981, Bani Sadr acted as an individual who happened to be the
President of the country. He grew more and more alienated from his
own cabinet, the parliament, and other institutions of state power.
Instead, he established a direct connection with his popular base through

daily columns published in his paper *Enqelab-e Islami* (Islamic Revolution). The more he took his grievances directly to the masses, the more he antagonized the leaders of the IRP and the clerical establishment in Qom.

The IRP believed that Bani Sadr's success in blocking Saddam's aggression was a double-edged sword. While the fate of the revolution became interlaced with the defeat of Saddam Hussein, they feared that success in the war would pave the way for Bani Sadr to complete his consolidation of power. Once again, like his Bonapartist move during the Cultural Revolution, Bani Sadr successfully rode the war machine under his command to expand his authority and to ridicule his opposition as naïve and simpleminded. The leaders of the IRP warned Ayatollah Khomeini of the perils the President posed to his leadership and pressured him to sack him as the commander in chief. As the Ayatollah's grandson, Hossein Khomeini, disclosed to a *Financial Times* reporter in March 1981, 'I have heard them say that it is preferable to lose half of Iran than for Bani Sadr to become the ruler.'[99]

The war changed the politics and political strategies of all parties engaged in the postrevolutionary power struggle. The IRP, the Mojahedin of the Islamic Revolution (not to be mistaken with the opposition group MKO), and the Society of Militant Clergy recognized that without winning the war, all other battles over the solidification of power would be rendered meaningless. At the same time, they realized that whatever faction declared itself responsible for the victory would be as important as the victory itself. Accordingly, they did not allow members of any of the opposition groups to participate in the war effort. Even though three main dissident parties, the MKO, the Fadā'iyan (the Majority faction), and the Tudeh Party announced that they would fight against the Iraqi aggressors, they were not allowed to join the army of volunteers or organize their own troops. Other smaller parties from the Left, such as Paykār, the Fadā'iyan (the Minority Faction), and a host of smaller communist groups condemned the war and, in the Leninist fashion of the 1917 revolution, called for turning the reactionary war into a revolutionary war to topple the regime.

In a statement issued on September 11, 1980, after expressing regrets for the tremendous loss of life and 'the country's resources,' the MKO leadership announced that 'if the government authorities allow them, they are prepared to defend the borders and cities against the aggression of the Ba'thist regime.'[100] One month later, on October 15, 1980, government authorities began arresting and sending MKO fighters home from the war front. In protest, the organization issued a statement condemning the government's monopolization of power.

> The Mojahedin-e Khalq regrets that our efforts to reduce the tensions and eliminate the obstacles for the participation of our members in the war have failed. Unfortunately, the divisive and exclusionary policies of some factions in the government have spread to the front and the defense of the country. We, hereby, ask the responsible authorities to end these disruptive actions and to create an environment conducive for all groups to fulfill their patriotic duties.[101]

The Tudeh Party supported the IRP and other opponents of the President, on the basis of a crude Leninist analysis, which deemed the former (including Ayatollah Khomeini) to be a revolutionary petit-bourgeois anti-imperialist leader. Despite the regime's anti-Soviet and anti-American positions, the Tudeh Party never relinquished its agenda to push the revolution forward against the American interests and alleviate tensions between Iran and its northern neighbor. The Iraqi invasion put the Party in an paradoxical position, since Iraq attacked Iran with a military largely built up by the Soviets during the 1970s. The Tudeh Party blamed the aggression on Saddam Hussein's deviation from earlier policies of peaceful coexistence and argued that the Americans designed the war in part to generate anti-Soviet sentiments in revolutionary Iran. In *Nāmeh-ye Mardom* (*People's Gazette*) published one month after the invasion, the party's Chairman, Nuroddin Kiyanuri, proclaimed that 'it was evident that the Pentagon and the followers of Zbigniew Brzezinski's doctrine had *anti-Soviet* intentions when they decided to ship weapons to Iraq.'[102] The Tudeh Party continued its long lasting practice of navigating between its political objectives domestically and advocating the Soviets' interest in the region.

In its more theoretical paper, *Donyā* (*The World*), the Party leadership falsely assured its readers that 'after Saddam Hussein launched his war against Iran, the Soviet Union and other socialist countries halted their military relations with Iraq.'[103] In reality, not only did the USSR continue to sell arms to Iraq through satellite states such as Poland and Czechoslovakia, the Kremlin never held Saddam Hussein responsible for instigating the war.[104] The Tudeh Party went even further to claim that it was the only political force in Iran that anticipated the war and, along with the Iraqi Communist Party, had warned the revolutionary regime about Saddam Hussein's ambitions. They asked their members and sympathizers to join the army of volunteers. However, both the regular army and the Revolutionary Guards viewed this move skeptically. They questioned the sincerity of the Party and accused its leadership of espionage for the Soviet Union.[105]

The Fadā'iyan Organization (the Majority) also asked its supporters to participate in resistance against Saddam Hussein's aggression, but at the same time it linked the war to the divisive policies of the government and to the 'liberal shortcomings' of the President. An editorial in *Kār* (*Labor*), the main political weekly of the Fadā'iyan, stated:

> The exclusionary and divisive policies, blind vengefulness against communist revolutionaries, and the execution and purging of revolutionary forces have inflicted heavy blows to the sustainability and progress of our revolution and the unity of the masses. As a result of these policies, the revolution has faced numerous obstacles and has faced imperialist and reactionary forces in the region that have targeted our country. Today, despite the divisive, camouflaged policies of liberals, who intend to monopolize state power, the responsibility of all communist revolutionaries is to fight the war against aggression.[106]

Only a week later, in the next issue of *Kār*, in a section called 'Notes from the Fronts,' a Fadā'i soldier wrote that 'the Fadā'iyan are the most active political and military group in mobilizing the masses. [...] Based on the recommendations of the Organization, hundreds of trenches have been dug and tens of thousands have been recruited to resist the aggression.'[107] The absurdity of the Fadā'iyan's claim that they had organized the most significant resistance against the Iraqi invasion is evident. But the fact remains that despite the Fadā'iyan's desire to be embraced by the Islamic Republic, the regime continued to view them as 'those who slaughtered the Revolutionary Guards in Kurdistan and now regard themselves the true guardians of the revolution.'[108]

Radical groups such as Paykār and the minority faction of the Fadā'iyan advocated turning the war into a revolutionary uprising against the Islamic regime. Evidently, they had relinquished their hope of sharing power with the ruling clerical establishment and tried to use all possible means to overthrow it. In its weekly paper, the leadership of Paykār denounced the war as the 'continuation of the reactionary policies of the two countries.' Only three weeks after the invasion, an editorial in *Paykār* (*The Struggle*) No. 74 declared, 'The war between Iran and Iraq is a war between two reactionary regimes on behalf of their bourgeoisie, to protect the interests of imperialism and global capital, and to maintain the oppression of the Iranian and Iraqi people.'[109] In the next issue of *Paykār*, No. 75, October 6, 1980, the group openly declared war against the Islamic regime. 'We are against this war;' *Paykār* declared, 'our goal is to unite Iranian and Iraqi workers against their respective capitalist classes.'[110]

The minority faction of the Fada'iyan also echoed the same sentiments. On October 22, 1980, in their weekly paper *Kār* (the minority edition), the Fadā'iyan (Minority) condemned the war as a device that would prolong the reactionary rule of the Islamic regime. They appealed to the Iranian people not to participate in the war and thereby strengthen the position of the Left against the regime.

> Wars are two types: just, revolutionary, and progressive versus unjust and reactionary wars. Iranian workers need to know that Iraqi workers are their brethren and Iraqi and Iranian capitalists their enemy. Only the two governments of Iran and Iraq and world imperialism benefit from this war. We plead with the workers and toilers of Iran and Iraq to do their utmost to expose the real nature of this war and avoid joining the war of two reactionary states.[111]

In their quest for power, the Islamic Republic Party and its allies found themselves in battle with a myriad of political and military forces. On one front, Saddam Hussein threatened the integrity of the country and its vital economic foundations. And internally, the only viable opposition to their total monopolization of power, President Bani Sadr, had achieved systematic resistance against the Iraqi aggression by revitalizing the old military under his own command. And finally, they witnessed the growing influence of opposition parties, which exploited the war to advance their grievances.

In response, the IRP launched a grassroots campaign to undermine the President and limit the opposition groups' access to the media. The IRP and its allies controlled a vast network of mosques, local councils, revolutionary committees, and the *hezbollahi* club-wielders. Aware of Ayatollah Khomeini's pragmatism, by mobilizing the masses against Bani Sadr, they hoped to persuade Khomeini of the popularity and legitimacy of their cause. Both Bani Sadr and the IRP faction realized that without his blessing, neither side could tame or eliminate the other.

For Bani Sadr, competing with his rivals' power of mass mobilization proved to be arduous. He came to power without a party and relied on his individual resources, especially his daily column, to generate sustained public support for his agenda. But after his return from the front to Tehran in March 1981, he realized that he needed a coordinated and well-disciplined group to ward off the organized attacks of the *hezbollahi* thugs against his popular base. In effect, the more the IRP stepped up its pressure against the President to circumvent his authority and to pressure Ayatollah Khomeini to withdraw his support, the more urgent it became for Bani Sadr to find a coherent organizational structure to fight for his political survival.

On March 5, 1981, during a rally in support of the President at Tehran University, for the first time the *hezbollahis* for the first time faced a fierce and concerted resistance. MKO members rounded up the attackers, confiscated their identification cards, handed them to the President, and announced that every single assailant was affiliated in one way or another with the IRP and its allies. At that decisive moment, it became evident that the potential for the two main factions in power to coexist had expired. The alliance between the Mojahedin and Bani Sadr proved to have dire consequences for both.

Bani Sadr's political capital depended heavily on Khomeini's support. Khomeini, who once called Bani Sadr his 'devoted son,' grew wary of his embrace of the Mojahediin, an organization that regarded itself as an *alternative to* rather than *a part of* the Islamic regime. Emboldened by Khomeini's unease, on June 7, 1981, the judiciary made the definitive move of shutting down *Enqelab-e Islami,* the only independent voice of the president. Not only did Khomeini support Ayatollah Beheshti who engineered the closure of the paper, two days later he issued a decree releasing Bani Sadr from his duties as Commander in Chief. Swiftly, only three days later, on June 12, 1981, the *majlis* moved to debate Bani Sadr's competence as President. But Khomeini blocked that effort and offered the President one last chance to recognize the limits to his authority and make amends with the leaders of the judiciary and the legislative power. Bani Sadr remained defiant. Eventually, on June 17, with the blessing of Ayatollah Khomeini, the Speaker of the *majlis*, Hojjat al-Islam Hashemi Rafsanjani scheduled a debate on the President's competence for June 20 and 21. The meeting occurred in the midst of violence and unrest on the streets of Tehran. But even before the impeachment proceedings had begun on the floor of the *majlis*, Bani Sadr's allies had already conceded defeat and mostly abstained from voting. He was impeached after two days of deliberation, which mostly entailed scathing attacks on his war record and his misuse of presidential powers.

With the impeachment of Bani Sadr, the Mojahedin lost their last ally among the ruling polity. In months of organizing dissent against the

IRP, the Mojahedin never openly declared their intention to overthrow the Islamic regime. On June 20, 1981, the day that the *majlis* opened the final deliberation on Bani Sadr's presidency, the Mojahedin called for a massive demonstration in central Tehran. The demonstrators were asked to resist by all means necessary any attempt by the Revolutionary Committees and the *hezbollahi* paramilitary mobs to disperse the crowds. Armed with clubs, razors, knives, and guns, the two sides clashed on the streets of Tehran. Hundreds of people were killed, wounded, or arrested. Intoxicated with their popularity and influence, the Mojahedin declared war on the Islamic regime. Confusion loomed over the Republic's houses of power. They seemed ill-prepared to repel yet another frontal attack on the foundations of the regime.

From the early morning of June 21, the indiscriminate execution of the members of opposition groups began at the notorious Evin prison in the northern hillsides of Tehran. A week later, in a devastating explosion at the headquarters of the Islamic Republic Party, Ayatollah Beheshti, the chief ideologue of the party along with seventy-two members of the Prime Minister Raja'i's cabinet and deputies of the Majlis perished.[112] June 28, 1981, marked the official beginning of the Reign of Terror. The MKO launched its most vicious campaign of assassination, by the end of which the government lost a President (Raja'i who replaced Bani Sadr), a Prime Minister (Mohammad Bahonar in Raja'i's government), a Head of the Judiciary (Ayatollah Beheshti), Friday imams of numerous cities, judges, prosecutors, commanders and members of the Revolutionary Guards, and neighborhood informants. The Islamic regime responded with the arrest and execution of all known members and sympathizers of opposition groups *en masse*. Dissent was no longer tolerated but met with the most atrocious punishments.

Chagrined by the government's brutally repressive response, Bani Sadr and the Mojahedin top leadership fled the country and sought refuge in France, perhaps with the hopes that with a Khomeini-like Paris-Tehran flight they could return victoriously and seize political power. That was not to be. According to one estimate, between the years 1981-84, more than 140,000 people were imprisoned. 12,000 members of opposition groups, most of whom were university and high school students, were executed.[113] Even smaller groups, which did not participate in the campaign of terror, fell victim to the brutality of the regime. For example, of 380 members of the *Paykār* party who were arrested between the summers of 1981 and 1982, 246 were executed.[114]

Not only did Soroush deliberately situate himself at the time in the camp of the proponents of the *velāyat-e faqih,* he continued to defend his position even after the Reign of Terror was terminated.   He was particularly hostile to Bani Sadr not only because of his actions as President, but more so as an intellectual rival. Often in his attacks on Bani Sadr, Soroush reminded the reader that his position was based on his scrupulous knowledge of the President's personality and ideas.   In his treatise *Bani Sadr, Mojahedin, and Hegelianism,* published one year after the impeachment of the first President of the Republic, he questioned Bani Sadr's sincerity before and after the revolution,[115] as well as his knowledge of Islam.[116]   He called him a 'bottomless power-monger,'[117] who suffered from the inability to connect to others in friendship,[118] and who fancied his Presidency as a 'cult of personality.'[119]

Soroush rejoiced at the President's impeachment and the arrest and execution of members of the Mojahedin and communist groups.   He justified the Reign of Terror as Divine Will, which brought love and kindness to those who assented, and agony to those who resisted.   'I need to emphasize,' he pointed out after more than one year of state-sponsored nightly executions,

> That God has consecrated the emergence and the establishment of the Islamic Republic.   This divine blessing has descended upon us like the coming of springtime to an arid land and it is the duty of all peoples of this country to be content and grateful for the blooming of this spring.   Like a tree, they ought to submit themselves to this breeze and wear the green garment of appreciation.   Otherwise, God forbid, they will suffer retributions if they show no gratitude towards God's benevolence.[120]

The Orwellian description that Soroush advanced in 1982 of the Islamic regime as a gentle, life-giving breeze could not be more in contradiction to the emerging totalitarian tendencies of the Iranian political apparatus. The young philosopher who condemned Marxism for its dogmatic core, and Hegelian philosophy for its historicist negation of freedom, found himself exulting in the disappearance of his philosophical rivals, through execution or exile. 'We are pleased now,' he exclaimed, 'that the pain of having such an undesired president is over'[121]... 'Like a healthy body that excretes its putrid parts, people have egested him.'[122] Bani Sadr was elected in January of 1980 with an unquestionable mandate.   He secured 75 per cent of the vote, easily defeating his rivals Hasan Habibi (whom Soroush endorsed) and Admiral Madani, a law and order candidate. Indeed, weeks before his downfall, thousands attended his rallies.   His popularity seemed intact after sixteen months in office. The president was ousted not by public expressions of discontent, but through a parliamentarian coup and the violent imposition of a new order at the top of which sat the leadership of the Islamic Republic Party.

Soroush castigated Bani Sadr not on any particular policy or political strategy. Rather, he psychoanalyzed the President as a man who saw himself above the ordinary masses, incapable of connecting to their needs and interests. At the time that the open criticism of Ayatollah Khomeini carried a mandatory sentence of fifteen years in prison, Soroush identified Bani Sadr's insusceptibility to criticism as one of the main reasons for his demise. In Khomeini, he saw all those qualities that Bani Sadr lacked. 'People see in the Imam,' he praised Khomeini, 'a leader whose unparalleled popularity has not affected his humility.'[123] In contrast, the masses lost their confidence in the President because they realized that 'he did not embrace the real virtue of the revolution—the fire that consumed all self-centeredness and egotism.'[124] 'Bani Sadr,' Soroush wrote, 'could not learn the art of loving and connecting with people from the Imam.'[125]

Soroush's critique of Bani Sadr was a mix of philosophical disagreement and disdain for his personality. He ridiculed Bani Sadr's credentials for his 'inadequate knowledge of basic philosophical concepts,' and his 'rudimentary competence in Arabic language,'[126] none of which disqualified one from holding the office of the president. One can easily detect the personal core of Soroush's disdain for Bani Sadr, the egotistic power-monger. But it remains unfathomed how Soroush could rejoice at the obliteration of his philosophical opponent without being perturbed by the brutality of such actions. 'This way of thinking,' to quote Soroush against Soroush, 'associates power with legitimacy and legitimacy with power, what exists with what is right and what is right with what exists.'[127] That perspective plagued Marxists, the Mojahedin, and Bani Sadr. Did the same plague infect Soroush?

The rise of the Reign of Terror should not be regarded as an inherent feature of the revolution. Different political parties and social actors asserted themselves to force the revolution towards their own goals and objectives. Soroush situated himself in the camp of the victors whose ultimate was decided by 'blood and iron,' and not by logical consistencies or philosophical clarity.

From an unknown, brilliant lay theologian and philosopher, thanks to the triumphant Jacobins of the revolution, Soroush was to become the court philosopher—to offer the Cultural Revolution legitimacy, and to ridicule Marxists on prime time television. In his defense, one might argue that his judgment was clouded by the unfolding struggle for power in a war-torn country, where civil war and urban unrest defined its daily routine. One need not approve the atrocities of the Mojahedin, the mismanagement and arrogance of Bani Sadr, or the waging of civil war in Kurdistan in order to condemn the executions of teenagers, the shutting down of all opposition papers, the criminalization of criticism, or engendering a segregated society by advancing legal measures and public ordinances that transformed women into second class citizens.

In his own defense, Soroush has argued that he had never taken part in purging or harming any of his detractors. He insists that, rather than being an apologist for the new regime, he contained the most belligerent factions during the Cultural Revolution by saving the universities from becoming the ideological tools of a select few. Most perplexing is the fact that even removed from the ardor of the moment, the man who has since put forward one of the most sophisticated conceptions of pluralism in contemporary Islamic philosophy, still fails to acknowledge his wrongs.

In 1994, Soroush gleefully began the introduction to the new edition of his *Satanic Ideology* with the reminder that 'the fifth edition of *The Satanic Ideology* is published during a time that the fever and fervor of Marxism and the sedition of Leftist political parties in our country has come to an end.' But, he warned his readers, Marxism was only one, and perhaps not the worst, expression of dogmatism. Attacked and eventually sacked from his professorial chair at Tehran University, Soroush later found himself the target of the same intolerant policies against which he had earlier remained silent. The 'fever and fervor of Marxism' was ended in Iran by an oppressive machinery that deemed the *Reign of Terror* to be an imperative of postrevolutionary state-building. We should neither discount the destructive role of the communist Left, nor should we condone the unprecedented violence that the Mojahedin organization inflicted on Iranian society. Nevertheless, the crimes of one should not justify the atrocities of the other. Soroush should have remained a critical voice against Marx*ism*, rather than a silent observer of the obliteration of Marx*ists*.

5

From the Reign of Terror to Let A Thousand Flowers Bloom

The coalition of forces that had instituted the Islamic Republic's *grande terreur* from 1981 to 1984 began to crumble with the first signs of their project's success. The goal of solidifying the new regime and consolidating all power in the hands of those who had demonstrated absolute loyalty to the Imam seemed complete. Although the Iraqi war continued to provide a common enemy around which all factions in power could exercise their solidarity, gone were the religio-nationalist fervors and revolutionary shibboleths that had shaped the political discourse of the postrevolutionary regime. Not only did the new regime survive the campaign of terror and assassination inflicted on them by the Mojahedin Organization, it also proved its resilience in holding together an otherwise fragile front under Khomeini's political edict *vahdat-e kalameh va `amal* (the unity of words and action).

While it served as an effective course in uniting revolutionary forces during the anti-Pahlavi struggle, Khomeini's *vahdat-e kalameh* became the foundation for unity among the dominant factions that erected the political structure of the new regime. Three factors contributed to the cohesion of the new republic: first, general acceptance of the principle of *velāyat-e faqih* under the leadership of Ayatollah Khomeini; second, the eight-year war with Iraq; and third, the suppression of opposition groups. With the fading of these foundations for unity, which began with the total annihilation of the opposition and ended with the death of Ayatollah Khomeini in June 1989, voices of dissent from within the polity gained significant strength.

Factions Within

The competing factions of the postrevolutionary regime diverged, at times radically, in the way they understood the sources of the legitimacy and the meaning of the Islamic Republic. These disputes erupted during drafting of the constitution as well as struggles over the institutional-ization of the revolutionary organizations, such as the revolutionary guards, courts, and militia committees.

Three major organizations formed the constitutive core of the new polity: *Jāme`eh-ye Ruhāniyat-e Mobārez* (The Society of Militant Clergy, SMC); *Mojāhedin-e Inqelāb-e Islami* (The Mujahidin of the Islamic Revolution, MIR); and most importantly, *Hezb-e Jomhuri-ye Islami* (The Islamic Republic Party, IRP).

Jāme`eh-ye Ruhāniyat-e Mobārez

The Society of Militant Clergy (SMC) was formed in 1977 as the organizational means to distribute and publicize Khomeini's decrees from Najaf in Iraq. In a recent interview with *Sharq* newspaper,[1] Ayatollah Mehdi Karrubi, one of its founding members, described the group's original purpose as an attempt to draw a distinction between the dominant conformist clerics in the seminaries with those who had accepted the leadership of Ayatollah Khomeini. The main activity of this group was the dissemination of Khomeini's political pamphlets and cassette-tapes. Clerics who considered themselves to be a part of this movement, delivered anti-Shah sermons and later, prior to the final collapse of the monarchy in 1979, mobilized neighborhood organizations for distributing heating oil and food rations.

More than an organization, the SMC was a *movement* that created a common mission for higher and lower ranking clerics who had divergent, and at times conflicting, social philosophies. Among SMC activists were fiery radicals such as Hadi Ghaffari as well as equable religious reformists such as Mohammad Bahonar. The SMC became the meeting place of clerics such as Mohammad Ali Montazeri and Mahmoud Taleqani, who welcomed even communists to the revolutionary coalition with those whose Islamic commitments were not to be perturbed by the expediencies of the revolution.

The SMC did not have bylaws or membership regulations. Rather sharing a conception of Islamic rule, it was based on an anti-monarchy agenda. From questioning the wisdom of republicanism to conflicts between *velāyat-e faqih* and democratic principles, significant differences arose among its members a few months after the revolution. Many, like Ayatollah Motahhari, argued that democracy is inherent in the Islamic nature of the republic, while the majority believed that democracy is inherently un-Islamic. But after the ratification of the constitution and the commencement of the eight-year war, these differences turned into topics of scholarly disagreements rather than political conflicts over governance.

In the early days of the revolution the SMC focused on generating institutional legitimacy for velāyat-e faqih. It succeeded. Prior to the establishment of the Islamic Republic, a number influential sources of emulation (marāje`-e taqlid) and grand ayatollahs, such as Ayatollah Golpaygani, Shari`atmadari, and Mar`ashi, remained aloof to the SMC apparatus. However, after the revolution, it became politically untenable to maintain a sphere outside the influence of the SMC. It successfully institutionalized Jāme`eh-ye Modarresin-e Howzeh-ye `Elmiyeh-ye Qom (The Society of Qom Seminary Teachers, SQST) as the only legitimate voice within the seminary community, thereby effectively suppressing the old tradition of multiple sources of religious seminarian authority.

Although faced with considerable opposition, the SMC and its parallel organization, the SQST, launched a campaign to generate a comprehensive official Islam, sanctioned by the new regime, and recognized as the only legitimate source of political and legal authority.[2] In order to achieve that, members of the SMC emphasized the fiqhi (jurisprudential) foundations of the constitution and challenged the authority of others (mainly the liberal nationalist parties) to interpret the constitution. They called this ideological foundation of the constitution islam-e feqāhati (the jurisprudential Islam), despite the fact that the document was more informed by the French, Soviet, Chinese, and Bulgarian constitutions than the credo of the shari`ah. As Rafsanjani, one of the founding members of the SMC, recalls in his memoir,

> [In early 1981] Mr. Mohammad Mojtahid Shabestari visited and asked for some clarification about the nature of our (the followers of Imam Khomeini) disagreements with the liberals (Mr. Bani Sadr, the Liberation Movement and others). I explained to him that the problem is simply about 'islam-e feqāhati.' They do not accept this premise and we do not have any other path in our Islamic rule except for following the same fiqh (with more work and a vibrant ijtihad).[3]

The SMC was responsible for the invention of what would later be known in the Iranian political discourse as din-e hokumati, or state-sanctioned religion. This move transformed the contested notion of *hokumat-e dini,* or religious state into a legalistic means for eliminating those who were deemed unqualified to participate in the debate over the political characteristics and social responsibilities of the postrevolutionary regime.[4] The SMC drew upon the religious authority of its members and the faculty of the Qom Seminary to establish the clergy not only as the interpreters of the Islamic state, but more importantly, as its agents.

Mojāhedin-e Inqelāb-e Islami

The Mujahidin of the Islamic Revolution (MIR) was established immediately after the victory of the revolution in April 1979. If the Society of Militant Clergy claimed the soul of the republic, the MIR intended to become its arms and legs. Its founding members belonged to small Muslim militant groups that were disillusioned by the ideological impurities of the *Sazmān-e Mojāhedin-e Khalq* (MKO) after a Marxist coup d'état in the mid-1970s rendered the remaining Muslim faction ineffective.[5]

Although the MIR manifesto stated that its main objective was the protection of the revolution from counter-revolutionary elements, only two weeks after its formation Ayatollah Khomeini ordered its rank and file to disarm and join the 'greater jihad of rebuilding the country.'[6] With automatic rifles in the hands of the thousands of people who had looted the military garrisons around the country, the last thing the postrevolutionary regime needed was militia. On May 5, 1979, Ayatollah Khomeini announced the establishment of the Revolutionary Guards (*Sepāh-e Pāsdārān*), institutionalizing the MIR into the body of the emerging polity. Its founding members[7] became prominent leaders in training the guards and organizing the urban militia of the Revolutionary Committees.

The leadership of the MIR met with Ayatollah Khomeini regularly and had no intention of challenging his social policies and political agenda. But the Ayatollah remained reluctant to bestow his blessing upon an armed organization without direct supervision by the clerical establishment. Thus he appointed a Qom seminarian, Ayatollah Rasti-Kashani, to be his representative within the MIR. Kashani was alien to the political-revolutionary culture to which the majority of the organization's leadership subscribed. Whereas the latter's ideas were inspired by Shari'ati's counter-hegemonic Islamic ideology, the former belonged to the conservative wing of the SQST who had negligible engagement in politics. Rasti-Kashani believed that his role was to contain the MIR within the boundaries of the Islamic revolution. He thought that 'innovative ideologies [a masked reference to Ali Shari`ati] that were the products of its free and widespread contacts with intellectual circles were risky.'[8] Khomeini's decision demonstrated another instance of the masterful balancing act which he perfected during the revolution.

The first sign of conflict among the MIR leadership appeared on the eve of the first May Day celebration after the revolution. Whereas a majority of the leadership, led by Behzad Nabavi, planned to release a statement recognizing International Workers' Day, others concurred with Ayatollah Khomeini's representative, who perceived such an acknowledgement to be a sign of the ideological impurity of the organization. As Mohammad Salamati recalled in 1995,

> Immediately after the establishment of the [MIR] organization, diverging viewpoints emerged in different arenas. The very first statements on International Workers' Day, and the martyrdom of Ayatollah Motahhari, and the anniversary of the passing of Dr. Shari`ati [...], each became a source of tension and conflict inside the organization. But as we faced common enemies and dangers, these differences did not manifest themselves in any serious ways.[9]

The more orthodox wings of the organization, which Rasti-Kashani hoped to bolster, viewed the preoccupation with the significance of the working class as the residual Marxism which had plagued Muslim revolutionaries for decades. In order to establish themselves as a historical force, they needed to liberate themselves from *satanic ideologies* and their materialist philosophies.[10]

The second moment that divulged internal friction within the organization came a few weeks later on the anniversary of Ali Shari`ati's death. While the majority him as the true 'teacher of the revolution,' others disparaged him for eclecticism and his relentless critique of the clergy. Upon the advice of the Leader's representative, the organization refrained from issuing an official commemorative pamphlet. But this latest conflict proved that the ideological currents inside the MIR were not easily reconcilable.

From these early discords, three factions emerged within the MIR: (1) Those who advocated the unqualified acceptance of Rasti-Kashani's views, even in cases that contradicted MIR' organizational principles, particularly in socio-economic matters; (2) Those who viewed Rasti-Kashani's role as merely consultative and disagreed with his orthodox respect for private property; (3) Those who had concluded that the differences between these factions were irreconcilable and that the organization could not operate as a single entity.[11]

Despite intervention by other high-ranking ayatollah's, particularly Ayatollah Musavi Ardebili, in March 1981 the predictions of the third faction materialized. Rasti-Kashani dissolved the central committee and nullified the leading role of its founders. While the second faction gained remarkable influence in the intelligence and security apparatus of the new regime, they refrained from engaging in MIR organizational politics. In December 1981, thirty-seven original members resigned and rendered the group ineffective until it was disbanded in September 1986 at the behest of the Supreme Leader's representative.

Hezb-e Jomhuri-ye Islami
If there ever was a state party in postrevolutionary Iran, it was the Islamic Republic Party (IRP). After the victory of the revolution in February 1979, the leaders of SMC and other activist clerics in Qom Seminary realized that their political future depended on the creation of an effective political party. Although their vast religious network allowed them to establish and maintain a leadership role during the revolutionary movement, in order to sustain that role, they needed to translate that power into an organizational vehicle within the new state apparatus. That led to the establishment of the IRP.[12]

The main ideologue of the IRP, Ayatollah Beheshti, and other founding members, Hashemi-Rafsanjani, Mohammad Javad Bahonar, Ali Khamene'i (the future Supreme Leader), and Abdolkarim Mousavi Ardebili, were all leading members of the SMC, but junior in rank within the seminary. They believed that in a republic informed and legitimized by the teachings of Islam, the lack of high religious credentials could limit their political influence. They doubted the revolutionary zeal of the older generation of seminarians, and distrusted their belated support for Ayatollah Khomeini. They also found objectionable Khomeini's reluctance to delegate executive responsibilities to revolutionary clerics.

Ayatollah Khomeini believed in the guiding role of the seminarians. He wished to involve them in the establishment of the legislative and judicial branches. He was also skeptical of political parties. He thought party politics would give rise to conflicts in a movement whose triumph depended on *the unity of word and action*. In one of his memoirs, Hashemi-Rafsanjani recounts how Khomeini offered his blessing to the formation of the IRP, despite his original reservations.

The first thing that occurred to us [the founders of the party] during those revolutionary days was an organizational vacuum. All of us believed that we were disorganized and a party would end this bedlam. Earlier, [...] we had planned to establish a party, but the Imam [Khomeini] objected. The Imam had always been suspicious of political parties and believed that they would inevitably create disunity. The Imam maintained that position so long as he was in Iraq. [...] Later, when I visited him in Qom and explained our organizational shortcomings and the necessity of a political party, he instructed us to establish it and that he would offer his blessing.[13]

One needs to read the memoirs of the leaders of the revolution with a critical eye. But Rafsanjani's recollection is consistent with postrevolutionary events, as well as early conflicts between members of the SMC and those to whom Khomeini entrusted the formation of the provisional government. In effect, the establishment of the IRP was the founders' response to two major threats: the 'ignorant fanatics' of the Qom seminary, a view shared by Rafsanjani and Beheshti, and the liberal nationalists who joined the revolution reluctantly and remained committed to a western-style democratic governance.

Even after it became evident during the negotiations of the Constitutional Assembly that the republic's liberal factions harbored strong aversion towards the principle of *velāyat-e faqih*, Khomeini continued to maintain his unspoken ban on the clerics' control of the executive power, particularly the office of the president. When the IRP contemplated nominating Ayatollah Beheshti for the first president of the republic, Khomeini reminded them that he would not support the candidacy of a *ruhāni*.[14] They lost the first presidential election in 1979 in a lop sided race to Bani Sadr. However, they came out of this humiliating defeat more determined to establish the IRP as *the* party of the state. In a revealing letter in March 1980, the IRP Chair, Ayatollah Beheshti, warned Ayatollah Khomeini of the dangers of prohibiting the clergy from assuming positions of responsibility in the executive power and of affording the liberals this uncontested privilege. He alerted the Supreme Leader that,

An idea is growing roots in the minds of your devoted followers that if you discern expedient the bearers of the 'second current' (*negaresh-e dovvom*) shall administer the affairs of the Islamic Republic, we should return to our job of religious learning (*talabegi*). We cannot witness anymore the squandering of our energy in the exhausting clash between these two currents.[15]

In the letter, Beheshti left nothing opaque about whom exactly he meant by the 'second current' or who the Leader's devoted followers were. He warned Khomeini that the liberals, led by President Ban Sadr, Provisional Prime Minister Bazargan, and the Minister of Foreign Affairs Ebrahim Yazdi, intended to abolish *velāyat-e faqih*. He also reminded him that the liberals were well aware that the only way they could realize their plan was to undermine the authority of the author of the letter and the other personalities who had formed the republic's most powerful political party.

The Supreme Leader's hesitation in containing the president puzzled the IRP leadership. In a series of letters, they reminded the Imam of their own sacrifices for the revolution and the perils of liberalism, whose most obstinate advocate was the president himself. They lamented that the leader's affection for them was fading and that others had succeeded in 'monopolizing his ear.' In a daring move, Rafsanjani pointed out to Khomeini, 'it seems as if you have forgotten, but the credibility of the Party depends on your influence. Your support has become pale in comparison to the early days. If you wish us to abandon the party, you need to persuade us, but if you believe that the existence of the party is necessary, then you must change the status quo.'[16]

In June 1981, the aggressive policies of the IRP together with the authoritarian tendencies of the President paid off. In an emergency session on June 20, 1980, the *majlis* passed with only one opposing vote a measure to impeach Bani Sadr. Only one month prior to this vote, Khomeini spoke of the President with respect and sympathy. He called him the son of a 'devout mullah,' and praised him for being 'unpretentious' and 'of the people.'[17] One day after the impeachment, when the Speaker of the *majlis* presented its decision to Khomeini, he added these few lines under the resolution without addressing it to any particular person: 'after the resounding vote of the majority of the respected representatives of the *majlis* in regard to the political incompetence of Mr. Abolhasan Bani Sadr, I dismiss him from the office of the presidency.'[18] Khomeini worded his reluctantly signed decree in such a way as to appear that he was only carrying out the wish of the *majlis*, rather than executing his own will.

Although the IRP acted with unity and clarity against Bani Sadr and other competing parties, it evinced considerable internal contradictions. From the beginning, its central committee was divided into two main currents of those who promoted a radical redistributive social justice agenda and others who questioned the authority of the state to engineer social justice.[19] Although these conflicting factions are often described as Left and Right, respectively, such categorizations obscure the distinctions between these them.[20] The dominant line in the party, led by Ayatollah Beheshti, was reflected in its manifesto. The IRP followed a Jacobinist politics, both domestically and internationally. But the established *Bazaaris* and the defenders of the old clerical establishment remained skeptical of the intentions and power of the party's young clerical leaders.

The IRP's manifesto articulated a Rousseauian vision in which it assumed a vanguard position in the total reconstitution of society. The manifesto depicted the masses as vulnerable to temptations, which they deemed, 'incongruent with Islamic values.' Against the liberals, it advocated the 'export of the revolution' and characterized capitalism as a system based on exploitation and corruption. To situate themselves as the true leaders of a foundational social transformation, against the old seminary establishment, the party leaders emphasized the necessity of a dynamic jurisprudence (*fiqh-e puyā*) and the competence, authority, and legitimacy of the *ruhāniyat* to respond to the needs and expediencies of the time (*masā'el-e mostahdaseh*).[21]

The party unambiguously translated these disguised declarations into the *realpolitik* of the postrevolutionary regime. But the more the IRP delegated key positions in the state to its own operatives, the deeper its internal frictions became. While the regime's three main organizational currents, the IRP, MIR, and SMC, formed an alliance to win the majority in the first *majlis* (1980-84), seldom did they manage to act in unison, particularly on economic issues.[22] The IRP's anti-free market, statist faction gained control of the government in 1981 after the first *majlis* successfully imposed its favorite candidate, Mir Hossein Musavi, for the influential post of the Prime Minister upon President Khamene'i. The MIR representatives in the *majlis* opposed the first IRP nominee, Ali Akbar Velayati, for the post of the Prime Minister. They had strong objections to Velayati account of his alleged affiliation with the conservative *Hojjatiyeh*. They formed a coalition with the statist faction of the IRP and narrowly defeated Velayati's nomination. [23] With Ayatollah Khomeini's blessing the IRP's statists dominated the legislative and executive powers, while the so-called right wing faction, bazaar merchants and members of the *Hojjatiyeh*, under the leadership of Asadollah Badamchian, gravitated towards the Judiciary, and began to invest their political capital in the Guardian Council (*Shurā-ye Negahbān*).

This investment bore fruit a few years later during the meetings of the Assembly for the Reappraisal of the Constitution in the spring of 1989.

Things Fall Apart
The Parties

In a span of less than two years, from 1986 to 1988, all three major organizational pillars of the republic lost their ability to maintain their partisan integrity. By the time of its dissolution in 1986, in the absence of the original founders who had earlier split from the organization in 1982, the Nabavi-Salamati faction, the MIR was reduced to an ineffective organization. Its collapse 'exemplified the disintegration of temporary alliances and the emergence of new boundaries among the revolutionary forces in power.'[24] It also triggered the emergence of new configurations among the dominant political parties.

Towards the end of the second term of the new *Majlis* in 1988, the divisions between the two main factions of the Society of Militant Clergy (SMC) reached an uncompromising point. A group of clerics, most notably Mehdi Karrubi, Mohammad Musavi-Kho'einiha, Mohammad Khatami, and Ayatollah Hasan Sane`i, who identified themselves as the proponents of *fiqh-e puyā* (dynamic jurisprudence) delivered an open letter to Ayatollah Khomeini. They reiterated their concern that a split in the SMC might appear as a sign of 'trouble for the revolution.' They assured the Supreme Leader that they have considered 'all possible compromises with other respected *ruhāniyun*.' 'But,' the letter explained, 'because of their uncompromising position and their non-conciliatory attitude towards nominating candidates for the next *Majlis*, we have decided to form a new association in the service of the Islamic revolution.'[25] They called the new organization *Majma`-e Ruhāniyun-e Mobārez*, or the Association of Militant Clerics (AMC).

Although Ayatollah Khomeini had worried that divisions and disagreements would eventually weaken the revolution, he gave his blessing to the new organization. 'Splitting [from the SMC] to express your views freely,' he advised, 'is not tantamount to conflict.'[26] Moreover, from his earlier emphasis on the *vahdat-e kalameh va `amal* (unity in words and deeds), Khomeini now drew different conclusions. He welcomed plurality of ideas and competing political agendas as a sign of a vibrant society and of the strength of the revolution. He declared: 'A society that does not have differences of opinion is imperfect. The *majlis* is also imperfect, if it does not reflect differences of opinions.'[27]

The leadership of the secessionists seized the moment and launched a campaign on the virtues of pluralism and the vices of the suppression of discontent. A leading member of the AMC, Abdolvahed Musavi Lari, recalled in an interview with the reformist daily paper *Salām* that 'the dissenting *ruhāniyun* of the SMC realized that with the Imam's consent they could easily argue that the establishment of the new organization would lead to the clarification of opposing views.' 'A healthy society,' he continued, 'should find ways to allow all voices to be heard.'[28] Echoing the same sentiment, another leading member of the AMC, Mohammad Musavi Kho'iniha remarked, 'Although the guidelines for both camps are Islamic tenets and Islamic action, disagreements on interpretation and rendition are inevitable.'[29]

Khomeini, as well as all others involved in the debate, recognized the irreconcilability of the friction between the two blocs of the *ruhāniyun*. While opposing factions often draped their conflicts in scholastic quarrels, they failed to coat the underlying power struggle that motivated these disputes. During the election campaign for the fourth *majlis*, the two sides of the militant clerical establishment accused each other of corruption while using Islam as an instrument for the control of the economic and political means of power. The rift between the newly formed AMC and the SMC after the fourth *majlis* election became so deep and their contentious political discourse so vicious that the AMC board of directors decided to halt their activities all together. One of its active members recalls:

> After the fourth *majlis* elections, and during the election campaigns, the political environment was so poisoned that it made any honest political activity impossible. [The SMC] campaign attacks turned a good-faith electoral into a struggle for positions of power for personal and partisan gains. The other reason for the Assembly's [of Militant Clerics] decision to halt its activities was the fact that more than eighty of its candidates were disqualified [by the Guardian Council].[30]

The AMC re-entered the political scene after close to five years in September of 1995.

The IRP could not remain impervious to the political and social changes that threatened the *vahdat-e kalameh* of those who had dominated the state power for half a decade. From its inception, despite its leaders' efforts, the party endured intense factional infighting. Established as an organizational arm of the postrevolutionary state, it embraced factions from the bazaari free-marketeers, such as Habibollah Asgar-Owladi, to radical statist Jacobins, such as the Prime Minister Mir Hossein Musavi. In the absence of common enemies, liberal nationalists and the militant Left, party unity had become unsustainable. As the state party, the IRP's internal tensions directly informed government debates and policies, the most vexing of which were the open hostilities between the President, Ali Khamene'i, and his Prime Minister, Mir Hossein Musavi. This conflict eventually led to the collapse of the party, ultimately giving rise in 1989 to the far-reaching revisions to the original constitution.

In 1987, with its internal conflicts had reached a debilitating point, the IRP's leadership concluded that it had fulfilled its original objectives. In May of the same year, the *majlis* Speaker Hashemi-Rafsanjani and President Khamene'i persuaded Ayatollah Khomeini to allow the party to shut its doors.

The dissolution of the IRP ended the era of *vahdat-e kalameh va `amal* in the political discourse of the republic. Although such unity never existed in practice under any postrevolutionary administration, the different factions that consolidated the political power temporarily suppressed their ideological and political differences. For much of the first decade of the revolution, the dominant political parties considered the *admission* of factionalism to be counter-revolutionary, divisive, and manufactured by 'foreign agents.'[31] But now, diversity of ideas, and competing interests, highlighted the strength and exuberance of the system.

The Iran-Iraq War

To a large extent, the state's newfound appreciation for diversity within the polity reflected the growing disillusionment among the masses with a revolution that had brought them the reign of terror, war, social restrictions, and economic hardship. The war continued to ravage the country and, for the first time, the republic found the recruitment of volunteer soldiers to be its most challenging task. While the earlier years of war required the management and organization of hundreds of thousands of volunteers from the remotest parts of the country, by the mid-1980s, mobilizing for war demanded considerable skill in selling martyrdom as the supreme honor.

In early 1984, it became evident that the fighting had entered into a long war of attrition. The *val-Fajr* and *Karbala* offensives, which repelled the Iraqi army from Khuzestan and Kurdistan, failed to achieve significant victories over the retreating army. Some 300,000 Iranian soldiers and volunteers and 250,000 Iraqi troops had been killed or wounded.[32] The *val-Fajr-5* offensive in February and March 1984 turned particularly deadly for the Iranian side, as the Iraqis with their heavy artillery, the French and Soviet-made helicopter gunships, and massive use of chemical weapons reportedly killed more than 40,000 Iranians within a four-week period.

The war, which at its inception threatened the existence of the postrevolutionary regime, had been transformed into a vehicle for the consolidation of power. The dominant factions that exploited it as a state-building tool, now had to face the reality of how its mounting casualties, in addition to its enormous economic price,[33] could cost them their very existence. With its political legitimacy at stake, and no opposition to blame, the regime could no longer sustain its prevarications on terminating the war.

Although world powers were indirectly involved in the eight-year war, neither the Reagan administration nor the Soviet Union saw any benefit in allowing the continuation of this war of attrition. Their concern became an urgent issue when the war developed into a Persian Gulf 'tanker war.' International pressure to end the conflict reached its highest point when the war directly threatened the free flow of oil from the Persian Gulf. Now American warships were involved in the protection of tankers. They directly handled any threats of disruption of oil export from the region. The Americans, with their forces in the region and their push for a final resolution at the Security Council made it clear that their tolerance for the continuation of the war had vanished.

On July 20, 1987, the UN Security Council unanimously passed Resolution 598, urging Iraq and Iran to accept a cease-fire, withdraw their forces to internationally recognized boundaries, and settle their frontier disputes by negotiations held under the auspices of the United Nations. Iraq agreed to abide by these terms if Iran followed suit. Iran, however, neither accepted nor rejected the resolution but demanded amendments condemning Iraq as the aggressor and called upon on all foreign navies to leave the Gulf. None of the demands it put forward as a precondition for accepting the resolution landed on sympathetic ears.

But making peace with Saddam Hussein was more of a domestic issue rather than an international dispute. The war had become the one, and perhaps the only, medium through which the state perpetuated the revolution and nurtured its legitimacy. The bifurcation of the conflict as the 'war against blasphemy,' as Prime Minister Musavi put it, and its ultimate purpose as 'the defense of the honor of the Qur'an and Islam,' as the Speaker of the *majlis*, Hashemi-Rafsanjani called it, served two distinct, but related, purposes. First, it stifled public debate on its real objectives and the means for ending the war, and second, by the Islamization of political discourse, it restricted all the discussion to the inner circles of the dominant factions in power.[34]

By 1987, it became evident that exploiting the war in order to maintain the unity and legitimacy of the regime had become an untenable strategy. In less than nine years, the population of the country grew by more than 14 million. Now, more than half of all Iranians were under the age of fifteen, the largest age group in the emerging demography of a nation weary of war and fading memories of the revolution. As Shahram Chubin noted in 1988,

> After seven years, the momentum of the war has not yet been exhausted. However, in the past year there has been a marked change in the tempo of the war, domestic politics of Iran, and what might be called psychological expectation. Within Iran there has been a quickening of the pace of domestic politics, as if the war was in its last phase and the domestic decks needed to be cleared for action. The Islamic Republican Party has been dissolved, conscription broadened, an anti-profiteering campaign initiated, a financial *jihad* proclaimed, a new will for Khomeini submitted. [...] The sense of urgency is unmistakable and derives as much from the pressures of the war as it does from anticipation of Khomeini's immanent demise.[35]

This sense of urgency intensified when the US navy attacked Iranian ships and oil platforms in October 1987 and April 1988. The fear of direct confrontation with the American forces in the Gulf against the backdrop of rising political factionalism and popular discontent forced Khomeini's close advisors to encourage him to accept resolution 598 unconditionally. The pressure on Ayatollah Khomeini culminated on July 3, 1988, when the USS Vincennes shot down an Iranian passenger plane killing all 290 people on board. Flight 655, a Boeing 747, en route from Bandar Abbas to Dubai, was apparently mistaken for an F-14 fighter plane. Whatever the circumstances and intentions behind the event, its result was unambiguous.

Three weeks later, in one of his most remarkable speeches, Ayatollah Khomeini accepted the terms of UN resolution 598. He referred to the ceasefire as a 'poisonous chalice' that *had* to be drunk:

> Accepting the UN resolution was truly a very bitter and tragic issue for everyone, particularly me. Only a few days ago, I was in support of the policy of the sacred defense, and saw the

interests of the country and the revolution in the continuation of
the war. But for reasons about which I cannot speak now, and
which will be clarified with the help of God in the future, at this
juncture, I regard [the ceasefire] to be in the interest of the
revolution and of the system. God knows that had it not been
for the desire to sacrifice our selves, honor, and credibility for
the sake of Islam and the Muslims, I would never have agreed to
this. Death and martyrdom would have been more bearable to
me. But what is the solution except that all of us should submit
to the satisfaction of the Divine Will [...] How unhappy I am
because I have survived and have drunk the poisonous chalice
of accepting the resolution.[36]

Khomeini's acceptance of the ceasefire was perhaps the most notable
manifestation of the appropriation of *maslahat-e nezām*, or the expediency
of the system, over what the leaders of the republic had once regarded as
the honor of Islam. Indeed, during the last year of his life, 1988-89,
Khomeini left a legacy of giving unprecedented priority to *maslahat* over
the demands of *feqāhat*. He left behind a republic in which temporal and
political necessities subordinated its transcendental and ideological
foundations. Volumes 20-21 of his proclamations, *Sahifeh-ye Nur*, are
filled with *fatwas* and rulings (*hokm*) on the significance of 'time and
place' in the Qur'anic exegeses and the urgency of contemporary
renditions of the Prophetic *sonnat* (tradition).

Maslahat over Feqāhat

Khomeini formulated his conception of the ever-expanding authority of
the *faqih* outside matters of jurisprudence and into social, political,
cultural, and economic matters as *velāyat-e motlaq-ye faqih*. Whereas his
notion of *motlaqeh* (absolute) was a reference to the expansion of powers
of the *faqih* within constitutional limits in matters outside jurisprudence,
after his death, this idea was translated into the absolute extra-legal,
divine authority of the *faqih*. This shift had dire consequences for the
political exuberance of electoral politics in post-Khomeini Iran.

During the revolutionary period, Khomeini had already shown his
mastery of strategic thinking. By 1987, he realized that he could not
restrict the creative and selective appropriation of Islamic text to his
inner circle. On November 1, 1988, he expressed his utmost contentment
when asked about the spread of discussions on Islamic views of state,
social rules, and regulations in the mass media and other institutions of
civil society:

The books of eminent *foqahā* of Islam are permeated with divergent ideas, temperaments, and renditions in different military, cultural, political, economic, and religious matters. Since in the past these disagreements were discussed exclusively in scholastic teaching and learning environments, inevitably, the masses of people were unaware of their existence. Even if they knew about them, these debates had no attraction for them [...] But today, with the highest joy, the Islamic Revolution has turned the dialogues of *foqahā* and other scholars into a topic of discussion on the radio, television, and newspapers. For today there is a scientific [`*elmi*] need for discussions such as limits of individual and social freedom [...] and the most important of all issues is the shape and determinants of the rule of *velāyat-e faqih.* All of these relate to a small corner of thousands of issues that involve people and were discussed by *foqahā.* We know that there were disagreements between our eminent *foqahā,* as we know that there are issues that they have not discussed before and that need to be resolved today. Therefore, under the Islamic Republic the doors of *ijtihad* ought to remain open, the nature of the revolution and the system necessitate that jurisprudent and interpretive ideas on different topics, no matter how diverse, engage with one another freely. Nobody should have the right or the ability to prohibit these engagements.[37]

For Khomeini, the *fiqhi* (jurisprudence) qualification, though required, did not legitimize the sovereignty of the Supreme Leader. Possession of authority in the matters of *fiqh,* did not legitimize *velāyat-e faqih.* Rather, it is the knowledge of and ability to respond to existing problems in all arenas of social life that would justify his rule. By stressing the centrality of political wisdom in place of religious knowledge, in anticipation of his own demise, Khomeini began to lay the foundation of an Islamic republic in which the preservation and interests of the state would eclipse the ordained obligations and duties prescribed in the *shari`ah.* Khomeini's new approach took the doctrine of *velāyat-e faqih* one step further towards the primacy of the *maslahat* (the political) over the authority of the *foqahā* (the religious). He marked this doctrine by placing the word *motlaqeh* (absolute) at the center of his old conception, calling it *velāyat-e motlaqeh-ye faqih* (the absolute rule of the *faqih*).

Khomeini's move appeared to expand the power of the *faqih* and the relevant religious institutions, in practice, it led to the separation of the *howzeh* (the seminary) from the state. By locating the supreme authority to determine state policies in the *political* sphere, the unintended consequence of the latest transformation in Khomeini's political philosophy was the secularization of *velāyat-e faqih.* In effect Khomeini transformed the idea of the religious state into the invention of a state religion (from *dowlat-e dini* to *din-e dowlati*).[38]

Before his death, between 1988 to 1989 Khomeini adopted the most radical positions on the issues of *maslahat* and the priority of the interests of the state over even the most fundamental Islamic principles, such as *hajj* (pilgrimage to Mecca) and daily prayer. He chastised the high-ranking clerics of Qom after they had lamented that the state-controlled television was endorsing un-Islamic behavior and spreading corruption by broadcasting western movies indiscriminately. In response Khomeini highlighted the educational significance of these programs and argued that it outweighed the depravities they might induce in people. He ruled that such programs were permissible, 'so long as they are not viewed with dissolute eyes.'[39] He also imposed, against the wishes of the Guardian Council, restrictions on the religious authority of the courts in matters of *hadd* (penalty for transgressing the limitations set by God) and *ta`zir* (discretionary punishment called for by a qualified *qāzi* or judge). 'During this period when the vast majority of the executors of our legal matters lack judicial religious qualifications,' he asserted, 'they do not have the right to determine the limits of *ta'zir* without the direct permission of a judicious *faqih*.'[40]

In another instance, in response to Hojjat al-Islam Mohammad Hossein Qadiri who had evoked Khomeini's own ruling on the unconditional prohibition (*harām*) of the game of chess, he advised the Hojjat al-Islam to follow the 'path of God and not the lures of pseudo-religious expressions of the *akhund* (an often pejorative reference to the clergy).' He rejected his own edict, reasoning that chess is permissible if it is not a 'tool of gambling.' 'With the way you interpret the ordinances and earlier rulings,' further ridiculing Qadiri, 'modern civilization must be completely annihilated, and people must remain in the Stone Age and forever live in the deserts.'[41]

Khomeini formulated all these new rulings in a thesis that recalled the postrevolutionary debates on the necessity of a *puyā* (dynamic and vibrant) jurisprudence. He argued,

> Time and place are two determining elements in *ijtihād*. We may reconsider a decree (*hokm*) on a specific problem if social, political, and economic circumstances change. This means that with a thorough understanding of social, political, and economic relations, the same problem, which has remained seemingly unchanged, demands a new decree. The *mojtahid* must scrupulously grasp the problems of his times.[42]

Although Khomeini's postrevolutionary politics often coincided with the advocates of *fiqh-e puyā* against the conservative guardians of the *fiqh-e sonnati* (traditional jurisprudence), there was an unmistakable feeling of openness in his final rulings on the contingencies of *ijtihad*. Most of his declarations on a *maslahat*-driven *fiqh* were directed explicitly as well as discreetly against the Guardian's Council. He considered obstructive the Council's unremitting exercise of its veto power over *majlis* resolutions. Members of the Council failed to realize the *contingencies* of Islamic rules and regulations, which resulted in 'narrow-mindedness,' 'mental ossification,' and 'reactionary politics.'[43]

Khomeini's critique of dogmatic *mojtahids* and those who found his *velāyat-e motlaqeh* troubling for the independence of the seminaries, generated confusion among the leaders of the three branches of the government. In February 1988, in a letter addressed to the Supreme Leader, the heads of the judiciary, legislative, and executive powers asked for guidance on how to approach the problem of *maslahat* institutionally. If precedence alone cannot offer solutions to contemporary problems, which institution was responsible for the determination of policies that were both right for the nation and sanctioned by Islam? In a short response, Khomeini announced the formation of the Council for the Discernment of the Expediency of the System, or as it later came to be known, the Expediency Council. 'Honorable gentlemen,'

> The expediency of the existing order (*maslahat-e nezām*) is the paramount issue whose neglect may cause the downfall of our precious Islam. Today the world of Islam regards the Islamic Republic of Iran as the best model whereby they may resolve their problems. The expediency of the system is of the highest importance, resisting it may weaken the Islam of the barefooted [wretched] of the earth [...] and will lead to the triumph of American Islam, the Islam of the arrogant and the powerful with the support of the billions of dollars of their domestic and foreign agents [...] The discernment of the *maslahat* of the system, in my opinion, must be under the supervision of *experts* (*kārshenāsān*) who are knowledgeable about specific matters.[44]

Thereby, he called for the formation of an expediency council to operate as an arbitration body between the *majlis* and the Guardian Council. The new council was to facilitate the government's implementation of legislation passed by the *majlis* without the impediments of Guardian Council's oversight. Khomeini appointed a thirteen-member assembly, headed by the President (Khamene'i), in which he designated a minority position to be held by the Guardian Council's. In response to this open hostility towards the Guardian Council, a few days after the decree creating the Expediency Council, the Chief Justice Ayatollah Sāfi resigned. Sa`id Hajjarian suggets, 'this resignation must be understood as a turning point in the relations between the two institutions of religion and state, a turning point which testified to the emergence of a structural differentiation between these two institutions.'[45]

Khomeini's attempt to institutionalize his *maslahat*-driven political philosophy met with open resistance from the jurists of the Guardian Council, who remained true to their postrevolutionary commitment as the sole arbiters of the compatibility of the laws of the land with the tenets of the *shari`ah*. The Head of the Guardian Council warned Khomeini that his far-reaching appropriation of the doctrine of *maslahat* 'threatens the integrity and authenticity of Islamic social order.'[46] In response, in a tone reminiscent of Lenin's critique of the British Left, Khomeini castigated the jurists for their infantile insistence on abstract principles at the expense of tangible changes in real life situation. He reproached the high-ranking ayatollahs of the Council that 'not only are these scholastic arguments of the seminaries, which belong to the theoretical realm, impossible to resolve, but they also draw us to a practical impasse that eventually would lead to the seeming violation of the constitution [...] In addition to safeguarding the sanctity and integrity of Islam, your responsibility is to assure the teachings of Islam are not rendered irrelevant in managing the meandering world of economics, military, political, and social relations.'[47]

These exchanges culminated in perhaps the most important and often cited *fatwa* Khomeini issued on the relation between state and religion. In mid-1987, the *majlis* passed a new labor law and sent it for approval to the Guardian Council. Anticipating its rejection, the Minister of Labor posed the question of the legitimacy of the state to intervene in private contracts. 'Does the state have the right to impose compulsory regulations on companies that benefit in one way or another from state-sponsored public services and facilities such as water, electricity, telephone, currency, fuel, ports, roads, piers [...], whether these services existed in the past and continue in the present or are newly established?'[48] In a brief response, the Supreme Leader affirmed that 'in either case, [in the extension of past benefits or in the installation of new services], the government can institute the necessary conditions.'[49]

In a move to redefine the significance of the law, in a rare explicit criticism of the Supreme Leader, the Council's Chief wrote the following:

Your *fatwa* affords the state the authority to institute any form of social, political, economic orders and a host of different labor relations, family laws, rural-urban affairs, and trade regulations, in exchange for the services it provides to the public [...] We fear that your *fatwa* would open the door to those who intend to undermine the Islamic principles of trade and investment, etc. We ask for clarification.[50]

Not only did the Council's warning fail to dissuade the Leader, it further determined him to expand his earlier ruling beyond the Minister of Labor's query. 'The state,' Khomeini declared, 'may deny its services to any entity that does not comply with its regulations. This applies comprehensively to all matters within state jurisdiction, above and beyond of what the Minister of Labor had previously inquired.'[51]

For the first time, a crisis of legitimacy was brewing, on one side of which stood the Leader himself. President Khamene'i tried to assure the jurists that the Supreme Leader had never intended to privilege a utilitarian view of Islam, or subordinate the universal principles of Islam to the immediate needs of the state. In a Friday prayer sermon, the President preached that Khomeini's views on the regulatory power of the state did not contradict the jurists of the Council's mandate to uphold the laws and tenets of Islam. He declared that, under the Islamic Republic, the state's interest ought to be consistent with the Islamically sanctioned laws.[52] For the Supreme Leader, who for almost a decade avoided direct confrontation with critics in his inner circle, the time for ambiguous declarations had ended. His pending demise would not allow him to continue exploiting the competing interpretations of his rulings. In a letter to the President, he laid out his most far-reaching defense of a utilitarian view of Islam. 'I did not intend,' Khomeini began, 'to engage in a quarrel at this sensitive time.'

Silence is the best manner, but that should not suggest that whatever we do we remain immune to others' criticism. Criticism is a divine gift for the growth of human beings. Therefore, I did not deem it right to treat your internpretation of my earlier ruling with silence [...] It appears from your sermon during the Friday prayer that you do not regard governance [...] as the greatest and the most important divine ordinance which has primacy over all other secondary injunctions. You attributed to me the idea that the state exercises its authority only within the limits of Divine laws. Your representation completely contradicts my original assertion [...] Governance demarcates a part of the absolute vice-regency of the Prophet of God, and is one of the primary injunctions of Islam and has priority over all other secondary injunctions, even prayer, fasting, and *hajj*. The ruler may demolish a mosque or a home to build a road and compensate the owner for his house; the ruler may shut the doors of mosques if necessary, and demolish a mosque that is the source of harm; the state may unilaterally annul religiously sanctioned [*shar`i*] contracts with people, if it discerns that the contract threatens the interests [expediencies] of the country and Islam. The state may temporarily suspend any religious matter, of prayer or otherwise, if it deems the practice contrary to the interests of Islam; the state may temporarily prevent *hajj*, which is one of the most important Divine responsibilities, if it is deemed contrary to the interests of the country. What is being said [about the limitations of the state's authority] is the result of lack of knowledge about the divine absolute *velāyat*.[53]

Taken together with his earlier statements on the condition of the *faqih*, Khomeini's open reprimand of the President and the Guardian Council laid out the most radical transformation of the republic from a state, conditioned, shaped, and informed by the teachings of Islam, to a state which sanctioned, defined, and implemented a contingent Islam. As the resignation of the Chief Justice of the Guardian Council indicated, the immediate effect, intentional or otherwise, of turning the theocratic principles of the republic up-side down was to transfer institutional authority from the politically independent seminaries to state political institutions. The last step towards the institutionalization of this transformation came with Khomeini's call for amending the constitution a few months before his death on June 3, 1989.

Amending the Constitution:
The Institutionalization of the Absolute Rule of the Faqih

The two most important revisions to the 1979 constitution, the addition of the velāyat-e motlaqeh and the Expediency Council, institutionalized the fundamental transformation of the Islamic Republic from a religious state, in which the state sought legitimacy from the religious establishment, to a political entity that prioritized its own interests by sanctioning a state religion.

Khomeini's late decrees generated additional confusion about the role of the Supreme Leader and its constitutional justification. On several occasions, he asserted that any form of exercising power, which at times appeared to be extra-constitutional, was related to the conditions dictated to the republic by the necessities of war.[54] But now that the war had ended and the remaining political prisoners executed,[55] the republic was ready to centralize a multilayered bureaucratic machine that had parallel sources of legal and extra-legal authority. In response to inquiries from parliamentarians and members of the High Judicial Council, on April 22, 1989, in a letter to the President, Ayatollah Khomeini appointed twenty representatives of different currents in the dominant ruling coalition along with five additional members to a Council for the Reappraisal of the Constitution (CRC). He asked the CRC to address five major themes and whether or not these topics should be constitutional amendments. They were, first, the conditions and qualifications of the Supreme Leader; second, the necessity of centralizing power in the executive and judicial branches of the government as well as in the management of state-run radio and television; third, the conditions and institutional means of revising the constitution; fourth, the constitutional establishment of the Expediency Council; and fifth, changing the name of the *Majlis-e Shurā* from *Melli* (national) to *Islāmi* (Islamic) and revisiting the district mapping and numbers of the representatives.[56]

From April 27 to July 11, 1989, in forty-one meetings, the CRC revised and added forty-eight articles to the first constitution of the republic. Khomeini's death in the midst of debates about the role of the *faqih*, and the constitutionality of *velāyat-e motlaqeh* (absolute), allowed for the first time different factions to voice their views. The two central provisions added to the constitution eliminated the requirement of *marja`iyat* (to be a source of emulation) from the qualifications of the Supreme Leader (article 109)[57] and eliminated the post of the Prime Minister, a major source of contention between the *majlis* and the President. It thereby reinstituted the earlier republicanism envisioned in the first draft of the 1979 constitution. With the elimination of the *marja`iyat*, the Islamic Republic in effect recognized Khomeini's irreplaceable, extraordinary charismatic leadership in which the credibility of a source of emulation had converged with an unparalleled political authority. His rule had blurred the distinction between an Islamically legitimized governance and politically sanctioned Islam.

While the new constitution lessened the significance of the religious authority of the *vali-ye faqih* (the Supreme Leader), it expanded his constitutional authority and added substantial institutional powers to his office (article 110). However, after seventeen meetings exclusively devoted to the meaning and institutional powers of *velāyat-e motlaqeh-ye faqih*, the final draft of the amended constitution remained ambiguous about the limits of the Supreme Leader's powers. Although article 110 of the new constitution afforded the *vali-ye faqih* unprecedented authority to determine and direct the policies and politics of the republic, it also required consultation with the Expediency Council as a condition for the exercise of its authority. The constitution left the legal-institutional course of this consultation unsolved.

While, according to article 107, 'in the eyes of law, the Leader is equal to the rest of the citizens,' article 110 allows him, if he deems necessary, to disregard the laws of the land. Article 107 also specified procedures for selecting a leader by the elected members of the Assembly of the Experts (*khobregān*). The Leader was to be appointed by an assembly elected by the direct vote of the citizens. The same body of experts was designated to determine grounds for the dismissal of the Leader (article 111). The evident tension between articles 107, 108, 111 and article 110, the inconsistencies between the accountability of the Leader and his rights and responsibilities, reflected two diverging views on the concept of *motlaqeh*. On the one hand, the majority view, which dominated the CRC, interpreted the concept as the *absolutist* rule of the *faqih*—thus the extra-constitutionality of his authority. On the other hand, according to the reading of a minority of high-ranking clerics, rather than an *absolutist* rule, *motlaqeh* referred to the extra-jurisprudent *scope* of the *faqih*'s rule. They emphasized the *political* core of the concept. They also laid stress on the constitutional accountability of the Leader's authority, for the political application of the *faqih* superseded his religious authority.

Those who envisioned a republic in which the Islamic sources of its legitimacy could be contested and debated in the public sphere—in the legislative process, in the institutions of civil society and the media—warned that the *absolutist* rendition of the *velāyat-e faqih* threatened the independence of the seminaries. The absolutists turned the sources of emulation into followers of a Supreme Leader, who lacked comparable credentials in jurisprudence but enjoyed the political authority to turn his rendition of the *fiqh* into the law of the land.[58]

Ayatollah Montazeri[59] played a central role in instituting the principle of the *velāyat-e faqih* in the first constitution by advancing an extra-constitutional theory of authority for the Supreme Leader. Now, he led the efforts to restrict the *absolute* powers of the *faqih* to the boundaries of the constitution. He lambasted those who negated electoral processes as the main source of the legitimacy of the *faqih*. Montazeri wrote:

> *Velāyat-e motlaqeh-ye faqih* does not mean an absolutist rule; it does not allow the *faqih* to carry out his wishes without any

accountability. It is not a license to disregard the constitution and Islamic laws. Rather, the meaning of *velāyat-e motlaqeh-ye faqih* is to govern the country based on respect for the highest interests of the nation within the frame of the constitution [...] The addition of *motlaqeh* was a response to those respected jurists who understood the jurisdiction of the *vali-ye faqih* within the limited scope of the *fiqh* (jurisprudence). It extends the scope of the Supreme Leader's authority, but it subjects him to the constitution like any other citizen.[60]

In order to limit the republicanism of the Islamic system while highlighting the divine sources of legitimacy of the Supreme Leader, during meetings of the Council for the Reappraisal of the Constitution, the absolutists (the Guardian Council, and their allies in the Assembly of Experts) followed two distinct strategies. First, they continued to voice their doubts about the principles of *zarurat* (necessity) and *maslahat* (expediency) as articulated by Khomeini. From the early days of the republic, ayatollahs of high stature believed that his reckless adoption of these principles undermined the authority of the clergy and would eventually lead to the complete secularization of society. To maintain their position of power, therefore, they resisted the legislative authority of the *Majlis* and used all their institutional power to impede the implementation of legislations they deemed 'un-Islamic.'

On numerous occasions, they questioned the wisdom of introducing *maslahat* as the guiding principle of the rule of the *faqih*. They believed that the more the republic shaped its policies in conforming to state interests, the more it departed from the teachings of Islam. The attack on *maslahat*-driven *fiqh* intensified after Khomeini's death on June 3, 1989. Only a few days after the funeral, during the twenty second session of reappraisal of the constitution, Mohammad Emami Kashani, once the Friday Imam of Tehran and an influential advocate of the absolutist power of the *faqih* and staunch critic of the *majlis*, raised the question of the legitimacy of the Expediency Council. The meeting was supposed to discuss the constitutional amendment on the composition and duties of the Expediency Council. But it turned into a forum cautioning against the overt use of *maslahat*. Kashani cast doubt on the constitutionality of a council whose responsibility was to reconcile the interests of the republic, as expressed in the *majlis* legislations, with the demands of Islam, as defined by the Guardian Council.

He objected to Musavi Ardebili, the chair of the commission in charge of drafting the amendment, for linking of the Expediency Council with the political will of Khomeini. Kashani believed that to prevent the institutionalization of the Expediency Council, he needed to sever it from Khomeini's legacy. He reiterated that there was an inherent structural contradiction in the composition and responsibilities of the Expediency Council. While he had not called for its abolition when Khomeini was still alive, he now rejected principally the idea of an arbitration body with authority over the Guardian Council and the *majlis*. He declared, 'In his political will, the Imam [Khomeini] clearly stated that with the consideration of the needs of the country, the Guardian Council shall advise the *faqih* in primary and secondary injunctions.' Therefore, in his view, in matters of conflict between the *majlis* and the Guardian Council, it was the latter that uttered the final word. Any other formation allows laypersons, such as elected members of the *Majlis*, to pose as experts on the *maslahat* of Islam and the nation.[61] In an earlier session, Kashani had ridiculed the institution of the Expediency Council for the schizophrenic position it imposed on the jurists of the Guardian Council.

> Today the Guardian Council's position is that [...] we cannot think of the *maslahat* of the nation in the afternoon in the Expediency Council while in the morning we defend the rule of Islam. That is to say, we cannot debate the right of the state to confiscate land in the Guardian Council and opine that it is un-Islamic and against the teachings of the sacred *shari`ah*, then in the evening when we arrive at the Expediency Council approve the state's action because we deem it to be in the interest of the country [...] I have one responsibility in the morning and another at night, in the morning I represent the *shari`ah*, and in the evening I need to recognize the *maslahat* of the nation.[62]

Many members of the CRC echoed Kashani's argument. A regime whose guiding principles were driven by the interests of the state instead of the mandates of Islam, would desacralize the republic and transfer the authority of the clergy to the 'experts' (*kārshenāsān*). In a blunt provocation, one day after Khomeini's death, Mohammad Yazdi, the one-time Chief of the Judiciary, pointed out, 'at its core, *maslahat* means crossing the line of constitutional and religious laws, it means committing acts against the *shari`ah* and against the law in response to necessities (*zaruriyāt*) of the time.'[63]

Many argued during these meetings that if the condition of *marja`iyat* (source of emulation) was to be eliminated from the qualifications of the Supreme Leader, and furthermore if the final approval of state policies was consigned to the Expediency Council, then on what basis could the republic be called *Islamic*? Ibrahim Amini, The first speaker of the fifth session, an opponent of the separation of *velāyat* from *marja`iyat*, warned his colleagues that their decision threatened the religious foundation of the republic. He spoke out against the general tenor of the assembly.

> Our Islamic system is based on a fundamental distinction from other political orders in the world. Neither do we simply abide by the will of the majority of people, nor do we simply respect the interests of the state. Other systems accept these without any other commitments. In an Islamic system, before acknowledging the necessities of the time and the interests of the nation, we need to be mindful of the Islamic sources of justification for these policies. Islamic sources in the *sonnat* and the Book are the foundational basis of the legitimacy of any policy— this is what it means to be Islamic. Therefore, we do not advocate the same kind of freedom; we recognize people's will and the nation's interest only within the boundaries of Islam.[64]

Asadollah Bayat took the point a step further and warned that this 'extreme *maslahat*-driven ideology' will lead to secularism. 'A leader without the authority to issue a *fatwa* will not have any legitimacy. The success of the Imam resulted from the credibility of his *marja`iyat*, not simply from his popularity, or his politics [...] The distinction between the two will lead to the separation of religion from politics.'[65]

But members of the Guardian Council and other supporters of a jurisprudential (*fiqhi*) interpretation of the Islamic Republic realized that anti-*maslahat* was increasingly becoming an untenable position. Particularly after the demise of the Ayatollah Khomeini, and the appointment of Ali Khamene'i, a junior cleric, as the Supreme Leader, the *Realpolitik* of the republic terminated the debate on the distinction between *marja`iyat* and *velāyat*.

With the realization that the principle of *maslahat* would remain as the central tenet of the Islamic Republic's political philosophy, its opponents turned their attention to the limits of its institutional practice. Although they were skeptical of the all-encompassing authority of the Supreme Leader, the important issue now was to restrict the power of decision-making to the ranks of the clerical establishment. In contrast to Khomeini's enthusiasm for 'the dialogue among *foqahā* and other scholars into a topic of discussion on the radio, television, and newspapers,' the authors of the revised constitution intended to block the possibility of widening access to interpretations of Islam.

Those advocating the separation of *marja`iyat* from *velāyat*, protested that they were honorably observing Khomeini's legacy. With a calm and self-assured manner, Hashemi-Rafsanjani, the vice chair of the Council, reminded his audience of his privileged access to the leader of the revolution. 'Recently,' he began,

> I was in [Khomeini's] presence and brought up the same issues that we are debating these days. He replied that the present situation of the country and the conditions of its management are fundamentally different from the qualifications of *marja`iyat*. Those in the position of leadership of the nation are unlike those in the position of *marja`iyat*, the latter must remain a source of emulation while the former ought to manage and lead the country.[66]

While Rafsanjani's recollection met with disbelief from other members, Mehdi Karrubi silenced the assembly by reading a passage from a letter Khomeini wrote in response to Hojjat al-slam Ansari, another critic of the separation of the two institutions of leadership and *marja`iyat*. 'The commonly practiced *ijtihad* in the seminaries,' he read, 'does not qualify anyone to discern the expediencies of our society. Those who do not have the depth of knowledge required for managing the world of politics and leading the society in this complicated world must not take over the responsibility of running the country.'[67]

Khomeini's words, even after his death, continued to carry an indisputable authority. His death inevitably set off a new struggle to claim his legacy. Unlike his other declarations, Khomeini's assertions on the separation between *marja`iyat* and *velāyat* did not leave much space for hermeneutic exercises of his words.[68] Nevertheless, the ambiguity in his conception of the *motlaqeh* (absolute or absolut*ist*) authority of the *faqih* allowed the two main factions to advance competing constructions. The pragmatist advocates of *maslahat*, led by Rafsanjani and Karrubi, argued for constitutional articles detailing the precise powers of the Supreme Leader, thus making his *office* legally accountable to constitutional checks and balances. Their opponents, led by the members of the Guardian Council, insisted on the *divinity* of Leader's political authority as the vice-regent of God's rule on earth, thus situating his *person* above the law.

In his call for the reappraisal of the constitution, Khomeini had indicated that the time had come to centralize (*tamarkoz*) the state institutions. From the tenor of the letter and his other statements at the time, it was evident that Khomeini had not developed a conceptual or practical elaboration of his theory of the *velāyat-e motlaqeh*. Rather, his intention was to integrate or eliminate parallel sources of authority in the judiciary and the executive power, such as the revolutionary courts and militia committees. In the twelfth session of the assembly, Mehdi Karrubi chastised those such as Ali Khamene'i who had interpreted the centralization of power as its concentration in the hands of a few. 'Centralization in each institution of the government,' Karrubi explained, 'does not mean unaccountability, or monopolization of power.' Rather, he proposed that Khomeini's call increased the accountability and transparency of government. Multiplicity in organs responsible for the same task 'affords everybody a way out when it comes to accepting responsibility.'[69]

The former Prime Minister Mir-Hossein Musavi endorsed Karrubi's interpretation and added

> Imam [Khomeini] demanded 'centralization in executive affairs,' not the centralization of executive matters in the hands of one person who manipulates all resources, responsibilities, and finances without any accountability. The meaning of centralization is not that people in charge are not accountable, and may disregard opposition to their policies. If we give authority to anybody in the government, we need to expect dissent and disagreement. Every person, including the Leader, in the government must be accountable to the law and act within the frame of the constitution.[70]

In order to bind the office of the Supreme Leader to the constitution, Hashemi-Rafsanjani and other pragmatist advocates of the doctrine of *maslahat,* even proposed a ten-year term limit for the *vali-ye faqih.* But such efforts met fervent resistance from the proponents of absolutism, who later extended their assault on the constitution by rejecting any mention of specific responsibilities for the *vali-ye faqih.* They argued that the *vali-ye faqih* is the embodiment of law originating in the Divine Book. They categorically regarded itemization of his duties and responsibilities as un-Islamic. In one instance, Azari Qomi objected to the line 'dissolving the Islamic Consultative *Majlis*' as one of the Supreme Leader's powers. 'Although I agree with the principle,' he reasoned,

> I object to its explicit mention in the constitution [...] If we accept the absolute rule of the *faqih,* dissolving the *majlis* is one of those occasions that might occur, but should not be mentioned in the constitution [...] I strongly disagree with these suggestions and believe that we are treating the Leadership like any other state position [...] I beg you not to be intimidated, debauching the authority of the Leader will have profound consequences for Islam and the nation [...] I am tired of reading in the newspapers

that Imam [Khomeini] was exceptional. Yes it is true, but the
Prophet (peace upon him) was also exceptional. Does that mean
that we should question the legitimate authority of the vice-
regent of God? We cannot impose limits and conditions on
velāyat. *Velāyat* is absolute with a Divine source of legitimacy.[71]

Azari Qomi's speech was interrupted several times by the vice chair and
the secretary of the assembly, who declared that he was out of order and
out of time. Bargaining for two or three more minutes, he concluded,
'those who contemplate the idea of a ten-year term for the Supreme
Leader have no sense of the true meaning of the absolute *mojtahid* [a *faqih*
with the legitimate authority of *ijtihad*].'[72]

Khomeini's death resuscitated the anti-republicanist sentiments of
the Guardian Council and its supporters in the clerical establishment.
They tried to limit the powers of the elected body of the polity and other
institutions in the government that drew their legitimacy from the
electorate and hence were responsive to its will. Ahmad Jannati,
Mohammad Yazdi, Imami Kashani, and their supporters each spoke at
length during the eighteenth and nineteenth sessions on the vices of
subjecting the Leader to the constitution and linking his legitimacy to the
will of the people. 'Specifying the responsibilities of the *faqih*,'
Mohammad Yazdi declared exasperatedly, 'might suggest that he may
not carry out his wishes above and beyond those stated matters. He
ought to be able to act even against the law.'[73]

Although Mir Hossein Musavi and others tried to emphasize the
constitutional dimension of the *faqih*'s authority,[74] the final draft of the
amendment left the ambiguity of the concept of *motlaqeh* untouched.
What remained unresolved was whether the addition of *motlaqeh*
allowed the *faqih* to be above the law (*absolutism*) or merely expanded the
scope of his authority to include extra-jurisprudent powers. The
assembly could not reach a final verdict. For the topic raised a
fundamental philosophical question as to the sovereign's sources of
legitimacy. On the one hand, it relinquished the charismatic power of
the Supreme Leader, the *vali-ye faqih*, and his legitimacy through his
religious stature (*marja`iyat*), but on the other, it expanded his authority
under the constitution. The degree to which the Supreme Leader was to
be held accountable to the will of the people was ultimately an issue that
the *maslahat* of the regime would have to define in practice.

From Mao Tse-Tung to Deng Xiaoping in One Friday Prayer Sermon
Not only did the end of the war force the regime to face the realities of a peacetime economy, it also ended the currency of an ideology of suffering and pain as a vehicle for mobilizing the masses. The appointment of Khamene'i as the Supreme Leader and the election of Rafsanjani in 1989 to the presidency realized two fundamental transformations of the republic. First, the office of the Leader was officially separated from the office of *marja`iyat,* as the new Leader lacked the credentials of a source of emulation. Second, a pragmatist President, who during the entire decade of the Islamic Republic stood on the side of *maslahat* of the state, rather than the realization of Islamic ideals, began his first term.

Conscious of Gorbachev's reform agenda in the Soviet Union, the new regime began a project of *perestroika* without *glasnost.* Rafsanjani initiated an economic reform agenda,[75] with the support of the newly established Expediency Council. Not only did he face legal and political opposition, he also needed to redefine a new religious justification for his administration's ideological transformation. Under his watch, the Islam of *maslahat,* peace, and prosperity would have to replace the Islam of ideology, war, and sacrifice.

Although Khomeini's late rulings, as Ervand Abrahamian observes, were meant to 'strengthen the *étatists* against the *laissez-faireists,*'[76] he also expanded the protection of individuals from the intrusions of the clerical establishment into their private lives (through rulings on music and the game of chess, etc.). Khomeini's *étatism* reflected his commitment to a *maslahat*-driven political theology in which the protection of the republic supplanted the interests of the clergy. It also inaugurated, intentionally or otherwise, contentious debates on how to negotiate and legitimize state policies. Rafsanjani successfully exploited the 'utilitarian aspects of the Imam's legacy,'[77] by emphasizing the need for economic reconstruction (*bāz-sāzi*) through a new language of Islamic virtues and vices.

In a Friday prayer sermon on November 9, 1990, for the first time Rafsanjani directly challenged the foundational ideology of post-revolutionary Iran. In what Mohammad Quchani has called the 'manifesto of the white collar *hezbollahis,*'[78] He transformed the revolutionary virtues of the *homo islamicus*—selflessness, austerity, and perpetual discontent—into a postrevolutionary ethos of the prosperous, joyful, and content subject. The *mostaz`af* (disinherited) no longer represented the symbolic (the export of the revolution) and real power (fighting at the front) of the republic. In the new era, the *mostaz`af* became the *āsib-pazir* (vulnerable), a pathology to be overcome. In his first few months, the *modus operandi* of Rafsanjani's rule became incongruous with the *modus vivendi* of the old *hezbollahis*. In his manifesto, Rafsanjani chastised those *hezbollahis* who praised asceticism over indulgence in what life has to offer, 'God's blessing [*ne`mat*] is for the people and the believers [to devour]. Asceticism and disuse [sic] of holy consumption will created deprivation and a lack of drive to produce, work, and develop.'[79]

He further ridiculed the old revolutionary *hezbollahis* for their lack of hygiene and proper etiquette in public. 'Being a revolutionary,' he scolded, 'does not mean that one has to live in poverty. There is nothing un-Islamic about the accumulation of wealth.' Those who advocate the idea that 'religion does not give serious consideration to production and proliferation of society's wealth [...] are propagating an un-Islamic viewpoint.'[80] He left nothing opaque about how he intended to close the first chapter of the postrevolutionary regime by ending the wartime mentality and institutions of governance. 'God has created in human beings an ornamental and beauty-seeking sense,' Rafsanjani advised the crowd during the same Friday prayer, 'with a disdain for ugliness.'

> Seeking beauty is a pillar [of Islam]. Now, if we object to beautiful sights, it is tantamount to fighting nature, something that God did not want [...] We suffer from a culture in which the style of living and the appearance of priests and *hezbollahis* should be unpleasant and ugly. If it becomes a cultural phenomenon that being a *hezbollahi* means looking unbearable, this is a sin and Islam has fought this [...] It would defame Islam [...] Luxury should exist, but not overt luxury [...] We have religious decrees that you must wear perfume, comb your hair, comb your beard, and wear a clean outfit. The Prophet himself looked at his reflection in water to make sure that he was presentable before his guests.[81]

These remarks deeply scandalized the Robespierres of the revolution who had remained powerful in the *majlis* and were by no means ready to hang up their revolutionary garb. Rafsanjani swiftly introduced a cabinet of *kārshenāsān* and *motekhassesin* (experts and specialists) to the *majlis* and maneuvered his way into getting the majority vote for its approval, even though only 4 of the 22 ministerial jobs went to clerics. More generally, he embarked on a campaign to move the center of expediency from the dusty, ugly, and smelly quarters of the clerics to the clean, bright, and fragrant offices of his technocratic allies. The discursive hegemony of the revolution was over.

Rafsanjani's proclamation did not go unnoticed by millions of war veterans who returned home in 1989 to discover that the revolution they had shielded on the war fronts was pronounced to be outdated and un-Islamic by the same leaders who had called upon them to defend it with their lives. The contradiction the veterans with their revolutionary ideals faced in the cities gave rise to a new grassroots and highly organized movement against what they described as the 'western cultural invasion.' The *hezbollahi* mobs that attacked the rallies and demonstrations in the early days of the revolution, now found themselves in direct conflict with the post-Khomeini regime. For the first time, this group organized itself to battle the cultural assault of capitalism and its corrupt sympathizers within the ruling coalition. The new group named itself *Ansār-e Hezbollah* and began publishing a bi-weekly called *Shalamcheh*.[82] In an interview in 1998, Mas`ud Dehnamaki, its forthright spokesperson, recalled, 'Ansar-e Hezbollah did not exist before 1989, the group came together around that time to defend the values [of the revolution] and fight those who betrayed it.'[83]

The *Ansār* viewed the post-Khomeini transformations as a prelude to the total secularization of the state. Hojjatolislam Rayshahri, whose organization *Jam`iyat-e Defā` az Arzesh-hāye Enqelāb-e Islami* (The Society for the Defense of the Islamic Revolution Values) continued to voice clerical anti-republicanism, put it bluntly a few years after the election of Rafsanjani. 'One of the most dangerous dimensions of the cultural invasion [of the west] was the separation between religion and politics. Unfortunately, our religious state has shown its failure in containing this horrific conspiracy.'[84] In an editorial in *Sobh,* a monthly journal of the same organization, Ruhollah Hosseinian, also accused Rafsanjani of exploiting *maslahat* in order to abandon the revolution. He wrote bitterly:

> Some cultural transformations happened in our revolution that affected our principles. Our revolutionary ideals were turned into mundane concerns, which created a variety of problems. At one point, sacrifice for and devotion to the revolution was every person's imperative, but today we are told that first and foremost people should satisfy their material needs, they should think of themselves [...] Mosques used to be the place for political, social, and cultural exchanges, but instead of promoting and supporting mosques, under his presidency, Hashemi Rafsanjani helped to establish other centers in which other worldviews replaced the religious spirit of our young generation [...] It is evident that a so-called worldly and utilitarian culture has taken the place of religion in our society.[85]

Rafsanjani's motto of *towse`h-gerā'i* (developmentalism) earned him the title *sardār-e sāzandegi* (the Commander of Constructiveness). But his development agenda bore an inherent contradiction on the basis of which unlikely coalitions emerged to sabotage his plan of *sāzandegi*. He had intended to bolster the authority of the state while at the same time he envisioned a *laissez faire* state to carry out his postwar reconstruction agenda through easing foreign investment and privatizating non-essential industries. He utilized the instruments of state power to contain the influence of the anti-republican clergy, and took liberties in expanding the 'expediency of the system' to limit literal readings of the Islamic character of the state.

With these contradictions, Rafsanjani further alienated the two competing factions, both of whom he had vanquished with his presidency. First, his *étatism* further antagonized the defenders of the absolutist interpreters of *velāyat-e faqih*. Secondly, his neo-liberal posture scandalized the former Jacobinists, who continued to believe in the revolutionary redistributive justice. The former prime minister, Mir Hossein Musavi, and the influential *majlis* deputy and former minister of Mines and Industry, Behzad Nabavi, were among the most vociferous critics of Rafsanjani's *laissez faire* agenda. They shared his vision of reconstituting the republic's international credibility, and they endorsed and widely benefited from the restrictions he had imposed on state intrusion into the public sphere. But the Jacobins, who were also struggling to reconcile their revolutionary dogma with the realities of the exchange rate and inflation, remained distrustful of the president's privatization agenda. They believed that personal gain, rather than economic reconstruction, motivated his development plans—hence his autocracy and the lack of transparency in his government.

Rafsanjani's reinvention of the revolution and his technocratic cadres, whom Mohammad Quchani calls 'necktie revolutionaries,' gave rise to an emerging civil society and a consumer middle class. His policies fomented a breach between the postrevolutionary *nouveaux riche* and the masses of *mostaz`afin* (the disinherited) as well as the millions of veterans of the eight-year war. Two factions opposing Rafsanjani followed different strategies mobilizing people against his policy of *bāz-sāzi* (reconstruction). The anti-republican absolutists raised the flag of Islam and situated themselves as the only true Muslims who were genuinely committed to the revolutionary ideals. They successfully coupled the *maslahat*-driven political philosophy of the new republic and its secularist undertone with the pauperization of *mostaz`afin*, the foot soldiers of the revolution and the war. This strategy bore fruit in the presidential election of 2005, whose victor was a former revolutionary guard and son of a blacksmith, Mahmoud Ahmadi-Nejad.

The former Jacobins, also committed to revolutionary ideals, sought to advance their cause by expanding the notion of *maslahat* into a theological intervention on religious pluralism. They believed that *velāyat-e motlaqeh-ye faqih* offered a form of secularization from within. They hoped to democratize access to religious knowledge, which would lead the country towards a sustainable religious pluralism. They found the most comprehensive theological articulation of their political agenda in the new voice of Soroush, and the most amenable constituents in the growing numbers of the urban youth and women, students, and other secular intellectuals. Their strategy resulted in the landslide victory in 1997 of Mohammad Khatami in the presidential election.

6

From Liberation Theology to State Ideology: Ali Shari`ati and the Emergence of New Religious Intellectuals

On May 23, 1997, Mohammad Khatami, the Director of the National Library, won a landslide victory in the presidential election against Nateq Nuri, the Speaker of the *majlis* and the Supreme Leader's favored candidate to replace Rafsanjani. Khatami's victory highlighted two major transformations in the postrevolutionary regime. First, by choosing the candidate of the opposition, the electorate, urban as well as rural, demonstrated that the nation had moved from a revolutionary mass society towards a civil society. Gone were the days when the Supreme Leader could carry out his wishes and legitimize them by mobilizing millions of people. Now institutional and structural means offered possibilities to a loyal opposition to muster popular support for their own political projects. Second, and perhaps politically more important, for the first time in the short history of the republic, the Supreme Leader sanctioned the results of an election that had brought into office a president whom he did not endorse.

It is now common wisdom that the growing numbers of educated youth and professional women played an instrumental role in electing Khatami. Along with structural and institutional changes in society, such as demographic changes in urban population growth, the high ratio of youth population, and massive increase in literacy, the dominant discursive shift from the old revolutionary *modus vivendi* to a more pragmatic *opus practicum* under Rafsanjani's administration paved the way for Khatami's platform of political reform. During the first term of Rafsanjani's presidency, while Khatami presided over the Ministry of Culture and Islamic Guidance (1988-1992) the number of daily newspapers and weekly journals grew from 102 to 369.

Rafsanjani, the champion of *perestroika,* realized that a movement for *glasnost* was in the making by an emerging class of public intellectuals and independent media. Rafsanjani's critics in Qom and the conservative clerical establishment, led by Ayatollah Jannati and his foot soldiers at the *Setād-e Ihyā-ye Amr-e be Ma`ruf va Nah-ye az Monkar* (The Headquarters for the Restoration of the Propagation of Virtue and Prohibition of Vice), feared the emerging public intellectuals for their rejection of the clerical monopoly of the interpretation of Islam. Rafsanjani dreaded their demands for transparency in governance. Under his presidency, the percentage of people living below the poverty line dropped from more than 27 per cent to less than 19 per cent, but that decrease occurred with a concomitant rise in the disparity between rich and poor.[1] Recall that Rafsanjani had extolled the virtues of prosperity, disdained revolutionary asceticism, and embraced the *laissez faire* Islamism of the *nouveau riche.* However, neither he nor Khatami after him abandoned altogether the extensive state-sponsored economic planning, which generally benefited the poor.

As Djavad Salehi-Isfahani has shown, in comparison to countries with similar economic and social resources, the Islamic Republic has the lowest percentage of population living in absolute poverty. Yet it shares the same rank with other nations in its distributive inequality (see the Gini index).[2] While successive administrations implemented various versions of privatization plans, they all blanketed their projects in a fog of secrecy that tainted these policies with nepotism and favoritism. In the mid-1990s, the term *Āqā-zādeha* (literally the Gentlemen's Offspring, or the Iranian version of the Soviet era *nomeklatura,* a neologism made popular by a new breed of investigative dissident journalists such as Akbar Ganji and Mohammad Quchani) perfectly captured the crony capitalism guiding Rafsanjani's policy of economic liberalization of. The President maintained tight control over mass media, and supported campaigns of intimidation against journalists who closely followed the terms and conditions of his privatization schemes. He also lifted many restrictions in the public sphere that had previously alienated the youth. He realized that *laissez faire* Islamism depended on the emergence of a consumer society that was secure from the assaults of *hezbollahi* vigilantes. While the transparency of state affairs remained the off limit to the exercise of civil liberties, Rafsanjani tolerated the public appearance of a generation of outspoken intellectuals who embarked on an Islamist revisionist project. Although they shared with Rafsanjani

**Table 1. The Growth of Literacy Rate
During the First Twenty Years of the Revolution (in thousand)**

	1976	1986	1996
Female	13187	18887	25761
Population	27113	38709	52295
Male	13926	19822	26534
Female	4679 (35%)	9835 (52%)	19118 (74%)
Literate	12877	23913	41582
Male	8198 (58%)	14078 (71%)	22465 (84%)

Source: *Markaz-e Āmār-e Iran* (Census Center of Iran)
http://www.sci.org.ir/portal/faces/public/sci/sci.gozide

Table 2. International Comparison of Poverty and Inequality

Country	GDP PC In 2003	Poverty Rate % under $2*	Gini Index
Iran	6608	7.2 (1998)	43.0 (1998)
Egypt	3731	43.9 (1999)	34.4 (2000)
Turkey	6398	10.3 (2000)	30.0 (2000)
China	4726	50.1 (1999)	44.7 (2001)
India	2732	80.6 (1999)	32.5 (1999)
Pakistan	1981	65.6 (1998)	33.0 (1999)
Venezuela	4647	30.6 (1998)	49.1 (1998)
Mexico	8661	26.3 (2000)	54.6 (2000)
Malaysia	8986	9.3 (1997)	49.2 (1997)

Source: The World Bank Report (2005),[3]
*The poverty rate is the percentage of individuals living under $2 per day.

political pragmatism and a feeling of postrevolutionary exhaustion, they were committed to the principles of re-distributive social justice.

While Abdolkarim Soroush gave voice to the emerging public intellectuals, by criticizing the now hegemonic Islamic state ideology, many of these same intellectuals saw their dissent as a continuation of Ali Shari`ati's counter-hegemonic Islam. As the ideologue *par excellence* of the revolution, Shari`ati introduced an Islamist liberation theology to which a generation of Muslim youth subscribed in the 1970s. While anti-monarchist and anti-imperialist students understood him in a Leninist-Jacobinist mode, postrevolutionary critics of the Islamic Republic interpreted the now deceased revolutionary as touting a Gramscian war of position. They learned that implementing social justice and democracy required discursive hegemony in society. Yesteryear's abolitionist revolutionary ideology had resulted in the despotic rule of the post-revolutionary regime. Abolitionism was now abolished, giving way to dialogue and discursive engagement. Most notable of among these developments was a new approach to the West, and a revisionist critique of *westoxication.*

Ali Shari`ati and Islamic Liberation Theology

In response to a colleague's query about his most significant achievement, Ali Shari`ati remarked, 'in one sentence: the transformation of Islam from a *culture* to an *ideology.*'[4] Through an innovative use of these concepts, Shari`ati located his political agenda between two major trends in Iranian politics. He believed that while the institution of the clergy had degraded Islam into a culture of stagnation, the Iranian Marxist-Leninists had failed to appreciate indigenous cultural resources in the formation of a counter-hegemonic ideology of emancipation.

Ali Shari`ati was born in 1933 in Mazinan, a small province in eastern Iran, and died on June 19, 1977 of a heart attack in London. He received his Doctorate in 1963 from the Sorbonne's *Faculté des Lettres et Sciences Humaines.*[5] Ali Rahnema, in his superb biography, carefully presented a view that Shari`ati's intentions may have been quite different from the way his ideology was appropriated by the revolutionary movement.[6] Indeed his life and works are shrouded in 'hagiographical and martyrological fantasies.'[7] Nevertheless, his influence remains significant decades after his death.

Shari`ati inverted the Marxian conception of ideology as a system of illusory ideas in conflict with reality into a revolutionary *tool* for the creation of new realities. Whereas Marx and Engels saw in 'morality, religion, metaphysics [...] and all their corresponding forms of consciousness' various manifestations of ideology,[8] Shari`ati used the term to denote a liberation *weltanschauung*. Ideology was not something to be overcome, rather, by bifurcating culture and ideology, he distinguished between two social states of being, one conformist and conventional and the other rebellious and critical. In contrast to Marxist-Leninists, he contended that ideology exists in a contested realm; appropriated progressively, it 'functions like a weapon against oppression.'[9]

Iranian communists seldom engaged theoretically with non-Marxist literature and often dismissed Islamic literature *in toto* as ideological superstructures of a decaying feudalist base. They regarded religion and religious thinkers, such as Shari`ati, to be not only theoretically, but also practically, misleading and misled.[10] Iranian communists perceived the revolution through a Leninist-Stalinist lens, which regarded the state as merely 'a manifestation of the *irreconcilability* of class antagonisms.'[11] In Lenin's reductionist view, the state maintained its power primarily through coercion. Consequently, Iranian communists believed that decapitating the head of this oppression machine was the first step towards emancipating the working class. In contrast, in a Weberian fashion, Shari`ati was more concerned, with the inner justifications of oppression.[12] Contrary to the Iranian communists' preoccupation with state coercion, Shari`ati's predicament was mass consent.

It was this preoccupation with legitimacy and mass consent that led him to formulate his theory of *Islam as ideology*. He maintained that structures of domination were based upon the triangle of economic power, physical coercion, and inner ideological/cultural justification. He expressed the three elements of a 'triangle of oppression' in Iran in different rhyming verses, *zar-zur-tazvir* (jewel-coercion-deception) or *mālek-malek-mullah* (landed gentry-ruler-clergy), or *tigh-talā-tasbih* (sword-gold-the mullah's rosary), in each of which the clergy represented the institutional force behind the ideological (inner) justification of political and economic oppression.[13]

Max Weber argued, 'Conceptions of legitimacy and their inner justification are of very great significance for the structure of domination.'[14] In his philosophy, Shari`ati depicted the *ruhāniyat* (the clergy) as apologists for oppression in Iran, a position they have enjoyed since Shi`ism became the official religion of the court under the Safavid Empire (1501-1736, AD). Therefore, in addition to physical means of coercion, the oppressive monarchy in Iran was maintained by the 'inner justification' of what Shari`ati dubbed 'Safavid Shi`ism,'[15] justified and advocated by the *ruhāniyat*.

Moreover, he believed that Safavid Shi`ism was exclusively engaged with the spiritual and metaphysical phenomena; its official exponents emptied Islam of its 'progressive and this-worldly essence.' Thus Safavid Shi`ism had turned Islam into a culture of 'unconsciousness,' and 'blind emulation.'[16] He contended that the Sunni as well as the Shi`ite *ruhāniyat*, legitimized unjust class-based social orders.

> For its own class interest and its own worship of the material world, and for its eternal coalescence with dominant powers and ruling classes, [the clergy] has transformed religion into individual piety, and an absolute worship of the hereafter.[17]

Shari`ati was profoundly influenced by the anti-colonial and liberation movements of the 1960s, especially that of Algeria and its effect on French progressive intellectuals with whom he strongly identified. His contribution lies neither in his sophisticated knowledge of western sociological theories, nor in his thorough re-examination of Islamic theology. Rather, in order to expose the repressive ideology of Safavid Shi`ism, Shari`ati took upon himself the task of re-writing the entire distorted history of Shi`ism, to re-claim its original revolutionary core, and to restore Alavi Shi`ism— the Shi`ism of Imam Ali, the true Islam of the disinherited.[18] He defined Alavi Shi`ism as an ideology of consciousness, a worldview through which Muslims would become aware of their social location, class position, national condition, historical and civilizational direction. 'Ideology,' he remarked, 'gives meaning to humankind's historical experience in the context of which one's ideals and values are constructed.'[19]

Shari`ati's distinction between the (Alavi) Islam of movement (*nehzat*) and the (Safavid) institutionalized Islam (*nahād*) defined the core of his hermeneutics. His Islam was Shi`ism conceived as a 'total party,' a movement of 'martyrs and blood,' rather than an institution of 'mourners' and 'opiates.' Instead of offering a scholastic discussion about the doctrines of *foqaha* and *ulama,* Shari`ati's historical narrative history consisted of a succession of martyrs and rebellions against tyranny. He was inspired by the St. Pauls and Aarons of Islam, rather than by its St. Augustines and Maimonides; by those who chose Islam consciously; by those whose Islam was realized in exile, prisons, and battle grounds rather than in the seminary quarters. Thus, he constructed an axiom of a true Islam of movement parallel to the succession of Caliphs and *ulama* of institutionalized Islam—an Islam of Abu Dharr[20] and Mansur Hallaj[21] versus Islam of Umar[22] and Ibn Sina.[23]

During a roundtable discussion in late 1960s, a historian criticized Shari`ati for reproaching traditional Islam and its institutions, i.e. the *ruhāniyat*. He ridiculed Shari`ati's *Islamology*. The critic insisted that he had not 'scientifically proven' his vaunted distinction between the Islam of movement and institutionalized Islam, that his theory was far from a 'neutral sociological scrutiny.' Shari`ati responded disparagingly,

> [...] I am not a scientific researcher, but I feel the heaviness of centuries of torture and martyrdom on my soul [...] This *qibla*[24] which symbolizes emancipation from thousands of years of enslavement has transformed into the house of oppression and ignorance, and now you demand calm and scientific research spiced by a respectful aristocratic etiquette [...] The logic of Shi`ites like myself is not the same as the logic of Ibn Sina, Ghazali, of the researcher or of the Orientalist, mine is the logic of Abu Dharr [...] O my brother, our quarrel is not over a 'scientific theory,' it is over the inheritance of [the Caliph].[25]

Shari`ati's words were generally misunderstood by his Muslim critics. Marxists castigated him for the liberties he took in moving from base (economy) to superstructure (politics and ideology) in his philosophy of history. Ali Akbar Akbari,[26] who knew Shari`ati from his participation in a study group,[27] offered the only systematic Marxist engagement with his ideas. Like many others, Akbari failed to understand Shari`ati's allegorical language, as well as his determination to pursue a counter-hegemonic project based on what he called the *estekhrāj* (extraction) and *tasfiyeh* (refinement) from Iranian history and cultural sources.

Shari`ati was less concerned with the consistency of his philosophy of history and often borrowed freely from Hegel, Kant, Marx, Trotsky, and Lenin without properly crediting his sources. Academic niceties were unnecessary, and impeded the effectiveness of his public sermons. Despite his appropriation of Marxian dialectical conception of history, he believed that his liberation theology needed to grow in Iranian soil, fed from its own cultural wellspring.

In his critique, Akbari repeated the same general arguments about the reactionary role of religion in history and accused Shari`ati of a futile attempt to revive an ideology whose time had passed with the end of feudalism. He mocked him for a lack of understanding of historical processes, not observing the difference between base and superstructure, and for failing to realize the incommensurability of socialism and religion. Despite Akbari's rudimentary knowledge and his determinist-scientific Marxism, along with Aramesh Dustdar, his book remained the only foundation for any other Marxist attempts prior to the revolution to discredit Shari`ati's work.

The *ruhāniyat* also chastised him for misusing the *hadith* (the Prophet's life narratives), for misappropriating the Qur'anic verses, and most importantly his downplaying Sunni-Shi`ite differences. Naser Makarem-Shirazi, one Qom's growing influential voices in the early 1970s, argued that Shari`ati's views on the democratic nature of Islam was based on an unreliable *hadith* and on a misunderstanding of the notion of *ijma`* (consultation).[28] Furthermore, he called Shari`ati's praise of the Sunni Saladin, the Muslim warrior who defeated the Crusaders and retook Jerusalem in 1187, distasteful and damaging to the souls of his young followers. Makarem's critique represented a typical failure of the *ulama* to grasp Shari`ati's conception of *Islam as ideology*.[29]

Another important clerical figure and a trustee of Ayatollah Khomeini, Morteza Motahhari, also rebuked Shari`ati for politicizing Islam.[30] Although he shared the same pulpit with Shari`ati at *Hossein-iyyeh-ye Ershād*, he remained conspicuously apprehensive about Shari'ati's denunciation of the clergy. In order to limit Shari`ati's growing influence, Motahhari tried and failed to impose regulations on the credentials of the speakers at the *Hosseiniyyeh*. He proposed to convene a board of directors for the *Hosseiniyyeh* composed of 'high ranking pious *mujtahids*, knowledgeable of both the necessities of time and the teachings of Islam.'[31] After he failed to persuade the managing director of the *Hosseiniyyeh*, Naser Minachi, to agree on imposing restrictions on Shari`ati, Motahhari made another effort to contain Shari`ati's popularity among young Muslims. In the winter of 1970-71, in a desperate move, he called him to a series of meetings attended by younger clerics who considered themselves a part of the new movement inspired by Ayatollah Khomeini. In the meetings, future leaders of the 1979 revolution, including Mohammad Beheshti, Hashemi-Rafsanjani, Mohammad Bahonar, and Musavi-Ardebili accused Shari`ati of instigating hostility towards the clergy.

In Qom and Mashad, the grand ayatollahs were perturbed by his scathing censure of Safavid Shi`ism. More shocking was his facile dismissal of the entire corpus of Shi`ite jurisprudence as mere superstition and its exclusive concern with ritualistic private matters of faith. The clerics assured Shari`ati that they considered him a good Muslim with good intentions, but believed he lacked a proper knowledge of theology and the history of Shi`ism. They also warned that him should he continue, the grand ayatollahs would destroy his reputation. Shari`ati knew that the grand ayatollahs could not dissuade his audiences from attending his lectures by accusing him of Wahhabism or apostasy. Obdurately, he rebuffed their offer of help.[32]

Soon thereafter, a number of grand ayatollahs launched a defamation campaign against him. They asked the Shah and his secret police to stop what they called the spread of Shari`ati's poisonous words and deceptive books. At the same time, they accused him of collaborating with the SAVAK with a mission to destroy Islam from within. A long list of ayatollahs lent their support to a petition to ban their followers from attending his lectures and issued *fatwas* condemning his heresy.[33]

While Shari`ati tried to appease them, he was incensed by the ayatollahs' complacency in matters of injustice and tyranny. In a letter to Ayatollah Milani, who had earlier forbidden his followers from reading Shari`ati's books or attending his lectures, he lamented that 'He still respects [the ayatollah]' and reminded him that his 'presence offered hope and support to all the youth who desired a safe haven in these bewildering times.' But a letter which had started with pleasant appreciation turned into a bastinade against the clergy. He wrote,

> Everybody is asking this question (and because of my gratitude towards you I have tried in vain to offer them a persuasive answer to them): why is it that pious people such as yourself, who sit on the cathedra of the deputy of the Shi`ite messiah (*imam-e zamān*) as a source of emulation, have not uttered a word about tyranny in this world? For eight years, the French army bloodied and massacred the Muslims of Algeria, ruined their cities, tortured their warriors, and the Algerians fought heroically. Even the enlightened Christian priests in France sympathized with the Algerians. The existentialist Sartre and the anti-religion Ms. Simone de Beauvoir defended them and endangered their own lives for the sake of the Algerians' cause. Even the French communist Henri Alleg joined the Algerian resistance and made the atrocities of the French, their torture of the Algerian *mujahidin*, known to the world. You, one of the leaders of the Shi`ite world did not even issue a meaningless statement of sympathy with them [...] For more than twenty years now the Muslims [sic] of Palestine have suffered at the hand of the Israelis. Their atrocities are so horrific that they compelled a young Japanese man to sacrifice his life heroically in defense of the Palestinians. But our clerical leaders do not show one-thousandth of the sensitivity they display in my condemnation in denouncing the brutalities of the Israelis [...] It perturbs

me deeply to witness that a great source of emulation writes on the pages of his book that 'the Prophet has advised *those who eat melon would go to the heaven!*' And then you have the audacity to call me an 'unfit element,' and condemn my *Islamology*.[34]

While motivated by professional rivalry at the *Hosseiniyyeh*, Motahhari recognized that the unprecedented popularity of Shari'ati's lectures could usher in a shift in authority of *ijtihad* from the clergy to lay theologians and intellectuals. He was infuriated by his disregard for the clerical hierarchy and his disrespect for the ritualistic aspects of Shi'ism. For the clergy, not only did the rituals of *rowzeh-khāni, va`z,* and *sineh-zani* (sermonizing, preaching, self-flagellation) underscore its distinction from Sunni Islam, more importantly, it perpetuated a social space for the *vo`āz* (the preachers), notably aiding them to earn their livelihood. After leaving the *Hosseiniyyeh,* Motahhari grew more suspicious of Shari'ati's motivations and began to accuse him of collaborating with the SAVAK. He asked Ayatollah Khomeini to issue a *fatwa,* banning his books. Although Khomeini trusted Motahhari's judgment in all political matters, he refused to censure Shari'ati publicly. But Motahhari continued his campaign even after Shari'ati's death and the collapse of the Pahlavi regime in 1979. In a letter to Khomeini, Motahhari called Shari'ati's death a 'Divine blessing' (`enāyat-e elāhi). 'The SAVAK had sent this man abroad,' he speculated, 'to propagate his degenerate thoughts around the world.'[35]

Shari`ati the Iranian Gramsci

Neither the Iranian Marxist-Leninist Left, nor the clerical establishment understood Shari'ati's intention to transform Islam into a revolutionary *counter-hegemonic* ideology. Whereas his lexicon troubled Marxist-Leninists, his idiosyncratic language in borrowing freely from Rousseau, Marx, Imam Ali, and Abu Dharr, scandalized his clerical detractors. Shari'ati consciously developed his historiography (his *Islamology*), his conception of Safavid Shi'ism, and his emphasis on the cultural-ideological basis of domination in terms of the Gramscian *war of position*.

Louis Althusser had already introduced Gramsci to French readers in late 1960s, but Shari'ati was not familiar with Gramscian ideas. Althusser and his so-called 'scientific Marxism' remained outside of Shari'ati's French intellectual milieu. Gramsci attracted the attention of neither existential Marxists nor the liberation movements, two sources of Shari'ati's intellectual inspirations. Nevertheless, independently from Gramsci, in his analysis of state power, Shari'ati shifted the question of oppression under the Shah from domination as coercion to leading as coercion bolstered by consent). The state expands its authority not only through political violent means, but also, in civil society in exercises ideological domination, through the trinity of *este`mār*, *estesmār*, and *estehmār*, that is colonialism, exploitation, and deceit. As Gramsci wrote, 'The general notion of the State includes elements which need to be referred back to the notion of civil society (in the sense that one might say that State = political society + civil society, in other words hegemony protected by the armor of coercion).' [36]

In Gramsci's theory, the state is not exclusively regarded as a *gendarme*-night-watchman organization. Rather, its dominance is maintained by means of the institutions and relations of civil society— schooling, family, churches and religious life, gender and ethnic identities, etc. Shari`ati echoed this idea when he wrote, 'An institutionalized movement disappears in the web of existing social institutions, i.e., state; family; language; banks and insurance; retirement plans; saving accounts; and even lottery tickets.'[37] Gramsci transformed the Leninist agenda of smashing the bourgeois state with a single blow, as he called it a *war of maneuver*, into the strategy of exercising 'leadership before winning governmental power.'[38]

Inspired by Marx's eleventh thesis on Feuerbach, Shari`ati described the philosopher and the *`ālem* as 'observers of this world.' The responsibility of the 'ideologue' was to stand in 'the position of God' and 'to demand the good and to destroy evil, to criticize and to correct, to define the ideals for whose realization the masses should be organized.' The Truth, he insisted, will emerge from neither scholastic debates nor scientific inquiry; 'truth manifests itself only in action.'[39] Accordingly, the Islamic ideal was a society based on the world-view of *towhid* (the oneness of God). However, instead of a mere demarcation of Islam as a monotheistic religion, he regarded *towhid* as a *weltanschauung* that reflected a utopian egalitarian social relation based on the unity of Man, Nature, and God.[40] He wrote,

> Social *towhid* negates the legitimacy of earthly gods and their authority in endorsing social orders that embody differences in class and other aspects of human life. In a word, a *towhidi* society negates human *shirk*.[41] [...] *Shirk* is a world-view that justifies [social inequality] and attributes class-ridden social orders to the divine will. In this way, not only does it justify such an order, but it worships it and calls it 'natural' and 'eternal' [...] The advocates of *shirk* 'naturalize' social inequalities

and create another god who forbids rebellion, and sanctifies the existing social orders.[42]

By politicizing *towhid*, Shari`ati called into question the authority of the *ruhāniyat* as official exegetes of the Islamic canon. He understood that legitimate *imam* is one who represents Islam in light of modern contingencies.[43] But the kind of legitimate imam he had in mind was an intellectual who rejected the Iranian practice of imitating the West as well as uncritically continuing old religious traditions. 'Intellectuals are those who think in new ways,' he wrote,

> It does not matter if they are illiterate; or not knowledgeable in philosophy; or are not a *faqih*, a physicist, a chemist; or a literary connoisseur, or a historian. Intellectuals need to be conscious of their time, of their people, they need to know how to think and how to appreciate the responsibilities that critical thinking bestows on their shoulders, and be ready to accept the sacrifices the realization of those responsibilities demand of them.[44]

Shari`ati's words resemble Gramsci's distinction between organic and professional intellectuals. In Shari`ati, intellectuals become organic not because they emerge from the classes they represent, but because they accept the responsibilities that their position as public intellectuals demand. Therefore, he strove to create a new Muslim leadership of young, educated who cast aside the habitual of blind emulation. Shari`ati's ambition was immensely successful. He never established a political party, but he considered his widely popular lectures to be the work of intellectual mobilization.

During his lecture series from 1967 to 1972, *Hosseiniyyeh Ershād* became the meeting place of a generation of young, otherwise Marxist, Muslim intellectuals. Shari`ati transformed the common understanding of Islam as the wisdom of ages into a dynamic (*puyā*) ideology of social change. In contrast to his detractors, he saw no contradiction in understanding Shi`ism as a revolutionary ideology, that was rooted in the past but still could herald a just future. He grasped the Qur'an as a Divine but historical text, revealed in allegorical verses and relevant to the generations in all ages.[45]

Ummah, Imamate, *and the Ideological Society*

After his death, Shari`ati was elevated to the status of the martyred teacher of the revolution. But his anti-clerical ideas remained controversial, and were swiftly marginalized after the triumph of the revolution in 1979. Ayatollah Khomeini's refusal to endorse a clerical admonishment and censorship of Shari`ati's work made the *ruhāniyat* more determined to cleanse the revolution of Shari`ati's heresies. Khomeini's pledge that he would assume only an advisory role and that the *ruhāniyat* would not partake in forming the postrevolutionary government,[46] added to their worry that authority for interpreting Islam would shift from the seminaries to the hordes of intellectuals.

However, Shari`ati's clerical opponents exploited his interpretation of the social role of *ummah* and *imamate*, which appeared to affirm their traditional functions. Shari`ati discussed the issues of *ummah* and *imamate* in three separate occasions.[47] Advocating a return to the progressive and democratic core of Shi`ism, Shari`ati nevertheless debated whether the principle of *imamate* in Shi`ite theology was truly compatible with representative and participatory democracy. 'I had doubt about *imamate*,' he once confessed, 'I thought it would be more democratic and progressive if people chose their own leaders [rather than pledging allegiance to a hereditary succession of *imams*].'[48] On several occasions he admitted that he had found the notion of *imamate* puzzling. He believed that it established a one-sided relationship between the rulers and their subjects. 'The idea of *imamate* used to be incomprehensible and even unreasonable to me.'[49]

Shari`ati's problem, what Reza Alijani has called the 'paradox of *vesāyat* [administration] and democracy,'[50] was the apparent conflict between the Shi`ite belief that the Prophet designated Imam Ali as his successor, and the democratic principles that he believed Shi`ism promoted. He found the solution in the debates at the Bandung meeting of the Non-Aligned Movement in 1955. One of the controversial issues that the delegates grappled with was the problem of freedom and democracy in the newly independent states. This debate inspired President Sukarno in 1957 to form an extra-parliamentary cabinet of experts for the establishment of a *guided democracy* in Indonesia.

The new governments found in Africa and Asia faced the predicament of reconstituting societies that had experienced the trauma of colonial violence democratically. Bandung debate about democracy became a touchstone with which Afro-Asian leaders justified their national policies. Gamal Abdel Nasser evoked Bandung when he nationalized the Suez Canal; Nehru never failed to mention the Non-Aligned Movement in his foreign relations speeches.[51] These evocations divulged the inherent contradiction between formal independence and its practical sustainability in the social, economic, and political arenas.

How was it possible to reverse the *real* influence of colonial powers in the post-colonial era? Many leaders in Bandung viewed democracy and freedom as institutions that would eventually return political authority to former colonial powers. In the words of the Philippine delegate, Carlos Pena Romulo, 'Does the road to greater freedom really lie through an indefinite period of less freedom?'[52]

These debates resonated with Shari`ati's analysis of *imamate* and *ummah*, specifically the contradiction between the guardianship of the leader and the will of the masses. Along with leaders of anti-colonial struggles, such as Franz Fanon, whose writings left a lasting mark on Shari`ati, and Sukarno, the President of Indonesia, he believed that the most enduring legaciy of colonialism was the alienation of colonial subjects from their own *selves*. Left to their own reasoning, he believed, the masses (`avām) would inevitably replicate the very same systems against which they had fought. The instinct of the liberated masses was to emulate European economic (capitalism) and political (electoral democracy) orders.

Sukarno's Rousseauian project to establish a social order 'in harmony with the soul of Indonesian people,'[53] Shari`ati thought, to be one of the significant contributions of the Non-Aligned Movement.[54] Sukarno was skeptical of the compatibility of Indonesian society with western-style democracy based on majority rule, what he often called 'majoricracy.' Shari`ati considered this to be a legitimate justification for a period of transition from liberation to self-governance, a period that made *imamate* (guardianship) a necessary step towards the realization of *ummah* (emancipated society). In this instance, he defined *ummah* as a *conscious* community of Muslims (i.e. those who realized their historical responsibilities), rather than the masses who were alienated from their earthly commitments to justice and equality.

Despite the clerics' open hostilities towards Shari`ati's rearticulation of Islam as ideology, they adopted his conception of *imamate* and *démocratie dirigée*. The appropriation was first manifested in the identification of Khomeini as *imam*. Although in Sunni tradition, the clerical leader of a community is known by the title of *imam,* in the years before Shari`ati it would have been considered heretical for any Shi`ite leader to claim *imamate*. The only *imam* recognized in Shi`ism was the absent Mahdi, the Messiah. The Iranian Islamic Student Associations in Europe and the US proffered the title of Imam to Khomeini after he moved to Paris in the fall of 1978. Although the clergy resisted this neologism (*bed`at*) in the Iranian-Shi`i tradition, later they adopted it, and in the process, distorted its link to Shari`ati's *Islamology*.[55]

While apolitical factions of the *ruhāniyat* rejected Shari`ati, others used him selectively and instrumentally. They appropriated Shari`ati's conception of *ummah* and *imamate* to justify the guardianship of the *faqih* and the restrictions imposed by the constitution on electoral politics. In later years, despite hostility towards his theology, the state-controlled radio and television broadcasted Shari`ati's lectures on *ummah* and *imamate* on the anniversaries of his death without informed commentary about his precise meaning. Shari`ati regarded the period of primacy of *imamate* as an 'ideological society,' a transitional period in which vanguards established political and social institutions that would guarantee the continuity of the revolution.

> After a resistance movement assumes political power, it will become static, it will become stagnant! It will become conformist! After a movement assumes political power, its main objective becomes the preservation of what it has gained. It becomes counter-revolutionary when it is institutionalized.[56]

Although he borrowed the idea of the routinization of revolutions from Max Weber, but unlike him, Shari`ati was not convinced of its inevitability or irreversibility. He wrote, 'we should not allow that revolutionary thoughts to transmute into a stagnant civilization.'[57] In order to disrupt this stagnation, he adopted an Islamized version of Trotsky's theory of permanent revolution.[58] He turned *amr-e be ma`ruf* (demand the praise-worthy), *nahy-e az monkar* (prohibition of the vile), *ijtihad* (historically contingent re-interpretation of the Text), and *hijrat* (transformative migration) into its defining principles.[59]

According to this schema, whereas *ijtihad* addresses the ideals goals of the ideological society, *amr-e be ma`ruf* and *nah-ye az monkar* define the specific ways through which the new social order should be realized. He linked *hijrat* to the national, historical, and social relations of the *ummah* and the *imam*. *Hijrat* occurs collectively or individually, internally (conscious raising) or externally (reconstituting the socio-historical situation). Ultimately, however, Shari`ati's permanent revolution not only promoted the institutionalization of his revolutionary ideas, but also, its top-down enforcement of the ideological commitments of the revolution encouraged the establishment of a massive bureaucracy.

In Shari`ati's utopian scheme, the same oppressed masses who must rise against oppression paradoxically become the chief obstacle to progress. In a Rousseauian twist, in the ideological society, the antagonism between the oppressed and the oppressor is transformed into 'the antagonism between a backward and stagnant society with the progressive ideology of a revolutionary regime.'[60]

> A guided democracy is the rule of a group whose intention is to condition and transform individuals' lives and their cultural views, language, [...] and social relations in the best possible way based on a progressive revolutionary program. To realize this goal, it has an ideology, a particular school of thinking, and a well-designed plan [...] the purpose of which is to lift the entire society towards its transcendental destiny. If there are those who do not believe in this objective and their thought and action corrupts the society, and if there are those who wish to abuse their freedom, their wealth and power, and if there are social obstacles and traditions which idles human beings, those traditions should be abolished, those ways of thinking should be condemned, and through whatever means this society should liberate itself from all petrifying constraints.[61]

Shari`ati was unapologetic in his rejection of liberal democracy. He contended that in a liberal democracy, electoral politics only assures the legitimacy of a state that exploits the 'uninformed vote of the backward masses.' A true democracy emerges through a 'transitional period of the revolutionary self-reinvention of the society.'[62] Without conscious and deliberate casting of their votes the backward masses could not realize democracy. Therefore, they should submit to the will of a revolutionary vanguard class (revolutionary party, leader, imam) who will never betray the historical mission of the liberated society.

Shari`ati devised the dichotomy of *demokrāsi-ye ra'y* versus *demokrāsi-ye ra's* to convey his notion of conscious democracy. *Ra'y* in this context suggests *conscious vote* and *ra's* (literally 'a head,' as in counting farm animals) represents the heedless constituents of a liberal democracy. It is only after the realization of 'the transitional revolutionary order,' he asserted, 'society reaches self-awareness and every person's vote is delivered willfully and consciously. At that time, the revolutionary period will end and a democratic system will be established.'[63] The establishment of a classless democratic society will conclude the revolutionary period; at that stage, society will reach self-awareness, and a just system will be realized. However, this stage will not be materialized in one generation; the reconstruction of a revolutionary society requires 'the devoted work of many generations.'[64]

The apparent shift in Shari`ati's views on the role of the masses in shaping their destiny—from a revolutionary force to an obstacle to be eradicated—indicates that when it becomes hegemonic, his utopian Islam would survive only through institutionalization, eliminating dissent, and instilling political quietism. He did not explain how he reconciled his emphasis on the revolutionary potential of the masses with his perplexing elitism. He went so far as to ridicule the people by declaring that their 'brain was as developed as that of a primitive Neanderthal.'[65]

The West and Gharbzadegi[66]

Gharbzadegi was the title of a monograph published in 1962 by Jalal Al-e Ahmad, an Iranian novelist and social critic. Al-e Ahmad viewed technology as the covert means with which the West was polluting and eradicating Iranian cultural authenticity and political sovereignty— hence the notion of 'Westoxication.' While Al-e Ahmad was not the first to coin the term, he should be credited for making *gharbzadegi* a popular discourse which constructed the West as the ultimate Other in Iranian dissident cultures, secular as well as the Islamic Left.

Al-e Ahmad admitted that he had borrowed the notion of *gharbzadegi* from Fakhroddin Shadman and Ahmad Fardid, neither of whom were prolific writers, and had remained obscure until recently.[67] Although Al-e Ahmad pays tribute to these two, he used *gharbzadegi* to address the predicament of colonialism and dependency rather than to underscore essential differences between the East and the West.

Fardid traced the roots of *gharbazedgi* to ancient Greece.[68] He conceived the history of the world as a struggle between idolatry-impurity (*tāghut*) and the sanctity of the Divine. From the moment human beings strove to place themselves in the position of God they became alienated from themselves. That desire to act like God belonged solely to the western civilization. Since its inception, God-like westerners have spread their idolatrous ideas around the world, either in the form of ancient Greece's polytheism or modern humanism. Either way, Fardid insisted, the result is the same: the incessant westoxication of the world, by blood and iron or words and ideas.[69]

According to Fardid, there were two important historical moments when Muslims succumbed to the temptations of westoxication. The first was the Middle Ages when rationalism and Greek philosophy influenced Islamic theology.[70] The second moment, specific to Iranian history, manifested in the early 1900s during the Constitutional Revolution. For Fardid, the Constitutional Revolution launched the project of 'double westoxication': belief in the Western idolatry of

Humanism *and* the attempt to transform Iranian society along the same lines. The power of modern westoxication overwhelmed even the most senior of Ayatollahs the most respected seminaries. 'Although some resisted,' he regretted, 'a significant number of *ruhāniyun*, most notably Ayatollah Na'ini, supported the revolution and saw no conflict between constitutionality and Islam.'[71] Fardid considered the Constitutional Revolution as the turning point of the 'double westoxication.' For him, a revolution inspired by the 'French Bill of Rights' lead inescapably to alienation.

Shadman's *gharbzadegi* was more nuanced and lent itself better to the construction of an anti-colonial discourse. Shadman saw a cultural and national continuity neither in Western nor Iranian ancient history. For him, the predicament of *gharbzadegi* had to be understood in a distinctly modern context. 'Cursing Alexander, the invading Arabs, or the Mongols,' he wrote in exasperation, 'will only hinder solving our current problems.'[72] In any case, *gharbzadegi* was a shallow emulation of the West. While they promoted western cultures and intellectual traditions through the negation of the self, Iranian intellectuals lacked a sophisticated knowledge of western traditions.

But in contrast to these two earlier conceptions, Al-e Ahmad viewed *gharbazedgi* as an historically distinct social and political phenomenon of *colonial* encounters. Although by the late eighteenth century European colonial powers had swallowed up Iran in their sphere of influence, Al-e Ahmad believed that westoxication penetrated the Iranian society after the CIA coup d'état in 1953 that toppled the nationalist administration of Prime Minister Mossaddeq and reinstalled the Shah. In retrospect, Al-e Ahmad became increasingly skeptical of the leaders of the 1906 revolution in their uncritical appropriation of western notions of rights and constitutionality. But rather than offering a totalizing discourse of a decadent West, he presented the concept of *gharbzadegi* in relation to the destruction wrought by colonialism.

During the 1906 Constitutional Revolution, divergent strands of Iranian intellectuals, from grand ayatollahs to western-educated secularists, evoked western ideas of democracy and rights to define their objectives. Although voices in the clerical establishment condemned constitutionality as inherently heretical, their reservations remained marginal. The constitutionalists even executed their most strident critic the influential Sheikh Fazlollah Nuri, with the silent blessing of seminarians. Early twentieth century intellectuals did not hesitate to declare they wished to create an Iran patterned after Europe. But after the 1953 CIA-led coup, Iranian intellectuals identified their politics with national liberation movements. Rather than idealizing the West, they allied themselves with its colonial victims' struggles for independence.

In the period of the Constitutional Revolution, Iranian intellectuals and political leaders embraced liberty and democracy as identifiably western ideas. In the years between the 1953 coup and the 1979 revolution, the West became exclusively associated with violence and decadence. Unlike Fardid, and his postrevolutionary counterpart Reza Davari, the revolutionary discourse of *gharbzadegi*, cast the west neither as an indivisible totality, nor as a degenerate essence beyond redemption. Al-e Ahmad captured the core of the shift from the first period of awe and inspiration to the second of contempt and rejection. He argued that for three centuries, Iranians 'looked at the West with languish, and subservience,' but the time had come for them to see the West with 'an eye of resentment and rivalry.'[73] Hossein Kachu`ian aptly observes, 'while during [the Constitutional Revolution], ideas and ideals of modernity informed the critical negation of the self in [the Iranian] discourse of identity, with the real experience of westernization, the second period was defined by a critical negation of modernity informed by a historical discourse of the self.'[74]

Rather than an essential Iranian or Muslim 'self,' defined against a supra-historical Western 'self,' Shari`ati argued that *gharbzadegi* plagued all humanity.  For Shari`ati along with Al-e Ahmad, *gharbzadegi* signified alienation induced by 'capitalist machinism' and reinforced by the violence of colonialism.[75] Rather than modern technology, the instrumental rationality of the machine-age had given rise to *gharbzadegi*. 'Machin*ism*,' Shari`ati responded to a Marxist critic, 'is a particular social order imposed onto machines.'[76] By linking it with 'machinism,' Shari`ati universalized *gharbzadegi* as a mental condition that affected people around the globe. He chastised his Marxist critic,

> I do not criticize 'machinism' because I resent technology (A modernist intellectual gentleman has written a critique of my *Islāmshenāsi* to prove that traveling from Mashad to Tehran is faster on an airplane than riding an ass, it is more comfortable and thus much better!). My argument against 'machinism' and 'scientism' is exactly because they withhold, rather than release, the emancipatory potentials of technology. 'Machinism' justifies and sustains the social system of capitalism, the fetishism of consumption, a philosophy of consumerism. 'Machinism' recognizes human beings only as 'consuming animals.'[77]

Shari`ati and Al-e Ahmad considered the critique of *gharbzadegi* as a universal struggle for the liberation of the colonized, who now bore the burden of emancipating the west from its own vices. In the following passage, Shari`ati historicized and located the discourse of liberation in the context of European *and* non-European intellectual traditions.

> Amongst us, there are 'wanderer intellectuals' who cannot accept their inherited ways of thinking or remain in those petrified frames. They are intellectuals because they cannot consume the ideological packages that the west has offered them in the last hundred years, because they intend to 'think,' to 'build', and to 'choose' their own paths. Recent experiences have shown that consumption [of others' ideas] cannot cure their pain, however much it might relieve them from the pain of 'obscurity.' That is why, as Jean-Paul Sartre wrote in his introduction to *Les Damnés de la Terre*, a new voice has arisen from Africa, Latin America, and Asia. Until a few years ago, Sartre confessed, the intellectual class of one-and-a-half billion indigenous people on all continents looked up to the intellectuals in Amsterdam, Paris, and London and repeated their progressive slogans and brilliant ideas. They just opened their mouths and repeated what western intellectuals had to say. But now, a new time has come. Intellectuals such as Fanon speak to us from Africa. This is a staggering moment that an African voice, not traditional and stagnant, an enlightened voice that is familiar with contemporary values and needs, speaks but does not repeat our words. It speaks the language of protest, and more importantly *against* metropole intellectuals! This is an historical moment, an important occasion for the West![78]

Al-e Ahmad regarded westoxication as a disease, 'as tuberculosis,' which infected the soul and the body, which turned people into strangers in their own land. The remedy to the disease was the preservation of 'our own historic and cultural character in the face of the machine and its onslaught.'[79] Both Shari`ati and Al-e Ahmad used critique of *gharbzadegi* in two ways, as a mean to negate *imposed* western modernity and as a critical rearticulation of the traditional Iranian self. 'If the return to self,' as Shari`ati underlined, 'means a return to who we *are*, to our existing national culture and religion, we are much better off to become western from head to toe.'[80] Al-e Ahmad reproached the westoxicated intellectuals as fervently as he chastised the orthodoxies of the *akhunds*. This double-edged critique of western modernity and a return to a *rearticulated* self distinguished Al-e Ahmad and Shari`ati's conception of *gharbzadegi* from other renditions.

They influenced Khomeini and his disciple Motahhari, despite the latter's reservations about their views of the clergy. On a number of occasions, Khomeini coupled his castigation of westoxicated intellectuals with an attack on clerics who blindly wished to preserve the old traditions rather than being conscious of the needs of the time. Khomeini bluntly said, 'Those pseudo-*ruhāniyun* and court *akhunds* are the worst enemies of Islam.'[81]

Motahhari also followed the same liberation discourse and developed a critique of *gharbzadegi* along the same social and political lines. Hostile to western-style democracy, he believed that secularism was a distinct historical experience of church and state relations Europe.[82] For him, Iranians experienced western modernity 'not in the Universal Declaration of Human Rights, but in the general behavior that the west imposes on human beings [...] Western conceptions of rights are intertwined with the primacy of capital over human interests, of money over human beings, of the worship of the machine, of the divinity of wealth, of exploitation, and of the limitless power of capitalism.'[83]

Despite their fundamental differences, Fardid's essentialist bifurcation of the East and the West and Al-e Ahmad's anti-colonialism shared a gendered understanding of the plague of westoxication. Whereas they represented the West as a totality with undisputed masculine power (associated with colonialism and imperialism), they regarded the loss of tradition as an injury to their manhood. Al-e Ahmad depicted the westoxicated as 'effeminate (*zan-sefat*),' 'licentious/unabashed (*bi shakhsiyat*),' 'wishy-washy/wimp (*hor-hory mazhab*),' 'comfort-loving (*rāhat-talab*),' 'sissy/dandy (*qerti*).'[84]

The triumph of the revolution in 1979 brought forward differences between these two distinct views. Now a nation that longed for independence and a return to the *self* had to decide which self it intended to resuscitate. Those who advocated a return to an *Islamic* self, in contradistinction to a national *Iranian* self, learned their mistake quickly after Saddam Hussein invaded Iran in 1980. Particularly after the war entered the period of the war of attrition in mid-1980s, those who condemned nationalism as a manifestation of *gharbzadegi* appealed to the citizens' sense of belonging to an ancient civilization. They recuperated the symbol of decadence of the Persian Monarchs, the ancient ruins of Persepolis, as an icon of national unity. The war taught the leaders of the Islamic Republic the identity to which they advocated a return could not exclude the Iranian self.

After the revolution, social critics and intellectuals grew increasingly skeptical of the anti-colonial idea of a return to self. Although it did not lose currency among leading intellectuals close to state power, most significantly Reza Davari, after the end of the war and the passing of Khomeini in 1989, a new generation of Muslim and secular writers grew weary of the abolitionist core of the westoxication discourse. Whereas before the revolution the rejection of *gharbzadegi* gave raise to an emancipatory ideology, the postrevolutionary regime exploited the same ideology to legitimize its rule and suppress its dissidents.

The end of the Iran-Iraq war in 1989 inaugurated a moment of self-reflection among emerging intellectuals who no longer sought to identify the roots of Iranian political, social, and economic problems in its colonial history. For many, the time had come to put *internal dynamics* rather than external interventions, at the center of the debate over the predicament of modernity and social change in Iran. Two best-sellers generated much interest in this topic: first, more scholarly and sophisticated, was Sadeq Ziba-Kalam's *Mā cheguneh mā shodim* (*How Did We Become Who We Are*), published in 1995 and reprinted five times in three years; and second, the more popular *Jāme`eh-shenāsi-ye nokhbeh-koshi* (*The Sociology of Killing Elites*) by Ali Rezaqoli, released in 1998 and reprinted twelve times in the same year. The subtitles of both books, *The Roots of Backwardness in Iran* and *A Sociological Analysis of the Roots of Dictatorship and Backwardness in Iran* unmistakably demonstrated the shift from anti-colonial, dependency theory to an internalist view of Iranian history. During the same period, significant attention was given to a critical social psychology of Iranians—that is the historical-cultural foundations of the self to which the entire society was to return.[85]

Rezaqoli ends his treatise with a long quotation from Shari`ati in which he expresses his reservation for 'blaming all vices on foreign agents.' In his typical dialectical approach, Shari`ati argues, 'Those who find colonialism and imperialism guilty of all things wrong in our society vindicate the internal reasons for our decaying society that they see before their own eyes.'[86] Although the thesis of Ziba-Kalam and others who emphasized the internal origins of backwardness in Iran lacked novelty, their ideas resonated with the political circumstances under the Islamic Republic and the growing discontent with its oppressive institutions.

Ziba-Kalam, a former militant Islamist student in Tehran who actively participated and later apologized for his role in the Cultural Revolution of 1980, links the anti-colonial and anti-imperialist revolutionary ideology to Marxian dependency theory and its communist advocates in Iran. In contrast to the old dependency thesis, he turns the causal relations of colonialism up-side-down, and argues that,

> Without negating the atrocities of colonial interventions in our land, we need to recognize that the catastrophe of colonialism was the *result* of our backwardness and weaknesses not its *cause*. *In reality, our backwardness led to, rather than being the result of, the advent of colonialism in Iran.*[87]

Ziba-Kalam sets out to develop a critique of dependency Marxist historio-graphy, a view that considered 'colonialism to be the cause of backward-ness,' and of its dominant political tradition of *gharb-setizi* (west-bashing).[88] To emphasize the internal causes of decay in Iranian society, he revives the classic Orientalist view of the genesis and decline of Islamic civilization. As a disillusioned child of the revolution, Ziba-Kalam, now a professor of the prestigious College of Law and Political Science at Tehran University, argues that radical Marxist anti-imperialism had profoundly informed and conditioned the Islamist revolutionary ideology in Iran. Such militancy, denied Muslim revolutionaries any the possibility of looking inward for the true historical causes of their nation's troubles.

Looking inward for the *causes* of problems rather than for their *solutions,* was a distinctly postrevolutionary agenda. Ziba-Kalam's book captured that moment of the inverted return to self. It was broadly appealing to Iranian intellectuals, as the remarkable sales of books in this genre suggest. The main premises of this inversion were borrowed from classical Orientalism, the discredited Marxian thesis of 'Asiatic Mode of Production,' and Karl Wittfogel's Weberian political elaboration of the same in *Oriental Despotism*.[89] Although representative books of this trend all share these premises, Ziba-Kalam's *Mā cheguneh mā shodim,* and its sequel *Sonnat va moderniteh* (*Tradition and Modernity*) are perhaps the most systematically articulated works of this genre.

In the same spirit of Orientalist historians and ideologues,[90] Ziba-Kalam located the points of Iranian decline in the 'closing of the door of *ijtihad,*' and its material foundation in the ecological conditions of 'hydraulic societies.' With geographical precision, he invoked Wittfogel's notion of 'hydraulic civilizations,' which was a methodical rendition of Marx's Asiatic Mode of Production. He argued that Iran served as an ideal type of a society in which arid lands had given rise to despotic political systems. Since large-scale irrigation required subs-tantial and centralized control, the state emerged as the sole institution that could vanquish other centers of power in society. Following the same internalist logic, Ziba-Kalam attributed the rise of Europe as a hegemonic colonial power to its internal (ecological, social, political, technological) dynamics. Accordingly, he speculated that the East and the West reached to their respective positions in world history *autonomously*. While the East mutated within itself and perpetuated its own stagnant social order, the West expanded its influence through the good fortune of sustaining a culture of innovation and critical engagement with tradition.

Rather than engaging with Ziba-Kalam's Orientalist and Eurocentric ideas, I wish to highlight how the reign of terror and the period of postwar reconstruction generated a sprawling skepticism of the revolutionary idea of the return to self. In less than a decade, the rejection of westoxication became the ideology of the established order. While the propagators and ideologues of the state disseminated their anti-colonial discourses, the disillusioned dissidents grew wary of the Republic's instrumental anti-westernism of the Republic. State-owned and other conservative newspapers accused Ziba-Kalam of 'baptizing the West by cleansing its sins.'[91] Although a host of Iranian historians questioned the validity of Ziba-Kalam's historiography and his empirical facts, the political significance of his argument muffled their criticism.[92]

What Shari`ati initiated in transforming Shi`i Islam from a religion of rituals and private piety into a theology of liberation and public good faced a crisis in postrevolutionary Iran. The realization of the Islamic Republic raised fundamental questions about the wisdom and feasibility of the revolutionary reconstitution of society. In postrevolutionary Iran, the totalitarian implications of what Shari`ati envisioned as *démocratie dirigée* materialized in the expansive role of the *faqih*, particularly after the institutionalization of its absolutist rule in the 1989 constitutional amendments.

While a growing number of revolutionary followers of Shari`ati regarded the Islamic Republic as the inevitable result of the politicization of religion, others rediscovered his Gramscian side. They began a project to expand the institutions of civil society. Indeed the presidential campaign of Mohammad Khatami of 1996-1997 emphasized the significance of the institutionalization of democratic change, both in the state apparatus as well as civil society. Women's organizations for equal rights, neighborhood associations, newspapers, professional journals, the omnipresent student movements, and more recently a massive labor union movement, have all opened a new space to criticize the program of the autocratic state as well as the religious foundations of its rule. In a true Shari`ati/Gramscian mode, competing interpretations of Islam now vie to become hegemonic not only in seminaries and the constitutional assembly, but inside family courts and schoolyards.

These changes could not have been realized without the fundamental transformation in religious interpretation, which was made possible by the daring critique of Islamic dogmatism put forward by Abdolkarim Soroush in the late 1980s. Those who took upon themselves the establishment of institutions of civil society, directly or indirectly, came out of the school of thought founded by Soroush. If before the revolution Shari`ati gave voice to the emancipatory potential of Islam as a liberation theology, after the revolution Soroush became the voice of a democratic change through a hermeneutical Islam. In the next chapter we shall scrutinize Soroush's ideas and examine the political consequences of his emergence as a leading dissident intellectual.

7

The Silence of the *Shari`ah*: Abdolkarim Soroush and the Theological Foundations of Political Reform

From early 1988, a group of Muslim intellectuals began to write for and congregate around the editorial board of *Kayhān Farhangi*, a monthly journal of culture and literary criticism, published by the daily newspaper *Kayhān*. In May 1988, it published a series of philosophical essays by Abdolkarim Soroush. His words proved to be one of most important theoretical foundations of political reform in postrevolutionary Iran.

Soroush had already become suspect during his short tenure at the Cultural Revolution Council (CRC) in the early 1980s. During the early years of the republic while the revolutionary fervor was at its height, and the advocates of Islamizing higher education pursued their purges and persecutions, Soroush cautioned his colleagues to moderate their unyielding determination to overhaul Iran's system of education. Informed by a Popperian education in the philosophy and history of science, he attacked the Islamization of the positive sciences, and, even more vigorously, defended the social and human sciences against the ideologues who believed that liberal arts directly challenged the seminaries and other clerical educational establishments. In two speeches at Tehran University marking the anniversary of the Cultural Revolution in May 1981,[1] and in May 1982,[2] Soroush told his revolutionary audience that the CRC must respect academic freedoms and encourage learning from the West and the East. An Islamic society needs to remain an *open society,* one in which 'freedom and truth both are respected, not at each other's expense. We should neither limit social liberties for the sake of the Truth, nor should we use our freedom to spread myths and fallacies as the Truth.'[3]

In his interviews and essays between 1982 and 1985,[4] Soroush linked plans to shutter university departments of humanities and social sciences to the dominant ideology that viewed the West as a totality with an unchanging *Zeitgeist*. While the condemnation of *gharbzadegi* proved to be effective in mobilizing the masses, Soroush saw its academic incarnation misguided and harmful. He criticized those who denounced the sciences for being rooted the western *Zeitgeist*. Their intervention in the higher education destroyed the integrity of a number of academic disciplines. Moreover, he taunted demagogues who recognized no distinction between the cognitive maps of scientific and historical inquiries and the geographical boundaries of East and West.[5]

Soroush's critique of the ideological attack on the social sciences and the humanities raised concerns both within the religious establishment and, more importantly, among the faculty of Tehran University's prestigious Philosophy Department and Divinity School. For decades, Heideggerian philosophers such as Ahmad Fardid and Reza Davari had dominated these departments. In an environment of purges and punishments, they worried that Soroush's hostility towards essentialist approaches to the East-West bifurcation could mean more than mere scholarly disagreement. While he continued to make known his displeasure with the philosophical characterization of sciences and technology as a *Gestell,* a Heideggerain notion of worldly 'enframing,' his critics began to question his revolutionary credentials and to 'expose' his liberal tendencies. Davari wrote a scathing review of a new translation of Popper's *Open Society and Its Enemies* in which he questioned those like Soroush who advocated a Popperian liberalism. 'Who is Popper?' Davari asked rhetorically. 'Our enemies abroad use him to oppose the revolution, and there are people within the ranks of the Islamic Republic who sanctify him and regard any attack on his ideas sacrilegious.'[6]

Like his mentor Ahmad Fardid, Davari viewed the perceived conflict between Islam and modernity as a manifestation of a larger and deeper contradiction between a western *weltanschauung,* rooted in the Greek philosophy and Hellenic culture, and an 'eastern cosmology.' During the early years of the revolution, he had identified the distinction between East and West along geographical lines.[7] But later he reformulated this dichotomy as two distinct 'states of being.'[8] The West was an indivisible totality at whose center was agnostic humanism.[9] He attributed the rise of technical societies to the emergence of a world in which individuals' rights of were prior to one's responsibilities to God. That was why, he remarked, turning Soroush into the strawman of the apologists of western culture, 'it would be mere simple-mindedness to draw distinction among western science, technology, and literature with its violence, colonial practices, vices and prostitution.'[10]

Fardid was another influential philosopher who became disillusioned with Soroush's politics and alarmed by his intention to rescue the human sciences from the onslaught of the Cultural Revolution. He turned Soroush's neo-Kantian orientation, via Popper, and his skepticism of Heideggerian phenomenology, into a test of his loyalty to the anti-colonial, anti-western core of the revolution. Fardid, who originally coined the term *gharbzadegi*, unashamedly accused Soroush for taking part in a freemason and Zionist conspiracy to destroy the revolution from within. 'I have a negative view of Kant and Hegel,' he declared, 'of the right and the left, and I interpret Heidegger through Islam.' He went a step further, 'Heidegger as the only thinker whose ideas are consistent with the Islamic Republic.'[11] In intellectual circles, Fardid attacked Soroush's integrity and questioned his intentions.

> Now we have a revolution and under its banner with Popper's philosophy some are determined to call for a *jihad* against *jihad-e nafs* (striving for self-perfection, or in this context purification) What is this rubbish they advocate as philosophy, these are insults to the history of humanity. One day they will be exposed, as I have said repeatedly before about the Freemasons. These people are managed by the international Jewish organizations and I shall inform Imam Khomeini of their conspiracies [...] I, Ahmad Fardid, have a short message to Imam Khomeini: Abdolkarim Soroush will destroy this revolution.[12]

These vicious, calculated, and concerted attacks on his person as well as his ideas proved to Soroush that intellectual debates could not resolve matters of politics, particularly in a revolutionary theater in which the blade of the guillotine terminated any discussion. He had considered *Kayhān- Farhangi* to be a tribune for intellectual engagement with ideas rather than an instrument for defamation and intimidation. Outraged, he scorned its editors for running Reza Davari's smear campaign. He announced that he would not reply to 'spiteful and malicious slander' which was masqueraded as philosophy. 'What purpose do these brothers have for printing those words? Are they trying to prove that they could steal the show from other journals by publishing baseless accusations and smear campaigns?'[13]

After Soroush's ultimatum, and an editorial change, *Kayhān-e Farhangi* became the voice of the postrevolutionary generation who feared the rising power of the advocates of absolutism, and their foot soldiers in the security and intelligence services. Soroush realized that in order to be effective, he needed a cadre of intellectuals who could rescue the revolution from the dogmatic clergy. He had already laid out his objection to the blinding fallacies of dogmatic Marxism-Leninism and celebrated the annihilation of its Iranian proponents, but another dogma, this time emanating from the inner circles of power, was about to determine his destiny. This time, he turned his attention to the problem of 'ideologization' of religion, and to its undisputed theorist Ali Shari`ati. Not only did he understand the significance of Shari`ati's doctrine of revolutionary Islam, he had learned from him how to turn his own idea into a counter-hegemonic program.

Having lost legal and constitutional struggles, a growing number of Islamist defenders of the Republic and secularized *velāyat-e faqih* formed an intellectual community of Muslim dissidents around *Kayhān-e Farhangi*. Among them were former intelligence officers, former leaders of Muslim student organizations, and Shari`ati followers who all shared Soroush's anguish over the totalitarian turn of the revolution. The intellectual defenders of Islam against Marxism and liberalism now had to defend their Muslimhood against a clerical establishment whose definition of Islam became increasingly exclusive.

From May 1988 to March 1990, in a four-part essay in *Kayhān-e Farhangi*, entitled *The Theoretical Contraction and Expansion of the Shari`ah*, Soroush laid out the foundation of a theoretical, political, and social engagement with the emerging totalitarianism. While he framed his argument as a matter of the epistemological problems of religious knowledge, his readers had no trouble reading the implications of his thesis. With these essays, Soroush inaugurated an intellectual movement the main premise of which was to salvage Islam from its *officially* sanctioned straitjacket. He knew that his ideas could not remain limited to the pages of a journal of social criticism. He congregated in the early 1990s with a number of key political, academic and intellectual figures and journalists in a group known as the 'Wednesday night circle.'[14]

Soroush did not advocate a political platform. He left the issues of politics and policies out of these meetings. Rather he intended to develop a community in which a 'thousand flowers could bloom.' The Muslim students, whose credentials included invading the American Embassy in Tehran, had reentered the political scene bearing postgraduate degrees in the humanities and social sciences from British universities. Soroush had left an important mark on their education abroad. With an invitation from the Islamic Student Association of the United Kingdom, for six months in the mid-1990s, he delivered a series of lectures and held seminars on his theological position in seventeen British towns and cities.[15] His formal and informal students emerged as the new voice of Islamism, ready to leave behind their Jacobin past and embark on the project of crafting the public sphere of Islam.

After Khomeini's death in June 1989, the Soroushians gradually lost their prominence at *Kayhān-e Farhangi*, the journal no longer welcomed their contributions. Soroush's circle therefore launched its own monthly journal called *Kiyān*. Although Soroush did not hold any official position at the paper, from the publication of its first issue it was conspicuously clear that the journal would express the views of these dissident intellectuals. *Kiyān*, which ran for more than ten years from 1991 until its closure by the order of Tehran's chief prosecutor in 2001, became one of the most contentious venues in which dissident Muslim intellectuals could address their critics. Although it was not the only opposition journal permitted to circulate in these years,[16] it occupied a distinct position among elite literary-political journals. First, the great majority of its articles used Islamic texts as the point of reference. Second, it was influential among Muslim students, who, along with the Muslim women's movement, had become the most organized and sustained political opposition in Iran.[17]

Despite the government's harassment, such as denying the journal its paper ration, *Kiyān* remained in circulation for ten years, a rarity in the oppositional press. Widely read by Muslim as well as the secular intelligentsia, it gave an effective voice to the new tendency among Muslim intellectuals to practice Islamic hermeneutics.

In a survey of its readers, the executive editors of *Kiyān* intended to demonstrate that the majority of its readers considered themselves to be practicing Muslims (80 per cent).[18] Although the majority believed that the journal's mission was *not* the secularization of society, they (68 per cent) also believed that secularization should not be regarded as an anti-religion movement. According to the results, readers who described themselves as not religious believed that *Kiyān* was working toward the privatization of Islam and the secularization of public sphere.

One of the most striking results of the survey was that students, graduates from four-year universities, and government employees made up the bulk of its readership. Recall that after the Cultural Revolution, these groups (students and government employees) were among the most ideologically committed supporters of the revolution, people whose loyalty to the government had been tested and proven. The conspicuous absence of women among *Kiyān's* readers could be explained by the fact that journals with similar critical views, such as *Zanān* (Women) (which focused on gender-conscious readings of Islamic literature, legal, and social women's issues) provided the same critical space for women.[19]

Kiyān's Readers' Survey (N 506)

Personal Data:	Education:	Residence:
Median Age 30	10% Ph.D.	51% Tehran
95% Male	55% BA	46% outside Tehran
56% single		3% abroad

Occupation:	Religious Conviction:
70% government	24% devout Muslim
employees	57% some religious tendencies
	19% non-religious

Source: Summarized from *Kiyān*, vol. 5, no. 26, pp. 46-49

Ten years after the Cultural Revolution, a majority of those who were involved in its implementation now voiced their opposition to its totalitarian implications. Soroush, who stumbled onto the revolutionary scene and became the reluctant spokesperson for the Cultural Revolution Council, was best situated to lead this movement—a movement of those who shared both the culpabilities of the past and the hope for the future.

The combination of his anti-totalitarianism and his unwanted role in a totalitarian project to Islamize higher education pushed Soroush into a contradiction. This socio-political location contributed to the formation of his hermeneutics, the central feature of which was rescuing the religion of Islam from its ideological renditions. Soroush advanced his critique of ideological Islam vis-à-vis two tendencies in Iranian politics and the religious establishment, both of which he condemned for their reductionism. The first was put forward by Shari`ati whose articulation of Islam as a liberation theology became the main ideological frame of the Iranian revolution. The second tendency transformed Islam as liberation theology into a state ideology created by a ruling cleric class of *nomenklatura* with privileged access to the meaning of Islam.

Soroush and the Critique of Islam as State Ideology

Both Shari`ati and Soroush were products of a mixed Islamic and Western education. Shari`ati was educated in rural schools in Khorasan province, its capital city Mashad, and Paris; Soroush attended a famous religious school in Tehran and completed his higher education in London. Both were enthralled by French and British political traditions, respectively, one became a religious sociologist whose agenda was to restore the revolutionary core of Islam, and the other became a Muslim analytical philosopher who advocated a pluralist open society. Whereas Shari`ati perceived religion and its historical mission as an ideology of liberation, in the postrevolutionary period, Soroush took it upon himself to salvage religion from its ideological manifestation.

Although coming from fundamentally different political backgrounds and theoretical orientations, both Shari`ati and Soroush shared a distinctive premise. They both rejected the Weberian perception of modern life as antithetical to religion. Whereas conventional sociological theories are primarily concerned with what religion *does,* and what its *function* in society is, both Shari`ati and Soroush highlighted what religion *is,* and how its believers understand and contest its *meaning*.

Although the Islamic Republic was not established on the basis of Shari`ati's political doctrine, in many respects it realized his conception of Islam as ideology and his Rousseauian 'reconstitution' (*bāz-sāzi*) of society, its goals and its institutions.[20] In contrast to its pre-revolutionary articulation, in its postrevolutionary manifestation, Islam as ideology became a *Sunnified* version of revolutionary Shi`ism.[21] That is, it had to reverse the revolutionary fervor of the masses and to re-orient their anti-establishment proclivities towards organized support for the state.

The Return from Ideology to Religion

> *The admirer of the flower deceives you*
> *If he is not tolerant of its thorn.* Sa`di

In a series of talks and articles, which were collected in the book *Farbeh-tar az eideolozhi* (*Loftier Than Ideology*), Soroush called into question Shari`ati's notion of Islam as ideology. Although formally composed as a critique of his philosophy, Soroush's underlying theme was his rejection of the ideological society established by the Islamic Republic. It is for that reason that since its publication, he has been the target of political and physical attacks by government officials and *hezbollah* mobs. Although Soroush denies that he has any political ambitions,[22] the intellectual community whose emergence he fostered has become the primary agent of political, social, and cultural change in Iran.

Rejecting Shari`ati's theory of permanent revolution, Soroush argued that although useful as a weapon to fight oppression, Islam as ideology and its prescribed establishment of an ideological society was a plague that must be eradicated in order to constitute a free religious society. He asserted that:

- Ideological societies are the breeding ground for the growth of totalitarian and tyrannical systems. Ideological societies do not tolerate diversity.
- Ideological societies become illusionary paragons. 'Opening the door of ideology inevitably results in shutting the door of free thinking. To enter the temple of ideology, human beings need to take off their shoes of reason.'
- In an ideological society, devotion to the cause takes precedence over the integrity of research and analysis.
- The survival of religion depends on its flexibility. When religion becomes a palpable, transparent totality, it will lose its depths and mysteries, and will fade into a mere ideological device for organizing a particular social order.
- In an ideological society, human beings serve ideologies, rather than vice versa. Ideological societies are exceedingly polarized. Ideological thinking is essentially partisan.[23]

Whereas Shari`ati defined ideology as a revolutionary rearticulation of culture, Soroush regarded ideology as distortion of reality. He regarded ideology as a systematic cognitive and epistemological matter rather than, as in Marx, a question of social and historical contingencies.[24] He argued that Marx presupposes a true reality of which ideology was a distorted, falsified representation. Emphasis on the illusory character of ideology suggests that Marx was comparing the ideological construction of reality with a correct non-illusory (more realistic or truthful) way of representation. Although later Engels linked, more explicitly, this non-illusory representation to the positive sciences, what generally legitimized Marxian truth was its privileged historical position. Marxian truth could be defined only from a teleological view, from a prior acceptance of historical determinism.

Soroush proposed that claiming the Truth has always been a part of all Islamic revivalist movements. These movements shared three basic elements. First, they campaigned against folk religious practices and rituals. Associated with *Wahhabism* and some trends of *Salafiyyah* movements, their aim was to create a homogenous and universal conception of Islam through strict and a literal reading of the Qur'an and the *Hadith*. Second, they emphasized the hitherto neglected dimensions of Islam, especially in the realm of *fiqh* (jurisprudence). They offered alternative genealogies of Islamic praxis, as for example in the case of Shari'ati, the Islam of Abu Dharr replaced the Islam of Ibn Sina, an Islam of the vanguard supplanted the Islam of the *'alim*. And finally, they appropriated selective Qur'anic verses which would justify the validity of their socio-political as well as scientific ideas. Thus for example, many proponents of Islamic revival located the root of liberal democracy and electoral politics in the Islamic notion of *shura* or *ijma'* (consultation).[25]

Whereas all Islamic revivalist movements had to separate what was permanently sacred from what was situational and changing in the Islamic text,[26] Soroush distinguished religion as intended by God from humanity's mundane knowledge of it. 'What remains constant is religion [itself] and what changes is religious knowledge.'[27] Humanity could not fathom God's true intentions. Therefore, those who ordain their ideology as the divine commandment of God laid the foundation for totalitarian-ism.[28] All possible interpretations of religion, both the permanent and the historically alterable components, are mundane and informed by socio-cultural particularities. Soroush argued that *any* claim to the truth of Islam transforms religion into an ideology as a falsified world-picture.

The most influential Muslim intellectuals before Soroush, Shari'ati and Motahhari had already emphasized the social, cultural and historical contingencies of religious knowledge. Shari'ati developed the idea in his sociology of Islam,[29] and Motahhari in his critique of *qeshriyyat* (fanaticism). For example, Shari'ati wrote, '*Towhid* descends from the sky and becomes earthly and enters into particular social relations in the context of which its meaning is constructed.'[30] Or in another place, Shari'ati retorted to a critic, 'I shall emphasize that I am a sociologist of religion and I understand *towhid* historically. I am not concerned with the Truth of the Book, or with the correct comprehension of the Qur'an, Mohammad or Ali. For me, the important matter is the social and historical *towhid*, it has always been the most important issue.'[31]

Similarly, on the problem of the cultural and historical contingency of religious knowledge Motahhari argued, 'If one compares *fatwas* of different *foqaha* and at the same time considers their personal lives and states of mind, it becomes clear that the intellectual presuppositions of a *faqih* and his knowledge of the external world inform his *fatwas*. That is why that the *fatwa* of an Arab has an Arab flavor and the *fatwa* of an

Ajam [non-Arab] has an *Ajam* flavor.'[32] Motahhari often compared the Qur'an to nature, a phenomenon that becomes increasingly comprehensible with the passage of time.[33] In contrast to the revivalists who considered pristine renditions of Islam to be more authentic than contemporary interpretations, Motahhari believed that *'future* generations will have a better grasp and a deeper appreciation of the Divine text.'[34]

But neither Shari`ati nor Motahhari developed an epistemological pluralism in which, as Soroush intended, *all* truth-claims become contingent. Soroush did not question the certainty of faith, but highlighted its ineffability. In this light, he rejected the revivalist (reformist or revolutionary) distinction between eternal and ephemeral, text and context. These binaries presuppose the responsibility of the reformist to define religion *as intended* by God in a modern formulation.

Soroush's Distinction Between Ideology and Religion.

IDEOLOGY	RELIGION
A weapon against oppression	Cannot be contained in any specific context
Elucidative, certain, and dogmatic	Intricate, enigmatic, and mystifying
Exclusivist, a 'garb' put on a particular society, reconstitutes society to fit its historical vision	Adaptive, it fits any society in every historical period, like the air all societies breathe
Theory of a movement, not seeker of the truth	A light for the movement and a guide for the seekers of truth
Requires official exponent	Requires neither the clergy nor any other institutionalized forum
Concerned with the shari`ah (canonized law)	More encompassing than the shari`ah (mysticism, folk cultures, theosophy, etc.)

Summarized and tabulated based on *Loftier Than Ideology*

In a series of contradistinctions, Soroush charted the differences between religion and ideology. The central point of these comparisons was the negation of any religious knowledge based on a privileged access to the essence of Islam. Such a privilege, he insisted, would inevitably lead to totalitarianism. Access to the essence of religion was neither conceivable nor desirable, he argued, for it only would give rise to a privileged *nomenklatura*, whether clerical or revolutionary.

In contrast to revivalists' Islamic ideology, which interprets the finality of Islam as a sign of its exhaustive rigidity, Soroush contended that Islam's finality signifies its indeterminate fluidity. The finality of Islam means that every generation experiences revelation *anew*. 'Thus,' he remarks, 'revelation incessantly permeates us, in the same way that it hailed the Arabs [during the time of the Prophet], as if the Prophet were chosen today. The secret of the finality of Islam lies in the perpetuity of the revelation.'[35] Accordingly, he transformed the *shari`ah* from a pre-conceived dogma into a continuously renewed and contested text.[36]

The Theory of **Shari`at-e Sāmet,** *the Silent Shari`ah*

In his opera *Moses und Aron*,[37] Arnold Schoenberg transposes the biblical verse in which Moses laments he is 'slow of speech and slow of tongue' into a philosophical statement about the ineffability of God. He transfers the power of communication over to Aaron, whose rhetoric inevitably distorts Moses' theology. The opera turns a heavy tongue into a potent symbol of the conflicts between thought and political action, revolutionary ideals and political realities.   In effect, Schoenberg invites his audience to hear the word of God in the silence of Moses.

By abandoning Islam as ideology, Soroush sought to reclaim the enigma of religion. Rather than being a manifesto for action, the *shari`ah* is silent, it is given voice by its exponents. It is like history, which is given voice by the historian, or nature, the laws of which are constructed by the scientist. The *shari`ah* does not put forward immutable answers to predicaments of all historical moments. That is not to suggest that 'The silence of the *shari`ah* empties it of any meaning. Rather, its silence impedes any particular group from claiming access to its essence whereby they would prohibit and condemn competing understandings of religion.'[38]  One cannot regard the *shari`ah* as an *a priori* knowledge. Religiosity demands an incessantly renewed exegesis. Accordingly, one cannot presuppose any particular meaning of the *shari`ah* and then consider changes in its interpretation to be problematic.[39]

Various movements to make religion contemporary were based on a fallacy: one cannot *make* religion contemporary, any comprehension of religion is already contemporary. 'The modernity of religious knowledge is a description rather than a prescription.'[40] Human cognition is contingent on time and place and it comprehends only what religion *is* rather than what it *ought to* be. In other words, one grasps the social-temporal existence of religion, not its divine-absolute essence.[41]

Soroush considered the religious text to be *hungry for* rather than *impregnated with* meaning. He believes that meaning is given to religion rather than extracted from it.[42] 'In every era,' he remarked, 'the *ulama* interpolate new questions and devise new responses from the *shari`ah* [...] The *totality* of these questions and answers define the contemporaneous religious knowledge.'[43] He argued that the mistaken identification of religion with the knowledge of it emanates either from '*fiqhi* positivism' or 'popular idealism.' Here Soroush borrowed from Allameh Tabataba'i's who defined Islamic realism in contrast to Berkeleyian idealism and positivist empiricism.[44] In Tabataba'i's view the proponents of neither idealism nor positivism recognized any difference between human representations of reality and brute phenomena. For the positivist, the real is the tangible, thus objectively comprehensible through its transmission by senses. In contrast, the idealist regards existential reality as the reflection of *a priori* ideas lodged in the mind. Thus Soroush referred to '*fiqhi* positivism' as a doctrine that highlights the primacy of jurisprudence (*fiqh*) in religion and equates jurisprudential knowledge of religion with religion itself.[45] It is only in the idealist's perception that subjectivity and existence were identical and inseparable. 'The minimum condition for a realist epistemology is the distinction between the object and the knowledge of it. Therefore, our understanding of the *shari`ah*, even if we consider it flawless, is distinct from the *shari`ah* itself.'[46]

History, Culture, and Religious Knowledge

> *O core of existence! It is a matter of point of view*
> *The divisions between the faithful, the heretic, and the Jew.*
>
>   Rumi

Soroush premised his philosophy on three ideas: (1) although religion is revealed by God, the moment it enters human subjectivity, it becomes particular and culturally and historically contingent; (2) religious knowledge corresponds to and is related and informed by other mundane forms of knowledge; (3) religious knowledge is progressive and its progress depends on changes in the human understanding of the physical world, i.e. science, and on new shared values of various societies, i.e. socio-political rights, and rights of women.

He proposed an epistemological pluralism based on what he recognized as competing interpretations of the *shari'ah*, so long as these interpretations are 'systematic' and 'methodical.'[47] 'A singular interpretation of the text is neither desirable nor possible.' Thus he advised, 'a wise *'ālim* of religion is conscious of his/her own standpoint, and does not deny the particularity of his/her view.'[48]

Soroush viewed the comprehension of religion as an historically progressive human endeavor that will inevitably lead future generations to a 'better and deeper grasp of the *shari'ah*.'[49] He skillfully wedded his Sufi language of skepticism with the Kantian neo-positivism of Karl Popper, to whose liberal political philosophy he subscribed. In his theory of the 'silent *shari'ah*,' Soroush was influenced by Popper's post-positivist doctrine of falsification.[50] He applied his principle of falsification to religious truth, arguing that the Truth of religion is not verifiable, and that *all* religious truth claims were falsifiable with reference to evolving scientific knowledge of the world.[51]

His main thesis is that human comprehension of religion is ephemeral, collective, and historical.[52] But neither his conception of collectivity nor his understanding of the historical character of this knowledge led him to abandon his methodological individualism. For Soroush, collective religious knowledge was imper-vious to actual lived religious experiences. In line with Shari'ati and Motahhari, he adopted an elitist understanding of knowledge. Collective knowledge of religion could only be institutionalized in the 'society of religious scholars' with the means to grasp Islam 'systematically.'[53]

Soroush also understood the historical character of religious knowledge in relation to the *accumulation* of knowledge over time, rather than to the socio-historical conditions of its production in each period. He emphasized the cultural particularity of religious knowledge, even to the extent of considering Arabic the 'coincidental' language of Islam.[54] But he ridiculed those who argued that 'knowledge is geographically bound and [...] history conditions the content of thoughts.' He reproached them as 'enemies of thinking. Their worship of the Golden Calf of history has now led them to worship the Cow of Fascism.'[55] He derided them that

> In their critique of ideas, our devout Hegelians[56] resort to the instrument of history rather than the device of logic. If they reject an opinion, it is not for the *fatwa* of reason, but for the necessities of an historical epoch. They put a stamp of 'reactionary' or 'progressive' on ideas based on their worship of the future, they leave the place of rationalism vacant [...] Their final

judge is history not reason, for they have decapitated reason by the order of the God of history.[57]

For Soroush, Reason is transhistorical. Accordingly, he rejected historical relativism as well as ideological absolutism. Both trends negate the independence of reason and are based upon the age-old tradition of 'intellectual-bashing' (roshanfekr-setizi).

Despite his hostility to Hegelian philosophy, like Hegel, he situated reason beyond history and culture.[58] Rather than a hermeneutical approach to religion, he regarded religious knowledge historically and culturally contingent to the extent that it corresponded to the historical March of Reason and reflected contemporary social and natural scientific knowledge. In a positivist vein, he bestowed on science and Reason the authority to arbitrate the correspondence between 'Religion Itself' and human knowledge of it. In Soroush's epistemology, the more religious knowledge corresponds to the sciences of time, the closer it becomes to Religion Itself. Whereas in his critique of ideology, human interest and political aspirations corrupt the true knowledge of religion, science and rationality remain devoid of politics.[59] As Hamid Dabashi aptly observes,

> Absent from Soroush's conception of social and biological sciences, with which he believes the religious sciences [sic] ought to converse, is any awareness of the presence, force, and ferocity of power in their very epistemic and operative parameters.[60]

However Soroush was not blind to the contradiction between the contingencies of human knowledge and the objectivity of scientific knowledge. To address this problem, he revived Hans Reichenbach's old debate between the social context of discovery and rational justification of scientific claims, in order to argue that only in the 'context of discovery,' could culture, politics, and history informed and condition scientific progress.[61] It is through 'epistemological rigor' that scientists exclude extra-scientific elements from their work and present an objective justification for their findings. In their rational justification the sciences were essentially aloof from contingency. It is the case because 'mathematics and the instruments of exact observation of natural and experimental sciences have made scientific claims stronger in the context of justification. Exact mathematization liberates meaning from its nebulous qualitative state.'[62]

While Soroush intended to liberate Islam from ideology by denying anyone, clerical or otherwise, privileged access to its essence, he offered parallel privileges to the heroic scientists who divulge the mysteries of nature.   His romanticized scientist, transcends the contingencies of power relations, culture, and history, practices his profession outside of his enabling social institutions suddenly emerges as the author of a model to which religious knowledge aspires.   In this way, Soroush elevated science in the 'context of justification' to the status of a neutral arbiter between competing interpretations of religion.   One may suspect that such a model would inevitably 'deplete Muslims of historical agency,'[63] for to act as a Muslim, one needs to have convictions about what Islam is.   While Soroush approved of competing interpretations of religion, he rendered irrelevant the everyday Islam of the masses by identifying scientific knowledge as the point of reference for the plausibility of religious knowledge.

Secularism, Democracy, and the Religious State

In spite of his pronouncements of his distance from politics, the most profound implication of Soroush's 'silence of the *shari`ah*' is political rather than philosophical.   Although he denied that he had any political ambitions, he recognized that 'to regard religious knowledge as ephemeral is to lay the foundation of a *democratic* religious state.'[64]   In 1992 and 1993, in two public lectures in Tehran and Hamburg, he introduced his idea of 'religious democratic state.'[65]   While this idea seemed to his critics to be an oxymoron,[66] Soroush defended it based on an idiosyncratic definition of the state.

Addressing the alleged contradiction between the religiosity and democracy, Soroush divided governance into three semi-independent spheres: (a) rights and responsibilities; (b) the scientific management of society; (c) and values.   Whereas in the realm of values the state may adopt religion as a guiding principle, in the 'scientific management of society' and citizens' rights governance should remain secular.

a. *Rights and Responsibilities:* The question of extra-religious rights preoccupied Morteza Motahhari, who profoundly influenced Soroush's notion of how citizens' rights should be conceived under an Islamic state.   He argued that his segregation of 'Religion Itself' from its human knowledge, and the transformation of the language of religion from 'obligations (*takallof*) to rights (*hoquq*)' would blur the conventional distinction between a Muslim and a non-Muslim.   An Islamic state may exclusively protect the rights of its Muslim citizens, but only if its administrators consider themselves in the position of determining who is a Muslim and who is not.   In a talk presented at a meeting with steel

industry trainees in Italy, where he addressed the question of
Muslimhood and Development, Soroush stated,

> In this world we need to draw a line between Muslims and
> apostates. This distinction, however, draws a partisan and
> political line, it conveys a worldly distinction, similar to physical
> boundaries between countries. But these distinctions would
> never become the basis of the Divine judgment. In the hereafter,
> these nominal differences are null and void.[67]

Questioning Sheikh Fazlollah Nuri's rejection of liberty and equality as
un-Islamic, he argued that 'there were no contradictions between Islam
and the ideas of the leaders of the constitutional revolution [of 1906].'[68]
Rather than a matter of jurisprudence (*fiqh*)(that is the knowledge of the
religion from within), he considered citizens' rights in a religious state to
be a political questions 'essentially based upon the knowledge of the
religion from without.'[69]

For Soroush, democratic Islamic state should derive its legitimacy
neither from a divine source, like the church in the European experience
of theocracy, nor from historical necessity, like Communism.[70] Rather, by
recognizing the divine origin of natural rights, a democratic Islamic state
should acknowledge the rights of its citizens to elect and depose their
leaders. 'The right of self-determination,' he insisted, 'is one of the non-
religious rights of people.'[71]

He acknowledged that the main predicament of the democratic
religious state was to establish a legal-political system that reconciled
respect for human rights with one's 'responsibilities towards the
Almighty.' For a believer, the question of rights (political freedom) is
intertwined with one's obligation to obey God. God's existence is an *a
priori* knowledge that inevitably would give rise to such questions as
'does God have any rights? Must we respect those rights? Does respect
for God's rights belittle one's concern for human rights?'[72]

While later in his career he would openly advocate political
liberalism, Soroush tried to separate the liberal from the Muslim political
subject. He argued that whereas liberal democracies are based on individualism and private religion, the pursuit of happiness under a religious
democratic state is inseparable from the religiosity of its subjects. Unlike
the religious person who searches for the ideal human being, he
advanced this distinction:

> The liberal does not seek the ideal, but the normal, a compliant,
> docile human in harmony with others. Sin is no more a sin but

an illness to be treated by psychologists and physicians who have taken the place of preachers of morality. Disease is not to be feared but to be looked upon compassionately and to be cured by doctors.[73]

How the rights of God are satisfied within a religious democratic state and what institutional means might there be for this satisfaction, remained opaque in Soroush's critique of liberal individualism.

b. *State as the 'Scientific Management' of Society:* He simply adopted a *laissez faire* philosophy in his depiction of the state administration as a non-ideological, independent system of organizing and maintaining the social contract. Whereas the religious state derives its values and ideals from religion, it borrows its operative methods from the 'science of management.' 'In the same way that there does not exist a *religious* thermodynamics, or *religious* geometry,' he remarked, 'governance [*hukumat*] cannot become religious.'[74] He asserted that the 'scientific management of society should be free from religious and ideological dogma.'[75] Thereby, he substituted the technocrat ('the scientist of social management') for the ideologue as the agent of state policy.

Soroush's preference for apolitical technocrats over ideological operatives to shape state policy is explicable only if one considers it in the context of the postrevolutionary regime in Iran. Each new administration since its founding has reinvented state bureaucracy by appointing their faction's operatives in managerial positions of the government. One of the key elements that has impeded the institution-alization of the revolution and continuity in state apparatus has been the absence of career bureaucrats in key decision-making and planning positions. But Soroush's *laissez faire* view not only empties the state of politics, it also naturalizes society as a mass entity requiring administrative management rather than recognizing it as a political phenomenon that is perpetuated by contestation and cooperation.

c. *Values and Goals:* Religion, he reminded his readers, gives society a sense of purpose and ideals. A democratic state should reflect these ideals and conform to the general spirit of a shared social conception of the 'good society.' He regards a state to be undemocratic if it does not reflect the general will. A state cannot be religious if it did not emanate from a religious society. In effect, Soroush rediscovered the early *Salafiyyah* doctrine that 'a religious state emanates from a religious society.'

Soroush leaves details of his conception of the religious democratic state unexplained. He offers no solution to the conundrum of fusing the religious and secular spheres of his three-fold division of governance into a practicable unity. How would the guiding religious values be defined? Which state institution would define them? How would they be integrated into the state policies? What would be the institutional means of resolving conflicts between the three constitutive elements of the state? For example, should an economist proposes an increase in production as the precondition of development, how would the reconcile this with the Islamic principle of modesty and contentment, of which Soroush himself is an advocate?

Soroush's democratic state is Islamic merely because it is instituted in a Muslim society. One does not *make* the state Islamic, in a Muslim society it simply *is*. The consequence of such an assertion in the post-revolutionary context was unambiguous. He intended to situate the sphere of religious articulation of the 'good society' outside of matters of governance and back into civil society. But as many of his own disciples point out, as a general theory of democratic state, his idea lacks consistency and clarity. If one does not *make* a state Islamic, Soroush's critics wondered, how could they justify the Islamic revolution? If a state is simply Islamic because it has emerged in a Muslim society, would that not lead to the political quietism against which Shari`ati and others rebelled?[76]

If we remain faithful to Soroush's own separation between Islam itself and Muslims' beliefs and practices, the Islamic character of the state should have nothing to do with Islam as intended by God but with how Muslims understand, contest, and rearticulate its meaning. In short, Soroush does not explicate whose version of Islam reflects the religiosity of the society and how that particular version becomes hegemonic in each historical moment.

Conceptions of Science and Technology
a. Science

In a journal called *Nur-e `Elm* (*The Light of Science*), Ayatollah Azari Qomi, an influential senior cleric, denounced the policies of the Iranian Central Bank un-Islamic. In a lecture delivered at Isfahan University on the anniversary of the unification of the seminary and the university, Soroush endorsed the remarks made by the President of the Central Bank to the effect that 'economic laws are unrelated to ideology.'[77]

Following the most prominent theoreticians of Islamic economy, Mohammad Baqir Sadr, Soroush argued that Islamic economics only furnishes economic values, 'the science of economics is external to religion.'[78] By the *science* of economy he meant econometrics, the mathematical schemes for measuring the degree of success or failure in achieving economic goals. Whether Islamic economy merely adds Islamic morality to capitalism (or socialism), or signifies a fundamentally distinct economic system, is not my concern here.[79] However, I would like to underline that the conception of a non-ideological, objective science informs Soroush's rejection of Islam as ideology.

Soroush learned from the experience of the Cultural Revolution that an Islamic Lysenkoism[80] was in the making under the Islamic Republic. He rigorously defended the integrity of the scientific method and chastised those who judged the results of a scientific experiment from an ideological standpoint. 'Science is validated and judged by experimentation,' and it is the community of scientists not party ideologues (Islamic or otherwise) who give meaning to these experiments.[81] He contended that western societies are 'science-based,' where 'politics, ethics, industry, development, art, and all other aspects of social life' are explained through references to science.[82] 'Yes,' he acidly declared, 'science is not neutral, but what is more neutral than science?'[83]

He regarded the social and cultural study of scientific knowledge as the latest incarnation of relativism. He therefore cautioned his readers against those Muslim intellectuals who 'naively believe that refuting the scientific character of human sciences is in the interest of Islamic thought.'[84] Although his fear of Islamic Lysenkoism should be taken seriously, his alternative, restoring the apolitical, ahistorical states of science, lacks novelty. Soroush's alternative stemmed from his misconception of the social studies of science: he mistakenly identified *reflexivity* with relativism; and he neglected the reciprocal and overlapping discourses of legitimacy in science, law, political power, and culture.

Rather than seeking neutrality, the social and cultural studies of science propose that scientific knowledge must be legitimized the realms of law and politics reflexively. As Jean-François Lyotard wrote,

> Since 'reality' is what provides the evidence used as proof in scientific argumentation, and also provides prescriptions and promises of a juridical, ethical, and political nature with results, one can master all of these games by mastering 'reality.' [...] This is how legitimation by power takes shape. Power is not only good performativity, but [it is] also effective verification and good verdicts. It legitimates science and law on the basis of their efficiency, and legitimates this efficiency on the basis of science and law. It is self-legitimating in the same way a system organized around performance maximization seems to be.[85]

In a speech for the first anniversary of the Cultural Revolution in 1980, Soroush compared science to a 'self-nourishing forest' which grows on its own will and does not 'conform to external demands.' But in order for this forest to grow, we need to Islamize its soil. 'Our responsibility,' he asserted, 'is to Islamize the environment (*faza*), after that all matters will naturally become Islamic and will bear the scent of this garden. If we plant a fig tree, the fruit of that tree will be figs.'[86] Science follows its own *internal* logic, but it blooms when it is placed in a conducive environment. Soroush's attempt to naturalize science and situate scientific progress outside human affairs is more striking when we take into account the fact that he, as a member of the Cultural Revolution Council, delivered his address a year after the massacre on the university campuses, as part of the campaign to 'Islamize the environment.'

Soroush's internalist/naturalist perspective on scientific progress is one of the reasons he considers science to be a point of reference for religious knowledge. Referring to Kuhn, Feyerabend, and Rorty, he lamented that philosophical critiques of the objectivity of science, 'have conquered the last entrenchment of rationality held by the neo-Kantian philosophy of Karl Popper.' Thomas Kuhn, Paul Feyerabend, Richard Rorty, and other proponents of post-empiricism, he declared,

> Sacrificed scientific methods and the logic of discovery for the sake of history and decapitated modern sciences, the purest signifier of rationality, at the feet of relativism. They argued that science is an ideological construct and, horrified at the consequences of their own deposition, they collapsed the bridges to the lost haven [of rationality].[87]

By contrasting post-empiricism with rationality and its 'purest signifier,' Soroush suggested that under the guise of *post*-modernism, these philosophers wished to revive *pre*-modern modes of expression. The impact of modern science on the human understanding of nature and of one's self is irreversible. But many believe otherwise, seeking to deprecate science as a socio-cultural ritual by linking it to 'power' (Foucault), to 'human interest' (Habermas), to 'cultural determinants and social relations' (the Edinburgh School, David Bloor and Barry Barnes), to 'the unconscious ideology of the community of scientists' (Thomas Kuhn), and to 'cosmology and sorcery' (Paul Feyerabend).[88]

Since Soroush conceived the advancement of science and rationality as a natural progression, any social, cultural, or historical qualification appeared to him to be both reactionary and futile. But as many critics of modern sciences have argued, neither science nor rationality offers universal measures of excellence. 'They are,' Feyerabend writes, 'particular traditions, unaware of their historical grounding.'[89] Science is not a 'fig tree,' it is a socially constructed enterprise upon which laws are written and political systems are legitimized.

One can extend Soroush's skepticism about ideological claims to privileged access to the essence of religion, to the realm of science (the religion of modernity) and argue for its social contingency. Soroush concedes that although 'science is logically distinct from values,' they are 'intertwined and inseparable in practice.'[90] Science here appears like revelation, logically pure, but profane in practice. But the question remains, does science exist outside its practice? When science steps out of the universe of logic, like religion, it enters the realm of human interest and fallibility. Reflexivity, which Soroush misidentifies as relativism, is about divulging values and presuppositions already embedded in science, and demystifying its claims. Far from responding to its *internal* logic, scientific knowledge is produced in a web of political, economic, and cultural networks.

b. *Technology*

Far from his philosophical abstractions about science, Soroush's remarks about technology were romantic and simplistic.

> If we define the happiness and the well-being of human beings in conquering and demystifying nature, dominating its forces and utilizing its energies, building machines, and alleviating human suffering, science would continue the same wrong path it has already taken.[91]

Such a perception of happiness in modern societies has led to the cultural dominance of technological thinking. Although critical of Heideggerian tendencies among Iranian intellectuals, in his own discussion, Soroush relied heavily on Jacques Ellul's classic Heideggerian study of technology.[92] He borrowed Ellul's five characteristics of technology (automationism; self-augmentation; universalism; autonomy; and monism) to argue that technology is a substantive totality—it implies a particular social order and human character. 'Ellul was right,' he stated, 'in asserting that in the pre-modern era, human beings were masters of their skills and instruments, but modernity brought the mastery of technology to dominate humanity.'[93]

Soroush considered technology to be a cultural system that restructures the social world according to its inherent characteristics.[94] One could not separate the application from the conditions of the emergence of a particular technology, each necessitated the other. He therefore chastised the crude naïveté of those who wished to adopt technologies for purposes other than their intended application. Whereas western science could be acquired *ad hoc*, 'utilizing technology demands the appropriation of the relations of its production.'[95]

Soroush drew a conceptual distinction between science and technology, between the way the two are politically and ideologically regulated and produced. Science responds to its internal dynamics, but technology engages all spheres of social life and transforms society into its object. Therefore, technology, unlike science, needed to be disciplined by cultural and political policy. Unlike science, which was organized from within, technology needed to be regulated from without. As a totality, technology could not be contained by its own internal logic; that is to say, there could be no technological solutions to the problems of technology. Harmless, environmentally friendly technology does not exist. Since modern technology was interrelated, its compartments could not be extracted for piecemeal use.[96]

Soroush provided a long list of grievances of the destructive consequences of technology. The following demonstrates how he considered modern technologies to be the origin of decadence.

> [Technology] pollutes the environment; it threatens personal and social security by the production of means of mass destruction and electronic surveillance devices; it emphasizes competition, speed, greed, envy, and development; it functions as the undeniable tool of oppression; it was born out of animosity with nature; its development disregards human values and traditions; it produces new needs and awakens lost desires; it assumes the divine role of creation; it has demystified the world and has created a meaningless, unholy, and dispensable world; it has alienated human beings from themselves.[97]

Although he acknowledged that 'ridding ourselves of the web of technological life is implausible,' he criticized the idea of 'catching up' with the West through technological advancement. 'The more we try to "catch up,"' he wailed, 'the farther we grow apart from ourselves.'[98] But what is the solution?

Although Soroush drew a bleak picture of modern life, he found relief from the tyranny of technology in simplicity (*sādegi*) and austerity (*qanā`at*). Similar to Ellul's 'technical phenomenon' and Weber's 'iron cage,' for him, retreat offers the only escape from technological society.

He put forward three provisions for the realization of contentment: (1) eliminate excess and clutter, both in production and consumption; (2) discourage the production of new needs, and the legitimation of speed and greed, the essential features of technology; (3) apply the principle of 'small is beautiful,' respect local technological know-how and self-reliance. One wonders how Soroush would reconcile an interventionist state that implements these 'contentment' policies with his *laissez faire* technocratic vision.

Although he typically avoids specific policy recommendations, he did admonish those who proposed the construction of a metro system to solve Tehran's traffic problem. Instead, he asked, 'could we not substitute bicycles for cars, to make the commute easier, the air cleaner, and our bodies healthier and stronger?'[99] Soroush's specific policy recommendations often contradict one another. While he believed that technology is a substantive, interrelated system, he insisted that in a hostile world Iran needs a strong military to defend itself against the 'evil forces of the enemies.'[100] He leaves unanswered questions about how it would be possible to discipline the adoption of sophisticated military technology and contain its civilian appropriation.

Just as he failed to show how the religious values of the state could be institutionalized, the *institutional* manifestation of Soroush's ideals of austerity and simplicity similarly remains unexplored. He refrained from reconciling his 'elimination of excess' with the 'flower of freedom,' which was the primary foundation of justice. Nor did he specify which institution would be responsible for defining excess and how would it enforce it? The Iranian government believes that satellite dishes open the door to corruption and decadence. Would Soroush support the removal the dishes from the rooftops? Should the government police cyberspace?

The emergence of Soroush as a globally recognized Muslim intellectual negates the unidirectional transformative authority of technology. Without electronic networking, thanks to which news of his travels, conference participation, *hezbollah* disruptions of his talks, and so on, have been widely publicized, Soroush might have remained a philosopher at the margins of Iranian politics. He has gained international recognition through the most sophisticated technologies of communication, so much so that *The New York Times* (11/8/1997) called him a leading dissident voice and on May 10, 1998, CBS's *60 Minutes* featured him as one of the central figures in Iranian politics. The transformative authority of technology is indeterminate, it is the result of competing interests in the sphere of social and political struggles.

The issues of production and consumption are particularly controversial in Iranian cultural politics. Production and consumption are a litmus test of Soroush's vision of a nation that does not value greed and competition, where the ideology of catching up has not colonized its soul. Many have criticized Soroush's technological romanticism, mostly from an instrumentalist perspective. As one critic argues, there is sufficient historical evidence to prove that technology is merely a tool in the hands of whoever utilizes it. 'So long as technology was situated within Islamic world,' N. Fakhroddin writes, 'it brought equilibrium and contentment, but in the hands of those who have abandoned their divine values it became the instrument of domination, oppression, exploitation, colonialism and the massacre of indigenous peoples.'[101]

Another critic warns that Soroush's conception of contentment and austerity is nothing but the romanticization of poverty. He ridiculed him for his sentimental Luddition and compared his vision of the good society to Amish life in Pennsylvania:

> Amish country is based on the condemnation of technology and the maintenance of their *ancien regime*. They are pious, do not drink alcohol, their men grow their beard, and their women wear *hijab* (they cover their hairs, wear long dresses and never use make up). They do not have electricity, do not use a car or ride a bus, and etc. [...] Iran cannot be transformed into an Amish country.[102]

In response to his critics, Soroush argued that those who separate technology from its destructive consequences believe that westerners are inherently evil and anything in their hands would become an instrument of oppression and exploitation. Technology would have the same effects on societies whether used by Muslims or Westerners.

On Westoxication

Although Soroush's conception of technology and development might suggest otherwise, he has been consistently critical of the notion of westoxication and its critics' representation of the West. He argued that the discourse of *gharbzadegi* was based on two false premises, namely (a) the conception of the West as an inseparable totality; and (b) the conception of the self as pure and authentic.[103] Consequently, the advocates of the discourse constructed a mutually exclusive conception of the self and the West, where the emancipation of the former was to be realized with the total negation of the latter. Soroush questioned fundamentals of the premise of the return to a pure, authentic self.[104]

The Conception of the West

Soroush argued that 'the West' as a singular and homogenous entity does not exist, neither geographically nor metaphysically. Conceiving the West as an evil essence perpetuates popular ignorance about its history and cultures, it only serves as a tool for political gain.[105] The critics of *gharbzadegi* objectify the West into a monolithic phenomenon to which they attribute all vices. They transform the West into an agent of history, with a shared transcendental *Geist*, who has controlled the destiny of all humanity. 'Can we say,' he asked, 'that the West is wherever there is vice? Or, conversely, wherever we find vice there is the West? Do we recognize the Western *Geist* from the West? Or the West through its *Geist*?'[106]

He pointed out at the center of the critique of *gharbzadegi* lied a demonized unified West, *independent from its actors*. This ahistorical perception generates the binary of total rejection versus wholesale acceptance of the West. 'The West,' he stressed, 'is not an entity, or a unified *Geist* embedded in all Westerners [...] such an underlying substrate of Being does not exist, *mā lā wahda lahu, lā wujud lahu* (a thing that does not have unity in substance does not exist).'[107] That West was a fiction that haunts its authors. We must engage the westerners who share a unified *Geist,* neither in their philosophy, nor in their cultural, traditional, artistic or intellectual expressions. 'The Western *Geist* is a trope that should not be taken seriously!'[108] Indeed, westoxication conveys a disease, 'but a disease created by the delusion of those who attributed an indivisible totality to the West and then found themselves entrapped by it.'[109]

By negating the existence of the West as a totality, Soroush intended to demystify its fictional substrate of Being. Rather than an existential reality, the West should be perceived as 'a compilation of thoughts, arts, techniques and industries, politics, manners and rituals, and etc., each of which may be espoused or rejected independently from the totality from which it has emanated.'[110] For example, one should not assume that embracing Kant ushers in an unmitigated acceptance of 'the West,' or the justification of European colonialism. Such a view suggests that 'Westerners are all aware of and subscribe to a Kantian philosophy,' or 'Kant should be held responsible for all the atrocities committed by Western powers.'[111]

Not only do the critics of westoxication interpret every aspect of the West as a manifestation of its totality, they also believe that the West has reached the end of its history. Soroush pointed out that by denouncing everything Western, the militant Iranian *gharb-setizān* (West-bashers)— rely on a determinist view of history through which they depict Westerners as homogenous and without agency. 'Gharbzadegi presupposes historical determinism.'[112] Echoing his earlier arguments against Marxism, Soroush reminded the West-bashers (*themselves a construct of the West*)[113] that 'the West did not emerge as an historical necessity, and it is not following a predetermined path of history; it could have been constructed differently and faces various paths in the future.'[114]

Nevertheless, he did not intend to discredit the entire critique of westoxication. He viewed Shari`ati and Al-e Ahmad in a different light from those, such as Fardid and Davari, who essentialize anything that emanates the West, particularly western humanism. Indeed Soroush endorsed Al-e Ahmad's oft-cited assertion that 'so long as [the Iranians] do not comprehend the philosophical essence [sic] and foundations of Western civilization, and only ape the outer shells of the West, we shall remain like the ass going about in a lion's skin.'[115] Whereas the *West-bashers* regarded modern technology as the physical manifestation of the metaphysical West, Al-e Ahmad and Shari`ati defined *westoxication* as technological determinism. 'We need to build and appropriate machines,' Al-e Ahmad remarked, 'but must not be enslaved by them.'[116] More than a rejection of the West, in his conception of *gharbzadegi*, Al-e Ahmad was concerned with the critique of the alienated self. 'One cannot find a single place in the work of Al-e Ahmad and others who followed him,' Soroush pointed out, 'where he deplored the West along with its technology.'[117] In effect, rather than regarding the West as a decadent totality, in his notion of *westoxication*, Al-e Ahmad was more concerned with the state of the Iranian self.

> In Al-e Ahmad's conception, *gharbzadegi* referred to the state of an alienated self in awe of the West [...] Al-e Ahmad spoke of the invasion of western technique, customs and rituals, the arts, science, and technology and how this intrusion has distorted our traditions, beliefs, and human relations. But he insisted that we have lost *ourselves* in our encounter with the West. Our connection with our tradition, with our past, with our history is severed. We have become people with neither a past to be proud of nor a future to look forward to.[118]

Thus Soroush inverted the critique of *gharbzadegi* from an anti-imperialist discourse into a device for self-criticism. His intervention became significant in the context of contentious politics of the postrevolutionary society in which competing views of national identity directly influenced and shaped state policies.

The Return to 'Authentic Self' (Bāzgasht beh khish)

The fallacy of the *gharbzadegi* discourse was rooted in a conception of an authentic Iranian self to which westoxicated society ought to retreat. 'Return to self,' Soroush complained, 'is an ambiguous message' which has been widely advocated by the world's most respected anti-colonial intellectuals, from Ali Shari'ati and Al-e Ahmad to Aimé Césaire and Frantz Fanon. These theorists never discussed what 'the "self" to which we need to return is [...] in these theories, the "self" and the "Other" substitute for "right" and "wrong," respectively.'[119]

Soroush provided a long list of these writers who appeared to promote the return to a culturally authentic self as the goal of decolonization. Yet his critique of these intellectuals is just as sweeping and oversimplified. Whereas Soroush was admirably thorough in laying out his own arguments, he is often hasty in treating others' ideas. Neither Fanon nor Aimé Césaire had misgivings about colonial encounters and the historical transformation of the colonial subject. Fanon stated that

> Decolonization is the veritable creation of a new man [sic]. But this creation owes nothing of its legitimacy to any supernatural power, the 'thing' which has been colonized becomes man during the same process by which it frees itself.[120]

> [...] We must not therefore be content with delving into the past of a people in order to find coherent elements which will counteract colonialism's attempts to falsify and harm. A national culture is not a folklore, nor an abstract populism that believes it can discover the people's true nature.[121]

> [...] The consciousness of self is not the closing of a door to communication. Philosophic thought teaches us, on the contrary, that it is its guarantee. National consciousness, which is not nationalism, is the only thing that will give us an international dimension.[122]

Soroush also misplaced Aimé Césaire in his long list merchants of authenticity. Echoing Fanon's skepticism about cultural authenticity, Aimé Césaire rejected his critics' assertion in which he was portrayed as a prophet of the *return to the pre-European past*. "For my part," Césaire replied in bafflement, "I search in vain for the place where I could have expressed such views; where I ever underestimated the importance of Europe in the history of human thought; where I ever preached a *return* of any kind; where I ever claimed that there could be a *return*."[123]

Despite his mistaken identification of Fanon and Césaire as advocates of an essentialist notion of national identity, Soroush rightly rebuked those who searched for authenticity on the basis of a dogmatic division of the world into mutually exclusive "East" and "West." For him return to self was meaningless. He emphasized hybrid sources and origins of culture, which was "changing and ephemeral."[124] "The "Self,"' he wrote, 'is born in every moment.'

> Rebelling against the 'self' is also part of the selfhood. Rectifying is an element of maintaining an identity, 'becoming' is part of 'being.' Therefore, cultural revival is a 'movement' and a 'transformation' of self and of culture [...] The problem arises from the historical awareness of the heterogeneity of the 'self.' It is the desire to privilege one element of the self over the others, i.e. communal or religious selves. That fosters cultural anxiety. There is an anxiety over the loss of the permanent and stable communal 'self' or permanent religious 'self,' none of which of course exists in reality.[125]

Rather than asking who Iranians are, how they have lost their identity, or how they can retreat to their former selves, as *gharbzadegi* theorists proposed, the point of departure for Soroush was how to *ascertain and construct* Iranian selves. An already enriched, flawless, and composed self, he asserted, 'never existed.' 'We need to prioritize the *articulation* of the self over the *return* to it.'[126]

Similar to Fanon, Soroush is anti-essentialism. He advanced an idea of Iranian national consciousness, which was constructed in the convergence of three sources: Iranian, Islamic, and Western. Accordingly, rather than an intrusive alien totality, he considers the West to be an eradicable element of Iranian intellectual production and cultural identity. Simliar to Morteza Motahhari's assertion about the reciprocal relation between Islam and Iran,[127] Soroush reiterates th idea that anything the origin of which is located outside one's cultural map should not be regarded pejoratively as the Other. Iranian might find the 'remedy' to the 'disease of *gharbzadegi*' in the West.[128]

Responses: From Prodigy to Pariah

> *We should cut out the tongue of those who speak of*
> *multiple interpretations of the Qur'an.*
>
> Ayatollah Mesbah Yazdi

The official responses to Soroush's theological interventions were uncompromising. Whereas hi critics in the late 1980s and early 1990s warned him of the slippery slope of relativism,[129] these debates soon turned into a coordinated mobilization of ideological apologists for the state, and their *hezbollahi* minions. On the anniversary of the unification of the seminary and the university, in December 1991, the Central Office of the Honorable Leader's Representatives in the Universities warned 'the spread of thoughts which consider religion to be a dependent variable of other human sciences is dangerous and it negate the legitimacy of the Islamic state.'[130]

A few years later, on September 9, 1995, in an editorial in Tehran's state-run paper *Ettelā`āt*, the Supreme Leader, Ayatollah Khamene'i, also cautioned Soroush not to criticize clergy's privileged social position and interpretive authority. In the aftermath of the publication of his *Qabz va bast*, the person of Soroush was transformed into a treat to national security. In the words of then Iranian Minister of Foreign Affairs Ali Akbar Velayati's, the 'Dr. Soroush issue' was a matter of 'national harmony,' and 'Iranian national independence.' After mob groups attacked Soroush during a lecture in Isfahan, Velayati warned him to cease 'dragging [issues of religious authority] into the daily newspapers.'[131] Soroush replied to this in a column published in the *Salam* newspaper on January 2, 1996. He wondered,

> Is it logical that a person who does not have access to the radio, to television, to newspapers, to mosques, to Friday prayer gatherings, and to religious delegations; a person who is constantly pounded by the mass media in the ugliest manner and is accused of spying, incompetence and treachery, of being a freemason, an American agent, a hypocrite, a liberal, a Salman Rushdie could weaken the basis of our independence and national harmony?[132]

In the introduction to the fourth edition of the *Contraction and Expansion*, published in 1996, Soroush expressed astonishment that his modest distinctions between religion and ideology, and between Religion Itself and human knowledge of it, should have fomented a 'wave of accusations, threats, and condemnations.' One critic, Hossein Ghaffari, chastised him for being 'westoxicated, more dangerous than Marx and Freud.'[133] Another, Sadeq Larijani, reprimanded him for advocating secularism and 'Popperian liberalism.'[134] Scores of treatises appeared from in the Qom Seminary and other publishers of orthodox theological texts in the early to mid-1990s. They uniformly attacked Soroush for calling foundational religious texts historically contingent and equally open to multiple interpretations. They also ridiculed him for turning the comprehension of Islam into a dependent variable of scientific know-ledge.[135] To discredit him, others simply trounced analytical philosophy and Popper's neo-positivism.[136] By way of Soroush and his critics, from the corners of philosophy of science departments, Karl Popper appeared in Iran as *the* leading Western philosopher. His ideas were widely championed by reformers who 'conspire' to secularize Islam.

Reminiscent of the collective admonition they raised against Shari`ati, the dominant clergy denounced Soroush's work as misguided and misleading. Two influential ayatollahs, Mesbah Yazdi[137] and Naser Makarem Shirazi,[138] both outspoken critics of Ali Shari`ati, warned their disciples and state officials of the perils of Soroush's 'relativization of religious knowledge,' and especially dangerous attempt to emasculate the interpretive authority of the clergy in religious matters.

During the 1990s, Soroush's theory of *qabz va bast* became the conceptual framework for debating the religious justification of the Islamic Republic. From the floor of the *majlis* to editorial pages, from seminary quarters to street corners in Tehran, friends and foes clashed over the question of the contingencies of religious knowledge. The speaker of the *majlis,* Ali Akbar Nateq Nuri, called for an end to competing interpretations of Islam and warned that they will weaken Muslims' faith in their religion. In a speech he delivered to the Revolutionary Guards, the speaker warned his audience that 'the enemies of the revolution are exploiting naive people with these complicated theories to undermine their faith in order to defeat the revolution [...] We need, to utilize new technologies of communication such as the internet to generate certainty in defending the principles of Islam and the revolution.'[139] A day later, in one of his repeated attacks on pluralism, Ayatollah Mesbah Yazdi began his Friday prayer sermon with the declaration that 'there is no room for fashionable ideas in the absolutes of Islam.' This leading critic of Soroush at the Qom Seminary cautioned his worshipers that

A number of Western-educated intellectuals are trying to taint the world of Islam with Western ideas. Rather than an unambiguous assertion about the realities of the world, they see our holy book as a compilation of mythical stories that are open to interpretation [...] We need to shut the mouth of anybody who claims that he has a new interpretation of Islam [...] The consequence of uttering words against the absolutes of Islam is nothing but burning in hell, we will throw these fashionable ideas into the dustbin of history.[140]

Another influential member of the *majlis*, Tehran representative Ali Movahhedi Savoji, scolded President Khatami for legitimizing his policies by referring to his *own* interpretation of Islam. After his remarks during the open session of the *majlis*, he told reporters: 'The President is not a theoretician of Islam. Even if we agree that different interpretations of Islam are permissible, Mr. Khatami is not a qualified source of emulation and thus not permitted to offer an opinion on matters outside his authority.'[141]

One can argue that before the appearance of Soroush's discussion of *qabz va bast*, there was a long tradition in Iran of competing schools of interpretations of canonical Islamic texts. But the significance of Soroush's intervention in the postrevolutionary period was that he expanded the exegetical authority to actors outside seminaries. As the many attacks on his person and his ideas demonstrate, what was at stake was the authority to produce religious knowledge, which Soroush expanded to civil actors without clerical religious training. The most influential authorities in the clerical establishment viewed Soroush's ideas as a political intervention, which, if realized, would lead inevitably to the secularization of the Islamic Republic. They were not wrong.

Not only did they try to contain the spread of his ideas in seminary quarters, they also made sure that their supporters would stop his corrupting influence on the streets and on university campuses, even by violent means.

A year after the publication of *Qabz va bast*, Soroush personally delivered to President Hashemi-Rafsanjani his grievances about the animosity he faced in the state-sponsored media. This move further antagonized his foes. A few weeks later, in November 1992, after a lecture at Isfahan University, the attacks on Soroush's idea turned into open threats against his safety. One *hezbollahi* proclaimed that 'the time for this insulting oratory is over, the authorities need to step in and stop this man.'[142] Another accused him of hypocrisy and sophistry in the tradition of Ahmad Kasravi.[143] Perhaps none of the verbal assaults against him were as disturbing to Soroush as those that evoke the name of Kasravi. In a letter to Rafsanjani and Mohammad Yazdi, the Head of the Judiciary, he asked the government to intervene and 'prosecute and punish those who threaten the safety of the citizens of this country.' In his letter, to which he attached a copy of his Isfahan lecture, he assured the heads of the executive and the judiciary that he would not 'succumb to the intimidations of fear-mongers.' 'I do not expect to live for ever,' he wrote bitterly, 'the only action I would consider is to revise my will.'[144]

Mohammad Yazdi, the conservative Head of the Judiciary, ignored the request to prosecute those who threatened his life, and bludgeoned his audience with knives and clubs. Soroush's failure to secure legal protection emboldened his detractors. In the spring of 1995, Isfahan University students invited him to speak about the legacy of Ali Shari`ati. Unknown pressure groups that operated under the generic name *Hezbollah* warned the university president that its members would not allow the university to become a tribune for anti-Islamic propaganda. The administration cancelled the talk. In response, the students changed the venue to a lecture hall outside the campus. But this did little to satisfy the *hezbollahis* who were determined to put an end to Soroush's unwelcome appearances.

A few dozen thugs stormed the lecture hall, which was packed with more than a thousand enthusiasts. They broke the windows and threw chairs first at the audience and then at Soroush who had just spoken his opening remarks. The *hezbollahis* fists landed on Soroush's face and head, and ripping his shirt. But before they could inflict further injuries, the student rescued Soroush and ushered him into a safe basement room until his assailants left the building.

Upon returning to Tehran, Soroush composed yet another open letter to the President. He complained to Rafsanjani,

> Those who live off of mayhem and raising havoc have expanded the encounters of ideas to animosity with our nation. In their vicious attacks and defamation of my character, they have affronted the dignity of our culture and our history. With their ugly actions, they have tarnished the beautiful image of our land to outsiders and to future generations [...] I have come to you in humility to seek justice, not for myself, but on behalf of our cultural pride and our dignity that have been subjected to these atrocities.[145]

More than one hundred prominent intellectuals also petitioned the President to take concrete action to curb these attacks. Rafsanjani showed neither the willingness nor the ability to intervene. Newspapers such as *Kayhān* and *Resalat*, which represented the seminarian's dogmatist views, accused Soroush of uttering inflammatory remarks and refusing to face his critics. Their editorials became the new blueprint for silencing Soroush. *Ansār-e Hezbollah* announced that its members would not allow him to speak at any public event so long as he refused to debate their representatives.

In the fall of 1995, the Islamic Student Association of the College of Engineering at Tehran University invited Soroush to deliver a series of lectures on 'Mysticism in Rumi's *Mathnavi.*' Three days before the first scheduled meeting, on October 8, 1995, the foot soldiers of the *Ansar* rallied on the Tehran University campus demanding that they be given the opportunity to debate Soroush. On the day of the lecture, scores of *hezbollahis* blocked the entrance to the auditorium, hoping to prevent Soroush from entering the hall. But he had already entered the building. His presence further fueled their fury. They stormed into the auditorium, and as they were throwing chairs onto the stage, their leader, Masud Dehnamaki, announced through a bullhorn, 'We demand a debate with Soroush, we are not here to sabotage the meeting, we ask to be heard.' Soroush refused, stating 'one cannot debate while his safety is at stake.'[146]

Meanwhile, his plight attracted denunciations of the Islamic Republic from renowned Islamicists around the world. The director of the Institut für Orient- und Asienwissenschaften of Bonn University wrote to President Rafsanjani. The influential Harvard professor of Islamic mystic traditions, Annemarie Schimmel, warned the Minister of Foreign Affairs, Ali Akbar Velayati, that the growing threats against Soroush would further deepen the regime's reputation for intolerance. But neither the President nor his Minister of Foreign Affairs was in a position to contain the increasing power of the *Ansar*.

The trauma of the College of Engineering incident kept Soroush out of lecturing circles for more than eight months. But in May 1996, students at the Polytechnique University invited him to speak at a ceremony to commemorate Ayatollah Motahhari's death. But even an event for commemorating a cleric whom Ayatollah Khomeini called 'dearer than his own son,' would not deter the *Ansar* from launching another concerted attack on Soroush. They occupied the campus and, in a scene from a theater of the absurd, while wielding their clubs and daggers, asked Soroush to debate his opponents. All he could do was to write yet another letter to President.

> Had the authorities punished the instigators of the hideous incident at the College of Engineering, instead of rewarding

them with freedom to terrorize, they could not become emboldened today to commit yet another vicious act of violence on another university campus [...] The triumph of worshippers of darkness conveys the defeat of our culture, the depletion of our hopes, and the decline of our thoughts. Remaining silent is not permissible, do not allow them to win.[147]

The *Ansar* also wrote to Rafsanjani: 'Haj Faraj [Soroush] intends to become the Galileo of your Excellency's medieval regime!! By raising the fear in you of looking like the European priests of the Middle Ages, he wants to create an arena for himself [...] In a two-page letter to you, our "secular mystic," with scores of lies and hundreds of insults, has accused the *Ansar* of plotting against his life. Why does not his Excellency respond to these baseless accusations?'[148]

By the end of 1996 it became apparent that the Soroush's public presence would be tolerated neither by his clerical detractors nor the vigilante guardians of the 'blood of the martyrs.' Even after the election of his friend and ally Mohammad Khatami to the presidency in May 1997, he remained as the main target of the 'pressure groups.' The failure of his friends in power to engender a safe, sustainable public sphere moved Soroush to head off for a fellowship at Harvard in 2000. For the first time, Harvard fellowship, and thereafter Princeton and the *Wissenschaftkolleg* in Berlin offered Soroush the possibility of situating himself within a global network of Muslim intellectuals.

Before his departure for Cambridge to assume his new appointment at the most prestigious academic arena in the United States, he published two of his most controversial books. Not only did the pressure fail to deter him from criticizing the orthodoxies of the Shi`ite clerical hierarchy, he continued to advanced a radical religious pluralism which scandalized even those who had politically and theologically invested in his project.

8

Islam, Democracy, and Religious Pluralism

You revealed Yourself in thousands of manifestations
With thousands of bewildering eyes, I behold You.

Forughi-Bastāmi

Straight Paths and Religious Pluralism

Earlier I shared how Soroush based his critique of dogmatic interpretations of Islam on the temporal contingencies of religious knowledge. He concluded that: (1) God revealed religion so it could enter the domains of human culture and subjectivity within which it is comprehended and observed. The moment religion enters human subjectivity inevitably it becomes particular, and historically-culturally specific. (2) Religious knowledge corresponds to other mundane forms of knowledge. It is related to and inspired by *non*-religious knowledge production. (3) Religious knowledge is also historically progressive. Its advancement depends on the evolution of scientific understanding of the physical world and ever-expanding notions of rights and mutual obligations in society such as civil liberties or the rights of women, etc.

In his earlier work, Soroush defined the epistemological contingencies of religious knowledge in an ambiguous relation with the historical and cultural contingencies of the divine text. Whereas he initially approached problems in attaining religious knowledge with logical and systematic reasoning, later on he became increasingly concerned with religious hermeneutics. Whereas he originally understood the diversity of religious knowledge as a reflection of historical progression, in his hermeneutics, he underscored regional, ethnic, and linguistic differences in exegesis of the sacred texts. He resolved the tension between temporal and spatial differences by adopting a hermeneutical approach. Whereas earlier he put forward epistemological questions about the limits and truthfulness of knowledge claims, later, in two important books *Straight Paths* (1998) and *Expansion of the Prophetic Experience* (1999), he emphasizes the reflexivity and plurality of human understanding. By pluralizing the Qur'anic phrase *Straight Path*, Soroush broke both modernist and orthodox traditions in Islamic theology.

The ambiguity in his writings on the universality of reason and the hermeneutics of the text reflected two moments in postrevolutionary Iran. The political context of his earlier work forced him to promote a supra-historical conception of reason against the onslaught of basic institutions of civil society. This is evident in his openly political writings in *Siyāsat-Nāmeh* (*Political Letters*), where he defines the goal of democracy as the establishment of procedures that guaranteed the free engagement of rational experts.[1] He believed that public deliberation of the meaning and social implications of religion and its social implications should take place in a secure arena for the exercise of public reason, as in John Rawls,[2] and within a public sphere that allows undistorted communication and deliberative politics, as in Jürgen Habermas.[3]

Soroush's thesis was shaped by multiple and at times contradictory sources drawn from Western philosophy and the Muslim Gnostic traditions. Although Soroush was profoundly influenced by Popper's post-positivism, his epistemological pluralism is more informed by Quine-Duhem's anti-foundationalism. Quine and Duhem proposed that given the totality of known and unknown auxiliary assumptions, all forms of knowledge are inevitably collective and thus based on a series of tacit, as well as explicit, presuppositions. In a recent interview, Soroush acknowledged the influence of Quine and Duhem in the formation of his theory of religious knowledge.

> When I was writing that book [*Qabz va bast*] I was unaware that I was under the influence of Duhem and Quine's theory; only in retrospect did I perceive this connection. [My] thesis poses the question as to whether there is such a thing as religious knowledge with a collective nature; my answer is *yes*.[4]

His reference to being *unaware* of the influence of Duhem and Quine's theory, demosntrates the ambiguity of both his understanding of epistemological pluralism and the collective nature of religious knowledge. Soroush continues to oscillate between a Hegelian perspective, in which he understands collectivity *temporally* as a historically progressive accumulation of knowledge transmitted from one generation to the next, and a Gnostic hermeneutical view, in which he highlights the *spatial* contingencies of meaning and interpretation. While collective nature of religious knowledge remains a central tenet of Soroush's doctrine, he has not yet defined the boundaries of this collectivity.

While his detractors continued their assault on paper and pavement, with the publication of *Straight Paths,* Soroush took a significantly greater step away from doctrinal renditions of Islam. As Said Amir Arjomand observes, in *Straight Paths* 'Soroush totally disregarded legalistic Islam and drew heavily on the tradition of Gnostic mysticism (`*irfān*), especially in the poetry of his favorite Rumi (d. 1273), to establish the principle of religious pluralism.'[5] Soroush had always referenced Rumi in his argument for plurality of paths to Truth, this time he radicalized his rendition of Rumi to establish the plurality of Truth itself. 'From the standpoint of Rumi,' Soroush wrote,

> The problem is not that some people have failed to find the Truth, [and] thus remained misguided and deprived. Rather, people's bewilderment results from the multiplicity of truths and the diversity in their manifestation. We are in awe of and attracted to different constituents of this divine diversity.[6]

Borrowing heavily from John Hick,[7] in a radical departure from dominant Islamic theological traditions, Soroush argues that rather than a sign of corruption of *the* Truth, the plurality of religion is the manifestation of a diverse set of responses to the Divine, experienced and comprehended in different cultural and religious traditions. His notion of experience and comprehension became the foundational element of his philosophy of religious pluralism. According to this view, the plurality of religions reflects different manifestations of the Divine in the phenomenal world. Rather than an aberration of God's intention, the varieties of religious experiences are consistent with the Divine Will. In effect, Soroush now sees different religions as 'related kin,' as discussed by John Hick,[8] rather than rival strangers, working toward the same goal of human transformation in mutually complementary ways.

Soroush credits Hick's Kantian philosophy as the primary source of his justification of ecumenicalism.[9] Hicks argues, 'The great world traditions constitute different conceptions and perceptions of, and responses to, the Real from within the different cultural ways of being human.'[10] Form this Hick and Soroush derive the distinction between ultimate reality *in itself* and ultimate reality as interpreted in human experience.[11] Although Hick originally constructed the idea of religious *pluralism* as a solution to the predicament of religious *relativism*, during the 1980s his doctrine provoked scathing soteriological questions about the moral responsibilities of the faithful.[12] In Hick's view, as adopted by Soroush, the soteriological questions of salvation, justice, liberation and the 'authenticity' of religious experience are explicable only with reference to the 'recognition of the mythological character of tradition-specific language about ultimate reality.'[13] Since all great religions envisage justice and salvation at the core of their belief system, in the absence of the experience of the ultimate reality *in itself,* all religions manifest true divine expression.

In Iran, Soroush's ecumenicalism came on the heels of controversies over his promotion of tolerance for diverse interpretations of Islam. Soroush wedds these two projects, in his most radical book *The Expansion of Prophetic Experience.* Walking on the razor's edge between heresy and faith, he ponders the moment when the earthly prophet encountered the Divine. Soroush regards the Prophet's life and character as absolutely central to the revelation of the Qur'an.

> Rather than a mere book or a collection of narratives, Islam represents an historical movement; it is the embodiment of an historical mission. Islam is the historical expansion of a *gradually-realized* prophetic experience. Pivotal to its meaning is the Prophet's persona [...] The Qur'anic revelation was woven around Prophet's life circumstances; it revolved around his internal and external life experiences.[14]

By linking revelation to the biography of the Prophet, he intends to bring to light the historicity of the Qur'an and the contingencies of its verses, as well as to draw distinctions between Islam, Christianity, and Judaism without questioning their inherent Truth. That is to say, by emphasizing the constitutive significance of the Prophet's life circumstances in shaping the Qur'anic text, he transfers the debate over theological incongruities of Abrahamic religions to the realm of history.

Soroush's assertion on the significance of the Prophet's life in shaping the message of the Qur'an revives two foundational debates from the formative decades of Islam. The first concerned the indeterminacy and rationality of human action, and the second was of the eternity (*qadim*) of the Holy Text. Under a political system that draws legitimacy from the scared canon, these questions drew immediate attention to the problems of civil liberty and sovereignty in contemporary Iran. Here again Soroush shrewdly extracts long-established theological conundrums from the seminaries and transforms them into a basis for the democratization of the Islamic Republic.

Reason and Religion

Since the emergence of the earliest Islamic schools theology, rationalist traditions, most notably the Mu`tazilites, thought that God's Justice (`adl*) required believers to be responsible for their own actions. In order to accept the princile that a just God rewards salutary deeds and punishes the sinful, one must possess the freedom to determine one's own destiny. The rationalists considered it a violation of the principle of justice, if God held people accountable for actions over which they had no power. Reason, the Mu`tazilites believed, was a constitutive faculty of humanity; its realization in action necessitated the recognition that life was essentially indeterminate.[15] An important corollary of this principle was the link between Divine revelation and the actions of the Prophet. The Qur'an could have been different had the Prophet made different decisions in his social and political career. Soroush writes,

> A person would come and ask the Prophet a question, someone brought an accusation against his wife, one would ignite the flames of war, the Jews or Christians made particular decisions, many accused the Prophet of lunacy […] they buried their sons and daughters alive, all these are reflected in the Qur'an and in the Prophet's words. Had the Prophet lived longer and faced more predicaments, those incidents would also have been reflected in the Qur'an. So, that is the meaning of the assertion that there could have been more written in the Qur'an. If `Āyesha had not been accused of having an affair with another man, would the early verses of the *Sura Nur* have descended? If the war of *Ahzāb* had not occurred, would the *Sura al-Ahzāb* have been revealed? If there had been no Abu Lahab in Hijaz and he and his wife had not behaved with animus towards the Prophet, would the *Sura Abu Lahab* have appeared? These were all unnecessary events the occurrence of which did not have any historical significance. Now that they have indeed occurred, their mark is left in the Qur'an.[16]

Soroush argues that all religions are comprised of two categories, `arazi*, the contingent or accidental, and *zāti*, the substantial or essential. Accordingly, while they differ in their contingencies, all religions in their essence promote the same principles. 'Religion,' he reiterates, 'does not have an Aristotelian nature, it only expresses God's *intentions*. These intentions define the essence of religion.'[17] Although he does not elaborate on what these essential elements of Islam and other religions might be, in a footnote Soroush identifies three basic substantive elements of faith: '1. Humankind is not God, but in His servitude (the element of *faith*), 2. Salvation defines the ultimate goal of life and the highest earthly achievement of religion (the element of *ethics*), 3. Religion protects and sustains reason, generations, belongings, and life (the element of *fiqh* or *jurisprudence*).'[18] The rest of religious content, their languages, the cultural and historical contexts of their revelations, particular juridical assertions, concrete teachings of everyday life, the wars they launch, and the peace treaties they forge are non-essential and contingent. And most importantly, he concludes, 'one may assert with certainty that essential (*zāti*) matters of religion cannot be deduced from its contingent (`*arazi*) elements.'[19]

The Eternity of the Qur'an

Muslim theologians who rejected the idea of indeterminacy and subscribed to the determinist doctrine of predestination (*Jabriyya*) argued that the principle of eternity of the Qur'an exposed the fallacy of the hermeneutics of the Divine text. They rejected the Mu`tazilite belief that the Qur'an was created (*hādeth*) by God, and arose with the prophethood of Muhammad. Rather they argued that the Qur'an was eternal, uncreated, and *qadim*. It was revealed in its entirety in one instant to the Prophet. The Ash`arite critics of the rationalists insisted that the Divine revelations speak eternal Truth without essential relation to the Prophet's biography and character. They evoked the Qur'anic verse from the *Sura al-Baqara*, to confirm the legitimacy of their position: *In the month of Ramadan the Qur'an was revealed, a Book of guidance with proofs of guidance distinguishing right from wrong* (2: 185).[20] Not only did they argue that the Qur'an was uncreated and eternal, more orthodox schools, such as Hanbalites and Zāhirites, went further to advocate that since speech was a Divine attribute, the Qur'an was Allah's spoken words.

The Mu`tazilites considered attributes, such as speech or beatific visions to be a direct violation of the unity of God (*Towhid*). God does not express Himself in the language of particulars—words will inevitably bind the Deity to cultural references and historical contingencies. The ninth century theologian al-Māturidi proposed, like God's other attributes, 'His attribute of speaking as well as His speech [*Kalām Allah*] are eternal without similitude and comparison. The exact nature of this eternal speech or the attribute of speaking is not known, but it is certain that Divine speech and letters are created. So, in reality,' al-Māturidi asserts, 'only the 'meaning' of which the words are an expression can be termed as the *kalām* of Allah.'[21] The Prophet did not hear the *words* of God, but had an inner experience of divinity, kindled by God, the meaning of which he was able to divulge to his contemporaries in comprehensible language. Arabic and its associated cultural norms, economic and political doctrines, symbols of beauty, and all the other particulars in the Qur'an have nothing to do with the unattainable eternal Truth.

Soroush's detractors did not misjudge the political implications of his theses of religious pluralism. If the word of God, *Kalām Allah,* was not to be understood literally as Divine words, but speechless mystic intuits known only to the Prophet, then no leader may justify his political authority as the exclusive and uncontested expression of the Divine Will. That would be tantamount to totalitarianism politically and religiously to blasphemy. 'A politically sanctioned official rendition of Islam,' he declares, 'is thus null and void.'

> Recently I read in a newspaper that an ignorant clergyman had claimed that 'if I sense a religious obligation, I shall not hesitate to desecrate my opponents.' These words mean precisely a declaration of prophecy–a conspicuous denial of the finality of Muhammad's prophecy.[22]

Soroush lays out the elements of a critique of what he aptly identifies as *'the fascist rendition of religion.'*[23] The blasphemy of putting one's self in the position of God inevitably breeds fascism. He further advances a political philosophy in which he considers the recognition of *religious* pluralism to be the prerequisite of *political* pluralism and tolerance.

The Critics: Relativism, Secularism, and Democracy
Critics of pluralism chastise Soroush from two distinct positions. The first group rebukes him from an *exclusivist* standpoint: they dismissed his notion of the plurality of Truth. They believe, with the exception of Islam, all religions are simply false. The second group, the *inclusivists,* is just as skeptical of the plurality of Truth, but they argue that each religion holds parts of *the* Truth which is ultimately unified only in Islam.

Exclusivism
In many respects, Soroush's exclusivist seminarian detractors anticipated his transformation from the distinction he made earlier in the *Qabz va Bast* between religion and religious knowledge to his pluralist theory of *Straight Paths.*[24]   For them, Soroush's arguments have its roots in philosophical relativism.[25] Once he recognized the legitimacy of multiple interpretations of Islam, they argue, the belief in the truthfulness of *all* religions would inevitably follow. Sadeq Larijani, an influential member

of the Guardian Council and one of Soroush's most prominent critics stresses that there is an inner connection between philosophical relativism, social secularism, and political democracy. Soroush knowingly or unknowingly advocates what Westerners desire.

> The discussion of relativism in religious understanding is one of the best weapons Westerners use in disarming our religious state. No device could be more effective than relativism for draining a religious state of its substantive core, thus our sensitivity about this topic. We are not engaged in a scholastic debate about religion, but troubled by a movement that is hampering our Islamic state by advocating relativism, which inevitably will lead to secularism and the separation of religion and state.[26]

Other critics share with Larijani this conspiratorial view, linking religious pluralism to a self-defeatist relativism that would eventually undermine the authority of the clergy and the legitimacy of the Islamic Republic. Mohsen Gharavian rightly contends that those who claim relativity of religious knowledge and the truthfulness of all religions intend to render those, particularly the *ruhāniyat*, who speak of faith with certainty as despots.[27] Soroush's scheme would leave the *ruhāniyat* with two undesirable options: either profess certainty in their beliefs as personal faith and become apolitical, or to advocate their faith publicly and be seen as tyrants. Another respected junior cleric of Qom Seminary emphasizes the same point.

> If we accept the relativity of interpretations, as intellectuals such as Soroush argue, nobody would have the right to claim the primacy of one interpretation over another. Rejecting the legitimacy of a dominant interpretation will inevitably restrict the involvement of religion in the political affairs of society. The entire premise of religious intervention in society rests upon the supremacy of one interpretation over another.[28]

Heidari Kashani highlights the main challenge of Soroush's latest books sharply and poses the question of the reconcilability of religion in public life with pluralism and secularism. Is it possible to accept religion as a point of reference for matters of justice and liberty without transforming it into an ideology of tyranny? Is salvation possible in one's own religion without denying the salvation of believers in other faiths?

Ali Rabbani Golpaigani objects to Soroush's appropriation of John Hick's *religious* pluralism as a means to solve the problem of *social* and *political* pluralism. He argues that Soroush misconstrues religious pluralism as a necessary condition for tolerance in this world and salvation in the hereafter. In order to recognize the social and political rights of all citizens, Rabbani argues, one does need not to doubt the Truth of one's own religion.

> Tolerance is a political and cultural issue which may be achieved without interrogating the certainty of a believer [...] Imam Ali regarded himself and his method of governance as purely and chastely Islamic, but nevertheless advised Malik Ashtar [his appointed governor of Egypt] to be kind to all people whether they shared his beliefs and practiced the same religion or not.[29]

Moreover, Rabbani and others do not consider the recognition of religious pluralism to be necessary for believing in the salvation of non-Muslims. Even the conservative member of the Guardian Council, Sadeq Larijani, acknowledges, 'Muslims do not have an exclusive claim for salvation.'

> God shall beatify a Christian who surrenders himself to the will of the Almighty, but because of social conditions, not of his making, is unable to see the Truth [of Islam]. Most of our *ulama* agree that adherence to another religion does not cause eternal anguish in Hell. It is possible not to see the Ultimate Truth, but be blessed by God; it all depends on one's actions in life.[30]

Inclusivism

One of the leading authorities in Islamic hermeneutics in Iran, Mohammad Mojtahed Shabestari argues that rather than reference to jurisprudence (*fiqh*), religious pluralism must be understood in the context of faith.[31] Without referring to Soroush, he emphasizes that tolerance does not need to be coupled with the recognition of religious pluralism. 'Tolerance,' he writes, 'is distinct from religious pluralism. One may be certain about the Truth of his religion, but at the same time be tolerant of other truth-claims.'[32] As a political problem, tolerance exists in a society in which 'the state acts as the protector of its citizens' liberties, not as the guardian of the multiplicities of Truth.'[33]

Shabestari stresses that by understanding pluralism in the context of faith, the debate shifts from the realm of *fiqh* to religious *experience*. 'Those who emphasize religious experience, regard religiosity as the outcome of humankind's experiential encounter with the Ultimate Truth, and consider those experiences as the source of their knowledge, inexorably believe in religious pluralism.'[34] Religion, as the inner experience of divinity, is inherently plural. Its diversity becomes a problem only when it becomes doctrinal and *shari`ah*-centered, where faith is mediated by a series of regulations that are constituted and maintained by enduring religious institutions. During the formative period of Islam, Shabestari comments, the *shari`ah* was understood as a means for the enrichment of faith, not as a tool for governance. However, in later periods, the *shari`ah* developed into a comprehensive juridical code with the authority to regulate all spheres of social and personal life. Faith, achieved through religious experience, is always fluid and conditioned by one's life circumstances; it is therefore practically conducive to pluralism. But the *shari`ah*-based religion reifies rules at the expense of diversity—hence the clergy's suspicion of pluralism.[35]

Although Soroush concurs with the basic premise of Shabestari's argument that a democratic state should not act as the arbiter of truth-claims, he insists on linking the principle of tolerance to the recognition of the multiplicity of truths. He does not deny that secular governance is the inescapable conclusion of his argument. But like Shabestari, his conception resonates more with 'objective secularism,' as a manifestation of institutional differentiation in modern societies, than 'subjective secularism,' as a cultural transformation detrimental to religious beliefs and practices.[36] At this point, Soroush abandons altogether the idea of 'secularism from within' that Said Hajjarian and other theorists of political reform had earlier promoted. They had argued that public contestation and competing interpretations of the religious justification of political authority necessitated Islamic secularism—a notion distinct from the French *laïcité* or more generally from the European experience of a separation of church and state.

Soroush faults his critics for failing to appreciate the distinction he had made between the separation and independence of the church and state. 'Instead of using the word 'separation,' it might be better to speak of the 'independence' of the institution of religion from the state.'[37] This distinction is imperative for protecting religion, and preventing the state from falling into totalitarianism. Religion must be independent from state, in the sense that the state must legitimize its policies independently from the religious convictions of its actors. Religious state actors may advocate policies that are informed and conditioned by their convictions, but they justify their initiatives by reference to pertinent social, political, and economic arguments. Both Soroush's and Shabestari's conceptions of faith as religious *experience*, call into question the possibility of a distinctly religious politics. Politics presupposes collective identity, which becomes unattainable in Soroush's notion of the individual's subjective, particular experience of God.

Perhaps the most important representatives of the inclusivist critiques of Soroush are Hasan Yusefi Eshkevari and Mohsen Kadviar. Eshkevari gained prominence after his arrest in August 2000 when he returned to Tehran from a conference in Berlin sponsored by the Heinrich Böll Foundation and the German Green Party. Eshkevari is an advocate of a democratic Islamic state, and an outspoken critic of the theocratic tendencies in the Islamic Republic,[38] He was first sentenced to death by the Special Court for the Clergy on apostasy charges, and later convicted of lesser charges and sentenced to seven years in prison. (He ultimately served more than four years before his release in February 2005.) Although Eshkevari has demonstrated his commitment to the transformation of the Iranian political system, he regards religious pluralism as a misguided attempt to establish democratic institutions. He argues that religious pluralism neither serves as a theological explanation of divergent religious beliefs and practices, nor is it particularly relevant to the problem of governance and democracy. He wrote, 'Not only does religious pluralism contradict the foundations of one's faith [in the absolute Truth], but it also has no practical utility.'[39]

Eshkevari takes Soroush to task for turning religion into a private affair in order to justify its plurality. Ever since his preoccupation with rejecting Islam as ideology, Soroush has feared, wrongly, that *any* collective assertion of religion poses a breeding ground for fascism.[40] Eshkevari writes:

> Friends who attempt to depict the prophets as preachers and teachers of individual ethics and confine the scope of religiosity to individual matters and a personal inner relationship with God, in other words, to 'inner religious experience,' should better analyze the indisputable struggles of the prophets and say what the Prophet of Islam's 23-year struggle was for, and finally what was the establishment of state and government for? Was it only to secure happiness in the hereafter, at the expense of accepting existing polytheistic circumstances?

> 'Justice' can be regarded in a broad and general sense as the 'social philosophy' of religion; the Koran is explicit about this. Justice is certainly not confined to the creation of a just and balanced world, but includes the realm of legislation, and according to the Koran implementing justice is closer than anything else to piety.[41]

By the intensity with which he situates social justice as the core of religion, one can immediately recognize the spirit of Shari`ati in Eshkevari. But while the emergence of a postrevolutionary *nomenklatura* and theocracy pushed Soroush to retreat from ideological certainties associated with Shari`ati's liberation theology, Eshkevari tries to resolve the problem of an Islamic democracy without relegating religion to private matters of personal faith.

Soroush replied to his most articulate critic, Mohsen Kadivar, in a debate later published in a book,[42] which was reprinted three times in less than a few months in 1999. By the time the third edition was published, Kadivar had been arrested for his widely publicized objections to the absolutist *velāyat-e faqih* and sentenced to eighteen months imprisonment at Evin prison. In his several treatises on political theology, Kadivar has meticulously mapped the jurisprudential foundations of different Shi`ite approaches to governance.[43] Unlike Soroush and Shabestari, who argue that the legitimacy of the state and its policies must be justified independently from religion, Kadivar believes that in a Muslim society, social change and democratic governance necessitated the perpetual transformation of *fiqh* (jurisprudence). Rendering *fiqh* irrelevant to democratic change would only contribute to its further ossification. In line with other critics of Soroush, Kadivar also stresses that tolerance does not require religious pluralism. In order to justify civil liberties, human rights, and democracy, one need not accept the relativity of Truth and plurality in religion. Indeed, the most enduring form of democratic transformation in Iran, he argues, is the one that would establish itself in relation to 'progressive' *fiqhi* traditions.[44] Kadivar declared in a debate with Mojtahed Shabestari that, 'It is imperative for a *faqih*, to attest to the consistency of the issues of civil liberties and rights with a theological-juridical framework. While a number of these rights may be recognized unequivocally in the context of traditional theology and *fiqh*, others could easily be granted by inference.'[45]

In a debate with Soroush, Kadivar cautioned him about moving from 'the plurality in the comprehension of Truth to the plurality of truth itself,' and 'from critical realism to absolute relativism.'[46] Weary of dogmatic, legalistic, official Islam under the Islamic Republic, throughout the debate Soroush insisted that the plurality of truth does not necessarily suggest relativism or lack of religious conviction. He recited Rumi's verse: *One who calls all righteous, foolish he is—One who calls all corrupt, treacherous he is.*[47]

He further reminded Kadivar that the promotion of religious pluralism should be understood irrespective of the Truth of each religion. Plurality of religions and the diversity of truth claims, he wrote in *Straight Paths*, is the consequence of neither the corruption of the Divine text, as many Muslims believe about the Bible, nor the result of historical and social accidents. 'It is the different manifestations of the Divine Will. He proliferated religions in the same way that He created a manifold nature, each of which manifests a dimension of His Truth.'[48]

Rather than historical aberrations or theological deviations, the truth claims of the world's great religions are part of a Divine plan. 'In matters of metaphysics,' following a Kantian line, 'by "parity of reasoning," no side can persuade the other of its own superiority.'[49] Competing truth claims should, as a Divine imperative, and will, as an historical fact, remain an integrated part of earthly life. The only alternative for the dominance of one Truth is coercive elimination, and not dialogical persuasion, of other claims.

Soroush Versus Soroush

Soroush's residence abroad took him far away from his colleagues and disciples. On two different occasions, in talks he delivered to enthusiastic audiences in London and Paris, he drew sharper and more nuanced distinctions between his conception of religious intellectualism and that of those who participated in political and social reform in Iran under President Khatami. In December 2003, disillusioned by Khatami's policies, Soroush openly criticized the President and his associates for not doing enough to contain the pressure groups, and to 'dry out their roots.' In an interview, he asserted that the reason for reformists' failure was their lack of strategic thinking. 'They failed because they shared the same system of thought with the dominant political order and were thus incapable of advancing a strong foundational critique of the system.'[50]

In a nine-part series, in London's *Towhid* Center, from April 10, 2004, to July 30, 2005, Soroush addressed the problem of what he called 'the historical failures of Muslims.'[51] By the end of twelfth century, Muslims had abandoned their creative, inquisitive spirit along with their culture of curiosity. He echoed the cliché of genesis and decline advanced by classical Orientalists such as Ernest Renan, Gustave von Grunebaum, and Bernard Lewis, and oddly enough, retold the story of how the West advanced independently while the East stagnated.

There are, however, important differences between Soroush's critical engagement with the Iranian Islamic-Shi`ite culture and the great

Orientalist apology for European colonialism. Soroush's struggle with orthodoxy in the Iranian religious establishment and political order situated him in a position to look inwardly and criticize the malaise of Iranian society. His approach also differs from Orientalists' teleological perception, in so far as they advance a Hegelian view in which 'the History of the World travels from East to West, for Europe is absolutely the end of History, Asia the beginning.'[52] For Soroush, 'history is the sphere of opportunities, not the domain of causes and effects.' He suspects historical narratives that conceive the 'failure' of the East in a causal relation to either ecology (arid lands that give rise to Oriental Despotism) or the depredations of colonialism. At the heart of these explanations, he believes, rests a historical determinism that renders Muslims' agency irrelevant. 'Things could have been different,' he speculates, questioning the inevitability of contemporary circumstances, 'had Muslims chosen a different path.'[53]

As in his writings, historical references in Soroush's lectures are often sketchy. The historical circumstances to which he refers often correspond to changes in theology and philosophy rather than in material conditions or power relations. Historical agency for Soroush belongs to philosophers and theologians who strive to institutionalize new ideas. Muslims failed because their theologians and philosophers failed to conceive a relation between humanity and God that was based on neither fear nor love. The Muslim world never conceived of humankind as independent rational agents in conversation with the Almighty. In a word, they failed because they did not have a Cartesian revolution. Only with the emergence of the rational subject, Soroush told his audience in London, could the principles of modernity materialize: 'experimental science, technological utilization of electricity, and finally a rights-endowed versus duty-driven subject.'[54]

The last point, the emergence of rights-endowed subject, was to become a central point of controversy in Iran. This was another of his attempts to distinguish legal political rights from the sphere of *fiqh*, which according to Soroush is limited to Muslims' religious duties and social obligations. The Muslim world never developed a sorely needed humanist tradition, he told his London audience, where a conception of rights could be articulated and institutionalized. So long as a conception of a 'despotic God' remained dominant in Islamic theology, democracy and humanism would never arise.[55]

Although Soroush remains committed to the project of religious intellectualism,[56] in recent years he has become increasingly less sympathetic towards those intellectuals who regard religion as a source of justification for social justice and the establishment of a democratic society. Rejecting these ambitions as a 'maximalist,' today he advocates a 'minimalist religion' the purpose of which is to enrich individual spiritual existence rather than to govern one's social life.[57] In his acknowledgment for receiving the Erasmus Prize in 2004, he identifies himself with Desiderius Erasmus of Rotterdam, the medieval theologian known as the prince of humanists, not only by sharing the same intellectual convictions, but also in Erasmus's refusal to join of the Lutheran party to mobilize the masses to institutionalize the Reformation. In his acceptance speech, Soroush, like Erasmus, described himself as an independent scholar who hoped to influence the reform of religion. In all humility,

> The Erasmus Foundation awarded me not only a prize but also an honorific title, namely, 'the Erasmus of Islam.' A few years ago, a correspondent of Los Angeles Times gave me the title 'the Luther of Islam.' I am, of course, innocent of all this but if I were to chose [sic] one of the two I would definitely opt for the Erasmus. The humanism, tolerance and more importantly the anti sectarian tendency of Erasmus attracts me more towards him than Luther, who was, no doubt, also a great man of European history.

> I am of the firm conviction [that] mankind today is in dire need of a spiritual interpretation of the universe as well as a spiritual emancipation (as Mohammad Iqbal once said). In my humble endeavors, therefore, I try to emancipate spirituality from the cage of official organized religions. As for [the] masses who seek the spirituality [sic] within an organized religion I offer a more tolerant interpretation thereof.[58]

After his short return to Iran in the summer of 2006, Soroush was obliged to defend his most recent words, not only because of his emphasized the spiritual dimension of Islam, but also because many had objected to his most controversial public lecture at Sorbonne in July 2005. Soroush was invited to Paris to speak about 'Shi`ism and the Challenge of Democracy.'[59] He began by reminding his audience that 'Iran is now governed by a regime whose rule is derived from the teachings of Shi`ism. On behalf of the Absent Imam, the *vali-ye faqih* reigns and administers the affairs of the land with the authority endowed upon him by the Shi`ite Messiah.'[60] These opening remarks scandalized religious intellectuals who believed that their responsibility was to show how the current regime in Iran must be regarded as an aberration, rather than a demonstration, of Shi`ite political thought. They objected to Soroush's characterization of the *velāyat-e faqih* as the only true manifestation of Shi`ite political philosophy. For them, *velāyat-e faqih*, with its anti-democratic core, was a Shi`ite political innovation gone awry. Prior to his Sorbonne lecture, only the high ranking clerics such as Soroush's nemesis Ayatollah Mesbah Yazdi and his influential defenders of the autocratic rule of the *faqih*, had described the Iranian regime as a true representation of Shi`i political philosophy.

In his address, for the first time, he linked the weakness of democratic institutions in Iran to Shi`ite messianism, one of it's essential differences from Sunni Islam. Revisiting earlier arguments he made in the *Prophetic Experience,* he described the finality of Muhammad's prophethood as 'the emancipation of humankind from the need for revelation,' and as the emergence of an 'inductive rationality.' But in Paris, he theorized that for Shi`ites, because of the belief in the Absent Imam (the Messiah), 'the significance of the finality of prophethood had faded.' To the chagrin of his audience, he recapitulated, Mohammad Iqbal's refutation of *mahdaviyat* (messianism),

> In the last part of chapter five of his book, Iqbal addresses the question of *mahdaviyat*. He admired Ibn Khaldun for identifying and debunking all narratives of the Hidden Imam. Praising Ibn Khaldun, Iqbal adds that if we believe in the return of *Mahdi*, who will be endowed with the same Divine authority as the Prophet, we are denying ourselves the benefits of the finality of prophethood, namely, the emancipation of humankind. Those who believe in the Return of Mahdi do not gain the liberties that the believers in the principle of finality enjoy. Accordingly, Shi`ites must resolve the predicament of *mahdaviyat* and examine its relation with emancipation and democracy.[61]

The theorist of the distinction between religion and religious knowledge, now in Paris attributed the failed liberalism of Mehdi Bazargan, the head of the short-lived Provisional Government in 1979, to the inherent contradiction between *mahdaviyat* and democracy. One who warned against drawing conclusions about the essence of religion from its contingencies, now at Sorbonne declared that *mahdaviyat* makes Shi`ism essentially anti-democratic and non-emancipatory.

A host of critics rebuked Soroush for strengthening the dogma of the orthodox religious establishment about the incompatibility of Shi`ism with democracy. In an open letter to his old friend and ally, Mohammad Saeed Bahmanpour, a cleric and lecturer at the Islamic College for

Advanced Study in London, called Soroush's Sorbonne lecture on the relation between Shi'ism and democracy disappointing. He wrote,

> Your lecture neither advanced the cause of democracy, nor did it resolve any political problems facing Iran [...] It is astonishing that a respected person such as yourself who advocated 'the expansion of prophetic experience' now has become the champion of *khātamiyat* [the finality of prophethood] [...] My dear friend, to reject the idea of *velāyat-e faqih*, do you find it necessary to condemn the entire tradition of Shi'ism? [...] You have put the Iranian people in an impossible position: abandon Shi'ism if you desire democracy.[62]

In his correspondence with Bahmanpour, Soroush tried to distance himself from his earlier assertion that there was an inherent contradiction between *mahdaviyat* and democracy. In his public reply to Bahmanpour, he highlighted his emphases in the London and Sorbonne on the benefits of 'legalism' in Islamic civilization and how the centrality of *fiqh* in this tradition could easily lend itself to the emergence of democracy. Repulsed by the suggestion that his ideas resonated with the hate-mongering words of Mesbah Yazdi, Soroush retorted,

> Yes, Mesbah Yazdi and I appear to be singing the same song that Islam and existing Shi'ism are irreconcilable with democracy. He is of the opinion that to be democratic one needs to disavow Islam and to remain a Muslim one needs to negate democracy. I insist that the establishment of democracy does not require the abandonment of Muslimhood. Which side are you on?[63]

Bahmanpour's criticism focused on Soroush's notions of *imāmat* and *khātamiyat*, and neglected his historical and sociological fallacies. One of the consistent themes in Soroush's work—from his early critique of Marxism to his objection to the Shi'ite messianic eschatology—has been his elitist depiction of history. In his London and Paris lectures, Soroush offers a historical narrative in which he establishes a direct correspondence between the makers of ideas, be it the humanist Erasmus of Rotterdam or the messianic liberal Bazargan of Tehran, and those who make history in their everyday lives. In Soroush, we find no sign of a Weberian indeterminacy, in which there can be no unmediated correspondence between ideas and objective realities, neither in their formation nor in their social consequences. He borders on offering a latter-day Berkeleyan idealism by asserting that Shi'ite messianic doctrinal conviction must be held responsible for the failure of Shi'ites to establish democratic political systems. Ideas do not make realities. The collapse of Bazargan's Provisional Government and with it the first postrevolutionary experiment in democracy had not in the least to do with messianic ideas of the revolutionary leaders, and everything to do with the particular social, political, and historical contingencies of the revolutionary Iran.

Mahmoud Sadri, the co-translator of Soroush's only book available in English,[64] was the author of another critical letter, objecting to his characterization of Shi`ite political philosophy and its social implications. Sadri writes that only with an essentialist Puritanism one could speak of an inherent contradiction between Shi`ism and democracy.[65] He reminds Soroush of the historical fallacies of his theory that a 'stronger belief in *khātamiyat*,' would result in a 'deeper commitment to democracy.' 'If we agree that the 'diluted' belief of Shi`ites in *khātamiyat* has weakened their commitment to democracy, this raises the question as to what have the Sunnis have achieved with their 'thick' devotion to *khātamiyat*?' How could he explain the despotic regimes in the Sunni world, since they, according to Soroush, appreciate the emancipatory rationality engendered by a 'thick' belief in the finality of the prophethood? 'On the opposite side of this fictitious distinction,' Sadri continues, 'behold the Constitutional Revolution [of 1906], the anti-neocolonial movement of fifty years ago, and the revolutionary movement of 1978. How could the 'diluted' commitment of Iranian Shi`ites to *khātamiyat*, which was supposed to make them oblivious to liberty and democracy, explain the liberation movements of the last one hundred years?'[66]

Soroush's denunciation of Shi`ites' historical failure is an unmistakable proof that he believes history is essentially the realization of ideas. As Sadri aptly puts it, 'it is the height of idealism to regard the formation of social and political realities as a direct consequence of ideas. Peoples' articulation of the historical meaning of their religion is mediated by and realized in the context of their social position as well as material and spiritual interests.'

Soroush's critique of Shi`ite messianism is even problematic if one reads him from a comparative standpoint. Messianism is one of the core principles of all Abrahamic religions. Certainly, Luther and Erasmus and the other Christian theologians of the Reformation did not abandon the messianic core of the Judeo-Christian tradition in order to encourage an unmediated relation between God and his human subjects. Messianic beliefs have both encouraged *and* prohibited critical engagement with the worldly affairs; they have inspired movements of liberation and

justified submission to oppression. As much as Shi`ite messianism has
counseled quietism, it has also fomented dissent and struggle. Even the
most significant ideological inspiration for liberation movements in the
twentieth century, Marxism is based on the secularized messianic
message of justice and liberty.

Whither Soroush?

Soroush has inaugurated one of the most important intellectual
movements in contemporary Iran. He began his journey with an
ideology critique first of Marxism and later of Islamism of pre and
postrevolutionary Iran. His hermeneutics and pluralist approach to
Islam encouraged a new generation of intellectuals to moderate the
Jacobin impulse of the postrevolutionary regime. They interpreted
Soroush as calling for struggle for participatory democracy through the
recognition of competing interpretations of Islam. For this generation,
revolutionary Islamism, with its exclusivist truth claims, provided the
ideological justification for totalitarianism. Rather than being an
epistemological or cognitive matter, they understood hermeneutical
Islam to be a deeply political issue. That is why the new generation of
religious intellectuals draw both from Shari`ati's notion of a resurgent
Alavi Shi`ism, *and* from Soroush's warnings of the fascist potentials of
dogmatic truth claims.

Both Shari`ati and Soroush conceive Islam in response to tyranny,
one against the despotic Pahlavi Monarchy and the other against
theocratic tendencies in Islamic Republic. Whereas Shari`ati argues that a
non-political articulation of religion provided the ideological justification
for a secular dictatorship, Soroush rejects the politicization of religion as
an inescapable ground for totalitarianism. On the strength of his Shi`ism
of the disposed, Shari`ati wished to demolish stagnant traditions and
reconstitute Iranian society, Soroush rejects every teleology and
advocates the intellectual pluralism 'let a thousand flowers bloom.'
Whereas Shari`ati positions himself as the bearer of the *True* Islam,
Soroush considers the Truth to be ineffable.

The most striking similarity between the two influential Muslim
theorists in contemporary Iran is their elitist perception of knowledge
and social change. Both suspicious of lived experiences as a source of
knowledge. For Shari`ati, the vanguard party holds the responsibility of
guiding the masses towards the 'classless *towhidi* society.' For Soroush,
the masses are 'emulators,' they perpetuate their culture and religion
uncritically, and follow the path of their leaders, imams, philosophers,

and theologians unconditionally. Not only are the masses are unconscious of their own realities, more importantly, he believes, the attain-
ment of such consciousness has destructive consequences.[67]

The longer the dogmatic clergy sustained their power in the Islamic
Republic, the more limited the public significance of Soroush's Islam has
become. Soroush's Islam retreats to the inner experiences of spirituality.
In spite of his trek towards the primacy of inner experiences of faith,
religion remains a prevailing force in Iranian politics. Who defines the
principles of this religion, and how those principles are implemented,
will be determined in struggles in the courthouses, on the streets and
public parks, in the factories, on university campuses, and in local-
regional councils.

9

Conclusion:
Social Change and the
Symbolic Universe of Religion

I started the book on a personal note; I would like to end it with another recollection from the revolutionary days of 1978 in Iran. It was after midnight and people in our neighborhood, like most other neighborhoods in Tehran, were defying martial law by staying out on the streets and shouting *Allah-o Akbar* (God is the Greatest). We saw military trucks approaching from the distance, then we heard gunshots and ran toward our homes. 'They martyred Mr. Bolouri,' our neighbor Atta shouted mischievously, mocking Mr. Bolouri's feeble character as a *chokh-bakhtyār*,[1] a low-ranking bureaucrat in the state-owned water company and the sole bread-winner for his wife and two young daughters. People rushed towards Mr. Bolouri's house to restrain the hysterical Mrs. Bolouri who had heard Atta, but failed to see the joke in his diabolic smile in the dark.

The soldiers left, and after a few minutes Mr. Bolouri triumphantly returned to his wife's curses. 'Don't you think of me and your children?' Mrs. Bolouri screamed at him with mixed emotions of anger and happiness. 'What business do you have staying out after midnight? You take care of your own family—let others do their revolution. Don't you think that they are going to kill you on the spot?' Expecting a hero's welcome, Mr. Bolouri, amused by his wife's outburst, retorted, 'I was not doing anything wrong, I was just praising the Lord.' Seeking approval from the crowd, he stretched out his arms towards them, 'Is it a crime in this country to say *Allah-o Akbar*?'

Mr. Bolouri's comment about his innocent involvement in the protest is what makes this incident revealing. As a *chokh-bakhtyār*, Mr. Bolouri was not particularly religious. He and his family did not observe Islamic codes of behavior, his wife and daughters were not *mohajjab* (veiled), and none of the members of the family was committed to daily prayers, or for that matter to any other Islamic-Shi`ite rituals. We must ask, then, why Mr. Bolouri jeopardized his life and his family's wellbeing by shouting *Allah-o Akbar* in defiance of martial law. Was it the integrity of Islam that was at stake for him? Was it the loss of identity due to the so-called 'rapid modernization' against which he was rioting?

I intend neither to psychologize nor to discover, in terms of rational choice, the tangible-material incentives behind one's participation in a revolutionary movement. The key to mass participation in a revolution is the creation of a safe space, a context within which one may culturally and politically justify one's presence. However, a safe space does not suggest that revolutionary participation occurs only if it is proven risk-free, for risk-free revolutionism is inherently contradictory. Rather, I want to emphasize the significance of cultural references and formal and informal institutions of the ethical order of society, norms and customs, in the transformation of the private individual into the public actor.

A master frame that Islamized the revolution of 1978-79 and defined its goals has been constructed retrospectively. It was also in retrospect that, to legitimize their victory, the *winners* wrote a new constitution, identified the ideologues of the revolution, devised a genealogy of its ideology, and named streets, parks, concert halls, university campuses, and public buildings after its martyrs. But the 'mullahs,' as a commonplace narrative of the Iranian revolution has it, did not steal the revolution from progressive, secular, and democratic actors. The symbolic universe of Islam in Iran had a constitutive significance in the formation of the revolutionary movement. Islam offered a cultural context within which a great majority of Iranians could identify with a call for justice and liberty and with the abolition of the *ancien régime.* But the Islam that won the revolution was distinct from the Islam that was institutionalized in the constitution. While the Islam of revolution was nebulous and indeterminate, the Islam of the Islamic Republic became prescriptive and doctrinal. The former was the Islam of negation, the latter affirmation.

The constitutive significance of Islam in the public sphere disturbs secular humanist sensibilities. The critics of public Islam often cite the Islamic Republic's *grande terreur* to justify their uneasiness about public religion as an emancipatory ideology, insisting that *religion in the public sphere breeds theocratic totalitarianism.* Islam is emancipatory when it is privatized, the devout secularists argue, social justice and democracy are essentially extra-religious.

The tragic events of September 11, 2001, and the Bush Administration's subsequent 'war on terror' [sic] reinforced the popular imperative to 'privatize' Islam. On March 1, 2006, in response to the Danish cartoon affair,[2] twelve writers, journalists, and intellectuals of diverse political background and national origin published a manifesto called 'Together Facing the New Totalitarianism.' The manifesto began with a provocative statement. 'After having overcome,' the signatories declared, 'fascism, Nazism, and Stalinism, the world now faces a new global totalitarian threat: Islamism.' They called for 'resistance to religious totalitarianism and for the promotion of freedom, equal opportunity and secular values for all. The recent events, have revealed the necessity of the struggle for these universal values.' With absolute clarity, the authors announced they 'reject "cultural relativism" which implies an acceptance that men and women of Muslim culture be deprived of the right to equality, freedom, and secularism in the name of the respect for certain cultures and traditions.'

The manifesto turned secularism into a universal right, conveniently neglecting to acknowledge the totalitarianisms they have overcome in addition to the entire failed mission of post-colonial nation-building were all secular projects. They brushed aside colonial atrocities committed under the name of Reason and Progress, and de-historicized Islamism as yet another ideology of intolerance rooted in the antiquated moral orders of fanatical bearded men and oppressed veiled women.

More intriguing than the text of the manifesto were the names of its twelve framers, a curious alliance between the old Left and the new Right, between self-proclaimed progressives and self-hating natives. It included Philippe Val, the founder of the leftist French weekly *Charlie Hebdo*, Irshad Manji, the author of the best-seller book *The Trouble with Islam Today*, the Muslim heroine of the American neo-conservatives, the French feminist sociologist Caroline Fourest, whose claim to fame was her controversial book *Frère Tariq*, an exposé of the Swiss Muslim theologian Tariq Ramadan, Ayaan Hirsi Ali, a right-wing Dutch politician of Somali origin who was elected to the Dutch Parliament on the anti-immigrant platform of the right-wing VVD and whose video *Submission* was widely distributed by the LPF, a Dutch neo-Nazi party, and finally, the omni-present Salman Rushdie, the rainbow politics of all-in-one.

The manifesto's revisionist history, which couples democratic-progressive politics with secularism and conversely, autocratic-reactionary politics with religious fundamentalism, fails to recognize the multilayered and politically contested manifestations of public religion. As I have tried to demonstrate in this book, rather than an example of the inherently oppressive core of public Islam, the Reign of Terror in the early 1980s and the longstanding of totalitarian tendencies in the Islamic Republic reflect the historical and political contingencies of the postrevolutionary regime's consolidation of power. From the formative days of the revolution to contemporary hermeneutical debates, public expressions of Islam had shaped the Iranian political landscape. From Mr. Bolouri's unsung courage during a midnight defiance of martial law to the courageous actors of civil society in today's Iran, competing meanings of Islam have been articulated, appropriated, and contested in the public sphere.

In this book I have highlighted the democratization of the entire edifice of Islamic knowledge production as one of the most enduring, albeit unintended, consequences of the Iranian revolution. From early discussions in the Constitutional Assembly to present day debates on the foundations of civil liberty, various groups have advanced their interpretations of Islam to justify their social and political agenda. Making Islam public, as a source of legitimacy of social action, undermines the authority of the traditional clerical establishment to legislate religious Truth. What Islam is and how it affords legitimacy is a topic no longer restricted to seminary quarters, but appears daily in a representative parliament, universities, courtrooms, street corners, radio and television, newspaper columns, and classrooms.

Not only could the Iranian experiment with public Islam usher in a democratic transformation of the Muslim world, it could also offer a new approach to in understanding public religion in general. The Enlightenment legacy of the privatization of religion as the precondition of democracy has left, in most cases, religion in the hands of anti-democratic and exclusivist clerical actors. The Iranian experience shows that secular humanism with its emphasis on the privatization of religion is not the only rejoinder to patriarchal advocates of politicized religion. The response to intolerant public religion must come from an inclusive, pluralist, and democratic public religion of justice. The social and political consequences of dogmatic orthodoxies need to be countered by a politics of competing interpretive religious hermeneutics.

Not only does a sustainable democracy depend on the constitutional and legal recognition of rights, it also needs to be perpetuated by private people promoting public good. The formal *recognition* of rights must give rise to the practical *exercise* of those rights. Those who advocate privatized religion believe, that the individual becomes a public actor only in the guise of a universal rational self equipped with moral autonomy to critique inherited beliefs and customs. For devout secularists, public action must be solely justified within the bounds of Habermas's 'modern structure of consciousness,' or be rooted in the individual's capacity to have an 'effective sense of justice,' as John Rawls once famously theorized. [3] But these conditions presuppose a *rupture* that transforms the old-traditional self into the new-modern actor; where the old is content with the *given* good life, while the new rationally strives for social justice. 'Under what conditions can we say,' Seyla Benhabib once remarked, 'that these general rules of action are valid not simply because they are what you and I have been brought up to believe or because they are what my synagogue, my neighbors, my tribe say so, but because they are fair, just, impartial, in the mutual interest of all?'[4]

The underlying and gendered elitism in this rationalist ethics is premised on the nineteenth century belief that the modern organization of social life has led or will soon lead to the decline of the explanatory authority of religion. Western modernity required the disengagement and differentiation of the public sphere from religion. Religion, once part of the public realm, must now work its enchantments—if at all—in a severely restricted private sphere. The masculine view of the segregation of public and private spheres, and the primacy of the former over the latter has in effect, as many feminist theologians have insisted, *feminized* religion by delegating it to the home, thus rendering it irrelevant to the public realm of politics.[5]

In an anti-colonial context, the Iranian revolution, along with Latin American Liberation Theology, deprivatized religion. It showed that rather than as being a residual tradition representing old social formations, one must understand public religion as emergent cultural practices, in which new meanings and values, new norms and traditions, new significances and experiences are continually being reinvented. As I have demonstrated in the preceding pages, public Islam derives its inspiration from the teachings of the Qur'an while implementing them with reference to the French, Bulgarian, or Chinese constitutions, it romanticizes the life of the Prophet while drawing upon the teachings of Fanon, it is mesmerized by Rumi while reading Wittgenstein, it appreciates Sufi mysticism while enjoying German and French hermeneutics. Both in its dogmatic-totalitarian practice, and in its hermeneutical-democratic manifestation, public Islam represents perpetually contested worldviews competing to become hegemonic.

Revolutions are motivated by Utopia, by a sense of justice and dignity which will be realized in an imaginary Promised Future, one that is inexorably linked to a romantic fantasy of Lost Heavens. While longing for the transcendental good society offers hope, believing in its existential reality generates Terror. The Iranian revolution gone awry was another totalizing attempt to reconstitute an entire society. This attempt created neither a homogenous society, nor a uniform polity. The Islamic character of the revolution and the postrevolutionary regime brought religion into the public sphere and empowered social groups who were otherwise disenfranchised and disengaged from civil society. But public religion also transformed Islam. It generated its own voices of dissent from within who advanced a far-reaching project of *hermeneutics as politics*.

Recognizing the multiplicity of meaning, and the negation of any claim of privileged access to truth—Historical Necessity, the Word of God, the Law of Progress, the March of Reason—lays the foundation for a viable democratic Islamic politics. Both a singular Islamist dogma, as well as a singular mode of modernity, are inherently totalitarian. They herald not the salvation of all, but the suppression of others; their Truth is realized only through terror. 'The "pluralizing hermeneutics,"' said Bauman echoing a Soroushian sentiment, 'augurs a "being towards the text" in lieu of the "being towards murder."'[6]

Notes

CHAPTER ONE

1   SAVAK was the Shah's secret police established with the help of the CIA advisors in 1958.   Under the SAVAK's control the prison was known as the Joint Committee Against Subversives.

2   The estimate was published in the spring 1982 issue of *Payām-e Enqelāb*, the journal of the *Sepāh-e Pāsdārān* (The Guardians of the Revolution Corps).

3   The pro-Soviet *Hezb-e Tudeh* (The People's Party), and *Sāzmān-e Cherik-hā-ye Fadā'i-ye Khlaq* (The Organization of the Guerrilla Devotees of the People).

4   Because of the vehement anti-American rhetoric of the regime, for the *Tudeh* party this meant as a step closer towards the Soviets.

5   I have borrowed this notion from Bjorn Hettne, *Development and the Three Worlds*, New York: Longman Scientific & Technical, 1991.   Hettne argued that the 'historical function of socialism has been to organize transitions to capitalism in backward areas.   This, however, does not mean that a future function of socialism may not still remain.   As long as the system of production and distribution is irrational from the point of view of human needs and ecological sustainability, the socialist tradition will always constitute a source of criticism and utopias' (p. 231).

6   Akbar Ahmad, *Postmodernism and Islam,* London: Routledge, 1992.

7   Ernest Gellner, *Postmodernism, Reason, and Religion,* London : Routledge, 1992.

8   Here I am not referring to the principle of *anything goes* as defined by Paul Feyerabend. Many Muslim critics of modernity and postmodernity, most notably Abdolkarim Soroush, mistakenly attack Feyerabend's use of the concept as a justification for the moral and cultural decadence of the west.   Rather than to a form of chaotic hedonism, *anything goes* in Feyerabend refers to a cosmological and historical principle.   He wrote, 'It is clear [...] that the idea of a fixed method, or of a fixed theory of rationality, rests on too naive a view of man [sic] and his social surroundings.   To those who look at the rich material provided by history, and who are not intent on impoverishing it in order to please their lower instincts, their craving for intellectual security in the form of clarity, precision, "objectivity," "truth," it will become clear that there is only one principle that can be defended under *all* circumstances and in *all* stages of human development.   It is the principle: *anything goes*' (Paul K. Feyerabend, *Against Method,* London: Verso, 1988 [1975], pp. 27-28).

[9] In 1985, *Sāzmān-e Mojahedin-e Khalq-e Iran* (The Organization of the Iranian People's Mujahedin, known in the West as Mujahedin Khalq Organization (MKO), published a list of more that 14,000 men and women who were executed between 1981-1984.

[10] For example, see Rosalind O'Hanlon's and David Washbrook's ('After Orientalism: Culture, criticism, and politics in the Third World,' *Comparative Study of Society and History*, vol. 34-1, 1992) critique of Gyan Prakash ('Writing post-Orientalist histories of the Third World: Perspectives from Indian historiography,' *Comparative Study of Society and History*, vol. 32-2, 1990) and Prakash's response ('Can the "subaltern" ride? A reply to O'Hanlon and Washbrook,' *Comparative Study of Society and History*, vol. 34-1, 1992).

[11] Derrida wrote, 'Metaphysics—the White mythology which reassembles and reflects the culture of the West: the white man takes his own mythology, Indo-European mythology, his own *logos*, that is, the *mythos* of his idiom, for the universal form that he must still wish to call Reason.' (*Margins of Philosophy*, Chicago: The University of Chicago Press, 1982, p. 213)

[12] Prakash, 'Can the subaltern ride?' p. 213.

[13] O'Hanlon & Washbrook, op cit. p. 150.

[14] Ibid, p. 152.

[15] Fredric Jameson, *Postmodernism, or the Cultural Logic of Late Capitalism*, Durham: Duke University Press, 1991, pp. 399-418.

[16] For a discussion on this topic see Patrick Williams & Laura Chrisman, eds. *Colonial Discourse and Post-Colonial Theory*, New York: Columbia University Press, 1994, especially their introduction to Part Four.

[17] G. C. Spivak, 'Can the subaltern speak?' in Cary Nelson & Lawrence Grossberg, eds., *Marxism and the Interpretation of Culture*, Urbana & Chicago: University of Illinois Press, 1988, p. 276. Commenting on Foucault-Deleuze conversation in 'intellectuals and power,' Spivak reiterated that 'a post-representationalist vocabulary hides an essentialist agenda.' (p. 285)

[18] Fredric Jameson, 'Marxism and postmodernism,' *New Left Review*, no. 176, 1989, p. 34.

[19] Jameson, *Postmodernism*, p. 401.

[20] Jameson, *Postmodernism*, p. 402.

[21] Habermas wrote, 'We cannot exclude from the outset the possibility that neoconservativism and aesthetically inspired anarchism, in the name of a farewell to modernity, are merely trying to revolt against it once again. It could be that they are merely cloaking their complicity with the venerable tradition of counter-Enlightenment in the garb of post-Enlightenment.' (*The Philosophical Discourse of Modernity*, trans. by Frederick G. Lawrence, Cambridge, MA: MIT Press, 1995, p. 5).

[22] Here Mannheim echoed Marx's dialectical understanding between social conditions and change in his famous theses on Feuerbach. In the third thesis Marx stated 'The materialist doctrine that men are products of circumstances and upbringing, and that, therefore, changed men are products of other circumstances [...] forgets that it is men who change circumstances and that it is essential to educate the educator himself.' (Karl Mannheim, *Ideology and Utopia: An Introduction to the Sociology of Knowledge*, New York, London: Harvest/HBJ Book, 1985, pp. 198-99.)

[23] Mannheim, Ibid, p. 253.

[24] Bloch offers an alternative to totalizing 'cognitive mapping' by incorporating folk culture into his conception of Utopia. In the introduction to his *magnum*

opus, The Principle of Hope, he wrote, '[*Wishful images in the mirror*] clear completely as soon as the mirror comes from the people, as occurs quite visibly and wonderfully in fairytales. The mirrored [...] common to all of them is a drive towards the colorful, representing what is supposedly or genuinely better. The appeal of dressing-up, illuminated *display* belong here, but then the world of *fairytale,* brightened distanced in *travel,* the *dance,* the dream-factory of *film,* the example of *theater* [...] However, if this sketching out turns into free and considered blueprint, then we find ourselves for the first time among the actual, that is, *planned or outlined utopias.*' (Ernst Bloch, *The Principle of Hope,* vol. 1, trans. N. Plaice, S Plaice, and P. Knight, Cambridge, MA: MIT Press, 1986, p. 13)

25 Edward Said, 'Orientalism reconsidered,' in Francis Barker *et al.,* eds. *Literature, Politics and Theory,* London: Methuen, 1986, p. 228.

26 Edward Said, *The World, the Text, and the Critic,* London: Faber & Faber, 1984, p. 30.

27 James Clifford, *The Predicament of Culture: Twentieth Century Ethnography, Literature, and Art,* Cambridge, MA: Harvard University Press, 1988, p. 263.

28 Ibid. p. 271.

29 This was a term coined by Homi Bhabha to describe Rushdie's *Satanic Verses.* He wrote, 'Where once we could believe in the comforts and continuities of tradition, today we must face the responsibilities of cultural translation... *The Satanic Verses* is a postcolonial work that attempts the onerous duty of unraveling this cultural translation' ('At the limits,' *Artforum,* vol. 27-9, 1989, p. 11).

30 For the most insightful discussion of the Rushdie Affair see Talal Asad, 'Multiculturalism and British identity in the wake of the Rushdie Affair,' *Politics and Society,* vol. 18-4, 1990. I shall emphasize here that Rushdie himself never intended to write a book that 'represents' the experience of a whole community. He wrote, 'Do not ask your writers to create *typical* or *representative* fictions. Such books are almost invariably dead books. The liveliness of literature lies in its exceptionality, in being the individual, idiosyncratic vision of one human being, in which, to our delight and great surprise, we may find our own image reflected' (*Imaginary Homelands,* London & New York: Granta Books, 1991, p. 412).

31 Rushdie as cited in Bhikhu Parekh, 'Reflections,' in L. Appignanesi & S. Maitland, eds., *The Rushdie File,* Syracuse, NY: Syracuse University Press, 1990, p. 122.

32 The observation put forward by Stuart Hall ('Our mongrel selves,' *New Statesman & Society,* vol. 5-207, 1992) and Homi Bhabha ('At the limits').

33 Bhabha, op cit, p. 12.

34 Cited in Asad, 'Multiculturalism,' pp. 458-460.

35 On January 9, 1998, the UK Education Secretary agreed to state funding of Islamic schools. The minister, David Blunkett, approved two schools, one in London and one in Birmingham, for the program. In an interview with Reuters, Iqbal Sacranie, Convenor of the United Kingdom Action Committee on Islamic Affairs, said that 'Such approval has been long overdue... It marks an important first step ... to build an equal and inclusive society.' (New York Times, 1/10/98)

36 Raymond Williams (*Culture and Society, 1780-1950,* New York: Harper and Row, 1958) redefined culture as a process, rather than a state, irreducible to 'its artifacts while it is being lived.' Postcolonial theory was profoundly

influenced by the notion of culture as lived experience, for it legitimized the self-awareness of the subaltern.

[37] Aziz al-Azmeh, *Islams and Modernities,* London & New York: Verso 1993, p. 3.

[38] Bhabha, op cit.

[39] Rushdie, *Imaginary Homelands,* p. 130.

[40] Rushdie, Ibid. p. 430.

[41] Pouyan was one of the founding members of *Fadā'iyan-e Khalq,* an urban guerrilla communist group established in 1970. In his manifesto on the necessity of armed struggle entitled *On the Refutation of the Theory of Survival,* written in 1969, he identified two principle causes that prevented the working class from rising against their oppression. '[Workers] presume,' he wrote, 'the power of their enemy to be absolute and their own inability to emancipate themselves [to be] absolute.' And then he asked, 'How can one think of emancipation while confronting absolute power with absolute weakness?' (p. 4). Pouyan was born in 1946 in Mashad and killed by the security forces in during a clash in the western part of Tehran in 1971.

[42] For a thoughtful review of the failure of the theories of social revolutions to explicate the origins and the dynamics of the Iranian revolution see Charles Kurzman's *The Unthinkable Revolution in Iran,* Cambridge, MA: Harvard University Press, 2004.

[43] An important example of this view is Misagh Parsa's *States, Ideologies, and Social Revolutions: A Comparative Analysis of Iran, Nicaragua, and the Philippines,* Cambridge, New York: Cambridge University Press, 2004.

[44] See three important books which gained canonical significance: Nikki Keddie and Yann Richard, *Roots of Revolution: An Interpretative History of Modern Iran,* New Haven, CT: Yale University Press, 1981; Ervand Abrahamian, *Iran Between Two Revolutions,* Princeton, NJ: Princeton University Press, 1982; and Said Amir Arjomand, *The Turban for the Crown: The Islamic Revolution in Iran,* New York, Oxford: Oxford University Press, 1988.

[45] Anthony Giddens, *The Consequences of Modernity,* Stanford: Stanford University Press, 1990, p. 4. In response to the question as to whether modernity is a *western* project, Giddens obstinately responded 'yes' (pp. 175-176).

[46] Aidan Foster Carter, *The Sociology of Development,* New York, NY: Causeway Books, 1985, p. 6.

[47] Robert Wuthnow, 'Understanding religion and politics,' *Daedalus,* no. 120, 1991, p. 3.

[48] Alasdir MacIntyre, *Whose Justice, Whose Rationality,* Notre Dame: University of Notre Dame Press, 1984, pp. 7-8.

[49] Bernard Lewis found the roots of Muslim rage in their irrational feeling of 'Humiliation—a growing awareness, among the heirs of an old, proud, and long dominant civilization, for having been overtaken, overborne, and over-whelmed by those whom they regarded as their inferiors' ('Roots of Muslim rage,' *Atlantic Monthly,* September 1990, p. 59).

[50] See for example, Patricia Crone, *Slaves on Horses: The Evolution of the Islamic Polity,* Cambridge: Cambridge University Press, 1980; Daniel Pipes, *In the Path of God: Islam and Political Power,* New York: Basic Books, 1983; Bernard Lewis, *The Political Language of Islam,* Chicago: University of Chicago Press, 1988; W. M. Watt, *Islamic Fundamentalism and Modernity,* London: Routledge, 1988.

51   Sami Zubaida, *Islam, the People and the State,* London: Routledge, 1989; Henry
     Munson, *Islam and Revolution in the Middle East,* New Haven, CT: Yale
     University Press, 1988; John Esposito, *Islamic Threat: Myth or Reality,* New
     York & Oxford: Oxford University Press, 1992; Joel Beinin & Joe Stork, eds.,
     Political Islam, Berkeley & Los Angeles: University of California Press, 1997.
52   See Keddie, *Roots;* Abrahamian, *Two Revolutions.*
53   Conventional wisdom renders revolutions as the result of both the intensifi-
     cation of class antagonism and the inability of the state to maintain its
     governing powers. In his book, *States, Ideologies, and Social Revolutions,*
     Misagh Parsa advances a theory that contradicts the main premises of this
     widely accepted conception of revolution. Parsa argues that the formation of
     broad coalitions is the most fundamental feature of Third World revolutions.
     Using three case studies of Iran, Nicaragua, and the Philippines, he
     demonstrates persuasively that, in contrast to all varieties of Marxian
     theories, a high level of working-class militancy and a strong ideological anti-
     capitalist commitment *impede* revolutionary transformation of state and class
     structure.
54   See *Taqvim-e tārikh-e enqelāb-e islami-ye Iran: Khabarhā va ruydādhā-ye ruzāneh,*
     Mordād-e 1356-Farvardin-e 1358 (*The Calendar and History of the Islamic*
     Revolution of Iran: Daily Reports and News from July 1978 to April 1979), Tehran:
     Soroush Publishers, 1991.

CHAPTER TWO

1   J. M. Blaut, *The Colonizer's Model of the World: Geographical Diffusionism and*
     Eurocentric History, London & New York: The Guilford Press, 1993.
2   That is, in its Weberian sense, the rational organization and administration of
     society (civic associations), economy (capitalism), and politics (the secular
     nation-state).
3   Edmund Burke III, (ed.), *Rethinking World History, Essays on Europe, Islam, and*
     World History: Marshall G. Hodgson, Cambridge, England: Cambridge
     University Press, 1993.
4   Eric Jones, *The European Miracle,* Cambridge, England: Cambridge University
     Press, 1981.
5   Hegel cited in Bryan Turner, *Orientalism, Postmodernism, and Globalism,*
     London: Routledge, 1994, p. 27.
6   From the word *salaf* meaning pious ancestors, early Islamic community.
     Salafiyyah suggests a call for a revitalizing the premises of the early Islamic
     community.
7   Although everywhere outside Iran Sayyid Jamal is known as al-Afghani,
     Iranians know him, after his native village, as Sayyid Jamal Asad-abadi.
8   Nikki Keddie, *An Islamic Response to Imperialism,* Berkeley & Los Angeles:
     University of California Press, 1968. Keddie also wrote another authoritative
     account *Sayyid Jamal ad-Din 'al-Afghani': A Political Biography,* Berkeley, Los
     Angeles: University of California Press, 1972.
9   On the significance of al-Afghani see Sami Zubaida, 'Islam and nationalism:
     Continuities and contradictions,' *Nations and Nationalism,* vol. 10-4, 2004.
10   Indian National Archives, Foreign Affairs Documents, G. Corderry's (sic)
     report to C. Grant, June 25, 1883, cited in Fereidun Adamiyyat, *Eideolozhi-ye*
     nehzat-e mashrutiyat-e Iran (*The Ideology of the Iranian Constitutional Movement*),
     Tehran: Payam, 1976, p. 33.

11   For the intellectual sources of the Constitutional Revolution see Fereidun Adamiyyat, *Fekr-e demokrāsi-ye ejtemā`i dar nehzat-e mashrutiyat-e Iran* (*The Idea of Social Democracy in the Iranian Constitutional Movement*), Tehran: Payam, 1976.

12   Keddie, *Islamic Response*, p. 1.

13   Keddie, Ibid. pp. 2-3.

14   Wilfred Cantwell Smith, *Islam in Modern History*, Princeton, NJ: Princeton University Press, 1957.

15   W. M. Watt, op cit, pp. 62-63.

16   W. C. Smith, op cit, pp. 47-51. For a lengthier discussion of early Islamic modernism see Fazlur Rahman, *Islam and Modernity, Transformation of an Intellectual Tradition*, Chicago & London: The University of Chicago Press, 1988, particularly pp. 43-83.

17   Al-Afghani, 'Lecture on teaching and learning,' November 8, 1882, Albert Hall, Calcutta. 'Commentary on the commentator,' 'The benefits of philosophy,' all English translations in Keddie, *Islamic Response*.

18   Some notions of this critique are present in his famous work called 'The truth about the *neicheri* sect,' 1880-1881, but he directly attacks Sir Ahmed Khan in his short essay entitled 'The materialist in India,' 1884. (in Keddie, op cit.)

19   Cited in Keddie, *Islamic Response*, p. 41.

20   In his theory of national liberation, Franz Fanon (*The Wretched of the Earth*, trans. Constance Farrington, Harmondsworth: Penguin, 1967 & *Black Skin, White Masks*, London: Pluto Press, 1986) also emphasized the predicament of cultural alienation and estrangement from the homeland. Al-Afghani's dialectical approach to the colonized and colonizer relation was also observed by Pierre Bourdieu in the establishment of the colonial relation in the Algerian countryside: 'The European gradually created an environment that reflected his own image and was a negation of the traditional order, a world in which he no longer felt himself to be a stranger and in which by natural reversal, the Algerian finally was considered to be a stranger' (*The Algerians*, Trans. A. C. M. Ross, Boston: Beacon Press, 1961, p. 131).

21   In Keddie, *Islamic Response*, p. 56.

22   Keddie, Ibid. p. 43.

23   Plural form of `ālim*, learned men of Islam, often used to refer to the Muslim clergy.

24   Keddie, Ibid. p. 65.

25   al-Afghani, *The Materialists in India*, in Keddie, 1968.

26   In Keddie, Ibid. p. 179. The idea that the colonizers did native people an unwanted favor by forcing modernization on them is the kernel of the western evolutionist perspective on history, either in its crude Marxian determinism or in its liberal-conservative version. The Marxian approaches are based on Marx's often cited journalistic writings on India. In his July 22, 1853 article, Marx asserted that 'modern industry, resulting from the railway system, will dissolve the hereditary divisions of labor, upon which rest the Indian castes, those decisive impediments to Indian progress' ('The British rule in India,' in *Karl Marx and Frederick Engels, Selected Works in Three Volumes*, Vol. 1, Moscow: Progress Publishers, 1983, p. 497). He concluded another article which was published in June of the same year with these words: 'Then, whatever bitterness the spectacle of the crumbling of an ancient world may have for our personal feelings, we have the right, in point of history, to exclaim with Goethe:

Sollte diese Qual uns quälen, Should this torture then torment
Da sie unsre Lust vermehrt, Since it brings us greater pleasure
Hat nicht Myriaden Seelen Were not through the rule of Timur
Timur's Herrschaft aufgezehrt Souls devoured without measure?
(Karl Marx, 'The future results of British rule in India,' Ibid. 1983, p. 493)

Far from a Marxian conception of history, Newton Gingrich, the onetime Speaker of the House, contended in his dissertation, 'Within the beliefs of twentieth century American liberalism, European colonialism is an unacceptable political policy, but what did it mean to the natives? Did the colonial powers perform a painful but positive function in disrupting traditional society and so paving the way for more rapid modernization?' (Newton Gingrich, 1971, *Belgian Education Policy in the Congo, 1945-1960,* Tulane University Ph.D. Dissertation, cited in Garry Wills, 'The Visionary,' *The New York Review of Books,* March 23, 1995.)

27 Fazlur Rahman, *Islam and Modernity,* pp. 50-51.

28 Jamshid Behnam, *Iranian va andishe-ye tajaddod* (Iranians and the Idea of Modernity), Tehran: Farzan, 1997, p. 94.

29 H. Enayat, *Modern Islamic Political Thought,* London: Macmillan, 1982, p. 1.

30 Enayat, Ibid. p. 69.

31 A revivalist movement named after its founder Muhammad ibn Abd al-Wahhab (1703-1792). In addition to its formative influence on Saudi Arabia, its significance is due to its role in the canonization of Islam and the attack on local Sufi practices.

32 For a classic treatment of al-Banna's ideas and the formation of *al-Ikhwān,* see Robert Mitchell, *The Society of Muslim Brothers,* New York & Oxford: Oxford University Press, 1969. To learn about al-Banna's ideas in the general context of Islamic political thought see Anouar Abdel-Malek, *Contemporary Arab Political Thought,* London: Zed Press, 1983.

33 In Mitchell, op cit, p. 30.

34 For most of Islamic history, both Sunni and Shi'ite theologians subscribed to the political doctrine of the primacy of order versus chaos. In this doctrine, the most eloquent proponent of which was Muhammad al-Ghazali (1058-1111), Muslims should obey their king/sultan/caliph for he provides security for the *ummah.* Even Ayatollah Khomeini, in the early days of his political career, advocated a similar position. In his 1943 *Kashf el-asrār* (*Revealing Secrets*) he reiterated that, 'Bad government is better than no government. We have never attacked the sultanate; if we criticized, it was a particular king and not kingship that we criticized. History shows that *mujtahids* have aided kings who did wrong: Nasir ad-Din Tusi, Mohaqqiq-i Sani, Shaykh Baha'i, Mir Damad, Majlisi [...] Mujtahids do not simply attack [the government], but if necessary help it as they did with semi-independent Iraq under the leadership of Mirza Mohammad-Taqi Shirazi. The ulama always cooperate with the government if that is needed.' (Cited in Michael Fischer, *Iran from Religious Dispute to Revolution,* Cambridge & London: Harvard University Press, 1982, p. 152. For a more detailed analysis of the evolution of Khomeini's ideas see Michael Fischer 'Islam and the revolt of the petit bourgeoisie,' *Daedalus,* vol. 3-1, Winter 1982.

35 John Esposito (ed.), *Voices of Resurgent Islam,* New York, Oxford: Oxford University Press, 1983, p. 10.

[36] John O. Voll, 'Fundamentalism in the Sunni Arab world,' in Martin E. Marty and R. Scott Appleby (eds.), *Fundamentalisms Observed,* Chicago: University of Chicago Press, 1991, p. 366.

[37] Abul Ala Maududi, *A Short History of the Revivalist Movement in Islam,* Lahore, Pakistan: Islamic Publications (PVT) Limited, 1963.

[38] Cited in Charles Adams, 'Mawdudi and the Islamic state,' in Esposito, *Voices of Resurgent Islam,* p. 108.

[39] For an extensive account of the evolution of Maududi't thought see Asad Gilani, *Maududi: Thought and Movement,* Lahore: Farooq Hasan Gilani, 1978, and Vali Nasr, *The Vanguard of the Islamic Revolution: the Jama`at-i Islami of Pakistan,* Berkeley, Los Angeles: University of California Press, 1994.

[40] For Maududi's doctrine on the Islamic state see A. A. Maududi, *First Principles of Islamic State,* translated and edited by Khurshid Ahmad, Lahore: Islamic Publications, 1974.

[41] A. A. Maududi, *Human Rights in Islam,* Leicester, UK: The Islamic Foundation, 1976.

[42] Enayat, *Islamic Political Thought,* p. 108.

[43] Yvonne Haddad, 'Sayyid Qutb: Ideologue of Islamic revival,' in Esposito, *Voices of Resurgent Islam,* p. 91.

[44] He wrote to his mother, 'Your greatest wish was that God might open my heart, that I commit the Qur'an to memory, and that I recite the Qur'an sitting before you in a beautiful intonation. so, I have memorized the Qur'an and fulfilled a part of your wish' (Sayyid Qutb, *Islam and Universal Peace,* Indianapolis, IN: American Trust Publications, 1993, p. ix).

[45] M. Siddiqui, 'Introduction,' in Qutb, *Universal Peace,* p. xii.

[46] Sayyid Qutb, *Milestones,* Salimiah, Kuwait: International Islamic Federation of Student Organizations, 1964/1978.

[47] Qutb, *Milestones,* pp. 13-14.

[48] Qutb, Ibid. p. 34

[49] Qutb, Ibid. pp. 81-83.

[50] Haddad, op cit, p. 88.

[51] Qutb, *Milestones,* p. 85.

[52] Qutb, *Milestones,* p. 84.

[53] Cited in Emmanuel Sivan, *Radical Islam: Medieval Theology and Modern Politics,* New Haven, London: Yale University Press, 1990, p. 129.

[54] Qutb, *Milestones,* pp. 96-102.

[55] Qutb, *Milestones,* p. 100.

[56] Many Muslim critics of Qutb have emphasized his esoteric interpretation of the Qur'anic notion of who is a Muslim. Hasan al-Hudaybi, a prominent *al-Ikhwān* leader, rejected Qutb's condemnation of self-proclaimed Muslims and adhered to the oft-cited Islamic principle that, 'We must consider any one who pro-claims that 'there is no God but Allah and that Muhammad is the messenger of Allah,' to be a Muslim . . . and must treat him on the basis of the *shari`a* since he is a Muslim' (Ibrahim Abu Rabi', *Intellectual Origins of Islamic Resurgence in the Modern Arab World,* Albany, NY: SUNY Press, 1996, p. 209).

[57] For a summary of his doctrine see Sivan, *Radical Islam,* pp. 94-113.

[58] Albert Hourani, *A History of the Arab Peoples,* Cambridge: Harvard University Press, 1991, p. 144.

[59] For a good representation of this approach see Michael Whine, 'Islamism and totalitarianism similarities and differences," *Totalitarian Movements and Political Religions,* vol. 2-2, Autumn 2001.

60 Sivan, *Radical Islam,* p. 27. On the issue of the continuity between Ibn
    Taymiyyah, Qutb's political philosophy, and the emergence of militant
    Islamist groups in the Middle East see Ahmed Moussalli, *Radical Islamic
    Fundamentalism: The Ideological and Political Discourse of Sayyid Qutb,* Beirut:
    American University of Beirut Press, 1992; Gilles Kepel, *Muslim Extremism in
    Egypt: The Prophet and Pharaoh,* Berkeley: University of California Press, 1986;
    Johannes Jansen, *The Neglected Duty: The Creed of Sadat's Assassins and Islamic
    Resurgence in the Middle East,* New York: Macmillan, 1986; Kenneth Cragg, *The
    Pen and the Faith: Eight Modern Muslim Writers and the Qur'an,* London: George
    Allen and Unwin, 1985; and Bernard Lewis, *The Political Language of Islam.*
    For the best critique of the depiction of Qutb as anti-modern, see Roxanne
    Euben, *Enemy in the Mirror,* Princeton: Princeton University Press, 1999.
61 Olivier Roy, *The Failure of Political Islam,* trans. Carol Volk, Cambridge, MA:
    Harvard University Press, 1994, p. 6.
62 Euben, op cit, p. 155.
63 Enayat, *Islamic Political Thought,* p. 150.
64 Qutb, *Milestones,* pp. 203-204.
65 Cited in John Esposito, *Islam: The Straight Path,* Oxford: Oxford University
    Press, 1988, pp. 168-69.
66 Henry Precht, 'Ayatollah *Realpolitik,' Foreign Policy,* no. 70, spring 1988, p. 113.

CHAPTER THREE

1   *Goftemān,* p. 10. All the citations are from the transcripts of the debates
    collected by Ali Zinati in a volume entitled *Goftemān-e rowshangar (The
    Illuminating Discourse),* Qom: Imam Khomeini Research Institute, 2000.
2   *Goftemān,* p. 11.
3   The invitation was extended to the representatives of the Liberation
    Movement of Iran (*Nehzat-e azadi*), National Front (*Jebhe-ye melli*), People's
    Mujahidin, JAMA, and Habibollah Payman a respected Muslim activist and
    intellectual, but they refused to participate so long as the organizers ignored
    their input in defining the agenda.
4   Each session was dedicated to a philosophical topic related to Marxian
    philosophy: 1. The Principles of Dialectics, 2. Evolution, 3. Contradiction, 4.
    The Relation between Contradiction and Motion, 5. Motion, The Generality of
    Motion, 7. The Transition from Quantity to Qualtiy.
5   During the same period, another series was also broadcasted on the issues of
    political economy and state policy. Participants in that series were, Babak
    Zahra'i, from the Trotskyite Iranian Socialist Party; Nur ad-Din Kianuri, the
    Chair of the Central Committee of the Tudeh party; Abolhasan Bani Sadr, the
    President of the Republic; and Ayatollah Mohammad Beheshti, the spokes-
    person of the newly founded ruling party Islamic Republic Party (IRP).
6   *Goftemān,* p. 11
7   *Goftemān,* p. 13.
8   *Goftemān,* p. 15.
9   Ruhollah Musavi Khomeini, *Hokumat-e Islami: Velāyat-e Faqih (Islamic Gover-
    nance: The Rule of the Jurist),* Qom: np, 1971.
10 Fanon, *The Wretched of the Earth,* p. 37.
11 Fischer, *Religious Dispute,* p. 184.
12 Arjomand, *The Turban for the Crown,* p. 137.
13 *New York Times Magazine,* October 28, 1979, cited in Arjomand, Ibid. p. 138.

[14] See *Mashruh-e mozākerāt-e majles-e barresi-ye nahā'i-ye qānun-e asāsi-e jomhuri-ye islami-ye Iran* (*Minutes from the Negotiations of The Assembly for the Final Examination of the Constitution of the Islamic Republic*), Vol. 1-4, Tehran: Islamic Revolution Documents, 1985 (henceforth *Mozākerāt*).   Also see *Asnād-e enqelāb-e Islami* (*Islamic Revolution Documents*), Vol. 1-5, Tehran: Islamic Revolution Documents, 1995.

[15] Motahhari was assassinated in May 1979 before the idea of *velāyat-e faqih* was seriously considered by the postrevolutionary regime.   However, in a controversial speech at al-Javad Mosque in Tehran he expressed his concern about the excesses of the revolution and the dominance of the notion of revolutionary Islam.   See Morteza Motahhari, *Pirāmun-e enqelāb-e Islami* (*On the Islamic Revolution*), Qom: Islamic Publishers, 1982.

[16] Ruhollah Khomeini, *Sahifeh-ye Nur: Majmu`e-ye rahnemudha-ye Imam Khomeini*, Tehran: The Organization of the Islamic Revolution's Cultural Documents, 1983, vol. 2, p. 351.

[17] Mehdi Bazargan, *Enqelāb dar dow harekat* (*The Revolution in Two Movements*), Tehran: Nehzat-e Azadi, 1984.

[18] According to Habibi, the five jurists who authored the first draft of the constitution were Ahmad Sadr Hajj Seyyed Javadi, Naser Katuzian, Mohammad Ja`fari Langarudi, `Abdolkarim Lahiji, and `Abbas Minachi (see Asghar Schirazi, *The Constitution of Iran: Politics and the State in the Islamic Republic*, translated by John O'Kane, London: I. B. Tauris, 1997, p. 38).   In an interview, Ezzatollah Sahabi recalled that Fathollah Bani Sadr, another liberal jurist, was also a member of the committee. See Bahman Ahmadi Amu`i, *Eqtesād-e siyāsi-ye Jomhuri-ye Islami: Dar goftegu ba Ezzatollah Sahabi* (*The Political Economy of the Islamic Republic: In Converstaion with Ezzatollah Sahabi*), Tehran: Jam-e No, 2003.

[19] For a history of the Fifth Republic see J.F. Hollifield & G. Ross (eds.), *Searching for the New France*, London: Routledge, 1991.

[20] For a brief history of the period see Schirazi, *The Constitution*, pp. 22-38 & Mehdi Moslem, *Factional Politics in Post-Khomeini Iran*, Syracuse: Syracuse University Press, 2002, pp. 11-46.

[21] See Amu'i, *Eqtesād-e siyāsi*.

[22] *Kayhan*, June 18, 1979, cited in Schirazi, Ibid. p. 23.

[23] Volumes 2 and 3 of Ayatollah Khomeini's *Sahifeh-y Nur* (collected volumes of his speeches and declarations) are largely devoted to his assertions about the meaning of an Islamic Republic and the role of the *ruhāniyat* in its affairs.   For specific references to his position on the advisory role of the *ruhāniyat*, see *Sahifeh-ye Nur* vol. 2, p. 250; vol. 3, pp. 110-111 and pp. 75-78.   Typical of these statements were: 'I, and other *ruhāniyun*, will not hold a position in the future government, the duty of *ruhāniyun* is to guide, I shall only take upon myself the responsibility of guiding the future government' (vol. 3, p. 135). On another occasion, he reiterated that 'I have never said that *ruhāniyun* are going to be in charge of the government, *ruhāniyun* have other responsibilities' (vol. 3, p. 140).

[24] Cited in Mohsen Kadivar, *Hokumat-e velā`i* (*Governance by Guardianship*), Tehran: Nay, 1999, p. 183.

[25] *Sahifeh*, Vol. 4, p. 463.

[26] Shaul Bakhash, *The Reign of the Ayatollahs, Iran and the Islamic Revolution*, New York: Basic Books, 1986, pp. 71-91.

[27] Bakhash, Ibid. p. 77.

28 At a meeting with the members of the Revolutionary Council and the Provisional Government on May 22, 1979, in Qom, Khomeini supported the idea of direct referendum in lieu of a constituent assembly. See Abolhasan Bani Sadr, *Khiyānat beh omid* (*The Betrayal of Hope*), np, 1982, p. 316 & Karim Sanjabi, *Omid-hā va nā-omidi-hā: Khāterāt-e siyāsi* (*Hopes and Disappointments: A Political Memoir)*, London: The National Front, 1989, pp. 332-33. According to Sanjabi, Mehdi Bazargan, the Head of the Provisional Government, played a significant role in changing Khomeini's mind on the issue of direct referendum of the draft (p. 334).

29 Bani Sadr, *Khiyānat*, p. 125. In interviews with Asghar Schirazi, other influential leaders of the revolution such as Ahmad Salamatian confirmed Bani Sadr's recollection. In his memoir, Karim Sanjabi (p. 333) the leader of the National Front also attributed the same position to Ayatollah Beheshti, the future vice-chair of the Assembly of Experts.

30 Cited in Bakhash, op cit. p. 78.

31 Daily *Jomhuri-ye Islami*, July 16, 1979, cited in Kadivar, *Hokumat-e velā'i*, p. 184.

32 Daily *Jomhuri-ye Islami*, July 15, 1979, cited in Kadivar, Ibid. pp. 186-87.

33 Daily *Kayhan*, September 15 & 29, 1979, cited in Kadivar, Ibid. p. 188.

34 *Sahifeh*, vol. 8, p. 75.

35 *Sahifeh*, vol. 3, p. 220.

36 *Mozākerāt*, vol. 1, pp. 5-6. Also printed in *Sahifeh*, vol. 8, p. 256.

37 *Mozākerāt*, vol. 1, p. 5.

38 *Mozākerāt*, vol. 1, p. 6.

39 *Surat-e mashruh-e mozākerāt-e bāznegari-ye qānun-e asāsi-ye jomhuri-ye eslami-ye Iran* (*The Complete Report of the Re-Appraisal of the Islamic Republic's Constitution*) (henceforth *Bāznegari)*, Vol. 1, p. 58.

40 Motahhari, *Eqelāb-e Islamic*, p. 78. In another speech at Tehran University's School of Divinity, he remarked, 'If in the early days of Islam, in response to non-believers, the Prophet had said: *kill them, destroy them,* Islam could not have survived. The only reason for the longevity of Islam is its audacity and clarity in engaging with opposing views' (Ibid, p. 14). Motahhari's post-revolutionary position was consistent with his idea of liberal and tolerant Islam on which he had written extensively. He believed the reason why secularism did not take root in Islamic societies was that, contrary to medieval Christianity, Islam recognized the diversity of ideas and did not identify any 'forbidden territories' in human thought (Motahhari, `*Elal-e gerāyesh beh māddi-gari* (*Causes of Attraction to Materialism*), Qom: Sadra Publishers 1978, p. 85).

41 *Sahifeh*, vol. 9, p. 88

42 *Sahifeh*, vol. 5, p. 125.

43 *Taqvim-e tārikh-e enqelāb-e islami-ye Iran* (*The Calendar and History of the Islamic Revolution of Iran*) (henceforth *Taqvim*), Tehran: Soroush, 1990, p. 298.

44 For the news of unrest immediately after the revolution and their media reports see *Taqvim*, pp. 290-98.

45 The delegation under the supervision of Ayatollah Taleqani arrived in Sanandaj on the first day of the Iranian New Year. Members of this delegation were Beheshti, Sadr Haj Seyyed Javadi, Bani Sadr, Hashemi Rafsanjani.

46 *Taqvim*, p. 290.

47 Cited in *Taqvim*, p. 298.

48 The Council was established to deal with the issue of labor conflicts and closures of factories due to capital flight. It had seven members from the

Ministry of Labor, Ministry of Industry, the Revolutionary Council, and two representatives on behalf of industry and labor.

49 Cited in Amu'i, *Eqtesād-e siyāsi*, p. 9.
50 Amu'i, *Eqtesād-e siyāsi*, p. 23.
51 *Sahifeh*, vol. 16, pp. 211-12.
52 For an account in English, see Schirazi, op cit. pp. 30-31.
53 *Mozākerāt*, vol. 1, pp. 375-76.
54 Ibid. p. 378.
55 The current version of Article 5 of the Iranian constitution states: 'During the Occultation of the *Vali-e `Asr* (may God hasten his reappearance), the *velāyat* and leadership of the *Ummah* devolve upon the just (`*ādel*) and pious (*muttaqi*) *faqih*, who is fully aware of the circumstances of his age; courageous, resourceful, and possessed of administrative ability, he will assume the responsibilities of this office in accordance with Article 107.' This version, which was debated by the Assembly, also emphasized that '*vali-e `asr* has to be recognized and accepted by the majority of people as their leader.' See *Mozākerāt*. vol. 1, p. 384.
56 *Mozākerāt*, vol. 1, p. 7.
57 See the invaluable essays collected in Charles Kurzman (ed.), *Modernist Islam, 1840-1940: A Source Book*, Oxford: Oxford University Press, 2002.
58 *Mozākerāt*, vol. 1, pp. 88-89.
59 *Mozākerāt*, vol. 1, pp. 520-21.
60 *Mozākerāt*, vol. 1, p. 375, my italics.
61 A derogatory reference to the *ruhāniyat*.
62 *Mozākerāt*, vol. 2, pp. 1122-23.
63 Not to be mistaken with Khomeini's successor, Ayatollah Ali Khamene'i.
64 *Mozākerāt*, vol. 1, p. 12.
65 *Mozākerāt*, vol. 1, p. 108-110.
66 *Mozākerāt*, vol. 1, p. 363.
67 *Mozākerāt*, vol. 1, p. 508.
68 *Mozākerāt*, vol. 2, pp. 1115-16.
69 *Mozākerāt*, vol. 2, p. 1118.
70 *Mozākerāt*, vol. 2, p. 1182.
71 *Mozākerāt*, vol. 2, p. 1184.
72 *Mozākerāt*, vol. 1, p. 293.
73 *Jomhuri-ye Islami*, July 15, 1979, cited in Kadivar, *Hokumat-e velā'i*, p. 187. In July 2001, in an interview with Françoise Germain-Robin of *l'Humanité*, Montazeri admitted that he was influenced by the revolutionary fervor of the time. He said, 'when power becomes absolute and concentrated in the hands of a fallible person, who is not accountable to any other institution. He might be the most pious, wisest, and the most knowledgeable person, it would inevitably lead to the rise of despotism and authoritarianism.' http://www.humanite.fr/journal/2001-07-19/2001-07-19-247608%20class=
74 *Mozākerāt*, vol. 1, p. 661.
75 *Mozākerāt*, vol. 1, p. 260.
76 Montazeri warned the Assembly, 'We will not approve a constitution which is not based on the principle of *velāyat-e faqih*.' *Mozākerāt*, vol. 1, p. 107.
77 *Mozākerāt*, vol. 1, p. 112.
78 *Mozākerāt*, vol. 1, p. 500.
79 *Mozākerāt*, vol. 2, p. 1092.
80 *Mozākerāt*, vol. 2, p. 1093.

[81] *Mozākerāt*, vol. 2, p. 1095.

[82] *Mozākerāt*, vol. 1, pp. 517-18.

[83] *Mozākerāt*, vol. 1, p. 519.

[84] *Mozākerāt*, vol. 1, p. 512.

[85] The representative from the state of Khorasan with 89 per cent of the vote, Dr. Rouhani had a Ph.D. in Public Health from Belgium. Before the revolution, he was the Associate Dean of Tehran University's School of Medicine.

[86] *Mozākerāt*, vol. 1, p. 343.

[87] *Mozākerāt*, vol. 1, p. 370-71.

[88] *Mozākerāt*, vol. 1, p. 377.

[89] All the following quotations are from the *Mozākerāt*, vol. 1, pp. 378-381.

[90] Beheshti was familiar with Marxist / Weberian critiques of liberal-democracy. As a young Muslim scholar with a Ph.D. in theology from Tehran University, he tried to broaden the scope of seminary teachings in Qom. In 1959, he founded the English language program and the *Din and Danesh School* for seminary students in Qom. And with the collaboration of Mohammad Bahonar and Morteza Motahhari, he revised the religious curriculum of modern state-sponsored secondary schools. In 1963 he immigrated to Germany and served as the director of the Islamic Center of Hamburg until 1970. He was killed, along with scores of other high-ranking government officials, in a blast that destroyed the headquarters of the Islamic Republic Party in June 28, 1981.

[91] *Mozākerāt*, vol. 1, p. 380.

[92] *Mozākerāt*, vol. 1, p. 383.

[93] *Mozākerāt*, vol. 1, p. 297.

[94] *Mozākerāt*, vol. 1, p. 297.

[95] *Mozākerāt*, vol. 1, p. 313.

[96] *Mozākerāt*, vol. 1, p. 313.

[97] For a substantive summary of these opposing views, see Gholam-Hossein Zargari-Nezhad (ed.), *Rasā'el-e mashrutiyat* (*The Constitutional Revolution Credos*) Tehran: Kavir, 1999, pp. 13-99.

[98] Janet Afary, *The Iranian Constitutional Revolution, 1906-1911: Grassroots Democracy, Social Democracy, and the Origins of Feminism,* New York: Columbia University Press, 1996, p. 71.

[99] Cited in Adamiyyat, *Eideolozhi*, p. 226.

[100] Abdolhadi Ha'eri, *Tashayyo` va mashrutiyat dar Iran* (*Shi`ism and Constitutionality in Iran*), Tehran: Amir Kabir, 1981, p. 239.

[101] Adamiyyat, Ibid. pp. 231-32.

[102] For Na'ini's argument on the sources of legitimacy of the constitution and the Islamic significance of equality and liberty, see Sayed Mahmud Taleqani's introduction to Na'ini's magnum opus *Tanbih al-ummah wa tanzih al-millah* (*The Admonition of the Public and the Refinement of the Nation*), Tehran: Enteshar, 1979, pp. 6-9.

[103] Molla Abdolrasul Kashani, *Resāle-ye ensāfiyeh* ('The credo of fairness'), in Zargari-Nezhad, *Rasā'el,* pp. 561-601.

[104] Cited in Adamiyyat, *Eideolozhi*, p. 253.

[105] Afary, op cit. p. 71.

[106] The Farsi notion of Nuri's political discourse, *saltanat-e mashru`eh,* was formulated in contradistinction to *saltanat-e mashruteh* or constitutional monarchy. Literally, the term *mashru`eh* refers to a religiously sanctioned law or ritual and in Nuri's discourse he advocated an Islamically sanctioned

(legitimized) monarchy. Since the reader is familiar with the term *shari`ah*, here I have translated the notion of *mashru`eh* as *shari`atized*. In Persian the notion of legitimacy, *mashru`iyat*, is derived from the word *shar'*, which is the root of the word *shari`ah*. However, in Persian political discourse, the notion of *mashru`iyat* suggests both religious and non-religious legitimacy.

[107] Sheikh Fazlollah Nuri, *Rasā'el, e`lāmiyeh-ha, maktubāt, va ruznāmeh-ha* (*Creeds, Pronouncements, and Papers*), vol. 1, edited by Mohammad Torkman, Tehran: Rasa Publishers 1983, p. 103. Mangol Bayat viewed Nuri's opposition to constitutional monarchy and its clerical supporters as merely a political feud over the control of power (*Iran's First Revolution: Shi`ism and the Constitutional Revolution of 1905-1909*, New York: Oxford University Press, 1991, p. 147).

[108] Nuri, Ibid. p. 64.

[109] Nuri, Ibid. p. 106.

[110] Afary, Ibid. p. 1. Afary begins her 450-page account of the Constitutional Revolution with the execution scene of Sheikh Nuri and ends it with the post-1979 revolution revival and celebration of his role as the martyr of the revolution. The saga of Nuri is pivotal to the central thesis of the book, the ever-present tale of the conflicts between secular, progressive, democratic tradition versus religious, conservative obstructionism in Iranian politics. Although her diligent reading of the historical events is quite illuminating, her comparison between Khomeini and Nuri does not take into account Khomeini's endorsements of the measures that were at the core of Nuri's opposition to the Constitutional Revolution. Afary's bifurcation does not correspond to the *Realpolitik* of either side of this dichotomy.

[111] *Mozākerāt*, vol. 1, p. 77.

[112] *Mozākerāt*, vol. 1, p. 318.

[113] *Mozākerāt*, vol. 1, p. 327.

[114] *Mozākerāt*, vol. 1, p. 316.

[115] *Mozākerāt*, vol. 4, p. 54.

[116] *Mozākerāt*, vol. 1, p. 210-11.

[117] *Mozākerāt*, vol. 1, p. 258.

[118] *Mozākerāt*, vol. 1, p. 213.

[119] *Mozākerāt*, vol. 1, p. 77.

[120] *Mozākerāt*, vol. 1, p. 676.

[121] *Mozākerāt*, vol. 1, p. 678.

[122] *Mozākerāt*, vol. 1, p. 716.

[123] *Mozākerāt*, vol. 1, p. 716.

[124] *Mozākerāt*, vol. 1, p. 718.

[125] *Mozākerāt*, vol. 1, p. 718-19.

[126] *Mozākerāt*, vol. 1, p. 719.

[127] *Mozākerāt*, vol. 1, p. 723.

[128] Article twenty, which was ratified with 58 votes, declared: All citizens of the country, both men and women, equally enjoy the protection of the law and enjoy all human, political, economic, social, and cultural rights, in conformity with Islamic criteria.

[129] Sami Zubaida, 'Is Iran an Islamic state?', in Joel Beinin & Joe Stork (eds.), *Political Islam, Essay from Middle East Report*, Berkeley & Los Angeles: University of California Press, 1997, p. 104.

[130] Arjomand, *The Turban*, p. 180.

[131] *Sahifeh*, vol. 21, p. 46.

[132] Said Hajjarian, *Az shāhed-e qodsi tā shāhed-e bāzāri: `Urfi-shodan-e din dar sepehr-e siyāsat* (*From the Divine to the Bazaari Witness: The Secularization of Religion in the Sphere of Politics*) Tehran: Tarh-e No, 2001, p. 83.

[133] *Mozākerāt,* vol. 1, p. 292-3.

[134] Jamileh Kadivar, *Tahavvol-e goftemān-e siyāsi-e Shi`i dar Iran* (*The Transformation of Shi`ite Political Discourse in Iran*), Tehran: Tarh-e No, 2000. Mohsen Kadivar, *Hokumat-e velā'i* and *Daghdaghe-ha-ye hokumat-e dini* (*The Anxieties of the Religious State*), Tehran; Nashr-e Nay, 2000.

[135] Hossein Mehrpour, ed., *Majmu`eh-ye nazariyāt-e shurā-ye negahbān* (*Collected Opinions of the Guardian Council),* Tehran: Center for the Islamic Revolution Documents, vol. 1, 1993, p. 73.

[136] Mehrpour, Ibid. pp. 68-80.

[137] Cited in Hajjarian, *Shāhed-e qodsi*, pp. 120-22.

[138] See Arjomand, *The Turban*, pp. 155-7.

[139] Cited in Arjomand, Ibid. p. 181.

[140] Cited in Arjomand, *The Turban*, p. 182.

[141] Hajjarian, op cit.

CHAPTER FOUR

[1] His real name is Hossein Haj-Faraj-Dabagh, but he has always been known by his pen name, Abdolkarim Soroush.

[2] Members of the Hojjatiyyah Society are often associated with a vulgar expression of conservative Islam. While the Society remained ambivalent towards the politicization of Islam, especially Khomeini's conception of *velāyat-e faqih,* after the revolution, a significant number of their members were elected to the *majlis* and held cabinet positions. Hojjatiyyah is associated with cultural traditionalism (in gender politics and religious freedom), political militancy (against freedom of expression), and economic conservatism (against land reform and state control of industry and trade). Therefore, while the nature of Soroush's involvement with the Hojjatiyyah cannot be independently determined, his retrospective disassociation is important in evaluating his current politics.

[3] Sadri & Sadri, eds., *Reason, Freedom, and Democracy in Islam: Essential writings of Abdolkarim Soroush,* Oxford: Oxford University Press, 2000, p. 8.

[4] Mohammad Quchani, *'qabz va bast-e perātik-e Soroush'* ('The practical expansion and contraction of Soroush') *Sharq,* (New Year Special Edition) March 2004, p. 50.

[5] Personal interview, Chicago November 1999.

[6] Mulla Sadra was a seventeenth century Persian Gnostic philosopher. Many contemporary Muslim philosophers believe that he was one of the greatest exponents of metaphysical doctrines in Islam. Henry Corbin compared Mulla Sadra to a combination of St. Thomas Aquinas and Jakob Boehme within the Islamic context. According to S.H. Nasr, 'Mulla Sadra's *Spiritual Journeys* [*al-asfar*] is the most monumental work of Islamic philosophy, in which rational arguments, illuminations received from spiritual realization and the tenets of revelation are harmonized in a whole which marks in a sense the summit of a thousand years of intellectual activity in the Islamic world' (*Science and Civilization in Islam,* New York: Barnes & Noble Books, 1992, pp. 335-6). While the great ayatollahs and other teachers at the Shi`ite seminaries were generally experts in *fiqh,* Motahhari's mentor, Allameh Tabataba'i, revived

Shi'i philosophical traditions, especially Mulla Sadra's illuminationist rationalism in the Qom seminary. Ayatollah Khomeini was another exponent of Gnostic philosophical traditions at Qom where, in addition to Mulla Sadra, he also taught Ibn Arabi's Sufism.

7   Abdolkarim Soroush, *Nahād-e nā-ārām-e jahān* (*The Restless Nature of the Universe*), Tehran: Qalam, 1982 [1977], p. 8.

8   Soroush, *Restless Nature*, p. 9.

9   Soroush, *Restless Nature*, p. 10.

10 Soroush, *Restless Nature*, p. 65.

11 For example, see Michael Fischer, 'Imam Khomeini: Four levels of understanding,' in Esposito, *Voices of Resurgent Islam*, 1983, pp. 150-174; and Hamid Dabashi, *Theology of Discontent, the Ideological Foundation of the Islamic Revolution in Iran*, New York: NYU Press, 1993, pp. 409-484.

12 Fischer, Ibid. p. 171.

13 Quchani, op cit, p. 50.

14 Included in these publications were: *Tazād-e diālektiki* (*Dialectical Contradiction*), Tehran: Serat, 1979; *Danish va arzesh* (*Knowledge and Value*) Tehran: Yaran, 1979; *Falsafeh-ye tārikh* (*Philosophy of History*) Tehran: Payam-e Azadi, 1979; `*Elm chist? Falsafeh chist?* (*What is Science? What is Philosophy?*) Tehran: Serat, 1979; *Eideolozhi-ye shaytani* (*The Satanic Ideology*), Tehran: Serat, 1980.

15 Soroush, *Dialectical Contradiction*, p. 13.

16 Soroush, *Dialectical Contradiction*, p. 13.

17 F. A. von Hayek, 'Scientism and the study of society,' *Economica*, New Series, vol. 9-35, 1942, p. 269.

18 Soroush, *What is Science?* p. 15.

19 Soroush, *Dialectical Contradiction*, p. 70.

20 Soroush, *Dialectical Contradiction*, pp. 20-21.

21 Soroush, *Dialectical Contradiction*, pp. 21-23.

22 Soroush, Ibid. pp. 30-31.

23 F. Engels, *Anti-Dühring*, Peking: Foreign Languages Press, 1976, part I. chapter 13.

24 For a detailed discussion on Engels' positivist approach to dialectics see Roy Bhaskar, *Dialectic: The Pulse of Freedom*, London: Verso, 1993; and Bertell Ollman, *Dialectical Investigations*, New York: Routledge, 1993.

25 Perhaps Marx's imprudent comment in his 1860 letter to Engels after reading Darwin's *The Origin's of Species* contributed to the emergence of determinist tendencies in Marxism. Marx wrote, 'Darwin's book is very important and serves me as a basis in natural science for the class struggle in history.'

26 F. Engels, 'Letter to P. L. Lavrov in London, November 12-13, 1875,' in *Marx, Engels, Lenin: On Historical Materialism*, New York: International Publishers, 1974, p. 289.

27 F. Engels, 'Speech at the graveside,' in Robert Tucker, ed., *The Marx-Engels Reader*, London, New York: Norton, 1978, p. 681.

28 *Evolutionary Socialism* was the title of Bernstein's 1899 book. Lenin formulated his Bolshevik ideology against Bernstein's anti-revolutionary position in his foundational 1902 treatise *What Is to Be Done?*

29 A group of Viennese lawyers and scholars led by Max Adler, Otto Bauer, Rudolf Hilferding, and Karl Renner, who formed a revisionist group within the Austrian Social Democratic party. This group was less concerned with

questions of revolution versus evolution and viewed Marxism as a theoretical tool in the analysis of society.

30 Marx and Engels both became weary of this economic determinism within their circles. In their correspondence, they tried to qualify their emphasis on the significance of relations of production in historical progress. For example in a November 1877 letter to Mikhailovsky, Marx chastised those who converted his 'historical sketch of the genesis of capitalism in Western Europe into an historico-philosophical theory of the general path every people is fated to tread, whatever the circumstances in which it finds itself.' In his often-cited letter to Joseph Bloch in September of 1890, Engels wrote that 'according to the materialist conception of history, the *ultimately* determining element in history is the production and reproduction of real life.' He disparaged those who twisted this into saying that 'the economic element is the *only* determining one,' and by saying so, they transform 'that proposition into a meaningless, abstract, senseless phrase.' (*Marx-Engels Reader*, op cit. pp. 760-764)

31 Soroush, *Dialectical Contradiction*, pp. 65-71.

32 Soroush, *Jahān-bini-ye Motahhari* (*The Worldview of Motahhari*), Tehran: np, 1979, p. 41.

33 Soroush, *Az tārikh-parasti tā khodā-parasti* (*From the Worship of History to Worshiping God*) Houston, TX: Islamic Student Association, 1980, p. 29.

34 Karl Popper, *The Poverty of Historicism*, London & New York: Routledge & Kegan Paul, 1957, p. 3.

35 See Popper's discussion in 'A pluralist approach to the philosophy of history,' in his *The Myth of the Framework: In Defense of Science and Rationality*, London: Routledge, 1995, pp. 130-153.

36 K. Popper, *Conjectures and Refutations: The Growth of Scientific Knowledge* New York: Harper & Row, 1968, p. 346.

37 Soroush, *Worship of History*, p. 51.

38 Prophecies such as what Marx wrote in the preface of the first volume of *Capital*, 'when a society has discovered the natural law that determines its own movement, even then it can neither overleap the natural phases of its evolution, nor shuffle them out of the world by a stroke of the pen. But this much it can do: it can shorten and lessen the birth-pangs.'

39 Cited in Karl Popper, *Open Society and Its Enemies*, Vol. II, Princeton, NJ: Princeton University Press, 1963, p. 109.

40 Popper, *Framework*, pp. 187-88.

41 *The Satanic Ideology* was the title of book published in 1980. It contained a series of talks and articles against the perils of Marxism, which he delivered soon after the triumph of the revolution.

42 *Masked Dogmatism* was the title of talk Soroush delivered in 1979 at the School of Economics at Tehran University, which was later published as a short monograph. *The Satanic Ideology* was an expanded version of the same monograph.

43 Soroush, *The Satanic Ideology*, p. 16.

44 Soroush, Ibid, pp. 18-20.

45 Soroush, Ibid, p. 27.

46 Soroush, Ibid, p. 71.

47 Karl Popper, 'Against the sociology of knowledge,' in David Miller's *Popper Selections*, Princeton, NJ: Princeton University Press, 1985, pp. 366-78.

48 Soroush, *The Satanic Ideology*, p. 39.

[49]   Popper, 'Sociology of knowledge,' p. 369.
[50]   Soroush, *The Satanic Ideology*, p. 40.
[51]   Soroush, Ibid, p. 66.
[52]   The exception in his polemical writings is his attack on then-President Bani
        Sadr and the Mojahedin-e Khalq Organization.
[53]   Mansoor Hekmat, 'We represent the majority of people!' Interview with
        Weekly International no. 59, June 20, 2001, http://www.iran-emrooz.de/
        khabar/hekmat800425.html. More than twenty years before this interview,
        Soroush questioned whether Marxists would respect the will of the people if
        it contradicts their own convictions. 'They believe that what the masses
        articulate and seemingly strive for is merely an illusion which needs to be
        overcome. Would these "populists" surrender to the demands of the masses?
        Would they honor the faith of the masses? Would they only become populist
        when people's demands fit their historical scheme? Which one takes
        precedence, people's outlook or their philosophy of history?' (*The Satanic
        Ideology*, p. 67.)
[54]   Transcribed from a four-part talk on the Islamic Republic Radio during the
        month of May of 1979 and published in *The Satanic Ideology*.
[55]   *Satanic Ideology*, pp. 89-90.
[56]   Soroush, 'The World,' in *Satanic Ideology*, p. 146.
[57]   Soroush, Ibid, p. 148.
[58]   Soroush, Ibid, p. 151-52.
[59]   For a detailed account see Shahrzad Mojab's unpublished dissertation *The
        State and University: The Islamic Cultural Revolution in the Institutions of Higher
        Education in Iran, 1980-87*, University of Illinois, Urbana-Champaign, 1991.
        For the events leading to the Cultural Revolution see Ali Rahnema & Farhad
        Nomani, *The Secular Miracle: Religion, Politics & Economic Policy in Iran*,
        London and New Jersey: Zed Books, 1990, pp. 176-82, and Bakhash, *The
        Reign*, pp. 117-24.
[60]   Abolhasan Bani Sadr, *Usul-e pāyeh va zavābet-hā-ye hokumat-e Islami* (*The
        Foundations and Principles of the Islamic State*), Tehran: np, 1975.
[61]   The most significant exception to this perception was the Toilers Party (*Hezb-
        e ranjbaran*), a Maoist party that openly defended both Bazargan's Provisional
        Government and Bani Sadr's presidency against their adversaries.
[62]   *Razmandegān-e Āzādi-ye Tabaqe-ye Kargar* (Warriors for the Liberation of the
        Working Class), message to revolutionary students, September 1979. James
        Hitselberger papers, Box No. 2, Hoover Institute, Stanford University.
[63]   *Sāzmān-e Paykār dar Rāh-e Azādi-ye Tabaqe-ye Kārgar Paykār* (The Organization
        of Struggle for the Emancipation of the Working Class), *Jonbesh-e dāneshju`ei
        va mas`ale-ye dāneshjuyān-e mobārez* (Student Movement and the Problem of
        the Militant Students' Organization), September 1980, p. 13. For a detailed
        analysis see Ghamari-Tabrizi, 'Between the Shah and the Imam: The students
        of the Left in Iran, 1977-1981,' in Gerald DeGroot (ed.), *Reading, Writing, and
        Revolution: Student Protest Since 1960*. London & New York: Addison Wesley
        Longman, 1998.
[64]   Cited in *Dānishgāh va `amalkardha-yi irtijā`* (University and the Actions of the
        Reactionaries) Ettehādieh-ye Anjomanhā-ye Dāneshjuyān-e Mosalmān (The
        Union of Muslims Students' Associations), Tehran: np, 1981, pp 25-26.
[65]   Ibid. pp. 26-27.
[66]   Bani Sadr, *Khiyānat*, p. 129.

67 Ruhollah Khomeini, *Islam and Revolution: Writings and Declarations of Imam Khomeini*, translated and annotated by Hamid Algar, Berkeley: Mizan Press, 1981, pp. 291-98.

68 Ibid. p. 298.

69 The student organization of the *Fadā'iyan Khalq,* was the largest leftist student organization.

70 According to a report posted on http://www.peikekhabari.com/a221.htm, Farrokh Negahdar the leader of the *Fadā'iyan* and Fatapour who was in charge of *Pishgam* met with Bani Sadr on April 20, 1980 and agreed to evacuate the campuses in order to avoid further escalation of the situation and to expose the plot against the President.

71 Pamphlet published by *Sāzmān-e Dāneshjuyān-e Pishgām (Rasht),* April 1980, James Hitselberger papers, Box No. 4, Hoover Institute, Stanford University.

72 Cited in Mojab, op cit, p.89.

73 Khomeini, *Sahifeh,* Vol. 12, p. 177.

74 Interview with author, November 1999, Chicago.

75 *Iranshahr,* Vol. 2, No. 17, pp. 2-5, June 28, 1980.

76 For Soroush's narrative of the Cultural Revolution see *Darbāre-ye enqelāb-e farhangi va chizhā'i keh qarār bud beshavad* (About the Cultural Revolution and What Was Supposed to Happen) in Soroush, *Siyāsat-Nāmeh (Political Letters),* Vol. 2, Tehran: Serat, 2000, pp. 323-44; and his *Darbāre-ye setād-e enqelāb-e farhangi* (About the Cultural Revolution Council) in *Siyāsta-Nāmeh (Political Letters)* Vol 1, Tehran: Serat, 1999, pp. 207-14. For controversies about his role, see Reza Farahani posted on:
http://www.iranian.com/BTW/June97/Soroush/Page1.shtml
for further discussions on the controversy see:
http://www.drsoroush.com/Farsi/Comments_by/Dr_soroush_comment_a bout_letter_to_khatami.htm
http://www.drsoroush.com/English/Articles/1997.04_Dr_Soroushs_Intervi ew_with_Seraj.htm

77 http://www.drsoroush.com/English/Articles/1997.04_Dr_Soroushs_ Interview_with_Seraj.htm

78 Farahani, op cit, p. 2.

79 Soroush, *Siyāsat-Nameh,* Vol 1, p. 337.

80 Farahani, op cit, p. 2.

81 http://www.drsoroush.com/English/Articles/1997.04_Dr_Soroushs _Interview_with_Seraj.htm

82 After Bani Sadr was forced out of power, Bahonar became the Prime Minister in the cabinet of Mohammad Ali Raja'ei, the Republic's second President. Along with Raja'ei, on August 30, 1981, he was killed in an explosion in the prime ministry offices.

83 Cited in http://www.peikekhabari.com/a221.htm.

84 All citations in the op cit pamphlet *Dāneshgāh va `amalkard- ertejā`,* p. 62.

85 Soroush, *Siyāsat-Nāmeh* Vol. 2, p. 333.

86 Ibid. p. 336

87 Khomeini, *Sahifeh,* Vol. 12, p. 177.

88 The proceedings were published in *Al-Samarāt: pirāmun-e vahdat-e hawzeh va dāneshgāh (On the Unification of the Seminary and the University),* Tehran: Jahad-e Daneshgahi, 1982.

89 Soroush cited in Mojab op cit, p. 164. I could not confirm the accuracy of these translations independently. In other occasions, I have found that in her

unpublished dissertation Shahrzad Mojab takes a more interpretive approach, which at times compromises the accuracy of her translations.

90 Soroush, *Bani Sadr, Sāzmān-e Mojāhedin va Hegelism* (*Bani Sadr, the Mojahedin, and Hegelianism*), Roma, Italia: Centro Culturale Islamic Europeo, 1983, pp. 69-70.

91 Soroush, Ibid, p. 70.

92 About his own role in the Cultural Revolution, Ziba-Kalam told an audience at the Teachers' Training College in Tehran, 'I ask God to forgive me for the role I played in the Cultural Revolution. I seek absolution from all those who suffered as the result of the closure of the universities and I hope that they will forgive me [...] Suffice it to say that only God knows my heartfelt intentions, that I believed that I was doing a service for the sake of the revolution and the country, and that I did not have any personal motives for individual gains. Later, I realized the futility of that effort and the damage it inflicted on the country' (Sadeq Ziba-Kalam, *Dāneshgāh va enqelāb* (*The University and Revolution*), Tehran: Rowzaneh, 2001, p. 84).

93 Ziba-Kalam, Ibid, p. 96.

94 Cited by Soroush in reference to the Cultural Revolution, in *Bani Sadr*, p. 70.

95 For an excellent summary of Bani Sadr's ideas and his short-term presidency see Bakhash, op cit, chapters 5-6.

96 Bani Sadr discussed his theory in depth in his *Usul-e pāyeh*.

97 Cited in Bakhash, op cit, p. 94.

98 See Bakhash, Ibid. p. 112-114.

99 Cited in Bakhash, op cit, p. 136.

100 Cited in The Ministry of Guidance Publications, *Jang-e tahmili dar tahlil-e goruhak-hā* (*The Opposition's Analysis of the Imposed War*), Tehran, 1985, p. 21.

101 Ibid. p. 21.

102 Ibid. p. 167, my italics.

103 Ibid. p. 167.

104 For a good collection of primary documents on the Soviet Union's position on the war, see *Gozari bar do sāl jang* (A Review of Two Years of War), Tehran: Political Office of the Revolutionary Guards, 1983, pp. 219-237.

105 See *Gozari bar jang*, pp. 235-37; and *Jang-e tahmili*, pp. 188-190.

106 *Jang-e tahmili*, p. 196.

107 Ibid. p. 196.

108 Ibid. p. 197.

109 Ibid. p. 81.

110 Ibid. p. 87.

111 Ibid. p.96.

112 Many believed that the number of murdered was much higher. But the government put the dead at seventy-two in order to evoke a similarity with the seventy-two martyrs of the `Āshura, Imam Hossein's battle in Karbala.

113 In a well-documented appendix to *Mojahed* No. 261, 5 September 1985, the journal of the Organization of People's Mojahedin, names and dates of the executions of 12,028 were published.

114 The official number announced by the government in *Ettela'at*, 5 May 1984. In its Winter 1982 issue, *Payam- e Enqelab*, the official organ of the Guardians of the Islamic Revolution admitted that more than 75 per cent of all the members of Leftist groups who had been arrested since the summer of 1981 had been executed.

115 Soroush, *Bani Sadr*, p. 31.

116 Ibid. pp. 41-43.
117 Ibid. p. 31.
118 Ibid. p. 23.
119 Ibid. p. 8.
120 Ibid. p. 5.
121 Ibid. p. 6.
122 Ibid. p. 8.
123 Ibid. p. 15.
124 Ibid. p. 20
125 Ibid. p. 26
126 Ibid. p. 42
127 Ibid. p. 64

CHAPTER FIVE

1   January 7, 2006. http://www.sharghnewspaper.ir/841017/html/index.htm
2   For a critique see Mohammad Mojtahid Shabestary, *Naqdi bar qarā'at-e rasmi az din* (*A Critique of the Official Reading of Religion*), Tehran: Tarh-e No, 2002, pp. 30-53. Also see Hashemi-Rafsanjani's *`Ubur az bohrān* (*Passing through the Crisis*), Tehran: Daftar-e Nashr-e Ma`āref-e Enqelāb, 1999, pp. 60-65.
3   Hashemi-Rafsanjani, *`Ubur,* p. 60.
4   For an excellent historical review of this transformation see Baqir Mu`in's *Hukumat-e Islami va Islam-e Hukumati,* Essen, Germany: Nima, 2004.
5   The MIR was established with the union of seven groups:: *Ummat-e Vāhedeh; Towhidi Badr; Towhidi Saf; Mansorun; Movahhedin; Falaq; and Fallāh.*
6   See Hojjat Martaji, *Jenāh-hāy-e Siyāsi dar Irān-e Emruz* (*Political Factions in Contemporary Iran*), Tehran: Shafi`i Publishers, 1999, p. 21.
7   Behzad Nabavi (the designated head of the organization), Mohsen Armin, Sa`id Hajjarian, Hashem Aghajari, Mostafa Tajzadeh, Mohammad Salamati were among the most influential of these members. They later became the political leaders of the reform movement during the 1990s.
8   In Amir Shahla, 'A glance at the history of the Islamic Revolution Mujahidin Organization,' *No Andish Monthly,* September 2001, p. 10.
9   Mohammad Salamati, interview with *`Asr-e Mā,* cited in Hamid Kaviani, *Pishgāmān-e eslāhāt* (*The Vanguards of Reform*), Tehran: Salam, 2001, p. 13.
10 Amir Shahla, op cit, pp.10-12.
11 For early factional disputes see Martaji, op cit, pp. 20-23.
12 In their manifesto called *Mavāze`-e mā* (*Our Positions*), published a few months after its establishment, the founders of the IRP clearly regarded themselves as state founders. Divided into eight sections, from Islamic ideology to foreign policy, the manifesto moved between the positions of a political party under the postrevolutionary regime and inaugural policies of the Islamic Republic. It is implicitly, and at times explicitly, written as program of the dominant party in power.
13 Hashemi-Rafsanjani, *Daurān-e mobārezeh* (*The Period of Struggle*), Tehran: Daftar-e Nashr-e Ma`āref-e Islami, 1998, vol. 1, pp. 336-37.
14 Mohammad Quchani, *Jomhuri-ye moqaddas* (*The Sacred Republic*), Tehran: Naqsh-o-Negar, 2003, p. 12.
15 Cited in Quchani, Ibid, p. 28.
16 Hashemi-Rafsanjani, *`Ubur,* pp. 21-24.
17 Khomeini, *Sahifeh,* vol. 8, 1995, p. 384.
18 In Quchani, *Jomhuri,* p. 39.

[19]   The first faction was most notably represented by Abolqasem Sarhadizadeh, Mehdi Hashemi, Mir-Hossein Musavi, Hadi Ghaffari, and the second by Asadollah Badamchian, Abdollah Jasebi, Asgar-Owladi, Jalalodin Farsi.

[20]   See for example Mehdi Moslem, *Factional Politics*; Bahman Baktiari's *Parliamentary Politics in Revolutionary Iran: The Institutionalization of Factional Politics*, Gainesville: The University Press of Florida, 1996; and Anoushiravan Ehteshami, *After Khomeini: The Iranian Second Republic*, London, New York: Routledge, 1995.

[21]   IRP, *Mavāze`-e mā*, Tehran: The Islamic Republic Party, 1979. The IRP manifesto consisted of eight chapters, from their 'worldview' to 'foreign relation policy.' The language of the text alternated between a revolutionary pamphlet to a state policy document.

[22]   For details of these factional debates see Baktiari, *Parliamentary Politics*, pp. 60-85.

[23]   The result of the vote was 80 opposed, 74 in favor, 38 abstained, and 15 were absent.

[24]   Kaviani, op cit, p. 17.

[25]   Cited in Martaji, op cit, p. 16.

[26]   Cited in Moslem, op cit, p. 69.

[27]   Cited in Moslem, op cit, p. 69.

[28]   Cited in Martaji, op cit, p. 18.

[29]   Cited in Moslem, op cit, p. 69.

[30]   Martaji, *Jenāh-hā*, p. 19-20.

[31]   The SMC continued to subscribe to this view and its members insisted that 'the ideas of Left, Right, traditional, and modern are fictional.' For a detailed discussion see Said Barzin, 'Jenāhbandi-hā-ye siyāsi dar jomhuri-ye islami-ye Iran' ('Political factions in the Islamic Republic of Iran'), *Iran-e Farda*, no. 17, May 15, 1995, pp. 36-41.

[32]   Global Security Report
http://www.globalsecurity.org/military/world/war/iran-iraq.htm

[33]   Because Iran purchased much of its arms on the international black market, estimates on the economic cost of the war vary significantly. As Baktiari noted, in his speech to the *Majlis*, '[Prime Minister] Musavi has stated that some 30 percent of the 1983-1984 budget... was spent on the war effort. Expenditures were 14 percent higher in 1984 than in the previous year' (*Parliamentary Politics*, pp. 119-20). Three years later, in 1987, the Prime Minister put the expenditure at '52 percent of the total allocations for the government to military and security affairs' of the war (see Shahram Chubin, *Iran and Iraq at War*, Boulder: Westview Press, 1988, chapter 7, pp. 123-138). Hooshang Amirahmadi ('Economic reconstruction of Iran: Costing the war damage,' *Third World Quarterly*, vol. 12-1, 1991, pp. 26-47) has offered one of the most plausible sets of figures. He estimated that by 1987, the cost of the war had reached $18 billion; its total economic cost topped $309 billion.

[34]   Chubin, op cit, pp. 79-83.

[35]   Chubin, Ibid, p. 252.

[36]   *Sahifeh*, vol. 20, p. 238.

[37]   *Sahifeh*, vol. 21, p. 46.

[38]   For two insightful discussions on this notion see Said Hajjarian's *Shāhed-e qodsi*, and Akbar Ganji, *Tallaqi-ye fāshisti az din va hokumat* (*Fascist Interpretations of Religion and State*), Tehran: Tarh-e No, 2000, pp. 32-56, 76-106.

[39]   *Sahifeh*, vol. 20, p. 89.

40 *Sahifeh,* vol. 19, p. 245.

41 *Sahifeh,* vol. 21, p. 34.

42 *Sahifeh,* vol. 21, p. 98.

43 *Sahifeh,* vol. 21, p. 61.

44 *Sahifeh,* vol. 20, p. 176. Khomeini's use of the word *kārshenās* for *expert* is quite significant. In the postrevolutionary political lexicon the word *khobreh* signified an expert in matters of social and political issues. But a *khobreh* also carried religious authority, one who becomes expert through education in seminaries. But a *kārshenās* evoked a more technocratic meaning for someone who has gained expertise through secular education.

45 Hajjarian, *Shāhed-e qodsi,* p. 89.

46 Hossein Mehrparvar, *Didgāh-hā-ye jadid dar masā'el-e hoquqi* (*New Perspectives in Legal Problems*), Second Edition, Tehran: Ettela`at Publishers, 1996, p. 56.

47 *Sahifeh,* vol. 21, p. 61.

48 Cited in Mehrparvar (ed.), op cit, p. 55.

49 *Sahifeh,* vol. 20, p. 163.

50 Mehrparvar, op cit, p. 56

51 *Sahifeh,* vol. 20, p. 165.

52 See Hajjarian, op cit, p. 116.

53 *Sahifeh,* vol. 20, p. 170.

54 See for example his letter to the Guardian Council in *Sahifeh,* vol. 21, p. 57.

55 Thousands of remaining political prisoners were executed in the summer of 1988 after the regime accepted the UN resolution 598. Estimates vary, but in a period of two months in August and September, between four to seven thousand members of opposition groups were retried in summary courts and executed. The executions were carried out with direct permission of Ayatollah Khomeini.

56 Introduction, *Surat-e mashruh-e mozākerāt-e shurā-ye bāznegari-ye qanun-e asāsi-ye jomhuri-ye islāmi-ye Iran* (*The Complete Minutes from the Meetings of the Council for the Reappraisal of the Constitution*), (henceforth *Bāznegari*) Tehran: Majlis Publication, 2001, no page number.

57 Khomeini was as advocate of the omission of *marja`iyat,* and had earlier indicated that he had always been principally against such a criterion (see chapter 3).

58 See Akbar Ganji's discussion on this point, *Fascist Interpretation,* pp. 80-85.

59 Ayatollah Montazeri was the heir apparent of Khomeini who was ousted from all his official positions after he openly criticized the continuation of the war and the massacre of political prisoners in the summer of 1988. In a letter to Ayatollah Khomeini dated August 14, 1988, he warned the Supreme Leader of the dire domestic and international consequences of mass execution of prisoners who had been serving time in prison. According to his account, between 2800-3800 members of the opposition groups were executed in a two-month period after summary trials that overturned earlier verdicts of ten or more years imprisonment. 'Our revolution was not about killing our own youth,' he reprimanded Khomeini (see Ayatollah Montazeri, *Khāterāt* (*Memoir*), Los Angeles: Sherkat-e Ketab, 2001, pp. 630-635.) Later, on February 13, 1989, he repeated his condemnation of the republic's policies and called on Khomeini to 'make up for the past mistakes,' and to create an 'open society.' 'The people of the world,' he warned the Leader, 'thought our only task here in Iran was to kill.' (Cited in Ahmad Ashraf, 'Theocracy and

charisma: New men of power in Iran,' *International Journal of Politics, Culture, and Society,* vol. 4-1, 1990, p. 141)

60 Ayatollah Montazeri, cited in Kadivar *Daghdagheha-ye hukumat-e dini (The Preoccupation with the Religious State),* Tehran: Nay, 2000, p. 133.

61 *Bāznegari,* pp. 837-838.

62 *Bāznegari,* pp. 208-211.

63 *Bāznegari,* p. 838.

64 *Bāznegari,* p. 175.

65 *Bāznegari,* p. 196.

66 *Bāznegari,* p. 196.

67 *Bāznegari,* pp. 197-98.

68 For an insightful discussion on claiming and reinventing Khomeini see the excellent book by Daniel Brumberg, *Reinventing Khomeini, the Struggle for Reform in Iran,* Chicago: Chicago University Press, 2001, particularly chapter seven, pp. 152-84.

69 *Bāznegari,* p. 452.

70 *Bāznegari,* p. 454-55.

71 *Bāznegari,* pp. 674-75.

72 *Bāznegari,* p. 675.

73 *Bāznegari,* p. 694.

74 *Bāznegari,* p. 691-92.

75 The main elements of Rafsanjani's economic reform were: encouragement of investment, the security of capital, securing loans from international sources, a controlled privatization, and the promotion of consumption.

76 Ervand Abrahamian, *Khomeinism: Essays on the Islamic Republic,* Berkeley: UC Press, 1993, p. 136.

77 Brumberg, op cit, p. 151.

78 Mohammad Quchani, *Yaqeh sefid-hā (The White-Collars),* Tehran: Naqsh-o-Negar, 2000, pp. 121-132.

79 Cited in Mehdi Moslem, op cit. p. 144.

80 Cited in Brumberg, op cit, p. 161.

81 Cited in Moslem, op cit, p. 145.

82 A reference to Shalamcheh valley in the Iranian Southwest in which *Karbala 8,* one of the last war campaigns, turned into one of the bloodiest last ditch efforts to push into the Iraqi territory before Khomeini's acceptance of UN Resolution 598.

83 Cited in Martaji, op cit, p. 39.

84 Cited in Martaji, Ibid, p. 24.

85 Cited in Martaji, Ibid, 30-31.

CHAPTER SIX

1 Parviz Piran, *'faqr va jonbesh-hāye ejtemā`i'* ('Poverty and social movements'), *Refāh-e Ejtemā`i (Social Welfare)* vol. 5-18, Fall 2006, pp. 2-29.

2 Salehi-Isfahani, Ibid.

3 Cited in Djavad Salehi-Isfahani, 'Revolution and redistribution in Iran: Poverty and inequality 25 years later,' working paper, August 2006.

4 Ali Shari`ati, *Mazhab alayh-e Mazhab (Religion Against Religion),* Tehran: n.p., 1977, p. 209.

[5] For a detailed biography and his intellectual development see the insightful work of Ali Rahnema, *An Islamic Utopian: A Political Biography of Ali Shari`ati*, London, New York: I.B. Tauris, 1998.

[6] Michael Fischer also cautioned his readers that Shari`ati's attempt to 'bridge the gap between traditional Shi`ism and contemporary sociology' was appropriated after his death by 'the more progressive wing of the religious movement,' and thereby transformed into a revolutionary ideology (Fischer, *Religious Dispute*, p. 5).

[7] Dabashi, *Theology*, p. 108.

[8] Marx & Engels, *The German Ideology*, in Robert Tucker, ed., *The Marx-Engels Reader*, New York & London: Norton & Company, 1978, p. 14.

[9] Shari`ati, *Tārikh-e tamaddon* (*The History of Civilization*) 2 vols. *Collected Works Nos. 11 & 12*, Tehran: Entesharat-e Agah, 1982, p.148.

[10] One of the exceptions was Ali Mirfetros's *Islam-Shenāsi* (*Islamology*). His book, which deliberately borrowed its title from Shari`ati's lecture series of the same title, was published in the spring of 1978 under the pseudonym Babak Dustdar. He debunked the kind of historiography that Shari`ati and other Muslims had devised to present Islam as a progressive, revolutionary ideology. Mirfetros argued that since its inception, Islam has been the ideology of the ruling classes and called any glorification of Islam as a civilization a pure fiction (Babak Dustdar, *Islam-Shenāsi*, Tehran: Kaveh, 1978).

[11] V. I. Lenin, 'The state and revolution' in *Marx, Engels, Lenin on Historical Materialism: A Collection*, New York: International Publishers, 1974, p. 526. Lenin's doctrine was based on the Engelsian view that '[the state] is the admission that this society has become entangled in an insoluble contradiction with itself, that it has split into irreconcilable antagonisms which it is powerless to dispel. [The] power, arisen out of society but placing itself above it, and alienating itself more and more from it, is the state.' (Engels, 'Origin of the family, private property and state,' in *Karl Marx and Frederick Engels, Selected Works*, vol. 3, Moscow: Progress Publishers 1983, pp. 326-7).

[12] Weber asserted that 'If the state is to exist, the dominated must obey the authority claimed by the powers that be. When and why do men obey? Upon what inner justifications and upon what external means does this domination rest?' (Weber, 'Politics as a vocation,' in *For Max Weber: Essays in Sociology*, edited and translated by H. H. Gerth & C. Wright Mills, New York: Oxford University Press, 1958, p. 78).

[13] Although occasionally Shari`ati compromised the content of his discourse for its poetic form, he believed that his rhyming allegories greatly deepened their rhetorical power.

[14] Weber Ibid, p.79.

[15] Shari`ati's notion of 'Safavid Shi`ism' resembles Abul `Ala Maududi's (d. 1979) and Sayyid Qutb's (1906-1966) re-appropriation of the concept of *jahiliyyah* in identifying the contemporary post-colonial secular/nationalist regimes in Islamic countries (see chapter 2). Both concepts of *jahiliyyah* and 'Safavid Shi`ism' are constructed not to depict a historical period, but to describe an omnipresent state of being.

[16] Shari`ati, *Tashayyo`-e Alavi va Tashayyo`-e Safavi* (*Alavid Shi'ism and Safavid Shi`ism*), Tehran: Hosseiniyyeh Ershad, 1971, pp .200-250.

[17] Shari`ati, *Tashayyo`*, p. 111.

[18]   The result of this endeavor was a three-volume book *Islam-shenāsi*, or *Islamology*, which was originally delivered in a series of lectures at *Hosseiniyyeh Ershād* from February to November 1972 (*Islam-shenāsi*, 3 vols. Collected Works Nos. 16-18, Tehran: Entesharat-e Shari`ati, 1981).

[19]   Shari`ati, *Islam-shenāsi*, vol. 1, pp. 28-29. In Shari`ati's view, ideology embodies a contradiction between the existing (*is*) and the ideal (*ought*) conditions [...] Anybody who has ideology believes in an ideal society and an ideal human being [...] therefore ideology is a belief based upon the *towhidi weltanschauung* and the determinant dialectics of history and class conflict and the transcendental responsibility of human beings (*Islam-shenāsi*, vol. 2, pp. 45-48).

[20]   Abu Dharr was one of the warriors of Imam Ali. Shari`ati's first published work (1956) was a translation from Arabic of a book by Joudah Al-Sahhar called *Abu Dharr Ghaffari*, which had been originally published in Mashad (*Abu Dharr*, Collected Works vol. 3. Tehran: Hosseiniyyeh Ershad, 1978).

[21]   Mansur Hallaj (d. 922), proclaimed *anal -haqq* (I have merged with, I am, the Truth), for which blasphemy he was executed by the ulama. This verse is attributed to him: 'Kill me, O my trustworthy friends — for in my being killed is my life' (trans. Annemarie Schimmel, *Islam, An Introduction*, Albany: SUNY Press, 1992, p. 108). Shari`ati transformed Hallaj's mystic 'death through love' into martyrdom for the Cause.

[22]   Umar was the first Muslim Caliph.

[23]   The Muslim philosopher (980-1037) known in the West as Avicenna.

[24]   Facing towards Mecca during daily prayers.

[25]   Shari`ati, *Ari inchenin bud barādar* (*Yes, Brother! This is How it Was*) Collected Works vol. 22, Tehran: Entesharat-e Sabz, 1982, pp. 309-313.

[26]   Ali Akbar Akbari, *Barresi-ye chand mas'le-ye ejtemā`i* (*An Analysis of Some Social Problems*), Tehran: Sepehr Publishers, 1977.

[27]   For a summary of the Left's engagement with Shari`ati's work see Rahnema's *An Islamic Utopian*, pp. 201-206.

[28]   Naser Makarem-Shirazi, '*Āyā hokumat-e islami bar pāye-ye shurāst?*' ('Is Islamic state based upon democratic councils?') *Maktab-e Islam* 13, no. 1, 1972.

[29]   For a summary of early clerical reactions to the rise of Shari`ati's influence also see Rahnema's *Islamic Utopian,* pp. 206-209 and pp. 266-276.

[30]   In an interview, Motahhari confided in Shahrough Akhavi that 'Dr. Shari`ati brought pressure to bear on the political aspect [of the *Hosseiniyyeh's* activities]' (Akhavi, *Religion and Politics in Contemporary Iran,* Albany: SUNY Press, 1980, p. 144. Hamid Algar also narrated an encounter with Motahhari in which he remarked that 'Dr. Shari`ati was an instrumentalist in the sense that he used religion as an instrument for his political and social objectives' (Algar, *The Islamic Revolution in Iran,* London: The Open Press 1980, p. 47).

[31]   Naser Minachi, *Tārikh-cheye Hosseiniyyeh-ye Ershād* (*A History of Hosseiniyyeh-ye Ershād*) Tehran: Ershād Publication, 2005, pp. 120-123.

[32]   Minachi, *Tārikh*, p. 149.

[33]   See Rahnema, *Islamic Utopian*, pp. 272-275.

[34]   Shari`ati, *Nāmeh beh Ayatollah al-Uzma Milani,* 'Letter to the Grand Ayatollah Milani,' in *Collected Works,* vol. 34, Tehran: Qalam, 1996, pp. 98-103

[35]   Cited in Abdolkarim Soroush, *Az Shari`ati,* Tehran: Serat, 2005, p. 260.

[36]   Antonio Gramsci, *Prison Notes,* edited and translated by Q. Hoare & G. N. Smith, New York: International Publishers, 1975, p. 263.

[37]   Shari`ati, *Tashayyo`*, p. 39.

38 Gramsci, *Prison Notes,* p. 207.
39 Shari'ati, *Shi'ah (Shi'ism)*, Collected Works vol. 7, Tehran: Hosseiniyyeh Ershad 1978, pp. 14-19.
40 Shari'ati, 'The world view of *Towhid*,' in *On the Sociology of Islam,* trans. H. Algar. Berkeley: Mizan Press 1979, pp. 82-87.
41 *Shirk* is the idea of polytheism. Shari'ati uses the term here to refer to societies stratified by class and race (Shari'ati, *Islamology,* vol. 1, p. 141.).
42 Shari'ati, *Islamology,* vol.1, pp. 131-132.
43 For discussion on that point see Sachedina, op cit. Also for his innovative use of the notion of *imamat*, see Reza Alijani's *Bad-Fahmi-ye yek towjih-he nā movaffaq* (*The Misinterpretation of an Unsuccessful Justification*) Tehran: Kavir, 2006. Here we also see the similarity between Khomeini's late *fatwas* on the qualities of the *vali-ye faqih* and Shari'ati's conception of imam.
44 Shari'ati, *Rowshanfekr va mas'uliyat-e ou dar jāme'eh* ('Intellectuals and their responsibilities in society') in *Collected Works,* vol. 20, p. 85.
45 Shari'ati remarked, 'The language of religion, and particularly the language of Semitic religions, in whose prophets we believe, is a symbolic language that expresses meaning through images and symbols—the finest and most exalted of all the languages that humankind has ever invented' ('Man and Islam,' in Algar, *Sociology of Islam,* p. 71).
46 Khomeini made several declarations in that regard in 1978 and 1979 after returning to Iran from Paris. See *Sahifeh,* vol. 3, p. 107, and vol. 4, p. 206.
47 First published in March 1969, in *Collected Works,* vol. 26, and almost a year later in winter of 1970, on the occasion of his pilgrimage to Mecca, he delivered two lecture series called '*Hijrat, ummat va imamat,*' ('Hijra, ummah, and imamate') and '*Vesāyat va shurā,*' ('Administration and consultation') both of which are published in *Collected Works,* vol. 29.
48 Shari'ati, *Collected Works,* vol. 28, p. 588.
49 Shari'ati, *Collected Works,* vol. 26, p. 492.
50 Alijani, *Bad fahmi,* p. 75.
51 For a review, see Roland Burke, '"The compelling dialogue of freedom": Human rights at the Bandung conference,' *Human Rights Quarterly,* vol. 28-4, 2006, pp. 947-965.
52 Cited in Roland Burke, op cit, p. 961.
53 Cited in Justus M. van der Kroef, '"Guided Democracy" in Indonesia,' *Far Eastern Survey,* vol. 26-8, August 1957, p. 113.
54 See Shari'ati's discussion on the emergence of democracy in Europe and its pitfalls for the newly independent states in *Vizhegi-hā-ye qorun-e jadid* (*The Distinctions of New Centuries*), Collected Works, vol. 31, Tehran: Daftar-e Tadvin va Tanzim-e Āsār-e Shari'ati, 1997, p. 219. Unlike his common practice of not mentioning specific references in his lectures and writings, here he made a direct reference to Sukarno's 'guided democracy.'
55 As part of the effort to erase the connection between Shari'ati and the designation of *imamate* to Khomeini, in his memoirs, Ayatollah Mahallati claimed that he was the 'first to use the title of *imam* for Ayatollah Khomeini.' See Alijani, *Badfahmi,* pp. 21-24.
56 Shari'ati, *Tashayyo',* pp. 31-39.
57 Shari'ati *Islamology,* vol. 1, p. 358.
58 Most often, Shari'ati was not explicit in referring to other works upon which he formulated his theories, especially if the reference was to prominent Marxists. For example on the notion of permanent revolution he stated:

'There is a thesis called "permanent revolution" which demonstrates how it is possible to intervene in the seemingly inevitable process of stagnation of a society. It is conceivable to exert a vanguard leadership over a society to sustain a permanent revolution by constantly reinventing the means of its livelihood' (*Islamology,* vol. 2, 65). Shari`ati might have also been inspired by Régis Debray's *Revolution in the Revolution,* which had significant currency in French Left intellectual circles during his residence in Paris from 1960 to 1965.

[59]   Shari`ati, *Islamology,* vol. 2, pp. 65-67.

[60]   Shari`ati, *Ali,* Collected Works, vol. 26, Tehran: Nilufar, 1984, p. 620.

[61]   Shari`ati, vol. 26, p. 618.

[62]   Shari`ati, *Tārikh-e tamaddon* (*The History of Civilization*) 2 vols. Collected Works Nos. 11 & 12, Tehran: Entesharat-e Agah 1982, p. 145.

[63]   Shari`ati, *Tārikh-e tamaddon,* pp. 145-48. Shari`ati's distinction between democracy of *ra'y* and democracy of *ra's* resembles Rousseau's distinction between the *will of all* and the *general will.* 'The latter,' Rousseau asserted, 'regards only the common interest; the former regards private interest, and is indeed but a sum of private wills [...] Our will always seeks our own good, but we do not always perceive what it is. The people are never corrupted, but they are often deceived, and only then do they seem to will what is bad.' (Rousseau, *The Social Contract,* trans. Maurice Cranston, New York, London: Penguin Books, 1968, p. 72)

[64]   Shari`ati, *Islamology,* vol. 1, p. 148.

[65]   For a discussion on Shari'ati's view on democracy and electoral politics see Rahnema & Nomani 1990, pp. 65-73.

[66]   Various English translations of the notion of *gharbzadegi* point to divergent interpretations of its meaning. These translations include: 'Westrusckness,' in Green & Alizadeh's translation (*Gharbzadegi [Westrusckness]*, Lexington: Mazda Publishers, 1983); 'Occidentosis,' in R. Campbell translation (*Occidentosis: A Plague from the West,* Berkeley: Mizan Press, 1984); 'Euromania,' in Roy Motahhadeh, *The Mantle of the Prophet* (New York: Pantheon Books, 1985), 'Westernmania,' in James Bill, *The Eagle and the Lion* (Yale University Press: New Haven, 1988), 'Westoxication,' in Nikki Keddie, *Roots of Revolution*, and many others. Keddie's translation captures the content of the Persian original better than other translations. (See Mehrzad Boroujerdi, '*Gharbzadegi,* the Dominant Intellectual Discourse of Pre- and Post-Revolutionary Iran,' in S. K. Farsoun & M. Mashayekhi (eds.), *Political Culture in the Islamic Republic,* London & New York: Routledge, 1992.

[67]   Ahmad Fardid's ideas became better known to English readers in Mehrzad Boroujerdi, *Iranian Intellectuals and the West, the Tormented Triumph of Nativism,* Syracuse: Syracuse University Press, 1996. A collection of essays transcribed from his lectures at Tehran University was published under the title *Didār-e farrahi va fotuhāt-e Sāheb-e zamān* (*The Glorious Meeting and the Triumphs of Mahdi the Messiah*), Tehran: Nazar, 2003. After more than six decades, Fakhroddin Shadman's *Taskhir-e tamaddon-e farangi* (*The Invasion by Western Civilization*) was reissued by Gām-e No, 2004, in Tehran.

[68]   Fardid, *Didār,* p. 348.

[69]   See chapters 18 and 19 in Fardid's *Didār.*

[70]   This is a reference to the rise of *Mu`tazela* school of theology whose most important proponent was Ibn Sina (Avicenna). A similar critique of rationalist school of Islamic philosophy was put forward by Seyyed Hossein Nasr in a number of his treatises most notably in his *Science and Civilization in*

Islam (New York: Barnes & Noble Books, 1992). Nasr refutes the idea that Greek scientific tradition and philosophy were deposited into the Islamic account in the seventh century and were withdrawn by Europeans in the sixteenth century and into the project of the Enlightenment.

71 Fardid, *Didār*, p. 358.

72 Shadman, *Taskhir*, p. 34.

73 Al-e Ahmad, *Gharbzadegi (Westoxication)*, Tehran: Ravaq, 1962, pp. 51-52.

74 Hossein Kachu`ian, *Tatavorāt-e goftemānhā-ye hoviyati-ye Iran (Transformations of Identity Discourses in Iran)* Tehran: Nashr-e Nay, 2006, p. 123-124.

75 See Shari`ati's *Māshin dar esārat-e māshinism* ('Machine in the captivity of machinism') in Collected Works, vol. 31, pp. 303-358.

76 Shari`ati, *Māshin*, p. 314.

77 Shari'ati, *Ensān-e bi-khod (The Estranged Humanity)*, Collected Works, vol. 25, p. 212.

78 Shari`ati, vol. 31, pp. 306-307.

79 Al-e Ahamad, *Gharbzadegi*, pp. 27-31.

80 Shari`ati, *Bāzgasht (Return)* Collect Works, vol. 4, p. 243.

81 See *Sahifeh*, vol. 9, pp. 488-489.

82 See his `*Elal-e gerāyesh beh māddigari (Causes of Attraction to Materialism)*, Qom: Sadra Publishers, 1978.

83 Motahahri, *Nezām-e hoquq-e zan dar Islam (The Order of Women's Rights in Islam)*, Tehran: Sadra, 1980, pp. 134-144.

84 'A westoxicated person is a wimp, he does not believe in anything. He wants to please others, and when he crosses the bridge does not care whether the bridge stands or collapses. He has neither faith nor belief. He cares neither for God nor for humankind. He is an observer, not a participant, he will never invest anything of himself' (*Gharbzadegi*, p. 144). Before the publication of *Gharbzadegi*, in his short stories and novels, particularly in *Modir-e madreseh (The School Principal)* published in 1958 and *Nefrin-e zamin (The Curse of the Land)*, a scathing attack on the devastating consequences of the White Revolution's land reform, Al-e Ahmad used fictional characters to depict the cultural and social dimensions of *gharbzadegi*.

85 Among these books, Hasan Qazi-Moradi's *Khodmadāri-ye Iraniān (The Self-Orbiting Iranians)*, Tehran: Akhtaran, 2000, and Ahamad Seif's *Pishdarāmadi bar estebdād dar Iran (A Preface to Despotism in Iran)*, Tehran: Cheshmeh, 2000 received considerable publicity. Both books argued that a prevailing culture of intolerance among Iranians has hindered the development of a civil society and a sense of public good. They both link this to the tradition of despotic political systems, from ancient monarchies to the postrevolutionary republic.

86 Shari`ati cited in Rezaqoli, *Nokhbeh-koshi*, p. 228.

87 Ziba-Kalam, *Mā cheguneh*, p. 36, emphases in the original.

88 Ziba-Kalam, Ibid, p. 36.

89 Karl Wittfogel, *Oriental Despotism: A Comparative Study of Total Power*, New Haven: Yale University Press, 1964 (1957).

90 Gustave von Grunebaum's *Modern Islam: The Search for Cultural Identity* (Berkeley & Los Angeles: University of California Press, 1962), W. M. Watt's *Islamic Fundamentalism and Modernity* (London, New York: Routledge, 1988), and more recently Bernard Lewis' *What Went Wrong: The Clash Between Islam and Modernity in the Middle East* (Oxford: Oxford University Press, 2002).

91 This was the title of a review originally published in the *Jomhuri-ye islami (The Islamic Republic)* morning newspaper in May 1995. The review was reprinted

in *Kayhan*, a state-sponsored newspaper, in the fall of the same year. The review was also included in the fifth edition of *Mā cheguneh mā shodim*, where the citation here originates.

92   See the appendix to the fifth edition of *Mā cheguneh mā shodim*.

CHAPTER SEVEN

1   Soroush, '`Ulum-e ensāni dar nezām-e dāneshgahi' ('Human sciences in the university system'), published in Abdolkarim Soroush, *Tafarroj-e son`: Goftārhā-ei dar Akhlāq va san`at va elm-e ensāni* (*Essays on Human Sciences, Ethics and Technology*), Tehran: Serat, 1987, pp. 190-202.

2   Soroush, 'Hoviyat-e tārikhi va ejtemā`ei-ye `elm' ('The social and historical character of science'), published in *Tafarroj*, pp. 203-227.

3   Soroush, *Tafarroj*, p. 227.

4   All collected in *Tafarroj*.

5   He developed this argument in a short essay called *Gharbiyān va hosn-o qobh-e sho'un va atvār-e ānān* ('The westerners and the vices and virtues of their manners and practices') published in *Kayhān Farhangi*, vol. 1-2, 1984.

6   Cited in Quchani, *prātik-e Soroush*, p. 50. Davari later developed a more comprehensive critique of Popper's philosophy in *Sayri enteqādi dar falsafeh-ye Karl Popper* (*A Critical Investigation of Karl Popper's Philosophy*). Davari also responded to the idea of geographical distinction between East and West in *Farhang, Kherad, va Āzādi* (*Culture, Reason, and Freedom*).

7   See his *Shemmeh-'i az tārikh-e gharbzadegi-ye mā* (*A Digest of the History of Our Westoxication*), 1984, Tehran: Soroush Publishers.

8   Davari refined his thesis after the publication of Huntington's 'Clash of Civilizations.' See Davari's 'Islam and the West,' pp. 139-152, in his *Farhang, kherad, āzādi* (*Culture, Reason, and Freedom*), Tehran: Saqi, 2000.

9   Davari, '*Postmodern, dowrān-e fetrat,*' ('Postmodernism the era of fortitude') *Mashreq*, vol. 1-1, 1995, p. 15.

10   Davari, *Shemmeh*, p. 22.

11   Fardid, *Didār-e farrahi*, frontispiece.

12   Fardid, Ibid, p. 168.

13   Cited in Quchani, *Prātik-e Soroush*, p. 50.

14   Among them were influential figures of the reform movement such as Reza Tehrani, Mashallah Shamsolva`ezin, Morteza Mardiha, Majid Mohammadi, Mostafa Tajzadeh, Hamid Reza Jala'ipour, Mohsen Sazgara, Akbar Ganji, Ahmad Borqani, Mohammad Abtahi, Said Hajjarian, and even Mohammad Khatami, who later was elected as the President in 1997.

15   See Hamid-Reza Jala'ipour, *Pas az dovvom-e Khordād* (*After the Second of Khordad*), Tehran: Kavir, 1999, p. 45.

16   Among other equally substantive and critical journals were: *Iran-e farda* (*The Iran of Tomorrow*); *Goftegu* (*Dialogue*); *Ādineh* (*Friday*); *Donyā-ye sokhan* (*The World of Discourse*), *Kelk* (*The Pen*); *Jāme`eh-ye sālem* (*The Healthy Society*), *Farhang-e towse`eh* (*The Culture of Development*).

17   Women and student movements were the main force behind the election of the philosopher-politician Mohammad Khatami to the Presidency in 1997.

18   The results of such surveys should be viewed critically. Questions regarding religious affiliation or the level of religious conviction are highly problematic. In a general sense, I am not satisfied with the measures used for quantifying religious conviction (which are most often based on external manifestations

of religious practices); more specifically, in the Iranian context, fear of persecution and distrust plays a major role in the correspondents' responses.

[19] For a review of the emergence of the Muslim feminist movement see, Ziba Mir-Hosseini, *Islam and Gender: The Religious Debate in Contemporary Iran,* Princeton: Princeton University Press, 1999; Valentine Moghadam, 'Islamic feminism and its discontents: Toward a resolution of the debate,' *Signs,* vol. 27-4, Summer 2002; Afsaneh Najmabadi, 'Feminisms in an Islamic Republic,' in Joan Scott *et al.,* editors, *Transitions, Environments, Translations: Feminisms in International Politics,* London: Routledge, 1997.

[20] Of course we should not discount the importance of electoral politics in Iran. In contrast to Shari`ati's vision, as the 1997 presidential elections in Iran demonstrated, the Islamic Republic seeks legitimacy through popular vote. This is not to suggest that elections in Iran are free and fair, but its constitution recognizes majority vote as the primary source of its legitimacy.

[21] Sami Zubaida, *Islam, the People and the State,* London: Routledge, 1989.

[22] In an interview with Kathy Evans of the London daily *The Guardian,* July 1999, Soroush said that 'I am just a theoretician, I let others draw their own conclusions from my ideas.'

[23] Summarized from Soroush, *Farbeh-tar az eideolozhi (Loftier than Ideology),* Tehran: Serat, 1994, pp. 135-154.

[24] For his critique of the Marxian conception of ideology see Soroush, *Dars-ha-ei dar Falsafeh-ye Elm-e Ejtema'* (Lectures on the Philosophy of Social Science) Tehran: Nay, 1995, pp. 291-384.

[25] Soroush, *Tafarroj,* p. 368.

[26] Jalal a-Din Farsi, a Muslim social critic and a historian of Islam, simplifies the matter by arguing that all the verses that were revealed to the Prophet in Mecca are permanently sacred and all the verses that were revealed to him in Medina are situational. The latter verses deal with the issues of governance and civic laws, while the former are about Islamic ethics and moral guidance. See his *Enqelāb-e takāmoli-ye Islam (The Evolutionary Revolution of Islam),* Tehran: Entesharat-e Elmi va Farhangi, 1983.

[27] Soroush, *Qabz va bast-e teorik-e shari`at (The Theoretical Contraction and Expansion of the Shari`ah),* Tehran: Serat, 1995, p. 52.

[28] Soroush *Bāvar-e dini, dāvar-e dini (Religious Faith, Religious Justification),* Ketab-e Ehya no. 5, Tehran: Yad-Avarn Publishers, 1992.

[29] Habibollah Payman argued that Soroush has discounted Shari`ati's contribution. He believes that there was nothing innovative about his 'new' hermeneutics. See Payman, '*Sobāt va tagh'ir dar andishe-ye dini*' ('Permanence and change in religious thought'), *Kiyān,* vol. 2-7, June/July, 1992.

[30] Shari`ati, *Islamology,* vol. 1, p. 140.

[31] Shari`ati, Ibid, p. 215.

[32] Motahhari, *Bahsi darbāre-ye marja`iyyat va rohaniyyat* (A Treatise on the Source of Imitation and the Clergy) Tehran: n.p. 1962. Also see Motahhari's *Dah Goftar (Ten Discourses)* Tehran: Hekmat, 1978, p. 101.

[33] See his *Khātamiyat,* Tehran: Sadra 1988, pp. 147-152.

[34] Motahhari, *Shesh maqāleh* (Six Essays), Tehran: Sadra, 1985, p. 134 (italics added). He also advanced his theory of historical contingencies of religious knowledge in *Islam va moqtaziyat-e zaman (Islam and the Necessities of Time),* Tehran: Sadra, 1988.

[35] Soroush, *Farbeh,* p. 78.

36   A similar notion of the continuity of revelation is suggested by Mohammad
     Mojtahid Shabestari, 'Modernism va vahy' ('Modernism and revelation'),
     Kiyān, vol. 5-29, March/April, 1996. He located this doctrine within the
     Christian and Islamic mystic traditions, the great twentieth century Muslim
     proponent of which was Mohammad Iqbal. Shabestari argued that in this
     tradition religious knowledge (faith) emerges from inner religious experience
     as the 'touch of the divine spirit.'
37   Schoenberg spelled Aron with only one 'a' to avoid the curse of 13 letters in
     the opera's title!
38   Soroush, Qabz va bast, p. 34.
39   Soroush, Qabz va bast, p. 186.
40   Soroush, Qabz va bast, p. 487.
41   Sorush, Farbeh, pp. 199-231.
42   See for example his 'Mā dar kodām jahān zendegi mikonim' ('In which world do
     we live?') in The Satanic Ideology. Mohammad Mojtahid Shabestari has
     introduced similar ideas in his thesis of taltif-e shari`at (The Benevolent
     Shari`ah).
43   Soroush, Qabz va bast, p. 442.
44   Tabataba`i's treatise, Usul-e falsafeh va ravesh-e reālism (The Principles of
     Philosophy and the Method of Realism), is heavily annotated by Morteza
     Motahhari and published in five volumes (Qum: Sadra Publishers, 1953-
     1985).
45   Soroush, Qabz va bast, pp. 342-344.
46   Soroush, Qabz va bast, p. 341.
47   He does not explain what the institutional means are whereby an interpreta-
     tion is considered systematic, or how such a criterion is employed in practice.
48   Soroush, Qabz va bast, pp. 305-06.
49   Soroush, Qabz va bast, pp. 302-310.
50   Adopting Hume's critique of inductive generalization, Popper argued that
     scientific theories cannot be verified by any accumulation of the observa-
     tional evidence. Rather, he argued, the basic process of science was the
     elimination of alternative theories by investigating as many of the empirical
     consequences of each theory as is practical, always trying for the greatest
     possible variety in the implications tested. The purpose of empirical work for
     Popper was to test the refutability of theory (The Logic of Scientific Discovery).
51   Popper himself used his falsification method to negate Marxist pseudo-
     scientific claims of materialist conception of history (The Poverty of
     Historicism).
52   Soroush, Qabz va bast, p. 106.
53   Soroush, 'Horriyat va ruhāniyat,' ('Freedom and the clergy'), Kiyān, 5:24, 1995.
54   It is extremely controversial to de-sacralize Arabic as the language of Islam.
     Nevertheless, Soroush remarked that 'the fact that the Qur'an was revealed to
     the Prophet in Arabic does not make this language an integral part of Islam.
     Had Islam been revealed in any other place, all of its literature and the ways
     through which it was expressed would have been different [...] Had the
     Prophet been German, the language of our daily prayer would have been
     German, there is nothing inherently sacred about Arabic.' (Farbeh, p. 59)
55   Soroush, Rāz-dāni, roshanfekri, va dindāri (Augury, Intellectualism, and Religious
     Conviction) Tehran: Serat, 1993. Here Soroush is referring to Davari, Fardid,
     and other Heideggerians who became closer to the clerical authoritarian
     renditions of Islam.

56   Although from the tenor and content of his critique, one may conclude that he was castigating the Heideggerian philosophers, such as Davari and Fardid, it is not quite clear why he referred to them as the Hegelians.

57   *Qabz va bast,* pp. 179-180.

58   Soroush's position strongly resembles Ernest Gellner's anti-relativist defense of 'Enlightenment Rationalist Fundamentalism.' Gellner argued that both religious and Enlightenment fundamentalism are 'committed to the denial of relativism.' The Enlightenment protagonist 'is committed to the view that there *is* external, objective, culture-transcending knowledge: there *is* indeed 'knowledge beyond culture'.' (*Postmodernism, Reason, and Religion,* London & New York: Routledge, 1992, p. 75)

59   See Ghamari-Tabrizi's 'Is Islamic science possible?' for a discussion of the objectivity of scientific knowledge. For Soroush's Hegelian approach and his meta-historical understanding of modernity and Reason see Hamid Dabashi's 'Blindness and insight: The predicament of a Muslim intellectual,' in *Iran: Between Tradition and Modernity,* R. Jahanbegloo, editor, Lexington Books, 2002.

60   Dabashi, *Blindness,* p. 110.

61   Popper wrote, 'The question how it happens that a new idea occurs to a man [sic]—whether it is a musical theme, a dramatic conflict, or a scientific theory—may be of great interest to empirical psychology; but it is irrelevant to the logical analysis of scientific knowledge.' He calls the former the 'context of discovery,' and the latter the 'context of justification.' (*Scientific Discovery,* p. 31)

62   Soroush, *Qabz va bast,* p. 96.

63   Dabashi, *Blindness,* p. 111.

64   *Farbehr,* p. 280 (italics added).

65   Seminar on Human Rights, Sponsored by the Iranian Ministry of Foreign Affairs, Tehran 1992; Seminar on Human Rights, Hamburg, The Institute of Oriental Studies, 1993.

66   The critics of Soroush's notion of democratic religious state, emphasize two contradictions, one being the old constitutional debate over the question of rights (of Muslims and non-Muslims, men and women) (Parvin Paidar, *Women and the Political Process in Twentieth Century Iran,* New York & London: Cambridge University Press, 1994), and the absence of structures through which the religiosity of the state is institutionalized (Maqsud Farastkhah, 'Rābeteh-ye din va siyāsat dar jām`'h-ye dini' ('The relation between religion and politics in a religious society'), *Kiyān,* vol. 14-18, 1994; Bijan Hikmat, 'Mardom-sālāri va din-sālāri' ('Democracy and theocracy'), *Kiyān,* vol. 4-21, 1994.

67   Soroush, *Farbeh,* p. 318.

68   Soroush, *Rāzdāni,* p. 38.

69   Soroush, *Farbeh,* p. 224.

70   Soroush, *Rāzdāni,* pp. 140-141.

71   Soroush, *Farbeh,* p. 51.

72   Soroush, *Farbeh,* p.273.

73   Soroush, *Rāzdāni,* pp.145-150.

74   Soroush, 'Ma`nā va mabnā-ye secularism' ('The meaning and the foundation of secularism'), *Kiyān* vol. 5-26, 1995, p. 8.

75   *Rāzdāni,* p. 150.

76   Majid Mohammadi, 'Ghosl-e ta`mid-e sekularism yā neāt-e din' ('The baptism of secularism or the salvage of religion'), *Kiyān,* vol. 4-21. 1994; Alireza Alavi,

1995, '*Hākemiyat-e mardom dar jāme`h-ye dindārān*' ('The sovereignty of the people in the society of the religious'), *Kiyān*, vol. 4-22. 1995.

[77]   Soroush, *Farbeh*, pp. 36-37.

[78]   According to Baqir Sadr, the problem with the capitalist economic system is not, as its Marxist critics argue, rooted in the principle of private property or in the commodification of labor-power. Rather the problem of socialist and capitalist economic systems is rooted in their philosophical materialism, on the basis of which its proponents envision only the pursuit of material pleasure and wealth. Islamic economy, according to Sadr, is the only system that takes into account the fulfillment of spiritual and moral needs of human beings. It is noteworthy that within the wide range of Islamic economic theories, which oscillate between socialism and capitalism, Baqir Sadr's borders on capitalism. See Baqir Sadr, *Eqtesād-e mā* (*Our Economy*), trans. from Arabic to Farsi by M.K. Bojnurdi, Tehran: Borhan, 1972.

[79]   For an excellent review of whether Islamic economy is conceived based on distinct economic principles (as a science of economy) or as a social system within which other economic principles are regulated and modified see M. A. Mannan, *Islamic Economics: Theory and Practice*, Cambridge: The Islamic Academy, 1986.

[80]   Lysenkoism is a reference to the ideological domination of Trofim Denisovich Lysenko over the Soviet genetics and agronomy programs. The Lysenko affair (1935-65) was one of the most blatant ideologically motivated attempts to manipulate and control scientific practices and to pre-determine the results of scientific research based on ideological commitments. See David Joravsky's *The Lysenko Affair*, Chicago: Chicago University Press, 1970.

[81]   Soroush, *Tafarroj*, p. 116.

[82]   Soroush, *Farbeh*, p. 329.

[83]   Soroush, '*Ma`ishat va fazilat*' ('Livelihood and wisdom'), *Kiyān*, vol. 5-25, 1995.

[84]   *Tafarroj*, p. 115.

[85]   Jean-François Lyotard, *The Postmodern Condition: A Report on Knowledge*, trans. Geoff Bennington and Brian Massumi, Minneapolis: University of Minnesota Press, 1991, p. 47.

[86]   *Tafarroj*, pp. 199-200.

[87]   *Farbeh-tar*, p. 359. Although Soroush is a great advocate of pluralism, epistemological and political, in his works he incorporates a masculine, militaristic language to describe his opponents. Phrases such as *sar boridan* (decapitating) of an idea or *qorbani kardan* (ritual sacrifice) of a goal are common phrases in his writings. One might argue that these are Persian tropes and do not necessarily connote the same signification as in English. However, given the current dominant political culture in Iran, there is more reason for Soroush to be more discriminating in his rhetoric.

[88]   Soroush, *Ma`ishat*, p. 8.

[89]   Paul Feyerabend, *Against Method*, London: Verso, 1988, p. 214.

[90]   *Tafarroj*, p. 173.

[91]   *Tafarroj*, p. 176.

[92]   Jacques Ellul, *The Technological Society*, New York: Vintage, 1964.

[93]   *Tafarroj*, p. 292.

[94]   For a discussion on different theories of technology see Andrew Feenberg's *Critical Theory of Technology*, Oxford: Oxford University Press, 1991.

[95]   *Tafarroj*, p. 292.

[96]   *Tafarroj*, pp. 281-304.

97 *Tafarroj*, p. 290.
98 Soroush, *Tafarroj*, p. 309.
99 Soroush, *Tafarroj*, pp. 32-33.
100 Soroush, *Tafarroj*, pp. 317-318.
101 N. Fakhroddin, *Khod-kafā'i va san`at* ('Technology and self-reliance') in *Tafarroj*, p. 484.
102 Reza Saberi, *Vahshat az gharb yā az teknology-ye gharb* ('The fear of the West or of its technology') in *Tafarroj*, p. 497.
103 A number of other Iranian intellectuals have also put forward arguments about the hybrid sources of Iranian culture. According to this view none of these sources must be considered primary, since they were integrated into one another. See Dariush Shayegan, *Bothā-ye zehni va khātereh-ye azali* (*Imagined Idols and Infinite Memories*), Tehran: Amir Kabir, 2003; Farhang Raja'i in *Moshkeleh-ye hoviyat-e Iranian-e emruz* (*The Predicament of Identity for the Contemporary Iranians*), Tehran: Nashr-e Nay, 2004; Mohammad Ali Nadushan in *Chehār sokhangu-ye vojdān-e irani* (*Four Spokespersons of the Iranian Conscience*), Tehran: Qatreh, 2003. There is a long list of others who also rejected a binary understanding of the West and the Rest.
104 Whereas in his critique of westoxication Soroush rejects the idea of purity and authenticity, on other occasions, especially in places where he addresses the issues of progress and development, he seems to be its advocate. For example in his lecture on 'Muslimhood and Development,' he offered the following definition of progress: 'a thing becomes complete when it progresses closer to its 'self' and rids itself of the alien tarnish [...] either through internal growth or by overcoming external obstacles [...] Think of a glass of water which is saturated with salt and has lost its original taste; when would this water become "water" again? When the salt in it is eliminated, when there are no alien element in it, then the water is pure [...] Progress is the movement toward "de-alienization," toward becoming pure' (*Farbeh-tar*, p. 331). In the same lecture, he also formulated a conception of the West that echoed the westoxication discourse. He argued that western civilization is founded on a triangle of technical and scientific progress, internal moral decadence, and external colonialism.
105 Soroush, '*Vojud va māhiyat-e gharb*,' ('The existence and the essence of the West'), *Kayhan Farhangi*, vol. 1-5, 1985, p. 15.
106 '*Gharbiyān va hosn-o qobh-e sho'un va atvār-e ānān*' ('The westerners and the virtues and vices of their manners'), *Kayhan Farhangi*, vol. 1-2, 1984, p. 15.
107 Soroush, *Gharbiyān*, p. 16.
108 Soroush, *Gharbiyān*, p. 16.
109 Soroush, *Tafarroj*, p. 235.
110 Soroush, *Gharbiyān*, p. 17.
111 Soroush, *Gharbiyān*, p. 17.
112 Soroush, *Az Shari`ati*, p. 176.
113 See Soroush, *Vojud va māhiyat*.
114 Soroush, *Gharbiyān*, p. 18.
115 Al-e Ahmad, *Gharbzadegi*, p. 28.
116 Al-e Ahmad, *Gharbzadegi*, p. 118.
117 Soroush, *Az Shari`ati*, p. 167.
118 Soroush, *Az Shari`ati*, p. 166.
119 Soroush, *Rāz-dāni*, pp. 115-116.

[120] Frantz Fanon, *The Wretched of the Earth*, trans. Constance Farrington, Harmondsworth: Penguin, 1968, p. 37.

[121] Fanon, *The Wretched*, p. 233.

[122] Fanon, *The Wretched*, p. 247.

[123] Aimé Césaire, 'Discourses on Colonialism,' [1972] in Williams & Chrisman (eds.), *Colonial Discourse and Post-Colonial Theory*, New York: Columbia University Press, 1994, p. 179, emphasis in the original.

[124] Soroush, *Rāz-dāni*, p. 116.

[125] Soroush, *Rāz-dāni*, pp. 116-117.

[126] Soroush, *Rāz-dāni*, p. 119.

[127] Morteza Motahhari, *Khadamāt-e moteqābel-e Islam va Iran* (*The Reciprocal Exchanges between Islam and Iran*), Qom: Sadra Publishers, 1983.

[128] Soroush, *Gharbiyān*, p. 17.

[129] Among these early critiques were: Hossein Ghaffari's *Naqd-e nazariyeh-ye shari`at-e sāmet* (*A Critique of the Theory of Silent Shari`ah*) Tehran: Hikmat, 1989; Ata'ollah Karimi's *Faqr-e tārikhi-negari* (*The Poverty of Historicism*), Tehran: Allameh Tabataba'i Publishers, 1990; and Hojjatoleslam Sadeq Larijani's *Ma`refat-e dini: Naqdi bar nazariyeh-ye qabz va bast-e teorik-e shari`at* (*Religious Knowledge: A Critique of the Doctrine of the Theoretical Expansion and Contraction of the* Shari`ah), Tehran: Ketab Publishers, 1991.

[130] Cited in Soroush, *Ghabz va bast*, p. 501.

[131] Ali AkbarVelayati, *Kayhan* editorial, Dec. 26, 1995. (Cited in Human Rights Watch Report, *Iran: Power Versus Choice*, March 1996, vol. 8-1 E, accessed via: http://hrw.org/reports/1996/Iran.htm.

[132] Cited in Human Rights Watch Report, Ibid.

[133] Ghaffari, op cit.

[134] Larijani, op cit.

[135] A good representative of these critical assessments are: Sayyed Hossein Musavi Zanjani, *Barkhord-e shāyesteh bā fāz-e farhangi-ye sarmāyeh-dāri: Barresi-ye mabāni-ye andishehā-ye doctor Soroush* (*The Appropriate Approach to the Cultural Phase of Capitalism: A Review of the Foundations of Doctor Soroush's Thought*), Qom: Howzeh Publishers, 1996; Ne`matollah Bavand, *Jāygāh-e `aql va demokrāsi dar nezām-e velāyat: Barresi-ye enteqādi-ye ārā'-e doctor Soroush* (*The Place of Reason and Democracy in the Velāyat System*), Tehran: Shurā-ye Tablighāt-e Islami, 1995; Hojjatolesalm Mohsen Gharaviyan, *Howzeh dar ma`raz-e hojum* (*The Seminary Under Attack*), Qom: Nashr-e Bargozideh, 1996; Ayatollah Mohammad Hossein Tehrani, *Negareshi bar maqāleh-ye bast va qabz-e teorik-e shari`at* (*A Review of the Expansion and Contraction Essay*), Tehran: Nashr-e `Ulum va Ma`āref-e Islami, 1994; Qader Fazeli, *Khatt-e qermez: Naqd va Barresi-ye ketāb-e farbeh-tar az eideolozhi* (*The Red Line: A Critical Assessment of 'Loftier Than Ideology'*), Tehran: Pelikan, 1996; Davoud Mahdavi-Zadegan, *Az qabz-e ma`nā tā bast-e donya* (*From the Contraction of Meaning to the Expansion of the World*) Tehran: Danesh va Andishe-ye Mo`āser, 2000.

[136] See Reza Davari, *Sayri enteqādi dar falsafeh-ye Karl Popper* (*A Critical Analysis of Karl Popper's Philosophy*), Tehran: Danesh va Andishe-ye Mo`āser, 2000.

[137] Mohammad Taqi Mesbah Yazdi, *Tahājom-e farhangi* (*Cultural Assault*), Qom: Imam Khomeini Teaching and Research Institute, 1999.

[138] Naser Makarem Shirazi, *Javānān va moshkelāt-e fekri* (*Youth and Problems of Mind*), Qom: Khorram, 1991.

[139] Reported in *Asr-e Azadegan*, no. 7, September 18, 1999, p. 3.

[140] Reported in *Asr-e Azadegan*, no. 7, September 18, 1999, p. 3.

[141] Reported in *Asr-e Azadegan,* no. 18, September 30, 1999, p. 3.
[142] For the chronology of attacks on Soroush I have relied on Reza Khojasteh Rahimi, *'Dāstān-e Soroush va sokhanrāni-hāyash'* ('The story of Soroush and his public lectures'), *Sharq,* October 24, 2004, p. 7.
[143] Ahmad Kasravi (1890-1946) was a historian and a philosopher whose magnum opus *The Constitutional History of Iran* served for many decades as the standard history of the Iranian Constitutional Revolution. During the 1930s and 1940s he emerged as an outspoken religious reformer with extreme anti-clerical sentiments. He was tried on the charges of slander against Islam and was assassinated during the trial by members of *Fadā'iyan-e Islam* (Devotees of Islam), a radical Islamist group.
[144] Cited in Khojasteh Rahimi, op cit.
[145] Cited in Khojasteh Rahimi, op cit.
[146] Cited in Khojasteh Rahimi, op cit.
[147] Cited in Khojasteh Rahimi, op cit.
[148] Cited in Khojasteh Rahimi, op cit.

CHAPTER EIGHT

[1] Soroush, *Siyāsat-Nāmeh (Political Letters)* Vols.1-2, Tehran: Serat, 2000.
[2] John Rawls, *Political Liberalism,* New York: Columbia University Press, 1993.
[3] Jürgen Habermas, *Between Facts and Norms: Contribution to a Discourse Theory of Law and Democracy,* Cambridge, MA: MIT Press, 1996. Whereas Habermas thinks truly legitimacy administrative power and law correspond with informal public opinion, Soroush still believes that for a society such as Iran, state power cannot be exercised outside of the religious context of Iranian society where public opinion is already religiously inscribed. Here he shows a closer affinity with Gadamer who asserts, 'That which has been sanctioned by tradition and custom has an authority that is nameless, and our finite historical being is marked by the fact that always the authority of what has been transmitted—and not only what is clearly grounded—has power over our attitudes and behavior […] Tradition has justification that is outside the arguments of reason and in large measure determines our institutions and attitudes.' (*Truth and Method,* New York: Seabury Press, 1975, p. 249.)
[4] Soroush, *Reason, Freedom, and Democracy: Essential Writings of Abdolkarim Soroush,* translated by Ahmad and Mahmoud Sadri, Oxford & New York: Oxford University Press, 2000, p. 16.
[5] Said Amir Arjomand, 'Reform movement in contemporary Iran,' *International Journal of Middle East Studies,* vol. 34-4, 2002, p. 723.
[6] Soroush, *Serāt-hā-ye mostaqim (Straight Paths),* Tehran: Serat, 1998, p. 27.
[7] John Hick has published controversial books and essays about the meaning of religious diversity. For a short summary see John Hick, 'The outcome: Dialogue into Truth,' in John Hick, ed., *Truth and Dialogue in World Religions,* (Philadelphia: Westminster, 1974). For a substantive discussion see his important books *God Has Many Names,* Philadelphia: Westminster, 1982; *Problems of Religious Pluralism,* New York: St. Martin's, 1985; and *An Interpretation of Religion,* New Haven: Yale University Press, 1989. In *Straight Paths,* Soroush included his own translation to Farsi of Hick's essay 'The epistemological challenge of religious pluralism,' pp. 285-295.

8   For an excellent review of Hick see Sumner Twiss, 'The philosophy of religious pluralism: A critical appraisal of Hick and his critics,' *Journal of Religion*, vol. 70-4, 1990: 533-568.

9   Soroush, *Straight Paths*, pp. 19-23. Hick also borrowed from Rumi the notion of God as the sun at the centre and different religions as planets revolving around it (Hick, *God Has Many Faces*, p. 52). In a talk delivered at the Theological Society in Norwich, England, he emphasized that the idea of religious pluralism and theological inclusiveness is not a Christian idea. He quoted Rumi, writing about the religions of his time, 'The lamps are different, but the Light is the same: it comes from Beyond.' (John Hick, 'Is Christianity the only true religion, or one among others?' http://www.johnhick.org.uk /article2.html, 2001.

10   Hick, *Interpretation*, p. 376.

11   Hick, *Interpretation*, pp. 233-51.

12   For a review of his critics see Timothy R. Stinnett, 'John Hick's pluralistic theory of religion,' *The Journal of Religion*, vol. 70-4, 1990: 569-588.

13   Hick, *Interpretation*, pp. 343-361.

14   Abdolkarim Soroush, *Bast-e tajrobeh-ye nabavi* (*The Expansion of Prophetic Experience*) Tehran: Serat, 1999, p. 19.

15   The doctrines of *Qadariyya* (free will indeterminacy) and *Jabriyya* (predestination and determinism) are often associated with the schools of the Mu`tazilites and Ash`arites, respectively. However, a careful examination of the adherents of these traditions shows that Muslim philosophers and theologians freely borrowed doctrinal elements from different schools to advance new philosophies.

16   Soroush, *Prophetic Experience*, p. 20.

17   Soroush, *Prophetic Experience*, p. 80, my emphasis.

18   Soroush, *Prophetic Experience*, p. 80.

19   Soroush, *Prophetic Experience*, pp. 81-82.

20   Others who believed in the gradual creation of the Qur'an and *did* link it to the Prophethood of Muhammad based their belief on another verse from the *Sura al-Isra'*: *We have divided the Qur'an into sections so that you may recite it to the people with deliberation. We have imparted it by gradual revelation* (17: 106).

21   A. K. M. Ayyub Ali, 'Māturidism,' in M. M. Sharif, editor, *A History of Muslim Philosophy*, vol. 1, Wiesbaden: Otto Harrassowitz, 1963, p. 217.

22   Soroush, *Prophetic Expansion*, p. 134.

23   Soroush, *Siyāsat-Nāmeh*, vol. 1, p. 215.

24   In addition to numerous articles in various journals published by Qom Seminary, four books about Soroush's new works are notable: Abbas Nikzad, *Serāt-e mostaqim, naqdi bar qarā'at-e Doktor Soroush az pluralism-e dini* (*Straight Path: A Critique of Doctor Soroush's Interpretation of Religious Pluralism*) Qom: Bustan (The Office of the Islamic Propagation of Qom Seminary), 2001; Hasan Hosseini, *Pluralism-e dini, yā pluralism dar din* (*Religious Pluralism or Pluralism in Religion*), Tehran: Soroush Publishers, 2003; Mohsen Gharavian, *Pluralism-e dini va estebdād-e ruhāniyat* (*Religious Pluralism and the Despotism of the Clergy*), Tehran: Yamin, 1998; Ja`far Sobhani, *Kesrat-gerā'i, yā pluralism-e dini* (*On Religious Pluralism*), Qom: Imam Sadeq Institute, 2002.

25   Often Soroush's clerical critics use relativism and pluralism interchangeably.

26   Sadeq Larijani, '*Naqd-e pluralism-e dini*' ('A critique of religious pluralism'), *Moballeghān*, a journal published by Qom Seminary, no. 25, January 2002, p. 2. (Accessed via http://hawzah.net/Per/magazine/index.aspx)

27   Gharavian, op cit.
28   Mohammad Javad Heidari Kashani, '*Naqdi bar pluralism-e dini*' ('A critique of
      religious pluralism') *Payām-e Howzeh Monthly*, no. 25, Winter 2000, p. 5.
      (Accessed via http://hawzah.net/Per/magazine/index.aspx)
29   Ali Rabbani Golpaigani, *Tahlil va naqd-e pluralism-e dini* (*A Critical Analysis of
      Religious Pluralism*), Tehran: Contemporary Thought Cultural Institute, 2000,
      pp. 63-177. Davoud Fairahi, a prominent faculty of Tehran University's
      School of Law and Political Science, puts forward a similar argument where
      he emphasizes that the legitimacy of political participation does not depend
      on the recognition of religious pluralism. One may recognize political rights
      of the opposition without sharing their conception of the nominal Reality.
      Davoud Fairahi, '*Moshārekat-e siyāsi dar dolat-e Islāmi*' ('Political participation
      under the Islamic state'), *Faslnāmeh Mofid*, no. 25, 2002.
30   Sadeq Larijani, *Naqd*, p. 7.
31   Mojtahed Shabestari is one of the leading Iranian advocates of the
      hermeneutic approach to Islamic theology. Influenced by Paul Tillich's
      Systematic Theology, and German phenomenological tradition, particularly of
      Friedrich Heiler, he argues that rather than from doctrinal debates,
      theological innovations emerge from the religious *experiences* of each
      generation of believers. The interpretation of the divine text is mediated by
      history, society, body, and language. While a hermeneutic approach
      acknowledges these contingencies, it also endeavors to transcend them.
      However, this transcendence can never be total and, accordingly, truth-
      claims may never be absolute. Truth belongs to God and remains inaccessible
      to human faculties. For an introduction see Farzin Vahdat, 'Postrevolutionary
      discourses of Mojtahed Shabestari and Mohsen Kadivar: Reconciling the
      terms of mediated subjectivity,' *Critique*, vol. 9-16, Spring 2000: 31-54.
32   Mohammad Mojtahed Shabestari, *Naqdi bar qarā'at-e rasmi-ye din* (*A critique of
      the Official Reading of Religion*), Tehran: Tarh-e No, 2002, p. 402.
33   Mojtahed Shabestari, 'On tolerance,' pp. 69-93, in *Qarā'at-e rasmi*,, chapter 2.
34   Shabestari, *Qarā'at-e rasmi*, p. 383.
35   Shabestari, *Qarā'at-e rasmi*, pp. 416-418.
36   For a discussion on this point see Mahmoud Sadri, 'Sacral defense of
      secularism: The political theologies of Soroush, Shabestari, and Kadivar,'
      International Journal of Politics, Culture and Society, vol. 15-2, 2001: 257-270.
37   Soroush, *Prophetic Experience*, p. 162.
38   For a comprehensive view of Eshkevari's theological and political writings
      see Ziba Mir-Hosseini & Richard Tapper, *Islam and Democracy in Iran,
      Eshkevari and the Quest for Reform*, London, New York: I. B. Tauris, 2006.
39   Hasan Yusefi Eshkevari, *Kherad dar ziyāfat-e din* (*Reason at the Banquet of
      Religion*), Tehran: Qasideh, 2000, p. 268.
40   For Eshkevari's rejection of Soroush's ideology critique see his *Shari`ati,
      eideolozhi, stratezhi* (*Shari`ati, Ideology, and Strategy*), Tehran: Chapakhsh, 1998.
41   Eshkevari cited in Mir-Hosseini & Tapper, p. 96.
42   Marziyeh Zojaji Qomi, ed., *Monāzereh-ye Soroush and Kadivar darbāre-ye
      pluralism-e dini* (*Soroush and Kadivar Debate Religious Pluralism*), Tehran: Salām
      Newspaper, 1999. Soroush included the debate in *Straight Paths*, pp. 69-135.
43   Among his books on the subject are *Hukumat-e velā'i* (*Governance by
      Guardianship*), Tehran: Nay Publishers, 1998; *Nazariyeha-ye dolat dar fiqh-e
      Shi`ah* (*Theories of State in Shi`ite Jurisprudence*), Tehran: Nay Publishers, 1997;

and *Daghdagheha-ye hukumat-e dini* (*The Anxieties of the Religious State*), Tehran: Nay Pubishers, 2000.

[44] *Monāzereh*, pp.10-20. Also see Kadivar's debate with Mojtahed Shabestari in Shabestari's *Qarā'at-e rasmi*, pp. 446-483.

[45] In Shabestari, *Qarā'at-e rasmi*, p. 476.

[46] *Monāzereh*, p. 79.

[47] *Monāzereh*, p. 36.

[48] Soroush, *Straight Paths*, p. 14.

[49] *Monāzereh*, p. 31.

[50] Reported by the Iranian Labor News Agency, Tuesday December 22, 2003. Accessed http://ilna.ir/shownews.asp?code=60892&code1=15.

[51] The audio links of these talks are available at http://www.drsoroush.com/Lectures-84.htm.

[52] Hegel, *The Philosophy of History*, New York: Prometheus Books, 1990, p. 163.

[53] Transcribed from Soroush, 'On the Historical Failure of Muslims,' Lecture Part 9, *Towhid* Center, London, July 30, 2005.

[54] All the above references are transcribed from Soroush's lectures in London.

[55] Soroush developed this point further in a talk delivered in November 2004, at the Deutsch-Amerikanisches Institut, Heidelberg. The text was accessed at http://www.drsoroush.com/English/By_DrSoroush/E-CMB-20041113-Rationalist_Traditions_in_Islam.html.

[56] Faced with skepticism by his colleagues and disciples, he defended himself in a widely publicized lecture on October 26, 2006 in Tehran which was attended by the most influential intellectuals and theorists of the reform movement. A report of the talk was published in one of Tehran's reformist-leaning newspapers *E`temād-e Melli*, November 4, 20006. The audio of the talk can be accessed via http://www.drsoroushlectures.com/Persian/Lectures/karnameye%20rosha nfekrane%20dini%20va%20ayandeye%20aan(85-08-04).mp3.

[57] For a discussion on the maximalist versus minimalist conception of religion see Soroush, *Prophet Experience*, pp. 82-122.

[58] Accessed via: http://www.drsoroush.com/English/By_DrSoroush/E-CMB-20041100-Acknowledgement_of_Erasmus_Prize_2004.html.

[59] The audio of the talk is accessible via http://www.drsoroush.com/Lectures-84.htm. For a summary report see http://www.baztab.com/news/27741.php.

[60] All the quotations are from the audio link http://www.drsoroush.com/Lectures-84.htm.

[61] Soroush, quoted in the Baztab's report, see http://www.baztab.com/news/27741.php.

[62] M. S. Bahmanpour letter to Soroush, August 15, 2005, accessed at http://www.baztab.com/news/27740.php.

[63] Soroush letter to Bahmanpour, August 23, 2005, accessed at http://www.drsoroush.com/Persian/By_DrSoroush/P-CMB-13830601-SoroushToBahmanpur.html.

[64] Mahmoud and Ahmad Sadri, editors and translators, op cit.

[65] Mahmoud Sadri, October 4, 2005, posted at http://iranian.com/MahmoudSadri/2005/October/Soroush/index.html

[66] http://iranian.com/MahmoudSadri/2005/October/Soroush/index.html.

[67] Soroush is profoundly influenced by the great Muslim theologian Imam Muhammad al-Ghazali's (1058-1111) neo-Platonic thesis of *gheflat* (the state of

unawareness). In his theory of *gheflat,* al-Ghazali emphasizes that only those who have reached the state of self-negation have the faculty of seeing the secrets of existence. If the secret is revealed indiscriminately, al-Ghazali argues, no one would participate in perpetuating humanity's livelihood. Social or communal life is reproduced unconsciously, or otherwise it would cease to exist. Although the great Sufi master poet Rumi is critical of al-Gazali's conception of God, he reinforces the Gazalian concept of *gheflat* as the Divine wisdom of life. Here are some examples in Rumi's poetry:

When we became aware of the world's *hows* and *whys*
Sealing our lips became the word of the wise,
The secrets of the unseen are not to be revealed
If the order of life is to remain congealed.
(Mathnavi, Book VI, Nos. 3526-3528)

In another poem, Rumi compares gaining knowledge of the mysteries of the world to the exposure of ice to the heat of the sun:
When the ice became aware of the sun, it remained naught
It melted, it became warm, it became soft.
(Mathnavi, Book V, Nos. 1941-1942)

For further discussion see Soroush, *Rāzdāni*, pp. 79-103.

CHAPTER NINE

[1] *Chokh-bakhtyar,* an Azeri term, literary meaning 'the very fortunate one,' was coined by Samad Behrangi (1939-1968), a leftist social and literary critic, to depict the hollow life of the newly formed Iranian technocratic class. Behrangi used the term pejoratively in reference to the conformist attitude of the new class.

[2] In September 2005, *Jyllands-Posten,* a Danish conservative daily, published twelve cartoons of the Prophet Muhammad, in all of which the Prophet was depicted in derogatory ways. One cartoonist portrayed him as an apparent terrorist with a bomb-shaped turban, and in another he appears above the clouds warning the apparent martyrs that heaven had ran out of virgins. In large demonstrations, Muslims around the world condemned the cartoons as anti-Islamic and racist.

[3] John Rawls, *A Theory of Justice*, Cambridge, MA: Harvard University Press, 1971.

[4] Seyla Benhabib, *Situating the Self: Gender, Community, and Postmodernism in Contemporary Ethics,* New York: Routledge, 1992, p. 6.

[5] For a feminist theology and theory of public religion see Linda Woodhead, 'Feminism and the sociology of religion: From gender-blindness to gendered difference,' in Richard K. Fenn (ed.), *The Blackwell Companion to Sociology of Religion,* Oxford: Blackwell Publishers, 2001; J. B. Elshtain, *Power Trips and Other Journeys: Essays in Feminism as Civic Discourse.* Madison, WI: University of Wisconsin Press, 1990; Mary Daly, *The Church and the Second Sex,* Boston: Beacon Press, 1985.

[6] Zygmunt Bauman, *Postmodernity and Its Discontents,* New York: NYU Press, 1997, p. 200.

Bibliography

Abdel-Malek, Anouar, *Contemporary Arab Political Thought*, London: Zed Press, 1983.

Abrahamian, Ervand, *Khomeinism: Essays on the Islamic Republic*, Berkeley: UC Press, 1993.

_____, *Between Two Revolutions*, Princeton, NJ: Princeton University Press, 1982.

Abu Rabi', Ibrahim, *Intellectual Origins of Islamic Resurgence in the Modern Arab World*, Albany, NY: SUNY Press, 1996.

Adamiyyat, Fereidun, *Eideolozhi-ye nehzat-e mashrutiyat-e Iran* (*The Ideology of the Iranian Constitutional Movement*), Tehran: Payam, 1976.

_____, *Fekr-e demokrāsi-ye ejtemā`i dar nehzat-e mashrutiyat-e Iran* (The Idea of Social Democracy in the Iranian Constitutional Movement), Tehran: Payam, 1976.

Adams, Charles, 'Mawdudi and the Islamic state,' in John Esposito (ed.), *Voices of Resurgent Islam*, New York, Oxford: Oxford University Press, 1983.

Afary, Janet, *The Iranian Constitutional Revolution, 1906-1911: Grassroots Democracy, Social Democracy, and the Origins of Feminism*, New York: Columbia University Press, 1996.

Ahmad, Akbar, *Postmodernism and Islam*, London & New York: Routledge, 1992.

Ahmadi Amu`i, Bahman, *Eqtesād-e siāsi-ye Jomhuri-ye Islami: Dar goftegu ba Ezzatollah Sahabi* (*The Political Economy of the Islamic Republic: In Converstaion with Ezzatollah Sahabi*), Tehran: Jam-e No, 2003.

Akbari, Ali Akbar, *Barresi-ye chand mas'le-ye ejtemā`i* (*An Analysis of Some Social Problems*), Tehran: Sepehr Publishers, 1977.

Akhavi, Shahrough, *Religion and Politics in Contemporary Iran*, Albany: SUNY Press, 1980.

Alavi, Alireza, '*Hākemiyat-e mardom dar jāme`h-ye dindārān*' ('The sovereignty of the people in the society of the religious'), *Kiyan*, vol. 4-22. 1995.

Al-e Ahmad, Jalal, *Gharbzadegi* (*Westoxication*), Tehran: Ravaq, 1962.

Algar, Hamid, *The Islamic Revolution in Iran*, London: The Open Press, 1980.

Alijani,Reza, *Bad-fahmi-ye yek towjih-he nā movaffaq* (*The Misinterpretation of an Unsuccessful Justification*) Tehran: Kavir, 2006.

Amirahmadi, Hooshang, 'Economic reconstruction of Iran: Costing the war damage,' *Third World Quarterly*, vol. 12-1, 1991.

Arjomand, Said Amir, 'Reform movement in contemporary Iran,' *International Journal of Middle East Studies*, vol. 34-4, 2002.

_____, *The Turban for the Crown: The Islamic Revolution in Iran*, New York, Oxford: Oxford University Press, 1988.

Asad, Talal, 'Multiculturalism and British identity in the wake of the Rushdie Affair," *Politics and Society*, vol. 18-4, December 1990.

Ashraf, Ahmad, 'Theocracy and charisma: New men of power in Iran,' *International Journal of Politics, Culture, and Society*, vol. 4-1, 1990.

Ayyub Ali, A. K. M., 'Māturidism,' in M. M. Sharif (ed.), *A History of Muslim Philosophy*, vol. 1, Wiesbaden: Otto Harrassowitz, 1963.

al-Azmeh, Aziz, *Islams and Modernities*, London & New York: Verso, 1993.

Bakhash, Shaul, *The Reign of the Ayatollahs, Iran and the Islamic Revolution*, New York: Basic Books, 1986.

Baktiari, Bahman, *Parliamentary Politics in Revolutionary Iran: The Institutionazation of Factional Politics*, Gainesville: The University Press of Florida, 1996.

Bani Sadr, Abolhasan, *Usul-e pāyeh va zavābet-hā-ye hokumat-e Islami* (*The Foundations and Principles of the Islamic State*), Tehran: np, 1975.

_____, *Khiyānat beh omid* (*The Betrayal of Hope*), N.P., 1982.

Barzin, Said, *'Jenāhbandi-hā-ye siyāsi dar jomhuri-ye islami-ye Iran'* ('Political factions in the Islamic Republic of Iran"), *Iran-e Farda*, no. 17, May 15, 1995.

Bauman, Zygmunt, *Postmodernity and Its Discontent*, New York: NYU Press, 1997.

Bavand, Ne'matollah, *Jāygāh-e `aql va demokrāsi dar nezām-e velāyat: Barresi-ye enteqādi-ye ārā'-e doctor Soroush* (*The Place of Reason and Democracy in the Velāyat System*), Tehran: Shurā-ye Tablighāt-e Islami, 1995.

Bayat, Mangol, *Iran's First Revolution: Shi`ism and the Constitutional Revolution of 1905-1909,* New York: Oxford University Press, 1991.

Bazargan, Mehdi, *Enqelāb dar dow harekat* (*The Revolution in Two Movements*), Tehran: Nehzat-e Azadi, 1984.

Behnama, Jamshid, *Iranian va andishe-ye tajaddod* (*Iranians and the Idea of Modernity*), Tehran: Farzan, 1997.

Beinin, Joel & Joe Stork (eds.), *Political Islam*, Berkeley & Los Angeles: University of California Press, 1997.

Benhabib, Seyla, *Situating the Self: Gender, Community, and Postmodernism in Contemporary Ethics*, New York: Routledge, 1992.

Bhabha, Homi, 'At the limits,' *Artforum*, vol. 27-9, 1989.

Bhaskar, Roy, *Dialectic: The Pulse of Freedom*, London: Verso, 1993.

Bill, James, *The Eagle and the Lion*, Yale University Press: New Haven, 1988.

Blaut, J. M., *The Colonizer's Model of the World: Geographical Diffusionism and Eurocentric History*, London & New York: The Guilford Press, 1993.

Bloch, Ernst, *The Principle of Hope*, vol. 1, translated by N. Plaice, S Plaice, and P. Knight, Cambridge, MA: MIT Press, 1986.

Boroujerdi, Mehrzad, *Iranian Intellectuals and the West, the Tormented Triumph of Nativism,* Syracuse: Syracuse University Press, 1996.

_____, 'Gharbzadegi, the dominant intellectual discourse of pre- and post-revolutionary Iran,' in S. K. Farsoun & M. Mashayekhi (eds.), *Political Culture in the Islamic Republic,* London & New York: Routledge, 1992.

Bourdieu, Pierre, *The Algerians*, translated by A. C. M. Ross, Boston: Beacon Press, 1961.

Brumberg, Daniel, *Reinventing Khomeini, the Struggle for Reform in Iran*, Chicago: Chicago University Press, 2001.

Brumberg, Daniel, *Reinventing Khomeini, the Struggle for Reform in Iran*, Chicago: Chicago University Press, 2001.

Burke, Edmund, III (ed.), *Rethinking World History, Essays on Europe, Islam, and World History: Marshall G. S. Hodgson*, Cambridge, England: Cambridge University Press, 1993.

Burke, Roland, '"The compelling dialogue of freedom": Human rights at the Bandung conference,' *Human Rights Quarterly*, vol. 28-4, 2006.

Campbell, Robert, *Occidentosis: A Plague from the West,* Berkeley: Mizan Press, 1984.

Césaire, Aimé, 'Discourses on colonialism,' [1972] in Williams & Chrisman (eds.), *Colonial Discourse and Post-Colonial Theory,* New York: Columbia University Press, 1994.

Chen, Weigang, 'Peripheral justice: The Marxist tradition of public hegemony and its implications in the age of globalization,' *positions,* vol. 13-2, 2005.

Chubin, Shahram, *Iran and Iraq at War,* Boulder: Westview Press, 1988.

Clifford, James, *The Predicament of Culture: Twentieth Century Ethnography, Literature, and Art,* Cambridge, MA: Harvard University Press, 1988.

Cragg, Kenneth, *The Pen and the Faith: Eight Modern Muslim Writers and the Qur'an,* London: George Allen and Unwin, 1985.

Crone, Patricia, *Slaves on Horses: The Evolution of the Islamic Polity,* Cambridge: Cambridge University Press, 1980.

Dabashi, Hamid, *Theology of Discontent, the Ideological Foundation of the Islamic Revolution in Iran,* New York: NYU Press, 1993.

_____, 'Blindness and insight: The predicament of a Muslim intellectual,' in R. Jahanbegloo (ed.), *Iran: Between Tradition and Modernity,* Lexington Books, 2002.

Daly, Mary, *The Church and the Second Sex,* Boston: Beacon Press, 1985.

Davari, Reza, *Sayri enteqādi dar falsafeh-ye Karl Popper (A Critical Analysis of Karl Popper's Philosophy),* Tehran: Danesh va Andishe-ye Mo`āser, 2000.

_____, *Farhang, kherad, āzādi (Culture, Reason, and Freedom),* Tehran: Saqi, 2000.

_____, 'Postmodern, dowrān-e fetrat,' ('Postmodernism the era of fortitude') *Mashreq,* vol. 1-1, 1995.

_____, *Shemmeh-'i az tārikh-e gharbzadegi-ye mā (A Digest of the History of Our Westoxication),* Tehran: Soroush Publishers, 1984.

Derrida, Jacques, *Margins of Philosophy,* translated by Alan Bass, Chicago: The University of Chicago Press, 1982.

Dustdar, Babak, *Islam-Shenāsi (Islamology),* Tehran: Kaveh, 1978.

Ehteshami, Anoushiravan, *After Khomeini: The Iranian Second Republic,* London, New York: Routledge, 1995.

Ellul, Jacques, *The Technological Society,* trans. J. Wilkinson, New York: Vintage, 1964.

Elshtain, J. B., *Power Trips and Other Journeys: Essays in Feminism as Civic Discourse,* Madison, WI: University of Wisconsin Press, 1990.

Enayat, Hamid, *Modern Islamic Political Thought,* London: Macmillan, 1982.

Engels, Friedrich, *Anti-Dühring,* Peking: Foreign Languages Press, 1976.

_____, 'Letter to P. L. Lavrov in London, November 12-13, 1875,' in *Marx, Engels, Lenin: On Historical Materialism,* New York: International Publishers, 1974.

_____, 'Origin of the family, private property and state," in *Karl Marx and Frederick Engels, Selected Works,* vol. 3, Moscow: Progress Publishers 1983.

_____, 'Speech at the graveside,' in Robert Tucker (ed.), *The Marx-Engels Reader,* London, New York: Norton, 1978.

Esposito, John (ed.), *Voices of Resurgent Islam,* New York, Oxford: Oxford University Press, 1983.

_____, *Islamic Threat: Myth or Reality,* New York & Oxford: Oxford University Press, 1992.

_____, *Islam: The Straight Path,* Oxford: Oxford University Press, 1988.

Euben, Roxanne, *Enemy in the Mirror,* Princeton, NJ: Princeton University Press, 1999.

Fairahi, Davoud, 'Moshārekat-e siyāsi dar dolat-e Islāmi' ('Political participation under the Islamic state"), *Faslnāmeh Mofid*, no. 25, 2002.

Fanon, Frantz, *The Wretched of the Earth*, trans. Constance Farrington, Harmondsworth: Penguin, 1968.

_____, *Black Skin, White Masks*, London: Pluto Press, 1986.

_____, *The Wretched of the Earth*, translated by Constance Farrington, Harmondsworth: Penguin, 1967.

Farastkhah, Maqsud, 'Rābeteh-ye din va siyāsat dar jām`'h-ye dini' ('The relation between religion and politics in a religious society'), *Kiyan*, vol. 14-18, 1994.

Fardid, Ahmad, *Didār-e farrahi va fotuhāt-e Sāheb-e zamān (The Glorious Meeting and the Triumphs of Mahdi the Messiah)*, Tehran: Nazar, 2003.

Farsi, Jalal a-Din, *Enqelāb-e takāmoli-ye Islam (The Evolutionary Revolution of Islam)*, Tehran: Entesharat-e Elmi va Farhangi, 1983.

Fazeli, Qader, *Khatt-e qermez: Naqd va Barresi-ye ketāb-e farbeh-tar az eideolozhi (The Red Line: A Critical Assessment of "Loftier Than Ideology")*, Tehran: Pelikan, 1996.

Feenberg, Andrew, *Critical Theory of Technology*, New York, Oxford: Oxford University Press, 1991.

Feyerabend, Paul, *Against Method*, London: Verso, 1988.

Fischer, Michael, 'Imam Khomeini: Four levels of understanding,' in Esposito (ed.), *Voices of Resurgent Islam*, 1983.

_____, *Iran from Religious Dispute to Revolution*, Cambridge & London: Harvard University Press, 1982.

_____, 'Islam and the revolt of the petit bourgeoisie,' *Daedalus*, vol. 3-1, winter 1982.

Foster Carter, Aidan, *The Sociology of Development*, New York, NY: Causeway Books, 1985.

Foucault, Michel, *The History of Sexuality*, vol. 1, New York: Vintage Books, 1990.

_____, *Discipline and Punish, The Birth of the Prison*, New York: Vintage Books, 1979.

Gadamer, Hans-Georg, *Truth and Method*, New York: Seabury Press, 1975.

Ganji, Akbar, *Tallaqi-ye fāshisti az din va hokumat (Fascist Interpretations of Religion and State)*, Tehran: Tarh-e No, 2000.

Gellner, Ernest, *Postmodernism, Reason, and Religion*, London & New York: Routledge, 1992.

Ghaffari, Hossein, *Naqd-e nazariyeh-ye shari`at-e sāmet (A Critique of the Theory of Silent* Shari`ah) Tehran: Hikmat, 1989.

Ghamari-Tabrizi, Behrooz, 'Between the shah and the imam: The students of the Left in Iran, 1977-1981,' in Gerald DeGroot (ed.), *Reading, Writing, and Revolution: Student Protest Since 1960*. London & New York: Addison Wesley Longman, 1998.

_____, "Is Islamic science possible?" *Social Epistemology*, vol. 10-3 & 4, 1996.

Gharavian, Mohsen, *Pluralism-e dini va estebdād-e ruhāniyat (Religious Pluralism and the Despotism of the Clergy)*, Tehran: Yamin, 1998.

_____, *Howzeh dar ma`raz-e hojum (The Seminary Under Attack)*, Qom: Nashr-e Bargozideh, 1996.

Giddens, Anthony, *The Consequences of Modernity*, Stanford: Stanford University Press, 1990.

Gilani, Asad, *Maududi: Thought and Movement*, Lahore: Farooq Hasan Gilani, 1978.

Gramsci, Antonio, *Prison Notes*, edited and translated by Q. Hoare & G. N. Smith, New York: International Publishers, 1975.

Green, John and Ahmad Alizadeh, *Gharbzadegi [Westrusckness]*, Lexington: Mazda Publishers, 1983.

Grunebaum, Gustave von, *Modern Islam: The Search for Cultural Identity*, Berkeley & Los Angeles: University of California Press, 1962.

Ha'eri, Abdolhadi, *Tashayyo` va mashrutiyat dar Iran (Shi`ism and Constitutionality in Iran)*, Tehran: Amir Kabir, 1981.

Habermas, Jürgen, *Between Facts and Norms: Contribution to a Discourse Theory of Law and Democracy*, Cambridge, MA: MIT Press, 1996.

_____, *The Philosophical Discourse of Modernity*, translated by Frederick G. Lawrence, Cambridge, MA: MIT Press, 1995.

Haddad, Yvonne, 'Sayyid Qutb: Ideologue of Islamic revival,' in Esposito (ed.), *Voices of Resurgent Islam*, New York, Oxford: Oxford University Press, 1983.

Hajjarian, Said, *Az shāhed-e qodsi tā shāhed-e bāzāri: `Urfi-shodan-e din dar sepehr-e siyāsat (From the Divine to the Bazaari Witness: The Secularization of Religion in the Sphere of Politics)* Tehran: Tarh-e No, 2001.

Hall, Stuart, 'Our mongrel selves,' *New Statesman & Society*, vol. 5-207, 1992.

Hashemi-Rafsanjani, Ali Akbar, `*Ubur az bohrān (Passing through the Crisis)*, Tehran: Daftar-e Nashr-e Ma`āref-e Enqelāb, 1999.

_____, *Daurān-e mobārezeh (The Period of Struggle)*, Tehran: Daftar-e Nashr-e Ma`āref-e Islami, 1998.

Hayek, F. A. von, 'Scientism and the study of society,' *Economica*, new series, vol. 9-35, 1942.

Hegel, G. W. F., *The Philosophy of History*, New York: Prometheus Books, 1990.

Heidari Kashani, Mohammad Javad, '*Naqdi bar pluralism-e dini*' ('A critique of religious pluralism') *Payām-e Howzeh Monthly*, no. 25, winter 2000.

Hekmat, Bijan, '*Mardom-sālāri va din-sālāri*' ('Democracy and theocracy'), *Kiyan*, vol. 4-21, 1994.

Hettne, Björn, *Development and the Three Worlds*, New York: Longman Scientific & Technical, 1991.

Hick, John, *An Interpretation of Religion*, New Haven: Yale University Press, 1989.

_____, *Problems of Religious Pluralism*, New York: St. Martin's, 1985.

_____, *God Has Many Names*, Philadelphia: Westminster, 1982.

_____, 'The outcome: dialogue into Truth,' in John Hick (ed.), *Truth and Dialogue in World Religions*, Philadelphia: Westminster, 1974.

Hollifield, J.F. and G. Ross (eds.), *Searching for the New France*, London: Routledge, 1991.

Hosseini, Hasan, *Pluralism-e dini, yā pluralism dar din (Religious Pluralism or Pluralism in Religion)*, Tehran: Soroush Publishers, 2003.

Hourani, Albert, *A History of the Arab Peoples*, Cambridge, MA: Harvard University Press, 1991.

Jala'ipour, Hamid-Reza, *Pas az dovvom-e Khordād (After the Second of Khordad)*, Tehran: Kavir, 1999.

Jameson, Fredric, *Postmodernism, or the Cultural Logic of Late Capitalism*, Durham: Duke University Press, 1991.

_____, 'Marxism and postmodernism,' *New Left Review*, no. 176, July/August 1989.

Jansen, Johannes, *The Neglected Duty: The Creed of Sadat's Assassins and Islamic Resurgence in the Middle East*, New York: Macmillan, 1986.

Jones, Eric, *The European Miracle*, Cambridge, UK: Cambridge University Press, 1981.

Joravsky, David, *The Lysenko Affair*, Chicago: Chicago University Press. 1970.

Kachu`ian, Hossein, *Tatavorāt-e goftemānhā-ye hoviyati-ye Iran (Transformations of Identity Discourses in the Iran)* Tehran: Nashr-e Nay, 2006

Kadivar, Jamileh, *Tahavvol-e goftemān-e siāsi-e Shi`i dar Iran* (*The Transformation of Shi`ite Political Discourse in Iran*), Tehran: Tarh-e No, 2000.

Kadivar, *Daghdagheha-ye hukumat-e dini* (*The Preoccupation with the Religious State*), Tehran: Nay Pubishers, 2000.

_____, *Hukumat-e velā'i* (*Governance by Guardianship*), Tehran: Nay Publishers, 1998.

_____, *Nazariyeha-ye dolat dar fiqh-e Shi`ah* (*Theories of State in Shi`ite Jurisprudence*), Tehran: Nay Publishers, 1997.

Karimi, Ata'ollah, *Faqr-e tārikhi-negari* (*The Poverty of Historicism*), Tehran: Allameh Tabataba'i Publishers, 1990.

Kashani, Molla Abdolrasul, '*Resāle-ye ensāfiyeh*' ('The credo of fairness'), in Zargari-Nezhad (ed.), *Rasā'el*, Tehran: Kavir, 1999.

Kaviani, Hamid, *Pishgāmān-e eslāhāt* (*The Vanguards of Reform*), Tehran: Salam, 2001.

Keddie, Nikki, *Roots of Revolution: An Interpretive History of Modern Iran*, New Haven, Conn: Yale University Press, 1981.

_____, *Sayyid Jamal ad-Din "al-Afghani": A Political Biography*, Berkeley, Los Angeles: University of California Press, 1972.

_____, *An Islamic Response to Imperialism: Political and Religious Writings of Sayyid Jamal ad-Din "al-Afghani"*, Berkeley: University of California Press, 1983.

Kepel, Gilles, *Muslim Extremism in Egypt: The Prophet and Pharaoh*, Berkeley: University of California Press, 1986.

Khomeini, Ruhollah Musavi, *Hokumat-e Islami: Velāyat-e Faqih* (*Islamic Governance: The Rule of the Jurist*), Qom: np, 1971.

_____, *Islam and Revolution: Writings and Declarations of Imam Khomeini*, translated and annotated by Hamid Algar, Berkeley: Mizan Press, 1981.

Kroef, Justus M., '"Guided democracy" in Indonesia,' *Far Eastern Survey*, vol. 26-8, August 1957.

Kurzman, Charles (ed.), *Modernist Islam, 1840-1940: A Source Book*, Oxford: Oxford University Press, 2002.

_____, *The Unthinkable Revolution in Iran*, Cambridge, MA: Harvard University Press, 2004.

Larijani, Hojjatoleslam Sadeq, *Ma`refat-e dini: Naqdi bar nazariyeh-ye qabz va bast-e teorik-e shari`at* (*Religious Knowledge: A Critique of the Doctrine of the Theoretical Expansion and Constriction of the* Shari`ah), Tehran: Markaz-e Tarjomeh va Enteshar-e Ketab, 1991.

_____, '*Naqd-e pluralism-e dini*' ('A critique of religious pluralism'), *Moballeghān*, no. 25, January 2002.

Lenin, V. I., 'The state and revolution' in *Marx, Engels, Lenin on Historical Materialism: A Collection*, New York: International Publishers, 1974.

Lewis, Bernard, *What Went Wrong: The Clash Between Islam and Modernity in the Middle East*, Oxford, New York: Oxford University Press, 2002.

_____, 'Roots of Muslim rage,' *Atlantic Monthly*, September 1990.

_____, *The Political Language of Islam*, Chicago: University of Chicago Press, 1988.

Lyotard, Jean-François, *The Postmodern Condition: A Report on Knowledge*, trans. Geoff Bennington and Brian Massumi, Minneapolis: University of Minnesota Press, 1991.

MacIntyre, Alasdir, *Whose Justice, Whose Rationality*, Notre Dame: University of Notre Dame Press, 1984.

Mahdavi-Zadegan, Davoud, *Az qabz-e ma`nā tā bast-e donya* (*From the Constriction of Meaning to the Expansion of the World*) Tehran: Danesh va Andishe-ye Mo`āser, 2000.

Makarem Shirazi, Naser, *Javānān va moshkelāt-e fekri* (*Youth and Problems of Mind*), Qom: Khorram, 1991.

_____, *'Āyā hokumat-e islami bar pāye-ye shurāst?'* ('Is Islamic state based upon democratic councils?') *Maktab-e Islam* vol. 13-1, 1972.

Mannan, M. A., *Islamic Economics: Theory and Practice*, Cambridge: The Islamic Academy, 1986.

Mannheim, Karl, *Ideology and Utopia: An Introduction to the Sociology of Knowledge*, New York, London: Harvest/HBJ Book, 1985.

Martaji, Hojjat, *Jenāh-hāy-e Siyāsi dar Irān-e Emruz* (*Political Factions in Contemporary Iran*), Tehran: Shafi`i Publishers, 1999.

Marx, Karl, 'The British rule in India,' in *Karl Marx and Frederick Engels, Selected Works in Three Volumes*, vol. 1, Moscow: Progress Publishers, 1983.

_____, 'The future results of British rule in India,' in *Karl Marx and Frederick Engels, Selected Works in Three Volumes*, vol. 1, Moscow: Progress Publishers, 1983.

Maududi, A. A., *Human Rights in Islam*, Leicester, UK: The Islamic Foundation, 1976.

_____, *First Principles of Islamic State*, translated and edited by Khurshid Ahmad, Lahore: Islamic Publications, 1974.

_____, *A Short History of the Revivalist Movement in Islam*, Lahore, Pakistan: Islamic Publications (PVT) Limited, 1963.

Mesbah Yazdi, Mohammad Taqi, *Tahājom-e farhangi* (*Cultural Assault*), Qom: Imam Khomeini Teaching and Research Institute, 1999.

Minachi, Naser, *Tārikh-cheye Hosseiniyyeh-ye Ershād* (*A History of Hosseiniyyeh-ye Ershād*) Tehran: Ershād Publication, 2005.

Mir-Hosseini, Ziba & Richard Tapper, *Islam and Democracy in Iran, Eshkevari and the Quest for Reform*, London, New York: I. B. Tauris, 2006.

Mir-Hosseini, Ziba, *Islam and Gender: The Religious Debate in Contemporary Iran*, Princeton, NJ: Princeton University Press, 1999.

Mitchell, Robert, *The Society of Muslim Brothers*, New York & Oxford: Oxford University Press, 1969.

Moghadam, Valentine, 'Islamic feminism and its discontents: Toward a resolution of the debate,' *Signs*, vol. 27-4, Summer 2002.

Mohammadi, Majid, *'Ghosl-e ta`mid-e sekularism yā nejāt-e din'* ('The baptism of secularism or the salvage of religion'), *Kiyan*, vol. 4-21, 1994.

Mojab, Shahrzad, *The State and University: The Islamic Cultural Revolution in the Institutions of Higher Education in Iran, 1980-87*, unpublished dissertation, University of Illinois, Urbana-Champaign, 1991.

Mojtahed Shabestari, Mohammad, *Naqdi bar qarā'at-e rasmi-ye din* (*A Critique of the Official Reading of Religion*), Tehran: Tarh-e No, 2002.

_____, *'Modernism va vahy'* ('Modernism and revelation'), *Kiyan*, vol. 5-29, March/April, 1996.

Montazeri, Ayatollah Hossein-Ali, *Khāterāt* (*Memoir*), Los Angeles: Sherkat-e Ketab, 2001.

Moslem, Mehdi, *Factional Politics in Post-Khomeini Iran*, Syracuse, NY: Syracuse University Press, 2002.

Motahhadeh, Roy, *The Mantle of the Prophet*, New York: Pantheon Books, 1985.

Motahhari, Morteza, *Khātamiyat* (*The End of Prophecy*), Tehran: Sadra, 1988.

_____, *Khadamāt-e moteqābel-e Islam va Iran* (*The Reciprocal Exchanges Between Islam and Iran*), Qom: Sadra, 1983.

_____, *Pirāmun-e enqelāb-e Islami* (*On the Islamic Revolution*), Qom: Islamic Publishers, 1982.

_____, *Nezām-e hoquq-e zan dar Islam* (*The Order of Women's Rights in Islam*), Tehran: Sadra, 1980.

_____, *Dah Goftar* (*Ten Discourses*) Tehran: Hekmat, 1978.

_____, *`Elal-e gerāyesh beh māddigari* (*Causes of Attraction to Materialism*), Qom: Sadra Publishers, 1978.

_____, *Bahsi darbāre-ye marja`iyyat va rohaniyyat* (*A Treatise on the Source of Imitation and the Clergy*) Tehran: n.p. 1962.

Moussalli, Ahmed, *Radical Islamic Fundamentalism: The Ideological and Political Discourse of Sayyid Qutb,* Beirut: American University of Beirut Press, 1992.

Mu`in, Baqir, *Hukumat-e Islami va Islam-e Hukumati,* Essen, Germany: Nima, 2004.

Munson, Henry, *Islam and Revolution in the Middle East,* New Haven, CT: Yale University Press, 1988.

Musavi Zanjani, Sayyed Hossein, *Barkhord-e shāyesteh bā fāz-e farhangi-ye sarmāyeh-dāri: Barresi-ye mabāni-ye andishehā-ye doctor Soroush* (*The Appropriate Approach to the Cultural Phase of Capitalism: A Review of the Foundations of Doctor Soroush's Thought*), Qom: Howzeh Publishers, 1996.

Na'ini, Mohammad Hossein, *Tanbih al-ummah wa tanzih al-millah* (*The Admonition of the Public and the Refinement of the Nation*), Tehran: Enteshar, 1979.

Nadushan, Mohammad Ali, *Chehār sokhangu-ye vojdān-e irani* (*Four Spokespersons of the Iranian Conscience*), Tehran: Qatreh, 2003.

Najmabadi, Afsaneh, 'Feminisms in an Islamic Republic,' in Joan Scott, Cora Kaplan, and Debra Keates (eds.), *Transitions, Environments, Translations: Feminisms in International Politics,* London: Routledge, 1997.

Nasr, S. H., *Science and Civilization in Islam,* New York: Barnes & Noble Books, 1992.

Nasr, Vali, *The Vanguard of the Islamic Revolution: the Jama`at-i Islami of Pakistan,* Berkeley, Los Angeles: University of California Press, 1994.

Nikzad, Abbas, *Serāt-e mostaqim, naqdi bar qarā'at-e Doktor Soroush az pluralism-e dini* (*Striaght Path: A Critique of Doctor Soroush's Interpretation of Religious Pluralism*) Qom: Bustan (The Office of the Islamic Propagation of Qom Seminary), 2001.

Nuri, Sheikh Fazlollah, *Rasā'el, E`lāmiyeh-ha, Maktubāt, va Ruznāmeh-ha* (*Creeds, Pronouncements, and Papers*), Mohammad Torkman (ed.), Tehran: Rasa Publishers, 1983.

O'Hanlon, Rosalind and David Washbrook, 'After Orientalism: Culture, criticism, and politics in the third world,' *Comparative Study of Society and History,* vol. 34-1, January 1992.

Ollman, Bertell, *Dialectical Investigations,* New York: Routledge, 1993.

OSEWC, *Jonbesh-e dāneshju`ei va mas`ale-ye dāneshjuyān-e mobārez* (Student Movement and the Problem of the Militant Student Organization), Tehran: *Sāzmān-e Paykār dar Rāh-e Azādi-ye Tabaqe-ye Kārgar Paykar* (The Organization of Struggle for the Emancipation of the Working Class), 1980.

Paidar, Parvin, *Women and the Political Process in Twentieth Century Iran,* New York & London: Cambridge University Press, 1994.

Parekh, Bhikhu, 'Reflections,' in L. Appignanesi & S. Maitland (eds.), *The Rushdie File,* Syracuse, NY: Syracuse University Press, 1990.

Parsa, Misagh, *States, Ideologies, and Social Revolutions: A Comparative Analysis of Iran, Nicaragua, and the Philippines,* Cambridge, New York: Cambridge University Press, 2004.

Payman, Habibollah, '*Sobāt va tagh'ir dar andishe-ye dini*' ('Permanence and change in religious thought'), *Kiyan,* vol. 2-7, June/July, 1992.

Pipes, Daniel, *In the Path of God: Islam and Political Power*, New York: Basic Books, 1983.

Piran, Parviz, '*Faqr va jonbesh-hāye ejtemā`i*' ('Poverty and social movements), *Refāh-e Ejtemā`i* (*Social Welfare*) vol. 5-18, Fall 2006.

Popper, Karl, *The Myth of the Framework: In Defense of Science and Rationality*, London: Routledge, 1995.

_____, 'Against the sociology of knowledge,' in David Miller (ed.), *Popper Selections*, Princeton, NJ: Princeton University Press, 1985.

_____, *Conjectures and Refutations: The Growth of Scientific Knowledge* New York: Harper & Row, 1968.

_____, *Open Society and Its Enemies*, Princeton, NJ: Princeton University Press, 1963.

_____, *The Logic of Scientific Discovery*, London: Hutchinson, 1959.

_____, *The Poverty of Historicism*, London & New York: Routledge & Kegan Paul, 1957.

Pouyan, Amir-Parviz, *Dar radd-e teori-ye baqā'* (*On the Refutation of the Theory of Survival*), Tehran: np, 1969.

Prakash, Gyan, 'Can the "subaltern" ride? A reply to O'Hanlon and Washbrook,' *Comparative Study of Society and History*, Vol. 34-1, January 1992.

_____, 'Writing post-Orientalist histories of the third world: Perspectives form Indian historiography,' *Comparative Study of Society and History*, vol. 32-2, April 1990.

Precht, Henry, "Ayatollah *Realpolitik*," *Foreign Policy*, no. 70, spring 1988.

Qazi-Moradi, Hassan, *Khodmadāri-ye Iraniān* (*The Self-Orbiting Iranians*), Tehran: Akhtaran, 2000.

Quchani, Mohammad, '*qabz va bast-e perātik-e Soroush*' ('The practical expansion and constriction of Soroush') *Sharq*, (new year special edition) March 2004.

_____, *Jomhuri-ye moqaddas* (*The Sacred Republic*), Tehran: Naqsh-o-Negar, 2003.

_____, *Yaqeh sefid-hā* (*The White-Collars*), Tehran: Naqsh-o-Negar, 2000.

Qutb, Sayyid, *Islam and Universal Peace*, Indianapolis, IN: American Trust Publications, 1993.

_____, *Milestones*, Salimiah, Kuwait: International Islamic Federation of Student Organizations, 1978 (1964).

Rabbani Golpaigani, Ali, *Tahlil va naqd-e pluralism-e dini* (*A Critical Analysis of Religious Pluralism*), Tehran: Contemporary Thought Cultural Institute, 2000.

Rahman, Fazlur, *Islam and Modernity, Transformation of an Intellectual Tradition*, Chicago & London: The University of Chicago Press, 1988.

Rahnema, Ali, *An Islamic Utopian: A Political Biography of Ali Shari`ati*, London, New York: I.B. Tauris, 1998.

Rahnema, Ali and Farhad Nomani, *The Secular Miracle: Religion, Politics & Economic Policy in Iran*, London and New Jersey: Zed Books, 1990.

Raja'i, Farhang, *Moshkeleh-ye hoviyat-e Iranian-e emruz* (*The Predicament of Identity for the Contemporary Iranians*), Tehran: Nay, 2004.

Rawls, John, *Political Liberalism*, New York: Columbia University Press, 1993.

_____, *A Theory of Justice*, Cambridge, MA: Harvard University Press, 1971.

Rezaqoli, Ali, *Jāme`eh-shenāsi-ye nokhbeh-koshi* (*The Sociology of Killing Elites*), Tehran: Nay, 1998.

Robert Wuthnow, 'Understanding religion and politics,' *Daedalus*, no. 120, summer 1991.

Roy, Olivier, *The Failure of Political Islam*, trans. Carol Volk, Cambridge, MA: Harvard University Press, 1994.

Rushide, Salman, *Imaginary Homelands,* London & New York: Granta Books, 1991.

Sachedina, Abdulaziz, 'Ali Shariati: Ideologue of the Iranian revolution,' in Esposito (ed.), *Voices of Resurgent Islam,* 1983.

Sadr, Mohammad Baqir, *Eqtesād-e mā* (*Islamic Economy*), translated from Arabic to Farsi by M.K. Bojnurdi, Tehran: Borhan, 1972.

Sadri, Mahmoud, 'Sacral defense of secularism: The political theologies of Soroush, Shabestari, and Kadivar,' *International Journal of Politics, Culture and Society,* vol. 15-2, winter 2001.

Said, Edward, 'Orientalism reconsidered,' in Francis Barker *et al.* (eds.), *Literature, Politics and Theory,* London: Methuen, 1986.

Said, Edward, *The World, the Text, and the Critic,* London: Faber & Faber, 1984.

Salehi-Isfahani, 'Revolution and redistribution in Iran: Poverty and inequality 25 years later," working paper, August 2006.

Sanjabi, Karim, *Omid-hā va nā-omidi-hā: Khāterāt-e siāsi* (*Hopes and Disappointments: A Political Memoir),* London: The National Front, 1989.

Schimmel, Annemarie, *Islam, An Introduction,* Albany: SUNY Press, 1992.

Schirazi, Asghar, *The Constitution of Iran: Politics and the State in the Islamic Republic,* translated by John O'Kane, London: I. B. Tauris, 1997.

Seif, Ahamad, *Pishdarāmadi bar estebdād dar Iran* (*A Preface to Despotism in Iran),* Tehran: Cheshmeh, 2000.

Shadman, Fakhroddin, *Taskhir-e tamaddon-e farangi* (*Invaded by the Western Civilization),* Tehran: Gām-e No, 2004.

Shahla, Amir, 'A glance at the history of the Islamic Revolution Mujahidin Organization,' *No Andish Monthly,* September 2001.

Shari`ati, Ali, '*Ensān-e bi-khod'* ('The estranged humanity'), *Collected Works,* vol. 25, Tehran: Qalam, 2000.

_____, *'Vizhegi-hā-ye qorun-e jadid'* ('The distinctions of new centuries'), *Collected Works,* vol. 31, Tehran: Chapakhsh, 1997.

_____, *'Māshin dar esārat-e māshinism'* ('Machine in the captivity of machinism') *Collected Works,* vol. 31, 1997.

_____, *'Nāmeh beh Ayatollah al-Uzma Milani'* ('Letter to the Grand Ayatollah Milani," in *Collected Works,* vol. 34, Tehran: Qalam, 1996.

_____, *Ali, Collected Works,* vol. 26, Tehran: Nilufar, 1984.

_____, *'Ravesh-e shenākht-e Islam'* ('The method of studying Islam'), *Collected Works,* vol. 28, Tehran: Chapakhsh, 1983.

_____, *'Mi`ād bā Ibrāhim'* ('Meeting with Abraham'), *Collected Works,* vol. 29, Tehran: Hosseiniyyeh Ershad, 1983.

_____, *Tārikh-e tamaddon* (*The History of Civilization*) vols. 1-2, (*Collected Works Nos. 11 & 12*), Tehran: Entesharat-e Agah, 1982.

_____, *Ari inchenin bud barādar* (*Yes, Brother! This is How it Was*) Tehran: Entesharat-e Sabz, 1982.

_____, *'Bāzgasht'* ('Return') *Collect Works,* Vol. 4., Tehran: Elham, 1982.

_____, *'Rowshanfekr va mas'uliyat-e ou dar jāme`eh'* ('Intellectuals and their responsibilities in society') *Collected Works,* vol. 20, Tehran: Entesharat-e Sabz, 1981.

_____, *Islamshenāsi,* vols. 1-3 (*Collected Works,* vols. 16-18), Tehran: Entesharat-e Shari`ati, 1981.

_____, *On the Sociology of Islam,* trans. H. Algar. Berkeley: Mizan Press 1979.

_____, *'Abu Dharr,'* in *Collected Works* vol. 3, Tehran: Hosseiniyyeh Ershad, 1978.

_____, *Shi`ah* (*Shi`ism*), *Collected Works,* vol. 7, Tehran: Hosseiniyyeh Ershad 1978.

_____, *Mazhab alayh-e Mazhab* (*Religion Against Religion*), Tehran: n.p. 1977.

_____, *Tashayyo`-e Alavi va Tashayyo`-e Safavi* (*Alavid Shi'ism and Safavid Shi`ism*), Tehran: Hosseiniyyeh Ershad, 1971.

_____, *Tashayyo`-e Alavi va Tashayyo`-e Safavi* (*Alavid Shi'ism and Safavid Shi`ism*), Tehran: Hosseiniyyeh Ershad, 1971.

Shayegan, Dariush, *Bothā-ye zehni va khātereh-ye azali* (*Imagined Idols and Infinite Memories*), Tehran: Amir Kabir, 2003.

Sivan, Emmanuel, *Radical Islam: Medieval Theology and Modern Politics*, New Haven, London: Yale University Press, 1990.

Smith, Wilfred Cantwell, *Islam in Modern History*, Princeton, NJ: Princeton University Press, 1957.

Sobhani, Ja`far, *Kesrat-gerā'i, yā pluralism-e dini* (*On Religious Pluralism*), Qom: Imam Sadeq Institute, 2002.

Soroush, Abdolkarim, *Az Shari`ati* (*For Shari`ati*), Tehran: Serat, 2005.

_____, *Siyāsat-Nāmeh* (*Political Letters*) vols.1-2, Tehran: Serat, 2000.

_____, *Reason, Freedom, and Democracy: Essential Writings of Abdolkarim Soroush*, translated and edited by Ahmad and Mahmoud Sadri, Oxford & New York: Oxford University Press, 2000.

_____, *Bast-e tajrobeh-ye nabavi* (*The Expansion of Prophetic Experience*) Tehran: Serat, 1999

_____, *Serāt-hā-ye mostaqim* (*Straight Paths*), Tehran: Serat, 1998.

_____, 'Horriyat va ruhāniyat,' ('Freedom and the clergy'), *Kiyan*, vol. 5-24, 1995.

_____, 'Ma`ishat va fazilat' ('Livelihood and wisdom'), *Kiyan*, vol. 5-25, 1995.

_____, 'Ma`nā va mabnā-ye sekularism' ('The meaning and the foundation of secularism'), *Kiyan* vol. 5-26, 1995.

_____, *Dars-ha-ei dar Falsafeh-ye Elm-e Ejtema'* (Lectures in the Philosophy of Social Science) Tehran: Nay, 1995.

_____, *Qabz va bast-e teorik-e shari`at* (*The Theoretical Contraction and Expansion of the Shari`ah*), Tehran: Serat, 1995.

_____, *Farbeh-tar az eideolozhi* (*Loftier than Ideology*), Tehran: Serat, 1994.

_____, *Rāz-dāni, roshanfekri, va dindāri* (*Augury, Intellectualism, and Religious Conviction*) Tehran: Serat, 1993.

_____, 'Bahsi darbāre-ye eideolozhi va din' ('On the relation between ideology and religion'), *Māhnāmeh-ye Farhang va Tose`eh* (*Culture and Development Monthly*), vol. 1-5, April-May 1993.

_____, *Bāvar-e dini, dāvar-e dini* (*Religious Faith, Religious Justification*), Ketab-e Ehya No. 5, Tehran: Yad-Avarn Publishers, 1992.

_____, *Tafarroj-e son`: Goftārhā-ei dar Akhlāq va san`at va elm-e ensāni* (*Essays on Human Sciences, Ethics and Technology*), Tehran: Serat, 1987.

_____, 'Vojud va māhiyat-e gharb,' ('The existence and the essence of the West'), *Kayhan Farhangi*, vol. 1-5, 1985.

_____, 'Gharbiyān va hosn va qobh-e sho'un va atvār-e ānān' ('The westerners and the virtues and vices of their manners'), *Kayhan Farhangi*, vol. 1-2, 1984.

_____, *Nahād-e nā-ārām-e jahān* (*The Restless Nature of the Universe*), Tehran: Qalam, 1982.

_____, *Az tārikh-parasti tā khodā-parasti* (*From the Worship of History to Worshiping God*) Houston, TX: Islamic Student Association, 1980.

_____, *Eideolozhi-ye shaytani* (*The Satanic Ideology*), Tehran: Serat, 1980.

_____, *Danish va arzesh* (*Knowledge and Value*) Tehran: Yaran, 1979.

_____, *Falsafeh-ye tārikh* (*Philosophy of History*) Tehran: Payam-e Azadi, 1979.

_____, *Jahān-bini-ye Motahhari* (*The Worldview of Motahhari*), Tehran: np, 1979.

_____, `Elm chist? Falsafeh chist? (What is Science? What is Philosophy?) Tehran: Serat, 1979.

_____, Tazād-e diālektiki (Dialectical Contradiction), Tehran: Serat, 1979.

Spivak, G. C., 'Can the subaltern speak?' in Cary Nelson & Lawrence Grossberg (eds.), Marxism and the Interpretation of Culture, Urbana & Chicago: University of Illinois Press, 1988.

Stinnett, Timothy R., 'John Hick's pluralistic theory of religion,' The Journal of Religion, vol. 70-4, 1990.

Tabataba'i, Alameh Mohammad, Usul-e falsafeh va ravesh-e reālism (The Principles of Philosophy and the Method of Realism), edited and annotated by Morteza Motahhari, vol. 1-5, Qom: Sadra Publishers, 1953-1985.

Tehrani, Ayatollah Mohammad Hossein, Negareshi bar maqāleh-ye bast va qabz-e teorik-e shari`at (A Review of the Expansion and Constriction Essay), Tehran: Nashr-e `Ulum va Ma`āref-e Islami, 1994.

Turner, Bryan, Orientalism, Postmodernism, and Globalism, London: Routledge, 1994.

Twiss, Sumner, 'The philosophy of religious pluralism: A critical appraisal of Hick and his critics," Journal of Religion, vol. 70-4, 1990.

UMSA, Dānishgāh va `amalkardha-yi irtijā` (University and the Plans of the Reactionaries) Tehran: Ettehādieh-ye Anjomanhā-ye Dāneshjuyān-e Mosalmān (The Union of Muslims Students' Associations), 1981.

Vahdat, Farzin, "Postrevolutionary discourses of Mohammad Mojtahed Shabestari and Mohsen Kadivar: reconciling the terms of mediated subjectivity,' Critique, vol. 9-16, Spring 2000.

Voll, John O., 'Fundamentalism in the Sunni Arab world,' in Martin E. Marty and R. Scott Appleby (eds.), Fundamentalisms Observed, Chicago: University of Chicago Press, 1991.

Watt, W. M. Islamic Fundamentalism and Modernity, London, New York: Routledge, 1988.

Watt, W. M., Islamic Fundamentalism and Modernity, London: Routledge, 1988.

Weber, Max, 'Politics as a vocation,' in For Max Weber: Essays in Sociology, edited and translated by H. H. Gerth & C. Wright Mills, New York: Oxford University Press, 1958.

Whine, Michael, 'Islamism and totalitarianism similarities and differences,' Totalitarian Movements and Political Religions, vol. 2-2, Autumn 2001.

Williams Patrick & Laura Chrisman (eds.), Colonial Discourse and Post-Colonial Theory, New York: Columbia University Press, 1994.

Williams, Raymond, Culture and Society, 1780-1950, New York: Harper and Row, 1958.

Wills, Garry, 'The visionary,' The New York Review of Books, March 23, 1995.

Wittfogel, Karl, Oriental Despotism: A Comparative Study of Total Power, New Haven: Yale University Press, 1964.

Woodhead, Linda, 'Feminism and the sociology of religion: From gender-blindness to gendered difference,' in Richard K. Fenn (ed.), The Blackwell Companion to Sociology of Religion, Oxford: Blackwell Publishers, 2001.

Yusefi Eshkevari, Hasan, Kherad dar ziyāfat-e din (Reason at the Banquet of Religion), Tehran: Qasideh, 2000.

Yusefi Eshkevari, Hasan, Shari`ati, eideolozhi, stratezhi (Shari`ati, Ideology, and Strategy), Tehran: Chapakhsh, 1998.

Zargari-Nezhad, Gholam-Hossein (ed.), Rasā'el-e mashrutiyat (The Constitutional Revolution Credos) Tehran: Kavir, 1999.

Ziba-Kalam, Sadeq, Dāneshgāh va enqelāb (The University and Revolution), Tehran: Rowzaneh, 2001.

_____, *Sonnat va moderniteh* (*Tradition and Modernity*), Tehran: Rozaneh, 1998.

_____, *Mā cheguneh mā shodim* (*How Did We Become Who We Are*), Tehran: Rozaneh, 1995.

Zojaji Qomi, Marziyeh, *Monāzereh-ye Soroush and Kadivar darbāre-ye pluralism-e dini* (*Soroush and Kadivar Debate Religious Pluralism*), Tehran: Salām Newspaper, 1999.

Zubaida, Sami, 'Islam and nationalism: Continuities and contradictions,' *Nations and Nationalism*, vol. 10-4, October 2004.

_____, 'Is Iran an Islamic state?' in Joel Beinin & Joe Stork (eds.), *Political Islam*, Berkeley & Los Angeles: University of California Press, 1997.

_____, *Islam, the People and the State,* London: Routledge, 1989.

Primary Material

Taqvim-e tārikh-e enqelāb-e islami-ye Iran: Khabarhā va ruydādhā-ye ruzāneh, Mordād-e 1356-Farvardin-e 1358 (*The Calendar and History of the Islamic Revolution of Iran: Daily Reports and News from July 1978 to April 1979*), Tehran: Soroush Publishers, 1991.

Goftemān-e rowshangar (*The Illuminating Discourse*), Qom: Imam Khomeini Research Institute, 2000 (transcript of philosophical debates on television, 1980).

Mashruh-e mozākerāt-e majles-e barresi-ye nahā'i-ye qānun-e asāsi-e jomhuri-ye islami-ye Iran (*Minutes from the Negotiations of The Assembly for the Final Examination of the Constitution of the Islamic Republic*), Vol. 1-4, Tehran: Center for the Islamic Revolution Documents.

Asnād-e enqelāb-e Islami (*Islamic Revolution Documents*), Vol. 1-5, Tehran: Center for the Islamic Revolution Documents.

Sahifeh-ye Nur: Majmu`e-ye rahnemudha-ye Imam Khomeini, Vol. 1-23, Tehran: The Organization of the Islamic Revolution's Cultural Documents, 1983-1994.

Surat-e mashruh-e mozākerāt-e bāznegari-ye qānun-e asāsi-ye jomhuri-ye eslami-ye Iran (*The Complete Report of the Re-Appraisal of the Islamic Republic's Constitution*), Vol. 1-2, Tehran: Center for the Islamic Revolution Documents.

Majmu`eh-ye nazariyāt-e shurā-ye negahbān (*Collected Opinions of the Guardian Council*), edited by Hossein Mehrpour, Tehran: Center for the Islamic Revolution Documents, 1993.

Jang-e tahmili dar tahlil-e goruhak-hā (The Opposition's Analysis of the Imposed War), Tehran: Ministry of Guidance Publications, 1985.

James Hitselberger Papers, Eight Boxes, Hoover Institute, Stanford University.

Gozari bar do sāl jang (A Review of Two Years of War), Tehran: Political Office of the Revolutionary Guards, 1983.

Newspapers

'Asr-e Āzādegān   *Salām*
Sharq   *Āftāb-e Yazd*
Kayhan   *Ettelā`āt*
Jomhuri-ye Islami

Index